Publications of the Milman Parry Collection
of Oral Literature No. 5

WILD SONGS, SWEET SONGS

D1453390

WILD SONGS, SWEET SONGS
THE ALBANIAN EPIC IN THE COLLECTIONS OF MILMAN PARRY AND ALBERT B. LORD

edited by Nicola Scaldaferri
with the collaboration of Victor A. Friedman,
John Kolsti, and Zymer U. Neziri

Published by
THE MILMAN PARRY COLLECTION OF ORAL LITERATURE
Harvard University

Distributed by
HARVARD UNIVERSITY PRESS
Cambridge, Massachusetts & London, England
2021

Wild Songs, Sweet Songs: The Albanian Epic in the Collections of Milman Parry and Albert B. Lord
Published by The Milman Parry Collection of Oral Literature, Harvard University
Distributed by Harvard University Press, Cambridge, Massachusetts & London, England
Copyright © 2021 The Milman Parry Collection of Oral Literature
All rights reserved

EDITORIAL TEAM OF THE MILMAN PARRY COLLECTION

Managing Editors: Stephen Mitchell and Gregory Nagy
Executive Editors: Casey Dué and David Elmer

PRODUCTION TEAM OF THE CENTER FOR HELLENIC STUDIES

Production Manager for Publications: Jill Curry Robbins
Web Producer: Noel Spencer
Cover Design: Joni Godlove
Production: Kristin Murphy Romano

ISBN: 978-0-674-27133-3

Library of Congress Control Number (LCCN): 2021941950

Table of Contents

Table of Contents

Appendices

Preface
Contents and Acknowledgments

Nicola Scaldaferri

Translated By Gregory Mellen

THIS VOLUME MARKS the conclusion of a project that has been long in the making. Its foundations were laid in August of 2003, at Prishtina, Kosovo, during the annual international seminar dedicated to Albanian language and culture. That seminar provided the occasion on which, at David Elmer's invitation, John Kolsti, Zymer Neziri, and I met for the first time. Then, in the spring of 2004, the four of us met once again, this time along with Gustavo Loria, to continue studying these materials together at the Department of Linguistics of the University of Calabria, thanks to the kind invitation of Francesco Altimari. These first two encounters were then followed by various trips to the United States and to Kosovo, which I made with the support of LEAV (Ethnomusicology and Visual Anthropology Lab) and the University of Milan; and it was in the course of those subsequent trips that the contents of the present publication were gradually brought into focus.

The resulting volume is the work of several scholars and thus is polyphonic in nature. Our collective goal has been to illustrate the various kinds of materials in the Albanian language that are contained in the Milman Parry Collection of Oral Literature (henceforth MPCOL)—both those that have been preserved in recordings and those that were taken down in writing. We have also attempted to provide tools that will be useful for the continued study and appreciation of these materials, and we hope that the volume may thus serve as a guide for other scholars and interested individuals when the contents of the MPCOL are made freely available online.

The contents of this volume include: first and foremost, indices of the MPCOL Albanian materials, which were realized in accordance with the criteria established by Matthew Kay (Kay 1995), with some slight adjustments rendered necessary due to the specific nature of these items; next, an anthology of selected texts, which is intended to be representative of the materials overall; and finally several appendices, which contain further items of a more documentary nature, such as photographs and letters. In addition, we have included an introductory section that contains several essays, the goal of which is to identify and highlight the unique qualities of these materials and to suggest potential areas of interest for future research.

The materials that required the greatest attention were the recordings. After all, whether they were sung or recited, the Albanian verses recorded by Milman Parry all form part of the documentation of the research that Parry was conducting specifically on bilingual singers; for that reason, these verses are generally found in the context of conversations and performances that were being held primarily in a Slavic language (generally referred to, by Parry's Muslim informants, as 'Bosnian'). Moreover, the recorded materials are of various distinct types—some consist of the recitation of a few isolated verses, others of extended sung performances—and they were executed by several different bilingual singers in different locations and times. It has been necessary to check and re-check the recordings with great care, and in numerous cases it was necessary to go directly to the source and listen closely to the original recordings that Parry had made on aluminum discs in the 1930s. The work on these recordings was conducted by myself, and was completed in large part during a period of research spent at the Music Department of Harvard University in 2006, thanks to a Fulbright grant; but I was also able to re-examine the recordings subsequently during several trips over the past decade, the last of which took place in December 2017. In this volume the recordings are identified with their Parry Number (PN), in accordance with the practice employed for other materials that Parry recorded and transcribed in the course of his fieldwork.

Among the recorded materials that we have decided to include in the anthology, pride of place must go to the songs performed in Albanian by the singer Salih Ugljanin. The publication of these Albanian songs fills a major lacuna in the attested work of this singer, who was of central importance in Parry and Lord's research, since hitherto only Ugljanin's performances in Slavic have been made known to the public. The anthology includes the Albanian versions of two songs that Ugljanin had also performed in the Bosnian language: namely, *Muji e Gavran Kapetani* ("Muji and Gavran Kapetan"), which is the first song of legendary epic in the Albanian language of which we possess a complete audio recording, and *Mark e Musa* ("Marko and Musa"), which is notable for the fact that in the course of his performance Ugljanin switches from singing to recitation, and in doing so he presents us with extremely interesting clues into the system of versification that he and other singers employed. In addition to these performances of Ugljanin, we have included three songs that were performed by

Fatima Biberović and were recorded at Gacko at the time when Parry was investigating the tradition of women's songs. Parry and his fellow researchers explicitly commented on Biberović's extraordinary singing ability, and they recorded over ten songs of hers; and yet these materials—precisely because Fatima sang in Albanian rather than Slavic—were not taken into consideration for the volume dedicated to women's songs that Bartók and Lord produced in 1951. That said, in that volume Bartók and Lord do make mention of one of Biberović's songs (describing the misfortune that befell a Turkish cake; see Bartók-Lord 1951: 251–252, 367), which is now published in the present volume.

The transcription of the texts of the recorded songs was carried out by myself and Zymer Neziri, in accordance with current standard Albanian orthography. We have tried to reproduce as accurately as possible the linguistic forms that are found in the recordings, and we refer our readers to other discussions for more detailed analysis of the issues that these songs raise, especially as regards the presence of dialect forms and the use of specific phraseology that is typical of this repertoire. My first draft of a translation of these songs into English benefited greatly from Victor Friedman's attentive eye and helpful suggestions.

The most substantial corpus of Albanian materials in the MPCOL is to be found in the documents Albert Lord produced during his trip to Albania in 1937. The index to these manuscripts was completed by myself in collaboration with Zymer Neziri; compared to the work conducted on the recordings, it was a relatively simple task and mainly involved examining in detail everything that Lord had taken down in his notebooks. In order to maintain a level of consistency with the other designations used in the MPCOL catalogues, we have decided to adopt the designation LAN (Lord Albanian Number) to identify these items (whereas in his notebooks Lord merely uses the Albanian term *dorëshkrim* 'manuscript').

When it came to selecting texts from those collected by Lord for inclusion in our anthology, we took into account above all the following three considerations: the representativeness of the singers, who are among the most important of their generation; the composition of the repertoires of the various singers, who applied themselves to a wide array of subjects within the two major genres of legendary epic and historical epic; and the connections between these texts and the other areas of research to which Parry and Lord dedicated themselves, especially the poetic repertoires of the Slavic community—and indeed, our work has brought to light themes and characters that transcend the two cultural and linguistic contexts. The texts we have chosen are seven in total, dictated by six different singers, each of whom is counted among the most significant of his time and is known to other scholars as well. The first five texts belong to the tradition of legendary epic: *Musa Qeshexhi dhe vlla Bergjanine Gjemi* ("Musa Qeshexhi and His Brother Bergjanine Gjemi," dictated by Gjergj Pllumbi); *Kanga e Halilit kur asht martue* ("The Song of the Wedding of Halil," dictated by Sokol Martini); *Kanga e Ali Bajraktarit me Krajlicen e Inglizit* ("The Song of Ali Bajraktari and the Queen of England," dictated by Ali Meta); *Kanga e Sirotin Alis* ("The Song of Sirotin Ali," dictated by Adem Brahimi); *Kanga e Halilit qi ka nxane Jovan Kapidanin* ("The Song of Halil Who Seized Jovan Kapidani," dictated by Rexhep Zeneli. Of the latter two items, the first is the longest and most complex epic song in Albanian that has hitherto been documented, whereas the second, according to Zeneli, is the Albanian version of a song performed by the famous blind singer Qor Hysa (Ćor Huso)—a figure who was at the center of Milman Parry's research interests, to such an extent, in fact, that Parry had used this singer's name as the title for his preliminary plan of research.

In addition to these five texts belonging to the tradition of legendary epic, we have included two songs that are inspired by historical episodes. One song is based on an event that was fundamental for the history of this region, namely the famous battle of 1389: this is *Kanga e Sultan Muratit* ("The Song of Sultan Murad," about the Battle of Kosovo, dictated by Ali Meta). The other song derives its content from historical events of the 1800s and is concerned with the border conflicts between Slavs and Albanians following the period of the league of Prizren: this is *Kanga e Ali Pashë Gusinjes* ("The Song of Ali Pasha of Gusinje," dictated by Marash Nika).

As a team we have discussed at length whether it was appropriate to intervene in the texts in order to emend the language that is contained in the manuscripts, since these present a certain degree of fluidity owing both to the conditions in which the dictation took place and to the fact that the researchers did not always possess an excellent knowledge of the *Geg* dialect used in Northern Albania. In the end we concluded that, at this point, it was best to reproduce the contents of the manuscripts as faithfully as possible, especially since the manuscripts themselves have documentary value of their own. In the future it will of course be possible to conduct a more detailed study of these materials from a linguistic point of view, especially when the MPCOL Albanian materials will have been made directly accessible online. The transcription of the songs collected by Lord was done primarily by myself, with some help from John Kolsti and Zymer Neziri; the translations into English, which were drafted initially by myself and Kolsti, have benefited substantially from the improvements suggested by Victor Friedman.

In the appendices we have included various documents, among which stand out in particular the letters that Albert Lord wrote to his family during his trip in 1937 (as we will see, these letters reveal important elements of Lord's plan of research) and the photographs that were taken by Lord during the same trip. In addition, we have included the historic photos of Gjergj Pllumbi that were taken by Shan Pici and were previously published in the periodical *Shêjzat* as accompaniment to texts written by Ernest Koliqi (and reproduced in this volume with thanks for the permission kindly granted by *Shêjzat*), as well as a few pictures that I took myself during a trip, eighty years later, in the very same regions through which Lord traveled in 1937. Lastly, the appendices include the photographic reproductions of a few of the original manuscripts dating to the time of Lord's collecting trip, since a close look at these documents can help us to better understand the spirit with which Lord undertook his research.

The volume opens with a collection of essays that examine various aspects of the research that Parry and Lord undertook and the materials that they collected. My introductory chapter reconstructs an overall picture of their research, by locating it within the context of its time and the methodologies that were then in practice; and I have tried to draw attention to some elements that could provide stimulus for future readings and re-examinations of these materials, not least with regard to new research paradigms that are being developed as we speak. In his essay, John Kolsti—who had the privilege of studying with Albert Lord and writing his doctoral thesis on the bilingual singer Salih Ugljanin—highlights some of the salient features of these materials, in part with reference to his own personal experiences in the field. Zymer Neziri, with his deep knowledge of the tradition of Albanian epic songs, contextualizes the collection that Lord made in Albania by identifying the contents and themes of the songs and the areas from which the various singers derived and also by examining in detail the biographies of the individual singers. An essay of mine then discusses certain specifics of performance and focuses in particular on the rhythmical and melodic components of the songs as observed in the light of new research frameworks. Lastly, Victor Friedman studies in his contribution a few elements of a more linguistic nature and examines in particular the admirative forms that are present in the narrative texts.

Last but not least, thanks are in order: to Gregory Nagy, Stephen Mitchell, and David Elmer, who have promoted and supported this project from the very beginning; to the family of Albert B. Lord, for granting us permission to use documentary materials that proved to be of the greatest interest; to Francesco Altimari, who has supported our work and has acted as a stimulating interlocutor from the time when the project was in its infancy. I would also like to express my own thanks personally to Kay Kaufman Shelemay for her frequent engagement with these issues and her crucial help during all of my stays at Harvard through the years; to Stephen Blum, Steven Feld, and Michael Herzfeld for their continual conversations on these and other related subjects; to Ardian Ahmedaja, Giovanni Cestino (to whom we owe also the graphic realization of the musical examples), Giovanni De Zorzi, Ardian Ndreca, Zef Çoba, Lorenzo

Ferrarini, Matteo Mandalà, Peter McMurray, Mikaela Minga, Isa Muriqi (Isa Elezi-Lekëgjekaj), Aferdita Onuzi, Besim Petrela, Stefano Vaja, and Aida Vidan—each of whom in various ways has contributed to this volume, whether with research or with assistance in the final production of the volume. Special thanks are due also to David Elmer and to his family—Bonnie, Rosie, and Nathaniel—for providing much-needed hospitality and tranquility in the crucial moments when the volume was nearing its final stages.

Lastly, on a more personal note I would like to mention Roberto Leydi and Ramadan Sokoli, since it was at their suggestion that, toward the end of the 1990s, I began to develop my own interest in the tradition of Albanian epic song.

Introduction

Nicola Scaldaferri

Translated By Gregory Mellen

1. Milman Parry and Albert Lord Encounter Albanian Epic Song

THIS VOLUME IS DEDICATED to the songs in the Albanian language that were collected by Milman Parry and Albert B. Lord and are now conserved in Harvard University's Milman Parry Collection of Oral Literature (henceforth MPCOL).[1] The volume contains the full catalogue of the materials collected by Parry and Lord as well as an anthology of the texts that were deemed of greatest interest; these texts, moreover, are accompanied by documents and photographs that illustrate the fieldwork conducted by Parry and Lord. In addition, the volume contains a selection of essays written by the team of individuals involved in preparing the publication of these songs. Each essay closely investigates certain specific aspects of the research undertaken and the materials collected herein.

These materials were gathered by Parry and Lord in the 1930s as a secondary pursuit alongside their main line of research, which, as is well known, was concerned primarily with investigating traditional Slavic oral epic as a living laboratory whose compositional processes could be examined in order to provide parallels for the study of Homeric epic. Parry and Lord came into contact with the Albanian tradition when they encountered bilingual singers during their travels in various areas of what was then Yugoslavia, in the period between June 1934 and September 1935. Some of the principal singers whom they encountered, in particular those of the former Ottoman Sanjak of Novi Pazar in the southern region of Serbia, knew how to sing in the Albanian language in addition to their local dialect of Serbo-Croatian.[2]

---

[1] For an overview of the MPCOL, see Elmer 2013.

[2] The term 'Serbo-Croatian' was used by scholars of this period to designate the language spoken in the Yugoslav context in which they found themselves at work. The term was used even in

Parry had no knowledge of Albanian; and yet he immediately became interested in this parallel tradition, especially since it offered the possibility to examine, in a border territory, the relationship between poetic texts and formulas as they passed from one language to another. The main protagonist of this undertaking would be the singer Salih Ugljanin, one of the central figures of his generation of singers, who was already known to researchers such as Matija Murko and Alois Schmaus. Ugljanin came from a family of Albanian origin. His native language was Albanian, and it was in Albanian that he had learned how to sing and that he continued to sing until around the age of thirty. But after his marriage to a Bosnian woman, he learned how to sing in Bosnian as well, and his reputation as a singer was owed to his activity in this second language.[3] It was precisely this encounter with Ugljanin, and the desire it created in Parry to investigate the relationship between two different languages, that motivated the first complete recording of an epic song in the Albanian language: this is the song *Muji and Gavran Kapetan*, which was performed by Ugljanin both in Albanian and in Bosnian in November of 1934 and was recorded by Parry on aluminum discs.[4]

Parry's continued interest in bilingualism would later motivate the decision to record, at Gacko, in Bosnia, during the spring of 1935, the repertoire of songs of Fatima Biberović. Fatima was originally from Prizren, a city in Kosovo, and spoke three languages (Bosnian, Turkish, and Albanian), but sang primarily in Albanian. The songs of female singers formed a parallel, secondary area of research for Parry and Lord, who dedicated specific attention to this phenomenon in the area of Gacko, since it was there that they discovered an extraordinarily rich presence of women's song. The repertoire of such songs would later produce significant analytical results in the volume *Serbo-Croatian Folk Songs*, which was the work of Béla Bartók and Albert Lord but was published only after Bartók's death.[5]

After Parry's early death in December of 1935 (shortly after his return to the United States), Albert Lord continued the work set in motion by his teacher.

---

connection with singers whom subsequent political and historical events would differentiate, for instance Bosnians and Montenegrins. Nowadays other designations have come into use (for instance, 'BCS', as a designation for 'the Bosnian, Croatian, and Serbian language') with the intent of doing justice to the complexity of the local context. Parry's Muslim informants generally referred to this language as 'Bosnian.' The former Ottoman Sanjak of Novi Pazar is often referred to locally simply as 'Sanxhak' (in Albanian) or 'Sandžak' (in BCS).

[3] For biographical information on Ugljanin, see *Serbocroatian Heroic Songs*, vol. 1 (hereafter SCHS I) 1954: 329.

[4] The song is identified as *Hrnjičić Mujo i Gavran Kapetan*, Parry Number (hereafter PN) 672. The Albanian version is recorded on discs 1205–1210, which is followed by the Bosnian version on discs 2011–2019. The song appears in the anthology included in this volume.

[5] See Bartók and Lord 1951. On the songs of female singers, see especially Vidan 2003, which is dedicated primarily to an analysis of the text of these songs.

In 1937 he traveled to Dubrovnik in order to work on the transcription of the materials that had previously been collected. As a coda to his stay in Dubrovnik, Lord spent six weeks in Albania during the months of September and October, in which he visited several different locations in the northern area of the country, near Montenegro and Kosovo; his travels, therefore, extended beyond the southern limits of the areas that had been explored by Parry a few years previously. Before undertaking this trip, while still at Dubrovnik, Lord began to study the Albanian language: his precise intent was now to collect materials specifically in Albanian, in order to follow up more closely the cues for research that had arisen during earlier investigations. However, during this trip Lord did not have at his disposal the technology required for sound recording; he resorted, therefore, to the method of transcribing, by dictation, only the texts of the songs, in addition to information about the singers themselves and their respective repertoires.

The corpus in Albanian that is conserved in the MPCOL comprises, therefore, two distinct sets of materials, which can be traced, respectively, to the research conducted in 1934–1935 and to Lord's travels in 1937.

a) The first set comprises the audio recordings made by Parry, with the help of Lord and the collaboration of Nikola Vujnović, during the period of time between September 1934 and July 1935, in the areas of Novi Pazar (Serbia), Bijelo Polje (Montenegro), Gacko (today located in Republika Srpska, the Serb-controlled territory within Bosnia and Herzegovina), and Aleksandrovo (Republic of North Macedonia). In total, these recordings consist of 70 items recorded on aluminum discs; these include songs and texts recited in the Albanian language, along with conversations and recitations in South Slavic languages. Of these, the materials performed by Salih Ugljanin at Novi Pazar (among which is the song *Muji and Gavran Kapetan*) and by Fatima Biberović at Gacko constitute the most significant part. The Albanian corpus, considered as a whole, represents only a small portion, quantitatively speaking, of the materials recorded during Parry and Lord's fieldwork, especially when compared to the more than 3500 phonograph discs documenting Slavic traditions.

b) The second set comprises the textual materials that were dictated by thirty-eight singers and collected by Lord in various areas of Northern Albania between September 4 and October 13 of the year 1937. These texts are now contained in nine notebooks that were compiled during Lord's travels (notebooks nn. 1–8, along with n. 12, which contains the index); in addition to these, there are three further notebooks (nn. 9–11), which contain materials that were collected at Lord's request by two local collaborators, Murat Paçi and Qamil Hoxha, and which were sent subsequently to the United States. The twelve notebooks are housed in a container that bears the label *Heroic Ballads and Folksongs from*

3

Nicola Scaldaferri

Albania. In total, the contents comprise, in written form, more than 22,000 verses of songs that belong in great part to the repertoire of legendary epic. Among these is included the longest epic text in Albanian transcribed from the oral tradition currently known to scholarship, namely *Kanga e Sirotin Alis* ("The Song of Sirotin Ali"), which was dictated by the singer Adem Brahimi.[6] Information about the singers and their repertoires turns out to be of the greatest interest; some of these singers were among the most important of their generation and were known to other scholars who conducted research on Albanian epic song in the same period. It is worth noting, furthermore, the numerous documents of a more private nature, including letters and photographs that Lord sent to his family, which were acquired recently by the MPCOL; these vividly flesh out the picture of a series of travels whose scientific results, as will be seen in the following pages, should be numbered among the fundamental steps in the documentation of Albanian epic.

In 1954 Lord published the first volume of the series *Serbocroatian Heroic Songs*, which was dedicated to the songs collected at Novi Pazar. In this volume Ugljanin's texts in Bosnian occupy a central role, and their significance is further increased by the text of one epic whose musical transcription was undertaken by Béla Bartók and appears in an appendix.[7] Although he specifies that various singers included in the volume were competent in two languages, in this work Lord merely mentions the existence of recordings in the Albanian language, recordings, he explains, that had been excluded from SCHS but would be published subsequently in a future book alongside the texts collected in Albania in the year 1937.[8] In the preceding years, Bartók and Lord had analogously excluded, on the basis of language, the Albanian songs of Fatima Biberović from their book *Serbo-Croatian Folk Songs*, which was dedicated in part to the women of Gacko.[9]

And yet the book with the Albanian songs, which Lord had announced as forthcoming, was never completed, and the Albanian materials therefore remained for a long time unpublished. These materials, of course, were always available to scholars, who were able to obtain direct access to them at Harvard in the MPCOL itself. Among such scholars, of particular note is John Kolsti, the author of the book *The Bilingual Singer: A Study in Albanian and Serbo-Croatian Oral Epic Traditions*, published in 1990. This book, which resulted from a doctoral dissertation directed by Lord, is devoted to the figure of Ugljanin as a bilingual

[6] *Kanga e Sirotin Alis*, Lord Albanian Number (hereafter LAN) 60, which appears in the anthology included in this volume.
[7] See SCHS I: 437–467.
[8] See SCHS I: 56.
[9] See Bartók and Lord 1951: 252.

4

singer, offering a close examination of the specific techniques involved in his use of formulae; these techniques are compared, in particular, to the corpus of materials collected by Lord in 1937. Although with respect to certain details it is now outdated, Kolsti's book remains to this day the most extensive work of analysis conducted upon the Albanian materials found in the MPCOL. In more recent years, Kolsti's research has been further developed by more sporadic contributions made by the other scholars who have collaborated in the production of the present volume.[10]

In fact, however, the materials in Albanian available in the MPCOL have remained at the margins of the principal lines of research dedicated to this epic tradition, which, despite a few important contributions by international scholars, has seen its most recent progress above all as a result of the persistent work of local researchers.[11] These researchers, for a long time, have had great difficulties in accessing materials conserved in an important American research university like Harvard. It was only in 2002, as a result of a long-desired trip to Cambridge, that Zymer Neziri was able to gain access in person to Albert Lord's notebooks and was thus able to verify and disseminate the fact that the version of *The Song of Sirotin Ali* collected by Lord in 1937 is effectively the longest Albanian epic text from the oral tradition transcribed under dictation and known to scholarship. The reasons for this delay are various, but they should be attributed in large part to complex and well-known political events, which have resulted in some significant barriers to communication—this, despite the fact that, at the same time, there was already a growing sensitivity to issues of repatriation and a general sense of the need to reconnect archival documents, collected in the past in the course of fieldwork, with the communities from which they derive.

For many years, the existence of the MPCOL Albanian materials—in part because of the reputations of the two scholars involved and the great impact their work had in the world of scholarship—haunted the scholarly discourse of those Albanian researchers who worked on the epic tradition. Indeed, references and allusions to these materials were not infrequent, even if these references and allusions were not supported by direct access to the documents themselves

---

[10]   See in particular the various articles in Neziri 2006, Scaldaferri 2012, Neziri and Scaldaferri 2016. Among the texts that make reference to Parry and Lord's research and that rely upon indirect sources in the form of published materials, see in particular Berisha 1998 and Halili 2016.

[11]   For an up-to-date overview of the research that, beginning at the end of the 1800s, has discussed Albanian epic—from Meyer to Palaj to Haxhihasani, from Çetta to Neziri—see the numerous articles included in Neziri and Sinani 2016, which offers the most recent overall survey of the subject. See also Section 3 of this introduction, "The Codifictation of Albanian Epic Poetry and the Mythic Year of 1937" (below), which discusses in particular the research that was undertaken in the years preceding Parry and Lord's own work.

but rather were often based on incomplete information, which could be derived from those texts that had in fact been edited. As often happens in the case of phenomena that are partly unknown, a kind of mythical aura grew around the MPCOL Albanian materials. This aura, moreover, was increased, unintentionally, by the greatest contemporary Albanian novelist, Ismail Kadare. The works of Kadare—from celebrated novels, like *The Palace of Dreams*, to his written essays and even his extemporaneous statements—are chock full of references to legendary epic song; they reveal Kadare's great passion for the subject as well as his close knowledge of it, and in some cases (especially in works of a more essayistic nature) they express opinions that must be understood in the context of the local culture and its specific debates.[12]

For our present purposes, the novel *Dosja H*, first published in 1981 and translated into English as *The File on H* in 1997, is of particular importance. This novel tells the story of two Irish scholars, both experts on Homer and professors at Harvard, who travel to Albania to study epic song. Loosely inspired by Parry and Lord's research, the novel also makes use of a fleeting encounter between Kadare and Lord, which took place in Turkey in 1979.[13] The relationship between the fictional story narrated by Kadare and the actual fieldwork carried out by Parry and Lord has been the subject of discussion, even in rather general terms, such as the manner in which a creative literary product can promote the diffusion of academic research, even as it may well, unintentionally, end up furnishing a distorted image of that research.[14] In fact, Kadare's novel, in part due to the author's reputation, has made the story of two professors who travel to Albania to study epic highly popular among Albanian readers, and in so doing

---

[12] See the essays collected in Kadare 2002, as well more extemporaneous remarks such as Kadare 1987.

[13] The episode is evoked in Eric Faye's preface to the novel: "There are books that arise from a spark, from a word, from a fleeting encounter. This is the case of *The File on H*. In August of 1979, at Ankara, Ismail Kadare met with an American, Albert Lord, who said that he had been in Albania in the 1930s with his fellow American Milman Parry, in order to study the traces of Homeric epic . . . . The conversation with Ismail Kadare lasted no more than five minutes. At that time, in particular when abroad, speaking with foreigners—especially Americans—was not allowed. From these few minutes of conversation would later be born the idea for a novel, which the writer would then complete upon returning to his homeland. That novel is *The File on H*" (Faye 2015: 7, my translation). Contrary to what Faye describes above, Parry of course never traveled to Albania with Lord. In November 1935, however, Parry wrote a short letter to his sister, the last surviving document that he wrote, in which he mentions his desire to spend the following summer extending his fieldwork to Albania (Reece 2019: 137).

[14] See Valtchinova 2002, which has the pointed sub-title "Variations on the Works and Lives of Milman Parry and Albert Lord." On the impact of the novel, see Kalfus 1998, a review in the *New York Times* entitled "Balkanizing Homer: An Albanian Novel Raises Questions about the Greek Epics," published after the release of the novel's English translation.

it has spread ideas about the research of Parry and Lord, as well as interpretations of that research, that are not always exact.

It should however be emphasized that, thanks to his sensibility as a writer, Kadare clarifies with great acumen some of the most controversial elements in the practice of epic song. Above all, he shows how the debate concerning epic, insofar as this phenomenon pertains to cultures situated along territorial boundaries, ultimately also involves debates concerning identity and ends up acquiring political implications; and he shows how the debate over epic has become inextricably involved in the often tragic events of recent history.[15] This is one of the reasons why passages from Kadare's novels are often cited (even as epigraphs) in significant scholarly works that, in recent years, have had as their subject the practices of epic song, as for example the volume *Balkan Epic: Song, History, Modernity*, edited by P. Bohlman and N. Petković.[16]

All this only strengthens the need to offer a complete and reliable description of Parry and Lord's actual research on epic song composed in the Albanian language. In particular, it is necessary to bring the two scholars' actual research back into the realm of scientific debate, by distinguishing that research from the ideas about it—ideas which have often acquired an almost mythical dimension, but are not in fact supported by any reliable data.

2. Aspects of the Fieldwork: Tangible Memory and the Archaeology of the Intangible

Parry and Lord's research has had a strong impact, with repercussions extending even beyond their specific areas of expertise. This has occurred principally as a

---

[15] In particular, the conflict between Serbs and Albanians in Kosovo, regarding which Kadare, in his narrative works, often makes intelligent and ironic references that mingle the historical past and contemporary situations. To give only one example, one can cite a brief passage from *Tri gёngё zie pёr Kosovёn* (translated as *Elegy for Kosovo*), in which the contradictions that arise between the rhetoric of epic song and real life become a metaphor for the confusion that exists between reality as it is experienced and narrative re-tellings of that reality (Kadare 2000: 19–20, 27):

The minstrels had already begun to compose their songs, each in his own language. They resembled the ancient songs; even the words were not that different. The Serbian elders changed: "Oh, the Albanians are preparing to attack!" and the Albanian *lahuta* minstrels sang: "Men, to arms! The pernicious Serb is upon us!"

"Are you out of your minds or are you making fools of us?" the people asked. "The Turks are marching on us, and you are singing the same old songs—'The Serbs are attacking, the Albanians are attacking!'" "We know, we know!" the minstrels answered. "But this is where we've always turned to find parts for our songs, and this is where we will always turn. These parts are not like those of weapons that change every ten years. Our models need at least a century to adapt!" ...

"This is how things come to pass in this world," one of the princes is supposed to have said. "Blood flows one way in life and another way in song, and one never knows which flow is the right one."

[16] Bohlman and Petković 2012: 1, 2, 13.

result of broadening the field to which one can apply the oral-formulaic theory, for which various additional uses have been hypothesized.[17]

Nonetheless, several decades after the fact, there remain in Parry and Lord's work certain elements that can be investigated further, beginning with the Albanian materials that are the subject of the present volume and certain aspects tied to Parry and Lord's research methods, which have hitherto remained somewhat in the dark and which lend themselves, now, to significant reinterpretations, not least thanks to new methodological approaches. In the first place one can consider the material components of the research itself and the issues that these present, such as, for example, questions bound up with the creation of the audio recordings that were fundamental for the success of Parry and Lord's travels in 1934 and 1935; these recordings were made possible by a technically ingenious system that allowed the researchers to record performances in their entirety. There are many aspects, therefore, that today can offer important subjects for inquiry and for discussion in areas of research that have undergone significant developments in recent years: from media archaeology to sound studies, from sensorial approaches to issues of repatriation, including reflections upon national patrimony and intangible forms of knowledge.

The contributions of Wolfgang Ernst and Peter McMurray, which re-examine the results of this research by making reference to media studies and sensory studies, constitute without doubt an innovative and highly interesting approach, marking the beginning of a direction of research that promises to produce important further developments.[18]

One particularly significant element in Parry's research is his intense rigor at the concrete level of fieldwork. Even though this fieldwork might seem to be lacking in apposite reflection and to be directed pragmatically toward the collection of materials, in fact it reveals methodological characteristics that are highly structured and that were probably not merely the product of Parry's brilliant intuitions. Indeed, it has been rightly emphasized that Parry's years of study at Berkeley had brought him into contact with the American tradition of anthropological research, in particular with the figure of Alfred Kroeber, who had studied with Franz Boas and was at the forefront of his field. Kroeber's ideas on the concept of culture seem to have left a trace in Parry's own ideas, and it is possible that Parry's use of two alternating disc-recorders, in order to solve the problem of the limited playing time of contemporary recording media, took

---

[17] There are notable connections, for example, with musicological research. Treitler 1974 is a classic example; see also Foster 2004b, Lawson 2012.

[18] Despite some inaccuracies, the relevant issues are introduced in Ernst 2013: 67–72, 181. See also McMurray 2015 and McMurray 2020. For materiality in research on music and audio recordings, see Roy 2015.

inspiration from Boas, who, already in 1893, had employed two phonographs in order to record a song in its entirety.[19]

Today, in numerous respects, Parry's work presents strongly modern characteristics, which one would not hesitate to describe as dialogical: his research, in fact, can be described at various levels as collaborative, thanks in no small part to the varied involvement of Nikola Vujnović, Parry's local collaborator.[20] It was a kind of research, moreover, that always focused its attention primarily upon the actual experience of the singer and thus led Parry to collect and record not only the songs themselves but also extended conversations concerning the biographies and the lived experiences of the singers themselves. These aspects of Parry's work remain to this day rather understudied, and yet they constitute one of the most exciting elements of the present collection and should prove capable of suggesting noteworthy new areas of investigation. In addition, the materials collected alongside the research proper—such as photographs, letters, and written accounts and reports—have a broad ethnographic interest that should not be underestimated; in fact, they open up important documentary windows, to which we shall return in the coming pages, especially as regards Lord's trip to Northern Albania, which functioned as an appendix to the trip Parry had made only a few years previously.

Certainly the most significant step forward, when it comes to the quality of Parry and Lord's research, was enabled by the use of audio recording, as opposed to the method of collecting the poetic texts alone via dictation. In what follows we will return to the issues that concern the textualization of the practice of epic song; here, I will merely point out that Jakobson, already in his preface to SCHS I, underlines how, thanks to the use of audio recording, the singers were spared the atypical situation in which they had found themselves previously, when they had been asked to dictate texts—a practice which inevitably led to a certain "deformation" of the songs; at the same time, Jakobson also emphasizes the importance of the presence of the singers' own testimony concerning their activity.[21] It should not be forgotten, however, that the practice

---

[19] The connections that link Parry's work and ideas to the American anthropological tradition are studied in García 2001.

[20] On the importance of Vujnović to Parry's fieldwork, see Tate 2010 and Ranković 2012: 12. On the dialogical approach and collaborative ethnography, see Tedlock 1979, Lassiter 2005.

[21] "In their overwhelming majority, the songs of those peoples with whom comparative epic study deals were considerably distorted when they were first collected. The songs and recitatives, instead of being delivered normally, were either artificially dictated, thus losing some of their most characteristic formal features, or they were sung or chanted expressly for dictation, that is, without *ritardando*, or special pauses. In both cases the form was violated. When the delivery of the lines was normal, the fieldworker often lacked skill in setting down an entire song with the necessary accuracy, and thus the texts were either marred by all sorts of gaps or subjected to later retouching. Finally, the rhapsode was sometimes required to repeat single

of transcribing the text alone under dictation was not abandoned by Parry once he had begun to have recourse to recording; to the contrary, some of the most important specimens in the collection were gathered by dictation (for instance, the well-known *Wedding of Smailagić Meho* dictated by Avdo Međedović), and in the case of the present volume the entirety of the materials collected by Lord in Albania were gathered in this manner. What is more, the possibility of multiple methods of textualizing these practices—practices which by their very nature may present the appearance of great multiformity, at least from the point of view of the researcher—can contribute to analytical distinctions that illuminate both the constitutive elements of the performances themselves and also the complex relationship that is created between the singer and the researcher in the course of the research.[22]

In the introduction to the second edition of *The Singer of Tales*, the editors cite a comment made by Parry regarding his request that the Harvard administration provide him with a half-ton of aluminum discs. It makes for an arresting image, and it would later be repeated several times by Lord, who defined the results of the research as a "half-ton of epic."[23] Far from exhausting itself at a merely anecdotal level, the image sheds light upon the 'epic' dimensions of Parry and Lord's research and it invites us to reflect upon the nature of the material components that make up the collection and that have strongly conditioned the entire course of the research. These material components constitute an important element in the relationship established by the researchers with their area of research at multiple levels: at the logistical level, in terms of the transportation, by ship, of delicate and onerous

---

verses or even entire epics, and then the two performances were artificially fused. In rarer and more recent instances, when a recording machine was employed, only isolated samples, or mere parts of epics, were recorded by this means. Parry, however, recorded on phonograph discs whole epics in their full length and also, when possible, the entire epic repertoire of a singer, in order to compare the rhapsode's delivery both of the various passages within one song and of different epic songs. Moreover, the language which is sung by an informant may be instructively compared with his spoken language. In addition to the epics, Parry recorded conversations with the singers about their lives and their art and about their personal attitudes toward this art, toward individual songs, and toward the subject matter of the poetry. In this way we learn the life of the reciter, composed and narrated by himself, and we observe the language in which he talks about his recitation, the 'meta-language', as the logicians would say" (Jakobson in SCHS I: xi–xii).

[22] Reflection upon the multiform nature of oral texts receives extensive treatment in Honko 2000 and Saussy 2016. For a few specific cases in Albanian, see Neziri and Scaldaferri 2016, which analyzes examples of recorded recitation and singing in comparison with the respective texts collected under dictation.

[23] "I have already written to the purchasing agent at Harvard instructing him to order for me from the aluminum company another half-ton of discs, which will be approximately 3,000 discs." Quoted in Lord 2000: x; see also Foley 2000: 77.

tools and apparatuses from the United States to Europe; at the organizational (and even the political) level, in terms of travel and collaboration, which of course could not have been organized without contact with local authorities and political figures;[24] and even at the concrete level of the recording technique employing aluminum discs: this format would ultimately constitute a new kind of memory, destined to become from that point onward the text of reference for all future analyses. The experience of recording in and of itself represents the fundamental step in the process of materializing and mediating performance, and this fact constitutes, more and more, a key element in the reflection upon sound and media.[25]

The topic acquires particular importance in the case of intangible forms of knowledge and spheres of activity that have been conserved and transmitted through time thanks to embodied knowledge (*le gramophone humain*, to use the words of Marcel Jousse) and that then become objectified in forms of memory that are by nature physical—and this importance is tied also to the reception of these new forms of memory and the cultural significance with which the new formats eventually become invested. The implications of this process are all the greater when the object that is rendered accessible by media is none other than the human voice, due to the dense and ambivalent relationship that is created between the disembodied voice and the format that grants it a new corporeal existence; however, it is also true that, in general, the very reflection upon orality itself should probably be reconsidered by taking into proper account its sonic and sensorial component, as has been opportunely suggested by McMurray.[26]

The procedures for recording sound, far from being neutral or merely instrumental, always prove to be tied to specific research hypotheses, whose results emerge from forms of interaction that come about in a manner that is influenced not least by the material conditions of the research itself. In Parry

[24] Concerning Lord's trip in Albania, one can deduce from the letters reproduced here in the Appendix the contacts that Lord made with the American Legation and with the local authorities in his effort to organize his travels and to provide for necessary protection during them. In Section 4 of this introduction (below), the various stages of the journey are reconstructed in detail, including Lord's contact with local researchers (in some cases accidental, in others organized in advance). See also McMurray 2020, which discusses the contacts—and the misunderstandings—between Lord and the Serbian Academy of Sciences at Belgrade regarding his journey in 1950.

[25] See Ernst 2013, Roy 2015. The study of the material components of recording involves various approaches that also concern other traditions and other musical practices; in the field of musicology, see in particular the influential treatment in Van Orden 2015.

[26] See McMurray 2020. On the complex debate concerning the voice, see in particular the anthology of fundamental texts in Clayton 2008. Among recent attempts to expand the debate, with particular regard for questions of technology and the body, see Labelle 2014, Scaldaferri 2014, Youngh 2015, Thomaidis and Macpherson 2015.

and Lord's time, researchers who carried out recordings in the field in similar situations always had to adapt their methods, in most cases, to the tyranny of the phonograph and the few minutes that it granted for recording; Parry, however, tried to "use" technology in order to find an adequate solution to the actual exigencies his research imposed.

As early as his first trip to the Balkans, carried out during the summer of 1933, Parry started to collect materials under dictation; however, he soon realized that transcriptions or dictated texts would not be sufficient for his purposes. He began therefore to use a mechanical phonograph, with wax cylinders, which he had bought in Zagreb. His first recordings were accomplished by methods similar to those employed by certain contemporary researchers who were making field recordings in Eastern Europe (such as Béla Bartók, Constantin Brăiloiu, and Zoltán Kodály). The phonograph had many limitations in the quality of its recordings: singers and instruments were required to perform almost inside the horn of the machine, with the result that some frequencies were captured better than others.[27] However, the crucial aspect concerned the temporal limits of the medium. Parry found singers able to sing songs that were hundreds of lines long; but the phonograph then in use among fieldworkers was unsatisfactory, because it allowed a maximum recording time of only a few minutes. To prepare for his second and more important stay in Yugoslavia (from June 1934 to September 1935) Parry carefully planned out his recording technology. First of all, he moved from wax cylinders to aluminum transcription discs, which represented the state of the art in audio recording of the 1930s. This system was especially apt for the purposes of fieldwork, because, compared to other media, the aluminum discs were of high durability and could not be re-recorded; moreover, the presence of the microphone resulted in a superior sound quality of the recordings.[28]

---

[27] Parry wrote about these limitations in his unpublished reports. Some remarks can be found in SCHS I: 7: "The singing, which itself brings out the vowels and obscures the consonants, was completely drowned out by the sound of the *gusle*. It was only when I had an electrical phonograph apparatus with a device for cutting down the low frequencies of the vowels and of the *gusle* and had a high-pitched microphone which could be placed near the singers' mouth and directed away from the head of the *gusle* that I was able to get transcribable recordings."

[28] Among folklorists and scholars who used aluminum discs for field recordings one should mention at least Charles L. Todd and Alan Lomax, as well as the Chicago linguist Manuel Andrade for his recordings of Mesoamerican languages in Mexico and Guatemala. One of the most noteworthy recording expeditions was surely the one undertaken in the 1940s by the brothers Bruce and Sheridan Fahnestock in the South Seas, during which they collected specimens of birdsong and local music in the course of their oceanographic surveys; in this expedition the disc-cutter was kept in the schooner and connected to the microphone on shore by wires that were two miles long. For a general introduction to the history of sound recording, see Hart 2003.

The way that the physical limits of recording formats condition the nature of recordings themselves has been a concern since the beginning of the history of recorded sound. A great number of musical pieces, especially of commercial music, have been restricted in scope to the few minutes allowed by the medium; on the other hand, long classical compositions have been cut and split into series of 78 rpm discs. Among the most famous cases, one can mention the portion of the Mass in B Minor by J. S. Bach, recorded by His Master's Voice at a Royal Albert Hall concert in 1926, which was split over four double-sided 12" 78 rpm discs.

Parry's solution to the issue of length, which allowed him to record long epics in their entirety, was unusual among the fieldwork of his time. He employed a special apparatus composed of two recording-head turntables; by switching between the two turntables, it was possible to record on a series of discs songs or conversations without any interruptions. He asked the Sound Specialties Company of Waterbury, Connecticut, to build this apparatus, which was likely designed by Lincoln Thompson, who was one of the greatest experts in recording at that time.[29] Parry's system attracted the admiration of Béla Bartók, who in more than one case wrote about the quality of these recordings, which were excellent for their time, both from the musical and from the technical perspective.[30]

From the descriptions of research methods reported by Lord on more than one occasion we know how Parry and Lord set up what constituted a veritable workshop, which contained two distinct areas: generally, in one area was situated the singer, along with Parry and Vujnović, whereas in the other area was situated the recording apparatus, which was operated by Lord. Drapes, hung up on the walls, helped to isolate the performance from extraneous noise, especially that which was produced by the power source necessary for the

---

[29] Roberts and Thompson 1935. Lincoln Thompson is also mentioned (merely as "Lincoln") by Lord in some unpublished texts in the MPCOL. Information about the techniques employed can be found especially in SCHS I: 7–11, and further in Parry 1971: xxxvi (where there is mention of the Ford V-8 automobile that Parry brought to Yugoslavia so that its battery might power the recording apparatus). Much of this information, as well as the reference to the article by Roberts and Thompson, was brought to my attention by David Elmer. In these same years, Thompson was also in touch with Alan Lomax, who mentions him and the Sound Specialties Company numerous times in letters concerning some equipment difficulties dating to the 1930s; see Cohen 2010: 16, 20.

[30] See the letter written to Kodály in December of 1941 (published in Bartók 1978: xxiv), in which Bartók attests that Parry was particularly good at choosing singers, as well as the article published on June 28th, 1942, in *The New York Times* (reprinted in Suchoff 1976: 148–151), in which he stresses the unique qualities of these recordings, namely: the registration of songs in their entirety thanks to the use of two turntables; the presence of many variants of the same songs; and the numerous conversations with singers that are included in addition to the songs themselves.

functioning of the whole apparatus; meanwhile, Parry and Vujnović formed a kind of small audience, which helped to create a situation that was more similar to a real performance.[31]

The aluminum discs conserved in the MPCOL, therefore, in addition to being the medium for the transcoding of the singers' performances, represent the physical record of complex experiences in field research and of a unique moment in the history of sound recording technology. The discs are all the more important if one considers the fact that the apparatuses Parry and Lord employed for recording have not themselves been preserved and that, therefore, we can get an idea of how they worked only by means of descriptions and photographs.

To listen to these discs once again is thus to undertake at more than one level a kind of archaeology of memory, in which it is impossible not to notice an analogy between, on the one hand, the digging of the groove that fixes the traces of the voice upon the rigid format of the disc and, on the other, the excavation of the researcher who gathers information in order to shed light upon performative procedures passed down through the ages. The singers had embodied old forms of knowledge in performative mechanisms whose nature was rhythmic, musical, and gestural; and now, by means of recording, these forms of knowledge have been transcoded into a tangible form of memory, which itself becomes the point of departure for new researches and new analyses; and these researches and analyses, in turn, contribute in a decisive manner to the creation of the myth, and of the very genre, of oral poetry. The content of the discs, however, cannot be separated from the recording procedures and formats that created them, nor from their own material history, insofar as all of these were elaborated by a researcher for specific objectives. At the end of the day Edgard Varèse's admonition regarding 'machines' remains valid: machines do not effect miracles; they can merely restore to us—in however different a form—that which we ourselves have introduced in them.[32]

3. The Codification of Albanian Epic Poetry and the Mythic Year of 1937

The materials collected by Parry and Lord, in particular the corpus of texts that were transcribed by Lord, should be numbered among the most noteworthy contributions to scholarship of that generation of researchers who, with their work, allowed for the construction of a national corpus of Albanian epic; and this is true despite the fact that these materials have for a long time remained

---

[31] See in particular the descriptions that are included in SCHS I: 10–11, Bartók and Lord 1951: 250.
[32] See Varèse and Wen-chung 1966: 18–19.

outside of the scholarly circles that have studied this subject. By re-situating these materials in their proper context we can better understand their importance and their innovative quality, which is tied in part to the specific nature of the research methods employed in order to gather them.

The years in which Parry and Lord encountered Albanian epic coincided with a crucial period in the construction of Albanian national culture. This national project involved texts that made use of the country's historical tradition as well as (and above all) the tradition of legendary epic, and in particular it entailed the formation of what is now considered the corpus of Albanian epic *par excellence*: namely, the epic songs that are identified as *këngë* (or *kangë*) *kreshnikësh* (or *të kreshnikëve*, or *kreshnike*), which can be translated as "songs of heroes" or "songs of the frontier warriors."[33] This genre is documented among those Albanians who live in the northern part of the country and in Kosovo and who use the Geg dialect[34]; it presents certain specific characteristics, which have been identified in numerous scholarly contributions, and it shares a great deal with Slavic epic. In fact, the connection with Slavic epic is quite clear even from a mere consideration of the manner of performance, which is carried out by a single singer (*lahutar* in Albanian, the analogue of the Slavic *guslar*) whose song is accompanied by a single-stringed instrument played with a bow (*lahuta*, identical to the Slavic *gusle*); and the connection is clear too in the case of the narrative content, which revolves around the experiences of the brothers Muji and Halil and the thirty Agas of Judbina. The complex (and controversial) relationship between the two traditions has given rise, as one might well imagine, to an intense debate, which is often slippery in nature and which has not infrequently extended into political discussions as well.[35]

Indeed, due to its history, the geographic region of south-eastern Europe has become known as a quintessential border zone, and it has entered into the global imaginary as an area of conflict (between East and West, between Christianity and Islam)—conflict that has had sometimes tragic results, which

---

[33] The adjective *kreshnik*, which has acquired in Albanian the definition 'heroic', has been the object of study on the part of numerous scholars and linguists, among whom some of the most important are Lambertz, Koliqi and Çabej; see Neziri 2003. On the relationship with the Slavic *krajišnik* ('border guard' or 'frontiersman'), see Skendi 1954: 99, Pipa 1984: 85.

[34] The Albanian language has two major groups of dialects: Geg, present in Northern Albania and the areas of the former Yugoslavia; and Tosk, present in Southern Albania. The two areas where these dialects are spoken are also called Gegëria and Toskëria. The official modern Albanian language, established during the period of the dictatorship of Enver Hoxha, is based on Tosk.

[35] On the relationship with the songs about the brothers Mujo and Halil Hrnjica that are present in Bosnia and Herzegovina, see Skendi 1954: 99–142, Pipa 1984. There is a very rich bibliography on these questions, beginning with the works of Cordignano, Skendi, Pipa, and Desnickaya, and extending down to the more recent works of Halili and Elsie. For an up-to-date overview of these issues, see the essays contained in Neziri 2006, Neziri and Sinani 2016.

have re-emerged once again in recent years. These dynamics have always found a catalyzing element, of an intensity perhaps known nowhere else, in the repertoires of epic song. It would be impossible to treat these issues adequately in the present pages, but they can be effectively summarized by Zumthor's celebrated formulation:

> ... epic song narrates combat against the Other, the hostile stranger, the enemy outside the group—whether the latter be a nation, a social class, or a family .... The epic tends toward the "heroic," only where "heroic" means the exaltation of a sort of community superego. It has been noted that it finds its most fertile grounds in border regions where there exists a prolonged hostility between two races, two cultures— neither of which obviously dominates the other. The epic song crystallizes this hostility and compensates for the uncertainty of competition; it foretells that all will end well, proclaims at least that we have righteousness on our side. In so doing, it forcefully arouses action.[36]

It is not an accident that it was precisely in border zones that Milman Parry discovered important traditions of epic song still active in the 1930s. These traditions continue to have contemporary relevance precisely in their being both ancient and modern at the same time, thanks to the way that they tightly connect historical realities with the blurry contours of myth.[37]

The first traces of the presence of *këngë kreshnikësh*, even if they were not yet known by this name at the time, are found in a work published by Gustav Meyer in 1897. Meyer thus inaugurated a line of research dedicated to this repertoire, which would continue to be studied intensely by foreign scholars (we will encounter later on figures such as Maximilian Lambertz and Fulvio Cordignano, not to mention Robert Elsie); and it is foreign scholars who were responsible for decisive contributions to the understanding of this repertoire and to its diffusion in the following decades. The work of such scholars supplemented the

---

[36] Zumthor 1990: 85.

[37] The connection between the modern world and the (more or less imaginary) ancient past, which can involve situations that are rife with strong symbolic valencies, does not only concern intangible traditions, which are mutable but also capable of being passed down through time via a system of practices and susceptible to becoming, in this way, powerful symbols in virtue of their relative manipulability; it also concerns physical objects, all the more so when they are endowed with monumental significance. Those who are old enough to have lived through the period of the breakup of Yugoslavia in the 1990s will remember the words issued from Mostar and diffused throughout the world by news media, after the famous bridge of Suleiman the Magnificent collapsed under bombing: "We'll re-build it, more beautiful than before, more ancient than before!"

fieldwork carried out by local researchers, who would arrive at the codification of the repertoire in written form in their respective collections.[38]

The consolidation and fixation of a system of poetic and musical practices follows a typical framework that is known to us from other periods and from situations different from the Albanian one; and such frameworks have often found their leading spokesmen in certain intellectual figures who act predominantly in the context of religious institutions. In Albania, a project of this type came into being naturally, soon after the country declared its independence from Ottoman rule in 1912, when the necessity came to be felt for a cultural program that was adequate to the new national context. This project acquired solidity thanks to the convergence of a wide variety of movements, which had as their respective objects issues involving literature, identity, and even politics, often influenced by the new balance of power that had taken shape in eastern Europe after the first World War; and it grew in strength in the years in which Ahmet Zog dominated Albanian politics. Zog had come to power in the 1920s, and, after he managed to proclaim himself king, he remained in that role until Italy occupied Albania in 1939. Zog's reign, with its mixture of light and darkness, represents the first important attempt to consolidate a unified Albanian state.

In this operation a key role was played by the religious figures of the city of Shkodër. This city, which was formerly the capital of an Ottoman *vilayet* and which was known for its important cultural traditions, had also a solid and long-standing Catholic presence. Particularly active in the local context, especially at the level of education, were the Jesuits and the Franciscans. Among the latter stand out in particular intellectual figures and scholars such as Shtjefën Gjeçov (1874–1929), Vinçenc Prennushi (1885–1949), Bernardin Palaj (1894–1946), and Donat Kurti (1903–1983), who were all tied in one way or another to the figure of the national poet, Gjergj Fishta (1872–1940).[39] Educated in Bosnia under the tutelage of the Franciscans, Fishta was a complex literary figure and a polyglot, and his activity included engagement with political and social issues; he represents one of the reference points of his era, and he deliberately embodied the role of the poet *par excellence*, up until the time when his work was banned during the years in which Hoxha dominated Albanian politics.

In order to celebrate the epic narrative of the new nation, between 1902 and 1937 Fishta wrote the epic poem *Lahuta e malcis* ("The Mountain Lute"), which relates the historical and legendary events that took place within the context of the struggles over the northern borders of Albania. The poem has deep roots in

---

[38] For a historical profile, see Neziri 2006, Neziri 2008.
[39] For Fishta's bibliography, see Gjecaj 2007.

the epic tradition of the northern mountains, as one can note from the title of the work itself; but it has also been correctly pointed out that a certain influence emanating from the work *Gorski vijenac* ("The Mountain Wreath"), composed by Petar II Petrović-Njegoš in 1847, is not lacking.

In 1913, just after Albanian independence, Fishta founded at Shkodër the periodical *Hylli i dritës* ("The Star of Light"). This would be followed a few years later, in 1916, by the opening of his printing house, which would prove to be very active. It was annexed to the local Franciscan convent and operated by Fishta thanks to the imprimatur granted by the local ecclesiastical authorities.[40] *Hylli i dritës* provided an important forum for discussions concerning various issues—political and cultural, literary and economic—which were aimed at furthering the goals of the new nation, and it constituted the central link that connected not only the numerous cultural initiatives that were undertaken by the Franciscan brothers of Shkodër but also the most vital cultural forces in the city as a whole. Parts of Fishta's epic poem appeared in *Hylli i dritës* as they were completed by the poet; and the periodical also published, among other things, excerpts of the *Iliad* and the *Aeneid* translated into Albanian. The periodical would later publish documents that were destined to become fundamental for Albanian identity; here it suffices to mention that in its pages were first published the customary laws of the mountain regions (now known generally as the *Kanun of Lekë Dukagjini*), which had been collected by Shtjefën Gjeçov and were posthumously gathered together in a volume that was edited and printed in 1933.

Starting in the year 1924, the periodical provided a space for the published texts of the songs of the legendary epic of Muji and Halil, which were brought to the public's notice for the first time with the generic description of *këngë kreshnikësh* and were presented as part of a cycle. The series was inaugurated with the episode of the wedding of Muji; the text opens with an introduction that highlights analogies with other projects to gather and catalogue European folklore, emphasizing explicitly the great significance of such work for the delineation of national identity. This fact is highlighted once again in a reference to the work of Vinçenc Prennushi, who in 1911 had published at Sarajevo an initial collection of folk songs that he called "National Treasure."[41]

---

[40] The digital version of *Hylli i dritës* is accessible online at the website of the Library of Shkodër: http://bibliotekashkoder.com/digital/hylli_i_drites/. For the complete catalogue of the digitized materials, see http://bibliotekashkoder.com/digital/ (accessed February 2021). For a guide to the century-long publishing activities of the Franciscan printing-house of Shkodër, see Gjinaj 2016.

[41] *Hylli i dritës*, 1924, V, 1–2, pp. 33–39. Prennushi's collection was titled *Visari komtaar* ("National Treasure"); it did not, however, include songs of the *kreshnike* cycle, even though in his introduction Prennushi makes mention of the songs of Muji and Halil (Prennushi 1911: xi).

The collection of *këngë kreshnikësh* was undertaken in a systematic fashion beginning in 1919, thanks to the work of the Franciscan Bernardin Palaj (1894–1946) and other collaborators. Palaj, who was a native of Shkodër but had been educated at Salzburg and Innsbruck, was a teacher along with other Franciscan brothers at Shkodër's Lyceum "Illyricum." A refined musician and man of letters, Palaj combined a passion for folklore with an intense poetic and literary activity of his own, which has only begun to become known and studied in recent years. In fact, Palaj, like many of his Franciscan brothers, would fall victim to the persecutions of Hoxha, and his literary work would remain for a long time in the dark.[42]

It is well known that the versions of *këngë kreshnikësh* published by Palaj are not mere transcriptions of popular texts taken down under dictation but rather re-workings that contain strong traces of his own literary sensibility. His approach to the transference of epic songs into textual form bears the marks of a refined aesthetic sensibility; his versions in the end contributed to the formation of a canon that was destined to have great influence on the diffusion of these songs and probably also influenced the criteria for the future collection and transcription of such songs when this was undertaken in the coming years. The Jesuit Fulvio Cordignano (who in the same period was employed in surveys in Albania, of which we shall speak further below), when discussing Palaj's work, points out an overlapping of popular practices and poetic retouchings in Palaj's versions and explains how this overlapping was able to influence even the work of the national poet in the very same years:

> And truly, the samples that are offered to us in the 1924 volumes of *Hylli i dritës* are among the choicest and the most beautiful . . . . They are not, however, entirely genuine songs, songs issued from the mouth of the people; rather, the compiler has permitted himself some rearranging and retouching, as is clear from a remark he makes in a note on p. 257: "this rhapsody gathered from the words of three rhapsodes of Curraj"; and, after all, it is immediately evident to anyone who has a deep knowledge of this genre of popular literature. In any case it must be said that the compiler reveals himself in these texts as an exceptional artist and poet. And not only an artist and poet, but also a very refined

---

[42] Palaj died in prison in 1946 after suffering mistreatment—a fate that later befell Vinçenc Prennushi in 1948. Both men were eventually recognized as martyrs of the Catholic Church and beatified in 2016. Donat Kurti spent seventeen years in jail, during which time he translated the Old Testament into Albanian. The tomb of Fishta, who passed away in 1940, was defaced during the years of the Hoxha regime and his work was prohibited. On Palaj's literary activity, see Palaj 2005 (along with the introduction to that work, written by Angela Cinnincione, which reconstructs its various phases).

critic and aesthete. And I do not hesitate a moment in dedicating the proper homage to Fr. Bernardin Palaj, who in his modesty does not sign his name to his compilation. . . . Fr. Fishta himself has not escaped the enchantment of these rhapsodies; indeed he has managed to make use of them in the most recent songs of his own *Lahuta*, in which one feels the influence of the expressive palette and the powerful images of these songs.[43]

In 1937, for the twenty-fifth anniversary of Albanian independence, the monumental series *Visaret e Kombit* ("The Treasures of the Nation") was inaugurated. This series would include, up until 1944, the publication of fifteen volumes dedicated to various aspects of Albanian folk culture; these volumes were accompanied by two volumes titled *Shqipenija me 1937* ("Albania in 1937"), which were published in 1938 and, significantly, open with a preface by king Zog.[44]

Of particular note is the second volume of *Visaret e Kombit*, which has the title *Kânge kreshnikësh dhe legjenda* and was edited by Palaj along with his Franciscan brother Donat Kurti. The volume contains 34 texts that have as their protagonists Muji and Halil. These texts were destined to become classics and points of reference in the following decades; they constitute only a portion of the materials gathered in the mountainous zones of Northern Albania by Palaj in collaboration with other Franciscans (Nikollë Dajçi, Bernard Llupi, Marin Sirdani, Simon Mikeli, Leonard Shajakaj, Rrok Gurashi). In the volume the singers from whom the scholars have gathered the texts are also mentioned: Pal Buli, Dodë Nikollë Loshi, Palok Ujka, Pal Duli, Gjergj Pllumbi, Marash Nika, Sokol Martini, Mirash Gjioni—the same names that we will find in other collections made by other researchers in those years, including that of Lord.[45]

The publication of this volume seems to have established unequivocally the correspondence between the term *këngë kreshnikësh* and the legendary epic that has at its center the figures of Muji and Halil—a fact that remained partly ambiguous in the previous volume of the series.[46] The adjective *kreshnik*,

---

[43] Cordignano 1943, vol. 1: 13–14.

[44] See the *Katalog i ekspozites dokumentore te Rilindjes Kombetare 1937*, which is accessible online at the website of the Library of Shkodër. Zog would guide the country for only a little longer, until the Italian occupation of the years 1939–1943.

[45] See the information that appears in the introduction to the volume (*Visaret II*: xii). As late as 2004 Elsie and Mathie-Heck would make use of the texts in *Visaret e Kombit* for their anthology of texts in English translation.

[46] In *Visaret e Kombit I*, edited by Karl Gurakuqi and Filip Fishta, there is a section with the title *Kânge trimije dhe kreshnikësh* (pp. 229–315). In this section, along with some songs that are clearly attributable to the cycle of Muji and Halil, there appear also the texts of *Kostadin e Jurndina*, collected from among the Arbëreshë in Italy. One may note that the tenth volume of the series,

however, was rather popular in those years, since it was central to Zog's rhetoric of power and was proposed by him as an honorific title for use especially in the northern areas of the country.[47]

Among the research of this era should be mentioned the work of Fulvio Cordignano (1887–1952), who has already been mentioned above. Cordignano was active for a long time in Albania as a priest and a scholar, and he would later find himself at the center of harsh controversies due to his ideas concerning the "non-homogeneity" of the new Albanian nation (ideas that were in part based on anthropometric studies that were quite fashionable in that era). Cordignano would effectively be ostracized, and this would hinder the circulation of his studies on epic. Cordignano's research, undertaken independently of the work done by the Franciscans, began in 1924; it would later result in two volumes entitled *La poesia epica di confine nell'Albania del Nord* and published at Venice in 1943. In the foreword Cordignano states that he had learned of other important research and publications (beginning with *Visaret e Kombit*) only after he had completed his own work and had intentionally not taken these other publications into account. Cordignano's text is highly significant, being rich in observations that have great relevance for the performative and musical aspects of the songs; Cordignano, moreover, collected epic songs of Muji and Halil from a single singer, Gjergj Pllumbi (or Pllumi), of Theth, with whom he had come into contact as early as 1925. However, Cordignano's work would not meet with a favorable reception in the debates that took place in Albania, in part due to the controversies that surrounded his name, and in part due to his tendency to maintain that the epic songs of Muji and Halil were of Slavic origin—a thesis that he supported in part by presenting the opinions he gathered when working with the singers themselves.[48]

Another scholar who paid close attention to Gjergj Pllumbi was Ernest Koliqi (1903–1975), a native of Shkodër. In addition to being a scholar Koliqi was also a poet and a politician, whose tasks included those of Minister of Education during the years of Italian occupation. He was educated in Italy and would later

---

edited by Myrteza Roka, is entitled *Lahuta e Kosovës* ("The *Lahuta* of Kosovo"), and yet, in spite of its title, contains only *kânge burrnije* (historical heroic songs), a fact that indicates the extent to which the term *lahuta* (perhaps in the footsteps of Gjergj Fishta's epic poem) had at this point acquired a strongly symbolic resonance that extended beyond its musical function of accompaniment for epic song.

[47] In 1925, as a gesture of reconciliation, Ahmet Zog (who at that time held the position of president) gathered together at Tirana prominent citizens, *bajraktars*, and *vojvodas* of Northern Albania, from whom he requested the *besa* (a solemn oath; see below, Ch. 1, p. 47) in support of the government; and in exchange he named them *kreshnike*, reserve officials, and granted them a pension. (This information has been kindly provided to me by Ardian Ndreca. See further Sirdani 1934.)

[48] See Cordignano 1943, vol. 1: 162–179, and vol. 2: 4.

return to live there after Hoxha became dictator. Already in the 1930s Koliqi was undertaking important research on epic song, publishing his first study in 1937; and in the same year he came into contact with Pllumbi, whom he defined as the king of the Dukagjin singers (*Mbreti e kângtarve të Dukagjinit*).[49] In the following years Koliqi would meet with Pllumbi numerous times in the course of his trips, which were almost pilgrimages, to the mountains of Theth. He dedicated important studies to Pllumbi's activity in the pages of the periodical *Shêjzat*, in which he included photographs taken by Shan Pici. Koliqi even dedicated a poem of his own to Pllumbi, and so too would Vorea Ujko (pseudonym of Domenico Bellizzi), one of the most important Arbëreshë poets—which just goes to show how Pllumbi, the singer from Theth, would enter into the shared imaginary as the rhapsode *par excellence* and would transcend the narrower context of his local fame.[50]

It is to Koliqi that we owe an important testimony to the manner in which Pllumbi conceived of the categorization of traditional songs. According to Koliqi, the singer in fact distinguished them into two groups: "*kânge t'egra* (wild songs) and *kânge të buta* (soft or gentle songs). The first group comprises the cyclic rhapsodies and the heroic songs in general . . . the second group comprises love songs."[51] In the categorization that the singer proposes we find once again a distinction that recalls the one between "men's songs" and "women's songs"—which is found in the work of Parry and Lord, and is analogous to the distinction already present in earlier work, such as that of Vuk Karadžić.[52] The "wild" genre includes both legendary epic and historical epic. Pllumbi and other singers seem effectively never to have used the term *kreshnik* when they referred to the legendary type of epic.

Koliqi was also in contact with Bernardin Palaj, whom he defined as *Frati i Kangve* ("the Friar of Songs"). He recognized that Palaj played a crucial role in valorizing Albanian legendary epic and in getting others to appreciate its quality—in part, perhaps, by means of his own aestheticizing interventions:

> The most beautiful songs, however, belong to the series that was
> collected and, it seems, reworked with a fine and masterful touch by

---

[49] The definition appears for the first time in Koliqi 1937, and the text *Në vis ku tingullojnë lautat...*, which dates to 1938 and was published serially by Koliqi (under the pseudonym Hilush Vilza) in the periodical *Shêjzat* in the years 1960-1961. The same contents are found also in Koliqi 1943. Additionally, Koliqi mentions other important singers with whom he had come into contact, including Prendush Gega and Sokol Martini, both of whom were met by Lord and figure in the photographic documentation of Lord's trip (see the Appendix). According to Koliqi, Martini was also an important informant for Palaj.

[50] These poetic texts would also be published in the periodical *Shêjzat* (IV, 9-10, and VII, 3-4).

[51] Koliqi 1960: 113.

[52] See the discussion at Bartók and Lord 1951: 248.

Father Bernardin Palaj. Palaj is called "the Friar of Songs," since it was he who first showed us, in the pages of the periodical *Hylli i dritës*, the stupendous beauty of that genuine poetry which hitherto had been unknown or passed over because it was thought to have consisted merely of servile and pedestrian translations from Serbo-Croatian. But instead, as we have maintained several times, this poetry is made up of migratory topics that are common to the entire Balkan world (we limit ourselves to this region even though one could also look further afield)—topics that are employed and elaborated by every people according to its own peculiar poetic genius.[53]

In 1937, in the pages of *Gazeta shqiptare*, Koliqi described the "pilgrimage" he had made to the mountains of Dukagjin in order to meet Palaj. From the description emerges a portrait of Palaj that is drawn with poetic color and forms a pair with the potrait of Pllumbi, "the King of Singers"; and in the portrait of Palaj it is evident that Koliqi had a clear sense of the role played by Palaj and by the religious figures of Shkodër in the codification of the corpus of epic texts and, more generally, in the study of Albanian folklore:

> Three days I stayed at Palç waiting for the friar .... And the friar arrived. In the early evening I heard him call as he came from the edge of the fields. The click-clack of the horse's hooves, quickly approaching the presbytery, filled my heart with joy: Father Bernardin Palaj, the parish priest of Merturi, with his residence at Palç. . . . He showed me a few piles of papers and old notebooks grown yellow with time. Together we leafed through those dusty pages, from which emanated a breath of eternal spring.
>
> The heroic cycle of Muji and Halil sung by the rhapsodes of Dukagjini in their pure and incisive language. . . . I don't know who said it, that elsewhere in the world the poets sing for the people, but in the Balkans the people sings for the poets. Even up to the present day, for me, the greatest Albanian poet is the Albanian people. This truth suddenly began to shine forth in my mind at Palç in the presbytery of the Friar of Songs.
>
> This man, in the course of his long solitude in the mountains, has lent his attentive ear to the inexhaustible song that springs from the depths of the hearts of the Albanian race, and he has snatched it from

---

[53] Koliqi 1960: 113–114.

the oblivion of time. On the disorderly shelves of the presbytery at Palçi there sleeps the seed of future springs of Albanian poetry.[54]

4. Albert B. Lord in Northern Albania: September-October 1937

The Preparation

The year of 1937, the twenty-fifth anniversary of Albanian independence, proved to be an important one in the history of Albanian culture and, in particular, in the history of Albanian epic song. While Fishta was putting the finishing touches on his more-than-thirty-year-long draft of his epic poem *Lahuta e malcis*, Palaj and Kurti published the volume of *Visaret e Kombit* with the first organic collection of *këngë kreshnikësh*, and in doing so they made this the official name for the genre; and at the same time Koliqi published his first work on epic and came into contact with the King of Singers, Gjergj Pllumbi, who was already being closely studied by Cordignano.

In the summer of the same year, the twenty-five-year-old Albert B. Lord found himself at Dubrovnik, probably ignorant of the events that were taking place just a little to the south and that, in short time, would deeply interest him. Lord was by now working alone, after the death of Parry, which had taken place in December 1935 soon after his return to the United States. In those months spent at Dubrovnik, along with Nikola Vujnović and a certain Jack (mentioned only by this name in Lord's letters), Lord was transcribing and typing out the texts of the songs that had been recorded a few years before. As a coda to this work, before his own expected return to the United States toward the end of October, Lord was planning to make a "collecting trip" in Northern Albania, with the goal of better understanding the local epic tradition there, whose existence had been revealed to him in his encounters with bilingual singers.

Lord recorded the various stages of his activity in those months with great meticulousness, and this allows us to reconstruct in detail both the phases of the work he was engaged in and also his preparations for his journey to Albania. A particularly useful source of information regarding Lord's preparatory work consists of private documents such as the letters he sent to his family (concerning both the preparatory phase and his journey itself), which have been made available to scholars only in recent times. As we will see in the following pages, these letters have proven to be of great importance. In addition to the letters we also have photographs (only recently rediscovered), which contain on

---

[54] Koliqi's text, initially published in *Gazeta shqiptare* in 1937, has been reprinted in an Italian translation by Angela Cirrincione (in the Introduction to Palaj 2005).

their reverse side handwritten notes with the names of people and places. It is from these documents that often emerge the most personal considerations and the most private glimpses into Lord's experiences as they took place, together with details that are of great interest from an ethnographic point of view; at times these documents contain significant information that was not included in the official research reports and that was subsequently forgotten. The authorization to publish these materials (especially the letters and the selection of photographs) was granted by Lord's family, who have thus permitted us not only to reconstruct Lord's experiences in great breadth and depth but also to supplement some noticeable lacunas: the most blatant previous omission concerns the identity of the collaborator who helped Lord in the transcription of the corpus of Albanian epic in the course of his trip, namely, Peter Preka. Preka in fact is nowhere named in the official documents and his identity appears only in a note in one of the documents of a more private nature.

It emerges from the letters that Lord prepared his trip to Albania with great care: one finds in them that Lord established contact with the American Legation of Tirana and acquired support, probably planned well in advance, at the administrative and political level.[55] It should be recalled that, in those years, the diplomatic relationship between the United States and Albania was excellent, and this surely encouraged visits from foreigners and favored their travels in Albanian territory. The American Legation was inaugurated in 1930 in the presence of King Zog, at a time when the highest echelons of Albanian diplomacy in the United States had as their protagonist the high-profile, enlightened intellectual Faik Konitza. In 1931 another Harvard researcher, the American anthropologist Carleton Coon, completed his anthropometric research in the mountainous areas of Northern Albania; these regions were considered, at the time, extremely conservative and had entered into the public imaginary as classic examples of areas that were primitive and impassable.[56]

At Dubrovnik Lord took lessons in the Albanian language in order to acquire the basic rudiments of everyday vocabulary, in part so that he might get around with ease, but also so that he might understand the content of the materials that he was preparing to gather. The notebook that Lord used for his practice exercises in Albanian is conserved in the MPCOL, and it testifies to his acquisition of the basic Albanian vocabulary necessary to get by in a new context; but in addition to basic vocabulary one also finds phrases and verses of epic poetry. Lord's method, the explicit goal of which was to learn the fundamentals in view of the work he was about to undertake, employed Serbo-Croatian as a linguistic

---

[55] See the discussion in McMurray 2020 regarding Lord's trip in 1950 and his preliminary contact with the Serbian Academy of Sciences at Belgrade.

[56] See Coon 1950.

starting point and made use of the language present in the texts of oral epic. At the same time, his notes from his lessons indicate that he paid great attention to certain aspects of phonetics, such as the different way of writing the two types of /e/ in order to highlight the accentuation as either acute or grave (see the page reproduced in Appendix 3)—a detail that later on in the actual transcriptions of the texts would not always be applied with perfect rigor.[57]

In addition to his linguistic study Lord probably also undertook readings that would give him information about the general situation of the area, as can be deduced from a note concerning *Some Tribal Origins, Laws, and Customs of the Balkans* by Edith Durham. In the first decades of the twentieth century, Durham, a famous traveler and writer, had undertaken extensive trips in the Balkan peninsula and had embraced the cause of the new Albanian state. She had spent time above all in the mountains of Northern Albania and had gained the respect of the local populations to such an extent that she acquired the nickname "The Queen of the Mountain Men" (*kralica e malesoreve*)—which is now inscribed on the monument dedicated to her that looms over the valley of the Shala river, an area that Lord also travelled through. Durham's writings, accompanied by photographs, had offered vivid depictions of these areas and had contributed in no small part to creating her reputation, which would come to be part of the shared imaginary, even at an international level.

That Lord felt he was well prepared for his Albanian experience—both at the linguistic level and at the level of organization—is well expressed in a letter he sent to his family on August 25th, a few days before beginning the trip to Albania. He had already arranged things in such a way that at Dubrovnik the work could continue to proceed during the period of his absence, and he wrote:

---

[57] The MPCOL conserves several notebooks containing preparatory materials that date to Lord's preliminary stay at Dubrovnik. One of them, with the title *Albanian* written on the cover, contains materials relating to Lord's lessons in the Albanian language. The content of the exercises consists, in fact, of epic formulae in Serbo-Croatian to be translated into Albanian, which shows that Lord was primarily concerned with internalizing the lexicon and the typical expressions of the language of epic song in its Albanian form. In addition to this one finds transcriptions of texts from a book of Albanian songs (among which one can see in one notebook *Skanderbegu e Ali Pasha and Skanderbegu e Ballabini*); Lord's purpose for these latter exercises was probably to familiarize himself with the language and the lexicon of Albanian poetry. Yet another exercise found in the notebooks consists of an initial transcription of a fragment (a few dozen lines) of an epic song, with an interlinear translation into Serbo-Croatian; evidently this was a test of Lord's work in learning to switch between the two languages. The fragment was dictated by the singer Kol Marku, whose name we will later see in the manuscripts among the first texts dictated at Shkodër. The song from which the fragment derives is identified as *The Song of Zuk Bajraktari* and is indicated by Lord as song no. 1, LAN 1. Lastly, it is also worth pointing out the notebook entitled *Addresser*, in which there appear writings of a more diaristic nature relating to the first part of the journey and containing names of singers, collaborators, and addresses.

Am well prepared for Albanian trip. Slight knowledge of the language. Am expected in Tirana, and even have a guide and interpreter, picked out by the American Legation, waiting for me there. Have the names of some singers all ready, and have even collected one Albanian song in Dbk [Dubrovnik]. Films and cameras are ready.

The Trip

After departing from Dubrovnik for Durrës by ship in the last days of August, Lord stopped first at Tirana where he was expected by the American Legation. Here, as is clear from his letters, Lord was provided with a person who would aid him in his travels by acting as guide and translator. In all probability this individual is to be identified with Peter Preka, of whom we will speak further below. From Tirana Lord travelled to Shkodër, at the feet of the mountains, the place that would serve as the starting point for his research. Many of the extant photographs were taken in these two cities, and for the most part they reveal market scenes.

At Shkodër, on September 4th, Lord began his work with the singers. Then he made his way eastward, heading through the mountainous interior and arriving at Prizren in Kosovo.[58] Next he made his way back through the Albanian mountains, stopping several times on his way back once again to Shkodër, and finishing his journey at Tirana in the middle of October. Lord had planned to stop also at Korça in southern Albania before returning to Dubrovnik, and he mentions this part of his projected journey in his letters; but in the end he had to cancel this stop due to lack of time. On October 16th Lord departed by ship from Durrës to Dubrovnik, and from there, on the 26th, he departed for the United States aboard the *Saturnia*, the ship that, together with its twin the *Vulcania*, operated on the Trieste-New York route; he arrived at his destination on November 9th.

Below we reproduce Lord's itinerary, with indication of the places and the days, as can be deduced from the documents we possess. In parentheses are added the territorial subdivisions that correspond to the administrative code that came into force in Albania in 2015 and that in large part differ from those current in the 1930s. In italics are indicated the stops that, although they are not mentioned in the notebooks containing the songs Lord collected, nonetheless can be securely identified from documents of a more private nature. (See also the maps printed at the end of this volume, pp. 384–385.)

---

[58] In the manuscripts there are no traces of the stay at Prizren, but that it took place is confirmed by Kolsti, who derived his information from personal communications with Lord that took place during his doctoral research.

Dubrovnik (Last days of August)
Durrës
Tirana

4-5-6 September

Shkodër

6-7 September

Bajza-Kastrat (Malësia e Madhe, Bashkia Koplik)

8 September

Pjetroshan-Kastrat (Malësia e Madhe, Bashkia Koplik)

Dedaj-Kastrat (Malësia e Madhe, Bashkia Koplik)

9-10-11 September

Boga (Malësia e Madhe, Bashkia Koplik)

12-13 September

Theth (Shala, Bashkia Shkodër)

14-15 September

Abat (Shala, Bashkia Shkodër)

16-17 September

Palç (Nikaj-Mërtur, Bashkia Puka)

19-20 September

Geghysen (Dukagjin, Bashkia Shkodër)

20-21 September

Kolgecaj (Bajram Curri, Bashkia Tropoja)

22-23-24 September

Tropoja

26 September

Pac (Bytyç, Bashkia Kukës)

Kam (Bytyç, Bashkia Kukës)

Prizren, in Kosovo; stop mentioned by J. Kolsti

1 October

    Bicaj (Luma, Bashkia Kukës)

3 October

    Va Spas (Mal i Zi, Bashkia Kukës)

4 October

    Spaç (Orosh, Bashkia Mirdita)

5-6-7 October

    Puka

    Shkodër, mentioned in the letter of October 5

10-11-12-13 October

    Gurrëz (Kurbin, Bashkia Laç)

    Kavaja, mentioned in the letter of October 5

15 October

    Tirana

16 October

    Durrës

    Dubrovnik

Lord's travels between the major towns took place by means of motor vehicles, whereas he made his way through the interior mountainous regions on horseback or by foot; all of his travels took place with the agreement of local authorities, who on more than one occasion, as is clear from Lord's letters, provided protection and guides. In a letter written from Shkodër on September 6th, Lord even informed his family—perhaps to reassure them of his safety—that he possessed a *laissez-passer* from the Minister of the Interior, the most important individual in the country after the king himself.

As has been stated above, during this particular trip, since he did not have at his disposal the means to make recordings, Lord dedicated himself exclusively to the collection of texts taken down under dictation. The handwriting of the notebooks reveals a collaborative effort: some parts were written by Lord, others by at least one other individual, whose name remained for a long time shrouded in mystery since it is never explicitly mentioned in the documents. Only in 2017, with the discovery of the photographs possessed by Lord's family, and thanks to the corresponding notes on the reverse of the photos, was it possible finally to give this person a name: Peter Preka.[59]

In the course of his "collecting trip," Lord continued to use the working methods that Parry had long employed, which allowed him to identify the most representative singers. For each singer the first items to be taken down were biographical facts: age, background, level of literacy (if literate), knowledge of other languages, travels, contacts with other singers, musical instruments played (*lahuta* or *çifteli*).[60] Then followed a full inventory of the singer's repertoire, which could vary from a few songs to several dozens. Also taken down was the singer's religion, which shows that in this area there were both Christian (Catholic) and Muslim singers; the latter, whom Lord considered more interesting for the purposes of his research, were encountered especially in the last part of the journey (see the letter of September 23rd, from Tropoja, included in the Appendix). Last but not least were transcribed, from each singer, under dictation, one or more songs that were considered to be representative. The songs that were transcribed derive in large part from the repertoire of legendary epic, though it is true that texts of historical songs and lyric songs are not lacking. As was true in the case of previous research as well, the singers were compensated for their participation.

The materials that were gathered therefore fit into the following three categories: biographies, repertoires, and transcriptions of songs. The first two always appear grouped together and, just like the songs, are identified by the Albanian term *Dorëshkrim* ('manuscript') and are numbered progressively. In order to be consistent with MPCOL conventions, it has been decided to use in this volume and in its catalogue the designation LAN (Lord Albanian Number).[61] From the point of view of cataloguing and numeration, the different types of material are all grouped together, as if (in accordance with the idea of the researcher himself) the information about the singer and his repertoire were equally important as the text of a song itself. Undoubtedly this view of the material differs from that of local researchers, who have been interested above all in the collection and codification of texts and, in accordance with a certain

---

[59] The name "Peter" is in fact mentioned in the accounts and in one letter (September 23); the name and surname appear together in the photographs that depict Preka several times at work alongside Gjok Pjetri and engaged in the task of transcribing texts under dictation (LAN 12–15, collected between September 6th and September 8th). It is very probable that Peter is to be identified with the translator and guide that is mentioned in the letters and was provided by the American Legation in Tirana.

[60] The *çifteli* is a plucked instrument with two strings; it is present in the Geg area, and is used to play instrumental music and to accompany singing.

[61] The numeration begins with no. 2, since Lord indicated the fragment transcribed at Dubrovnik as no. 1.

viewpoint tied to a romantic conception of popular poetry, have generally not concerned themselves with the concrete experiences of the singers and have therefore not collected information about them as individuals—with the partial exception of the work of Cordignano and Koliqi, who both occupied themselves with the figure of Gjergj Pllumbi. The centrality of the figure of the singer, his background, and his repertoire would be an important part of Lord's mature reflections in this field; moreover, in the research carried out in 1934–1935, one of the most important elements is to be found in the conversations held by Parry and Vujnović with the singers (*pričanja*), which were recorded on discs just as the songs were. These conversations can reveal, at one and the same time, noteworthy facts both about the dynamics of the creation and the transmission of the texts and also about the personal histories of the singers themselves. Lord began his collection at Shkodër when he met the fourteen-year-old Pjeter Trepshi. Trepshi is preserved to memory in one photograph, and he dictated a few lyric verses to Lord; a player of the *çifteli*, he was the son of the owner of the hotel in which Lord had stayed. Lord then continued on his journey, making his way toward the central area of the mountains, in the heart of the regions called Malësia e Madhe and Dukagjin, where he obtained his most significant results. The stops on Lord's journey touched places that were fundamentally important for the cultural history of Gegëria—from Theth to Kukës to Tropoja—in years in which the traditional social structure of the clans and their territorial rootedness were still very much solid and stable. Lord encountered dozens of singers, and though they were not all at the same level, there were among them some of the greatest singers of that generation; and we will re-encounter them ourselves in the studies of other researchers.

It should be emphasized that, in the information gathered by Lord, the singers do not seem to have made any distinction between historical and legendary epic. To the contrary, the contiguity that can be observed between historical and legendary texts seems to confirm the formulation proposed by Pllumbi, who distinguished between lyrical or love songs, on the one hand, and heroic songs, on the other, where the latter category includes both historical and legendary works. As one might easily suppose, the term *kreshnik* is almost entirely absent; it appears, in the course of all the notebooks compiled by Lord, only a single time, and at that only in passing, among the biographical information gathered about Prendush Gega, whom Lord had met at Puka on October 7th (LAN 84).[62] Of Gega, however, though he is listed as a "poet," no songs appear to have been transcribed.

---

[62] While none of Lord's informants used the term *kreshnik* as a generic label for songs in the repertoire, the singers did occasionally use the term within their songs to designate 'heroic' individuals; see, e.g., LAN 60, line 1359, and LAN 79, line 31.

Nicola Scaldaferri

Some Glimpses into the Personal Side of the Research

It is worthwhile to focus for a moment upon a few significant facts, of which we can discern traces above all in the more private documentation kept by Lord, and which can offer us some hitherto unrecognized but very illuminating perspectives on Lord's journey. In particular, the following materials are of great use: the pages of a more diaristic kind contained in the notebook entitled *Addresser*; the eight letters Lord sent to his family (which frame Lord's entire experience in the field); and above all the photographs, which are a newly revealed corpus of the utmost interest. There are nearly 100 photographs in total, and they were found, along with their negatives, at the beginning of 2017 by Lord's family. There are images of Tirana and Shkodër that date to the beginning of the trip and depict for the most part market scenes; there are landscapes and pictures of individuals from the trip; there are portraits of singers (though unfortunately not all of these are accompanied by a clear identification of the individual depicted); there are scenes from the collecting work; and finally there are details of private life. At the moment, we do not possess any technical information concerning the type of camera that Lord used. This body of photographs firmly places Lord in his own right among the gallery of travelers and scholars—from Durham to Lambertz to Coon, to cite only a few of the most well-known—who in the first decades of the twentieth century journeyed through Albania and left behind photographic documentation of the greatest interest. Such pictures, in fact, help to provide a counterweight—an alternative view—to the "official" Albanian image of the period, which is represented in large part by the famous pictures of the photographers of the Marubi dynasty.[63] For our present purposes, however, Lord's pictures, along with the annotations that he made on the reverse, provide illuminating information about his research and about a few crucial moments on his journey—information that does not emerge from any other materials.

One thing to point out concerning this kind of documentation (especially the notes and photos) is that it is quite copious for the beginning of the trip but it diminishes in quantity as the research progresses, precisely, in fact, when Lord was arriving at the most significant results as far as the collection of songs is concerned. In fieldwork it commonly happens that, toward the beginning, one is struck by the newness of the situation, but as one progresses, one's energies

[63] A panorama of photographic journeys undertaken in Albanian territory, curated by Robert Elsie, can be seen on the website http://www.albanianphotography.net/ (accessed February 2021). On the activity of the Marubi and their collection of photographs, see http://www.marubi.gov.al/ (accessed February 2021).

32

and concentration get absorbed by the data that is being accumulated. As far as the photographs are concerned, though, it is certainly also possible that the rolls of film may simply have run out and it was not possible to acquire others on the spot.

Undoubtedly one of the most crucial stages of the trip began on September 13th, the date when Lord met with Gjergj Pllumbi at Theth. Pllumbi's name appears in the notes before this date and is indicated as a singer to be sought out (in addition to being mentioned in the first pages of the *Addresser* notebook); for example, he was mentioned by the young singer Pjeter Trepshi, who, in the course of giving his biographical information, named Pllumbi as one of his teachers.

Soon after, on September 14th and 15th, Lord would stop at Abat, where an exceptional event took place: Lord encountered the "Friar of Songs," Bernardin Palaj. Thus far no trace of this meeting has been found in the official reports, but the photographs possessed by Lord's family and discovered in recent months leave no doubt that it took place. The name "Palaj" appears in the *Addresser* notebook, where Lord mentions having met his collaborator, Rrok Gurashi, at Boga, on the way to Theth and Abat, just a few days beforehand. Also in the *Addresser* notebook there appears Palaj's address, and so too does the Franciscan printing house, *Shtypshrkonja francescane*, and the title of the work *Visaret e Kombit*. Nevertheless, while this information might have been provided indirectly by third parties, it is the photos that Lord took at Abat that testify directly to an actual meeting between the two men (photograph nos. 14 and 15 in Appendix 1). It may not be entirely an accident that the most important results for Lord's research, and the meetings with some of the principal singers, took place after Lord had met with Pllumbi and Palaj, who may well have provided Lord with important guidance regarding the continuation of his journey and the singers he should contact.

It is once again the photographs (and their corresponding notes written on the reverse) that testify to the presence, at Abat, of Adem Brahimi, along with Palaj and Rrok Gurashi (photograph no. 15). Brahimi was one of the key figures for the success of Lord's trip in Albania. He was the most skilled singer that Lord encountered, and he accompanied him as a guide on horseback for at least two weeks in the most difficult and most remote interior areas—certainly from mid-September, the time of the meeting with Palaj, to the end of that month, during the period that was without doubt the most productive of the trip. But most importantly, in the course of the journey, on several occasions, Brahimi would dictate two extensive epic songs, one of which was the *The Song of Sirotin Ali* (LAN 60), already mentioned above as the longest song of the collection. Brahimi is moreover the only singer that Lord mentions in his letters to his family, and he does so with explicit praise.[64]

Among the photographs is found a pair of pictures (taken in the area of Kastrat, in Malësia e Madhe, toward the very beginning of the trip) in which the subject is none other than Lord himself in traditional garb. Lord thus situates himself in the group of foreign travelers, writers, and scholars who were unable to resist the temptation to photograph themselves in local dress. Such images begin with the well-known portrait, from 1813, that Byron had made of himself after he visited Ali Pasha of Tepelena; they continue, with another case being that of Maximilian Lambertz, who had himself photographed in 1916 in the traditional garb of Shkodër; and they arrive, finally, at the case of Robert Elsie, who had himself depicted in the traditional dress of Theth, the location in which, moreover, he was buried after his premature death in September of 2017. The most immediate inspiration for the images of Lord, however, may be the portrait for which his teacher, Milman Parry, posed, in local dress, in 1935.[65]

Lord's Letters: An Attempt To Take Stock

The information that emerges from Lord's private correspondence is various and important. We find in the letters logistical details, like those concerning the routes that Lord took, especially on foot and on horseback, in the more remote interior areas, and references to difficulties and personal risks, which are mentioned especially in the last letters, when the end of the journey was already in sight.[66]

We also find in the letters a reference to two teachers from local schools, Murat Paçi and Qamil Hoxha, from Shkodër and Tropoja respectively, to whom Lord entrusted the task of collecting further materials to send him when he was back in the United States, in order that the work could continue in his absence.[67] Also not lacking are passages of a more descriptive kind, incidental curiosities, and details of ethnographic interest, such as the mention of the well of Skanderbeg at Boga, which is depicted in the photos (photograph number 10 in Appendix 1). Lord describes the story of this well in the *Addresser*:

> Story of well at Boga with three goats' heads. The first settlers were shepherds. They could find no water for their herds. One young goat

---

[64] See the letter of September 23 written from Tropoja.
[65] This image appears on p. 438 of the first, hardcover edition of Parry's collected papers (Parry 1971). It does not appear in the later paperback edition.
[66] See the letters of October 5 from Puka and of October 15 from Tirana.
[67] See the letter of September 23 written from Tropoja.

found this spring, then returned to the herd. The shepherds noted that his beard was wet, waited and traced him to the spring.[68]

Then too there is the description of local events, rites, and beliefs: for example, Lord describes hospitality rites and notes the similarity between these rites and those described in the texts of the songs that had been collected so far. This similarity has been noticed by numerous travelers, who have pointed out the strong connection between local practices and certain narrative elements of the oral tradition. In this regard, the two long letters that Lord wrote at the beginning and end of the central part of the trip (from Boga, on September 11th, and from Tropoja, on September 23rd) are of great significance; the latter of the two is accompanied by a detailed sketch (reproduced in Appendix 2) of the interior of the *kulla* (a traditional stone house of the mountain regions) in which Lord had spent the night.

From the private correspondence there also emerge significant considerations regarding the results of the trip. The letters in fact reveal Lord's immediate impressions of his experience as it took place stage by stage during the journey. Writing from Boga on September 11th, before heading into the depths of the mountains, Lord expressed uncertainty about the value of the materials he was gathering, stating that he was not yet in a position to determine whether the trip ought to be considered a success or not; and it is true that, at this point, he had not yet made his way into the areas where he would have his most fertile encounters. Around a month later, however, a letter sent from Puka on October 5th reveals Lord's sense that he had now arrived at significant results, even though there still remained ten or so days before the end of the trip. And it was in fact during the period of time between September 11th and October 5th that the most significant encounters had taken place and the most important materials had been gathered, from singers like Gjergj Pllumbi, Sokol Martini, Adem Brahimi, and Ali Meta.

Lord's firm conviction that he had definitely made significant progress is expressed later, in the last letter sent from Albania, written at Tirana on October 15th, just before his return to Dubrovnik, where he would spend the last part of his European trip before returning to the United States. It is a letter of great significance, and it has the ring of a kind of attempt to take stock of a research experience to which, ultimately, Lord would never return.[69] It may, perhaps, help

---

[68] Manuscript notes that appear in the *Addresser* notebook, p. 11.

[69] Lord returned to Albania in June 1966, but only for a few days, in order to participate in a folklore conference. On that occasion he met with the young scholar Agron F. Fico, who later, in the 1990's, was in contact with Mary Louise Lord and scholars affiliated with the Milman Parry Collection of Oral Literature (see Fico 2016: 15–42).

us to find an explanation for Lord's subsequent lack of interest in the Albanian tradition and in his research on that tradition (research which, in fact, he would not go on to publish, even though he had announced his intention to do so). In this letter Lord admits, effectively, that in the course of the trip he had not found exactly that which he "was looking for, only traces of it"—despite being fully aware of the limitations of a period of fieldwork that was probably, in fact, too short in duration:

> [the trip] was highly enlightening and successful, though actually I did not find the exact thing I was looking for, only traces of it. For various reasons it is harder to get at than I had expected, and needs more time in "breaking ice."

It is difficult to know exactly what Lord was looking for in Albania and exactly what its relation might have been to the overall vision of his research, which saw him occupied for many years in the wide-ranging exploration of various and distinct kinds of poetic practices. Above all, it is difficult to know what he was hoping to find in the Albanian tradition, as a particular kind of poetic system and cultural phenomenon, and how this might have illuminated the tradition that formed his starting point—namely, the Slavic tradition, which would always continue to be Lord's essential point of reference.

All this, however, does nothing to diminish the value of a corpus of materials that belongs by right among the principal collections of Albanian epic. Its importance consists in the first place in the uniqueness of its texts, in the significance of the singers who were involved, and in the richness of the information that was collected; but equally important is the methodology employed in collecting the material, since this methodology has the merit of focusing on phenomena that were not always at the center of the attention and the concern of local researchers, especially as regards the background of the singers, their activity, and their repertoires.

Moreover, in the texts collected and transcribed by Lord and his collaborator, there is no trace of that attempt to retouch, to correct, and to polish, which more or less explicitly characterizes the work of local scholars, above all that of Palaj. Thus, even if Lord's materials are sometimes marked by uncertainties and inconsistencies, due perhaps to a level of linguistic preparation that was not quite up to the task, nonetheless they reproduce the words dictated by the singers in a manner that is more faithful than the polished and attractive versions published by local Albanian researchers.

PART ONE

ESSAYS

1

Milman Parry, Albert Lord, and the Albanian Epics

John Kolsti

IN THE FALL OF 1960 a course in Serbo-Croatian taught by Albert Lord led me into the world of Serbian and Croatian literature and South Slavic, primarily Bosnian, oral traditional poetry. When I learned that singers interviewed and recorded by Milman Parry and Lord, then a twenty-three year old graduate student, in the Sanjak of Novi Pazar in 1934–35 included bilingual Albanians whose line and scene-building skills were later analyzed by Lord in *The Singer of Tales*, I was surprised to read that one of them, Salih Ugljanin, had recited and sung songs for Parry in both Bosnian (*bosanski*) and Albanian (*arnautski*). When I mentioned to Lord that Albanian had been spoken in my childhood home, he invited me to walk with him over to Houghton Library to leaf through the small notebooks he had used in the mountains of North Albania in 1937 to record songs sung and dictated by Geg, or North Albanian, singers, young and old, novice and experienced, Muslim and Roman Catholic.[1]

Lord's first contact in Shkodër involved a fourteen-year-old Catholic boy who arrived at his father's hotel with a *çifteli*, a two-stringed long-necked lute, and sang a rhymed twenty-three-line ballad and a rhymed twenty-line lyric (Nos. 2 and 3 in the collection). These initial songs, which, Lord notes, were "sung in the same style," were far removed from the long traditional epic poems which Albanian singers accompanied on the bowed *lahuta*. But the boy, who learned

---

[1] The books by Edith Durham (1909) and Joseph Swire (1930) served as excellent introductions in the 1930s to High Albania before and after World War One and up to the expulsion of King Zog (1928–1939) by Mussolini. Durham's classic book was doubtless Lord's travel guide for the clan territories he ventured into after setting out from Shkodër. Swire provided readers in the 1930s an informative account of the social and political turmoil inside Europe's newest nation state.

such songs "from clients who come to the hotel," including Gjergj Pllumbi, had in all likelihood met there the old *lahutar* whom Lord found and recorded in Theth one week later (LAN 28, "Musa Qesexhi and His Brother Bergjanine Gjemi," included in this book).

I quickly realized the value of Lord's collection. Over the next five weeks he found what he had hoped to find: long epic poems, most of which echoed the Bosnian material he and Parry two years earlier had recorded on phonograph discs. One had 2163 lines (LAN 60, "The Song of Sirotin Ali," dictated by Adem Brahimi and included in this book), another 1753; two had over 1,000 lines. The experienced singers he encountered, both Roman Catholic and Muslim, had to have influenced and been influenced in return by Albanian singers in the Sanjak of Novi Pazar and Montenegro. Unlike short ballads and lyric songs, epics of this length were nowhere to be found in the few published Albanian sources at that time. It is fair to say, however, that except for Albanian Franciscans in Shkodër and in Bosnia,[2] little attention had been paid to the epic songs of North Albania by Albanian or foreign collectors.

Ugljanin had informed Parry that his family had migrated to the Sanjak from Northern Albania. He boasted of contacts with a renowned Muslim singer in Montenegro, Ćor ('Blind') Huso (Qorr Hysa in Albanian) and of having served along the Austrian Military Frontier in northern Bosnia before its occupation by Austria in 1878. Lord describes the monolingual blind singer as follows:

> [Ćor] Huso was from Kolašin in Montenegro, and he wandered from place to place singing to the *gusle*. His fame spread abroad, and some of our best singers had learned songs from him. . . . He seems to have been a good showman. His dress and the trappings of his horse were distinctive, and he cut a romantic picture. It is a great pity, of course, that someone did not collect songs from him a couple generations ago, but he seems to have escaped the attention of collectors—just why it would be interesting to know. . . . From later accounts of singers who learned from him, we can get some picture, however inaccurate, of the songs which he sang and the influence he had on the tradition.[3]

---

[2] Fr. Vinçenc Prennushi's collection, which was published in Sarajevo in 1911, contains only lyric poems and short narrative poems. In Shkodër, *Hylli i dritës* (The Star of Light), a Franciscan publication founded in 1913, ran scholarly articles on songs collected and edited by priests in North Albania and included epic songs about the border warriors later edited and published in Tirana in volume two of *Visarët e Kombit*.

[3] Lord 2000: 19–20.

A note after Rexhep Zeneli's 424-line song about Halili's capture of Jovan Kapidani (LAN 79, included in this volume) states that "this song was learned from Qorr Hysa." Unfortunately, no further information was offered.

Lord, like Ugljanin, was not particularly interested in the short songs about turn-of-the-century skirmishes along the volatile Montenegrin border or ballads about local outlaws and outcasts. The unusual song he recorded about the expulsion just twelve years earlier of Albania's first elected president Fan Noli (a Harvard-educated head of the Boston-based Albanian Orthodox Church) by a Muslim chieftain, Ahmed Bey Zogolli,[4] must have fallen well outside his primary focus, as did the few short songs in the collection about local Albanian heroes who defended the sultan's border with Montenegro (for example, LAN 34, "The Song of Ali Pasha of Gusinje," included in this volume).

Lord had recorded Ugljanin's conversations with Parry and heard the singer at times reluctantly, but nevertheless effortlessly, recite pastiches of short balladic songs in 4-3 and 4-4 rhythms in both languages. But when Parry asked him to recite and then sing one of his long Bosnian songs, "Ramo of Kovač," he did so reverting to the longer rhythm of the epics (see below). Ugljanin's ability to "fix" (*ujdisati* in Bosnian) half lines, changing from four to six, or six to four syllables, may be seen in the following example, when he *recites* the opening scene of the tale (PN 656, disc 980)[5]:

Lum për ty, more, i lumi Zot.	Blessings on you, o blessed Lord!
Kur o bô nji sabah i bardh,	When morning came
koka çue Çeto Bashe Muja	Çeto Bashe Muji arose
e në kull-o zjarmin e ka dhez,	lit the fire in his *kulla*
e n' oxhak-o kave qi po pî.	drank coffee by the hearth.
Qather Muja n'kom-o qi o çua,	Then Muji rose to his feet
edhe Muja vetën e shtrëngoj	and Muji girded himself
e silahin Muja e ka ngjesh.	he put on his gun belt
Dy pistole i ka pa shti,	and stuck two pistols in it

---

[4] Gjok Pjetri's song (LAN 15) about Zogolli's expulsion from Albania of Bishop Fan Noli, in December of 1924, is perhaps more political than historical. The song ends: "He became our sovereign king (*mbret*) / sovereign king, Zog the First / may he live long together with the Albanians / may he live long, King Zog the First" (ll. 197–200). Zog proclaimed himself king in 1928. Pjetri then adds in verse form his reasons for composing the song: "I am from High Albania (*Malsia*) / I have never been to school / I can't read and I can't write / I wish to leave it as a reminder / to sing the song of our king / ever to be told in song to the *lahuta*."

[5] On the difference between singing and recitation as two distinctive performance modes, each with its distinctive rhythms, see Chapter 3 in this volume.

shpatën Muja bytyn i ka lidh . . .	he tightly strapped on his sword . . .
(a break in the recording)	
e tëposhtë koka djerg.	and climbed downstairs.
N'kapi Muja po shkon,	Muji went to the gate
fushës bardh ju ka luftu,	he struggled across the white plain
fushës madhë ju ka shkua . . .	Muji passed through the long plain . . .

Ugljanin was clearly uncomfortable when he assumed he was being asked to demonstrate the different rhythms he associated with epic tales accompanied by the *lahuta* (*gusle* in Bosnian) and with ballads and short balladic epics accompanied by the *çifteli.*

When Ugljanin then *sings* in Albanian the opening scenes of a long epic he had recited in Bosnian (*bosanski*), Parry's surprised assistant Nikola Vujnović exclaims, "*Dobro, dedo!*" ("Well done, grandpa"). The lines Ugljanin slowly composed (see below) give the listener a good idea of the rhythm of the long songs Lord's assistants transcribed in the notebooks. Listening in Widener Library to Ugljanin recite and sing traditional epics as well as the border ballads and even a lyric song he had remembered from his youth was my first contact with a dialect and culture markedly different from the southern, or Tosk, experience of my parents that Lord knew I was somewhat familiar with.

When Lord encouraged me in 1962 to study Albanian along with Croatian and Serbian literature at the University of Belgrade, my interest in expanding South Slavic studies to include Albanian oral traditional literature followed. Questions that interested me were those that had motivated Lord to collect his own material in High Albania: How does the transmission and recreation of long Balkan narrative songs change from one language to another, and from one ethnic group to another? How are the local dialects reflected in the formulaic lines and the essential passages of shared traditional tales whose pattern "has a genesis . . . in myth and not history."[6] In an excellent study of traditional narrative songs of Bosnian women recorded by Parry and Lord, Aida Vidan notes that Parry points out the need to study the transmission of narrative poems across different dialects and localities. This is precisely what she does in her comparison of songs recorded in the Gacko region, which was mostly Muslim and Serbian Orthodox, and in the nearby Roman Catholic, coastal area around Dubrovnik, noting how the two locales "provide a striking example of how the fluidity of oral poetic practices could traverse even very strong cultural borders." She continues: "Many formulaic expressions, even blocks of lines, undergo minimal changes when they cross from

---

[6] Lord, n.d.: 34.

one tradition to another, particularly if these traditions share a broad linguistic base. Others, however, become colored by local dialects."[7] Interestingly, Parry's description of the transmission of poems between speakers of different dialects of the same language applies perfectly well to a shared traditional poetry that crosses from one *language* and ethnic group to another in the same or neighboring territories: "In some way, then, the foreign poems are heard by the local singers and repeated more or less as they have been heard . . . they make the foreign poetry fit their spoken language in so far as they can do so without any too great loss. . . . In time these poems, by the unending process of change . . . become fused with the local poetry, yet even when they have been lost as poems, they leave their mark upon the poetic language."[8]

Ugljanin certainly made traditional Albanian ballads and lyric songs follow the rhythm of octosyllabic lines in Bosnian, and traditional decasyllabic Bosnian epics "fit" into longer lines in Albanian. A good example of his ability to adjust (*ujdisati*) lines is readily seen in his variations on traditional opening invocations and essential scenes in "The Song of Bagdad" and "The Captivity of Đulić Ibrahim" (both performed in Bosnian):

> Jednom vaktu a starom zemanu (PN 277a, line 1)
> O starome vaktu i zemanu (PN 659, line 1)
> Once in days of old

And likewise in his performances (in Albanian) of "Muji and Gavran Kapetan" and "Marko and Musa":

> Oj lum per ty o Zot mor-oj lumi Zot (PN 672, record 1205, line 1)
> E lum për ty-o moro j-lumi Zojote (PN 659, record 1056, line 1)
> Blessings on you, o blessed Lord

Adem Brahimi adds equally familiar formulas in "The Song of Sirotin Ali" (LAN 60, lines 1–2):

> Lum të na për të lumin Prendi
> qi s'jem kon e aj na ka falë

> Blessed be our blessed God
> we would not be had He not granted us life

---

[7] Vidan 2003: 63.

[8] Parry 1971: 337–338; cf. Vidan 2003: 63n140.

The once ritual *function* of the traditional Bosnian and Albanian invocations remains the same, and the audience is well aware of what kind of tale follows.

And listeners will not be surprised when Ugljanin elsewhere ends a Bosnian tale with the equally familiar closing formula *ej, tako ćuo, tako ti kazao* ('that's how I heard it, that's how I told it to you', PN 668, line 1177), which echoes those used by Ali Meta (LAN 57, lines 287–289):

> Keshtu kan than atje s'jam kan
> por pa kan nuk din me than
> gjithmone Zoti neve na ndimoft
>
> This is how they told it, I was not there,
> but had it not happened, they would not know how to tell it,
> may the Lord always help us.

And by Lord's favorite traveling companion in Tropoja, Adem Brahimi (LAN 60, lines 2159–2160):

> Keshtu ka than atje s'jam kan
> por pa kan nuk kishin than
>
> This is how they told it, I was not there,
> but had it not happened, they would not have told it.

Lord's collection, like Parry's, clearly indicates a strong interest in short (200–400 line) as well as longer songs, including those with balladic themes, as long as the tale was "told fully" and had as its basic story pattern "the quest of a bride which ends with a conflict between rival suitors," and had as its final concern "the heroic action involving a large group that transcends the purely intimate family group."[9] Indeed, many of the songs in the collection tell of hunting or raiding parties by border warriors, the stealing or return of brides, and happy, even when embarrassing, endings (LAN 57, "The Song of Ali Bajraktari and the Queen of England," included in this volume). Older singers in North Albania, not unlike Ugljanin in nearby Novi Pazar and singers who lived along the Montenegrin and Austro-Hungarian (Croatian-Bosnian) borders, probably were attracted to the story patterns of the mythic epics as the world of the Seven Kings (Hungarian and Christian Slav princes in the songs) and Seven Kingdoms (Europe) was steadily expanding into shrinking Ottoman territories and increasingly threatening a way of life. The heroic actions of larger-than-life

---

[9] Lord, n.d.: 33.

border warriors such as the brothers Muja and Halili along with their companions, the thirty *agas* (LAN 39, LAN 79) defend rather than rebel against a once-powerful Ottoman presence, which in the lifetime of many of the more experienced singers still reached as far north as Transylvania. The formal greeting, hosting, and departure of guests, the assembling of an army or hunting party, the defense of the Empire or a household, the capture of a city or of a bride, the rescue of a captured hero, the celebration of weddings or of the defeat of enemies or supernatural creatures—such is the thematic material of most of the mythic songs in Lord's collection.

Lord, we read in his correspondence home to his family (in Appendix 2 of this volume), was particularly struck by the custom-bound hospitality he was shown, particularly in Muslim areas: "We are in exclusively Mohammedan country now, and the tradition is more interesting for me. In the mountains I have sat next to the fire with our man Adem opposite [me] brewing coffee, while others sat about on cushions in true Turkish style and talked of heroes and exploits, smoking and sipping coffee constantly. Such scenes are described in the poems. . . . At meal times, in the large part of a Muslim house reserved for males, they sit around a round table on the floor and the host divides the food . . . and the youngest son, or brother[,] stands and waits, brings water to wash our hands, and to drink. Whenever an important person enters this 'selamlik', all jump to their feet and salute with a 'long life to you!' This is all in the poems also" (letter from Tropoja, 23 September). He adds a sketch of the *selamlik*. Three weeks later Brahimi, described earlier by Lord as "the best singer we've struck yet," recounts the scenes of hospitality this way in his song of Sirotin Ali (LAN 60) when the hero Muji's signal rifle summons his companions to his fortified tower (*kulla*). Muji tells his younger brother to go out and greet them:

Shpejt Halili para u paska dal	Halil quickly went outside to meet them
e hozhgjelden tridhete Agalar	and he welcomed the thirty Agas.
e atlaret Halili jau ka marre	He took their thoroughbreds
e rahat n'podrum jau ka bâ	And made them comfortable in the stables.
Agët jan hip shkallave perpjete	The Agas climbed up the steps
ne atë kalla te Muja kenkan shkue	and went to see Muji in the fortress.
ne divehane Muja i paska ndesh	Muji greeted them in the anteroom.

o hozhgjelden tridhete more Agë	"Welcome, o thirty Agas."
e mire selamin Muja jau ka marre	And Muja nicely received their greeting.
në ode te Mujes q'atherë kenkan shkue	They then went into Muja's room.
ne minere gjith rreth jan ndej	They sat down all around on cushions.
me sheqer kafe po me u pjekin	Coffee with sugar was being made for them,
po ju pjek aj Bylyk Basha Muji	Bylyk Basha Muja making it,
po ju shkep aj Halili i ri	and Young Halil kept serving it.
e ne lafe q'athere jan ra	Then they all fell to talking,
duhan të kuqë Muja qi jau ka dhan	Muja gave them red tobacco.

(lines 1362–1377)

Much of what Lord heard around the fireplace and in a home indeed is an echo of what the singers recall while performing and, perhaps more importantly, it is a reflection of the society at the western edge of a once dominant Ottoman Empire that surrounds them. In Boga, Lord comments on another ritual duty of the host: the host keeps the brandy glasses of guests completely full, to avoid any hint of the dishonor signaled by a half-full glass; custom demanded that, during a blood feud, a man who had yet to avenge a killing must be served with a half-full glass, "to ever remind him of his duty (letter from Boga, 11 September). Lord is intrigued by another side light gained while in the more primitive high mountain areas: "An old man here in Boga has the power given him by a Turkish priest[10] to 'tie up' a fever. He ties a piece of red string around the right wrist of the patient. It's as simple as that—and he takes no pay. I was present talking with him when one mountain woman came and had her fever 'tied up.' And a singer who has just now left us had the same red string around his wrist" (ibid.). Parry's conversations with Ugljanin had already revealed to Lord how closely the singer—and his Slav and Albanian neighbors—identified with the ritual acts described in the songs of bygone years, something he would continue to examine at the opposite end of the Turkic world in Central Asia.[11]

---

[10] Most likely a *heçim* 'faith healer' in Turkish (the term is used in LAN 39).
[11] See Lord 1991: 211–244.

While Ugljanin's songs may recall distant Ottoman borderlands (Baghdad) and campaigns in northern Bosnia he vaguely remembered, or larger-than-life heroes assisted by woodland sprites and their intended brides disguised as warrior maidens, or a wonder horse that flies and speaks Turkish, songs from North Albania at the beginning of the twentieth century also looked towards the nearby Montenegrin coast across a volatile, "cursed" (*proklet* in Serbian) mountainous terrain inhabited by infidels and by benevolent and equally malevolent mythological creatures that come out of the sea. Lord's collection indeed suggests that the mythic story patterns and deep structure of the fantastic epics that survived in the Muslim and Roman Catholic clans of High Albania had far more in common with magical tales, or tales of enchantment for children, than the few songs he recorded of local heroes in the recent past. He concludes his study of the interrelationship among the sometimes blurred narrative genres of Balkan oral tradition by stating:

> The traditional epic and the traditional ballad, as well as the traditional prose tale . . . may all take their origin from mythic story patterns of great antiquity. Such patterns arose from the beliefs of a people, and as beliefs changed the outward manifestations changed, but the patterns of action remained stable . . . . Quests to the other world and captivity there or escape and rescue—to use but one of the basic groups of patterns—continued on because the fundamental message of man's overcoming the threat of oppression and death and surviving as a race is inherent in these narrative patterns, and it is too important to the group for it to be lost.[12]

The messages directed at men, women, and children in heroic epics, ballads (often called 'women's songs' in scholarship on South Slavic traditions), and fairy tales, respectively, are "too important to the group" because the actions described take place not only "in days of old" or "once upon a time" but also around the performer and his or her audience. Children are gently introduced to the often frightening world around them, women to their roles in society, and young men into the interpersonal and family bonds of loyalty sealed by the *besa* ('oath') and blood-taking. The *besa* can range from a simple promise, a sacred oath, or a temporary or permanent truce between feuding households or extended families. It was "not only a moral virtue, but also a particularly important institution in Albanian customary law. Among the feuding tribes of

---

[12] Lord, n.d.: 39.

the north it offered the only form of real protection and security to be had."[13] Ottoman pashas and the Turkish central authorities before 1920, to say nothing of King Zog's police posts that tracked Lord's small party, never had complete control over the remote mountain areas visited by Lord. What protection the group had while moving mounted or on foot from one clan's territory to another's came, Lord more than once remarked in his letters home, from armed escorts that were provided by families inside clan territories and by commonly accepted laws of hospitality.

Lord had ventured into an unchanged area of the Balkans that British Foreign Bible Society missionaries in the mid-nineteenth century had called Europe's "Dark Hole."[14] What he witnessed there was "the only true example of a tribal system surviving in Europe until the mid-twentieth century. In these remote valleys with inadequate communications has survived a group of people whose whole life was organized in terms of kinship and descent."[15] Relationships between kinship groups were governed by the vendetta, from which custom generally exempted women. "The only possible exception to this was when, if all a woman's brothers had been killed in a feud, she might, if she had no husband, take their place. Then by swearing perpetual virginity, and by assuming man's clothing, she could be treated socially as a man, and kill and be killed."[16] Lord indeed found a maiden warrior in songs he recorded, a disguised warrior bride who, in the service of the sultan or emperor (*mbret* in the tales), saved the Empire and then revealed her identity to her hapless fiancé in their wedding chamber (LAN 57, "The Song of Ali Bajraktari and the English Queen"). The social order in the songs, the fortified, multi-storied household *kulla* (tower), the clan (*fis*), clan assembly (*kuvend*), and clan subgroup (*bajrak*), along with names, official titles, or military ranks (*bajraktar, kapidan, pasha, dezdar, bylykbasha*), all recalled a time that was about to run out. Lord describes in detail the hospitality (and protection) he received as he moved from one location to another. Twenty-five years later he would, with mixed feelings, show me his photos of Albanian singers and mountain pastures and shepherds with their flocks and relive moments he had experienced in a prewar world he knew no longer existed.

Lord's field work in North Albania and his later analytical study of how singers Parry interviewed "comprehend the manner in which they compose, learn, and transmit their epics" applies to bilingual as well as monolingual singers.[17] But even though just one of the Albanian singers he encountered

---

[13] Elsie 2001: 35.

[14] For the designation, see Wolchik and Meyer 1985: 147, with note 20.

[15] Whitaker 1968: 254.

[16] Whitaker 1968: 267.

[17] Quotation from Lord 2000: xxxv. On bilingual singers, see Kolsti 1990.

understood and easily demonstrated for Parry the art of line-building and scene-building in different languages, we may safely assume that others like him were completely at ease while recreating tales and transmitting them across cultural-linguistic (Muslim-Christian, Albanian-Slav) divides. The vast collection of songs recorded by Parry and Lord in Bosnia and Hercegovina, Montenegro, and the Sanjak of Novi Pazar provided Lord with enough material to analyze how singers there composed decasyllabic lines and developed scenes or themes essential to the songs during the act of recreating tales they had just heard performed by another singer. Singers asked to recite as well as sing the same song revealed that while they faithfully, if hardly "word for word," as they might boast, repeated the essential themes in the song—e.g., the assembly of a raiding or wedding party, the arrival of a messenger, the delivery of a letter, the journey, the duel or battle, the return, the wedding celebration—they did not hesitate to lengthen or shorten scenes and songs alike, depending as much on their own mood as that of their audience. An irritated Ugljanin, thinking he was being asked to show Parry how the songs he had sung in his youth differed from the songs he heard in his thirties after he had learned to speak *bosanski*, demonstrated that he was true not only to the genre (ballad/epic) but also to the "shorter" or "longer" rhythm in which the tale must be dictated, recited or sung.[18]

I believe that because of Ugljanin's clearly demonstrated ability to "fix" lines, had he been pressed by Parry to do so, he could have recreated in *arnautski* as well as *bosanski* all the songs he had learned listening to Slav or Albanian singers. Unfortunately, Ugljanin contributed far too little material that could be used to analyze the formulaic style of his "fixing," that is, line-building, skill in Albanian. In light of Lord's material, however, there is no question about his rightful place as an experienced singer in the oral epic tradition of North Albania, his place of origin. The twenty thousand-plus lines Lord collected from forty different singers in Albania two years later certainly serve as an adequate touchstone for examining the extent to which Ugljanin's half-lines and whole-lines correspond to those of monolingual singers in neighboring North Albania. The lines clearly show that Ugljanin composed traditional Albanian half-line and whole-line formulas and substitution patterns that served as the building blocks of the recurring scenes and actions in the collection. We may conclude, then, that Ugljanin's recreation of oral epic songs for Parry and Lord in Albanian echoed the tales not only of the Slav performers he had learned from but also their North Albanian counterparts.

---

[18]   On rhythm in connection with the recitation, singing, or dictation of a song, see Chapter 3.

If Ugljanin's line- and scene-building skills serve to connect shared oral narrative traditions between the highlands of North Albania and along the Dinaric Alps to the Austrian Military Frontier, so do the musical instruments which, as Lord notes, Albanian and Slav singers used in these areas: the one-string, bowed lute (called *lahuta* in Albanian and *gusle* in Bosnian) and the long-necked plucked lute (called *çifteli* in Albanian and *tambura* in Bosnian). It is not surprising that the fourteen-year-old boy Lord met in a hotel in Shkodër had brought along his *çifteli*, an instrument not used in remote regions by experienced singers to accompany the singing of the mythic epics. Lord, as did Ugljanin, makes a clear-cut distinction between narrative traditions which minimized or maximized musical accompaniment: "In northern Albania the epic of the past is differentiated from the historical songs, which tend to be balladic, by two oppositions, (1) decasyllabic/octosyllabic, and (2) *lahuta/çifteli*. The distinction between the two genres is thus maintained."[19] The recordings Lord made of Ugljanin in Novi Pazar give the listener some idea of how the rhythm of the long narrative songs he collected in North Albania, when recited or sung, might have sounded.

The traditional epics themselves, the lengths of which in some cases far exceeded those that had been published by Albanian Franciscans in Shkodër before Lord's trip, gave every indication that singers in High Albania, while sharing traditional singing styles and musical instruments with distant as well as neighboring Slavs, were preserving local customs and, in some locales, archaic dialects that continued to instruct and entertain their audiences. Indeed, when the few short ballads in the collection are put aside, the mythic epics, which have no regard for geographical, chronological, or historical accuracy, show that tales "of olden times" in the Parry and Lord collections reflect their ancient ritual roots and common narrative patterns.

When Lord left Dubrovnik and ventured into the vendetta-bound, clan-dominated mountains, he entered what was left of a semi-independent, militarized society that for over five centuries had both plagued and maintained Ottoman-controlled territories in Europe. Its way of life had all but disappeared after the Second World War, but in its mythic epics, family, clan, and territorial rivalries survived in the world of the supernatural. In his later writings Lord extended that world of oral traditional epic far beyond the Balkans, Turkey, and Baghdad to Lake Baikal and Turkic groups along the Soviet-Chinese border. He notes that the long-necked bowed instruments similar to the *gusle* which are found at both ends of Turkish lands are closely associated with horses, be it a wooden horse made to jump by a performer's fingers in the Caucasus or the *gusle*

---

[19] Lord, n.d.: 28–29.

string which is made from a horse's tail.[20] Ali Meta's song about Ali Bajraktari and the Queen of England (LAN 57), which tells of dragons battling each other in the sea and the hero's disguised bride flying on a winged horse onto a ship off the (Adriatic) coast, serves as an excellent example of a multiform of Ugljanin's song about Ðerđelez Alija's disguised bride, who salvages his stalled military expedition by taking Baghdad and stealing its queen to present her as a bride to the emperor (sultan). Lord notes also that whereas heroes and heroines in Balkan songs change clothes to conceal their identity, in Central Asia they change shape, which to him suggests that "the element of the shamanistic and fantastic . . . may be beneath the surface of some Balkan Slavic narratives."[21] The same, I offer, may be said of some early Russian narratives. The oldest accounts of Russian heroes who change shape revolve around the mid-eleventh century werewolf prince, Vseslav of Polotsk, in Kievan chronicles of the time, and a century and a half later in the rhythmic prose account of the ill-fated expedition of Prince Igor' into the steppes against the nomadic Polovtsians. Both ancient heroes, Vseslav and Igor', operate in the real and supernatural worlds.[22] Vseslav reappears as Volkh (<*volhv* 'magician') Vseslav'evich in nineteenth-century collections of Russian *byliny*, magical tales in verse form of the bygone heroes of Kiev's and early Muscovy's border lands.

When Lord returned from North Albania to Dubrovnik, where he had earlier delivered to Nikola copies of Parry's field recordings in Novi Pazar to be transcribed, he was just beginning his life-long, multi-disciplinary journey into oral traditions and performers who continued to recreate narrative songs which crossed cultural, linguistic, and ethnic borders. His concluding remarks in *Epic Singers and Oral Tradition* give some idea of the directions he explored after assisting Parry in the former Yugoslavia and his own collecting in North Albania two years later, and of his life-long theoretical, analytical, and comparative approaches to oral traditional poetry and the verse-makers and societies that preserved it:

> The Central Asiatic epic traditions can be invaluable in reaching a full appreciation of the history of some of the stories and story elements in South Slavic epic and lyric song, and of the techniques of their composition and transmission. This would include possible vestiges of shamanic motifs, which would explain some puzzling situations in Balkan epic

---

[20] Lord, n.d.: 18.
[21] Lord 1991: 213.
[22] Jakobson and Simmons 1949: 13–86.

and ballad. Much remains to be done as we continue to increase our knowledge of this extraordinarily rich cultural continuum.[23]

Lord's valuable collection of unedited Albanian songs and ballads, some undeniably raw and others of high artistic quality, is a cultural monument which comes directly from the Roman Catholic and Muslim singers who contributed to it, and from the remote localities that influenced them. While he did not come across singers comparable to the best he had recorded on phonograph discs for Parry in 1935, he did return to Dubrovnik from High Albania with a deep appreciation for the world of healer-priests (Turkish *heçim*), singer-seers, and mythic story patterns that continue to this day to instruct and entertain. Lord would move on to reflect on "the deeper meaning of the poetry" and the still dynamic story patterns in a predominately Muslim cultural continuum that stretches from Bosnia and Albania to the easternmost ends of the Turkic world. In *The Singer of Tales* he indicates in his concluding remarks that his focus on how *oral* literature is created will turn towards what is behind a literature that remains *traditional*:

> When we know how a song is built, we know that its building blocks *must* be of great age. For it is of the *necessary* nature of tradition that it seek and maintain stability, that it preserve itself. And this tenacity springs neither from perverseness, nor from an abstract principle of absolute art, but from a desperately compelling conviction that what the tradition is preserving is the very means of attaining life and happiness. The traditional oral epic singer is not an artist; he is a seer. The patterns of thought that he has inherited came into being to serve not *art* but religion in its most basic sense.[24]

What Lord saw, heard, and sensed all around him during his six, physically difficult but intellectually fruitful weeks in North Albania never left him. To be sure, the singers he met there, both Roman Catholic and Muslim, continued to validate a shared way of life that had managed to survive for centuries beyond the reach of the Seven Kingdoms, Stamboll, Byzantium, and perhaps even Ancient Rome.

---

[23] Lord 1991: 238.
[24] Lord 2000: 220.

The Albanian Collection of Albert B. Lord in Northern Albania

Context, Contents, and Singers

Zymer U. Neziri

1. The Collection of Albanian Epic Songs

ALBERT B. LORD BELONGS to the first important group of collectors of Albanian legendary epic songs, the cycle of *kreshnike*, during the period between the two World Wars, a group which also includes Bernardin Palaj, Donat Kurti, Karl Gurakuqi, Filip Fishta, Hasan Reçi, Prenk Qefalia, among others. His collection, made in 1937, is equal in importance to works such as *Visaret e Kombit* (volumes I, II, IV 1937-1944, published by Bernardin Palaj and others), *Zana popullore* (by Kasem Taipi), *Hylli i dritës* (by Gjergj Fishta), *Edukata e re* (by Sadi Pejani). The generation of Lord precedes those of the great collectors, with names such as Zihni Sako, Qemal Haxhihasani, Gjergj Komnino, Anton Çetta, and Demush Shala, who collected and published epic songs in the second half of the last century.

The beginning of the collection of epic songs in Albania—especially the legendary epics belonging to the cycle of *kreshnike*—started late, when in other parts of Europe many national corpora had already been created. The first fragment in Albanian from these cycles was published by Gustav Meyer in 1897 (*Tha, drit ka dal e dielli nuk ka ra* ["He said, 'there is light, and the sun is not out'"])[1]; the first Albanian scholars to collect epic were Gaspër Jakova-Mërturi, who published

---

[1] Meyer 1897: 52.

the song *Të lumët na për të lumin Zot,* ("May We Be Blessed for Blessed God") in 1904,[2] and Nikollë Ivanaj, who published the song *Vuko Harambashi dhe Hajkuna e Dezdar Osman Agës* ("Vuko Harambashi and Hajkuna, Daughter of Dezdar Osman Aga"), in 1905.[3] Also worthy of note is Hasan Fejzullahu (Hasan Fejzulović), an Albanian student from Aleksinac, who collected in 1901 a song, dictated by his father, dealing with Gjergj Elez Alia.[4] Under the title *Bola Husen-Aga,* this song was published by T. Đorđević in Serbian as a variant of a Serbian song.[5]

The preoccupation with this tradition among Albanian intellectuals of that time was expressed by the Franciscan priest Shtjefën Gjeçov.[6] Gjeçov was a teacher and collector of folkloric, archaeological, and historical materials who was shot in 1929. The echo of Gjeçov's concern for the collection of *kreshnike* songs and their translations was fully felt after the first World War, when eventually this work started to be done systematically.

Lord had planned to publish this collection of the Albanian epics at the beginning of the '50s.[7] For unknown reasons, Lord never saw this plan through to fruition; possibly the difficult relationship between Washington and Tirana played some role.[8] In any case, his collection ranks among the great collections of Albanian epic made by foreign scholars.

A considerable part of the Albanian songs present in Lord's collection belongs to the legendary-heroic cycle of songs of the *kreshnike.* This cycle is one of the pillars of Albanian cultural and artistic heritage. In it we can recognize, in many poetic aspects, the echo of a historical period of many centuries ago, a period of ethnic contacts and conflicts.[9] According to scholars such as Aleks Buda, we can find here the echo of conflicts and battles between the local (Illyrian-Albanian) population of this part of the Balkans and the Slavic populations, from their first arrival in the Balkans until the 13th and 14th centuries, when conflict intensified in the period of Serbian feudal power and the Nemanjić dynasty.[10] Among other scholars, Maximilian Lambertz recognized

---

[2] Jakova-Merturi 1904: 183–184; the original title of the song was *Chéto Bashé Muji (Kangha e Malesoresh)* "Çeto Basho Muji" ("The Song of the highlanders").

[3] Ivanaj's publication appeared in a journal printed in Dubrovnik, *Shpnesa e Shqypëniis,* 9 September 1905: 3–4. The original title was *Te vedhaznuomit é Vuko Harâmbashit e Hajkunes te Dizdar Osman-ages.* Nikollë Ivanaj (1879–1951) was a democratic patriot and journalist.

[4] See Neziri 2006: 36.

[5] Đorđević 1932: 66.

[6] Sako and Haxhihasani 1966: 8.

[7] SCHS I: 56.

[8] Stephen Mitchell, personal communication, Cambridge, MA, Harvard University, 23-2-2007.

[9] Sinani 2006: 66; Uçi 1986: 28; Gjergji 1986: 117; Neziri 2001: 75.

[10] Buda 1986: 54: "The strong conflicts of the 13th–14th centuries . . . in the Northern and North-East Albanian areas have been the main stimulus for the formation and the maturation of the cycle of the *kreshnike.*"

that these songs could derive from the period of the migration of Slavic populations across the Danube, preserving the memory of ancient battles among local populations and the Slavs, which occurred around the years 700-800.[11]

The origin of the cycle, however, is a controversial matter; other scholars—including some Serbian scholars—have a different opinion, and claim that the Albanian epics originated in the seventeenth century.[12] Nevertheless, during that period evidence points not so much to conflicts between Albanians and Serbs as to closeness among them, with figures such as Pjetër Budi and Pjetër Bogdani.[13] The result of this *rapprochement* was the common rising against the Ottomans in 1689. The first phase of the long conflict between Albanians and South Slavs came to an end in the fourteenth century, considering that the Battle of Kosovo (1389) marks the beginning of the alliance of the Balkan populations against Ottoman power. If we want to situate the epics in a historical frame, we could speculate that the historical epics originated after 1389, while this year marked the end of the formation of the legendary songs (like the cycle of *keshnike*), which should belong to a prior phase.

This cycle is among the few traditions of oral poetry still surviving in Europe at the beginning of this new millennium. It has been said, correctly, that the area of these songs is among the most important in the world for epic tradition.[14] During the twentieth century, more than 500,000 verses belonging to the legendary cycle of *kreshnike* were collected, in different variants.

It has even been claimed that the *kreshnike* cycle is a continuation of ancient Illyrian epics. Despite the lack of documentary evidence for ancient Illyrian epic, local scholars have tried to uncover evidence in the fields of history, archaeology, and linguistics. The Albanian folklorist Demush Shala pointed out mythic-legendary elements of the *kreshnike* cycle that could recall ancient heroic actions;[15] the Croat scholar Radoslav Katiçiq [Radoslav Katičić] tried to reconstruct ancient formulas of hypothetical Illyrian epics on the basis of anthroponyms and homonyms.[16]

Historical Albanian epic songs originated with the Battle of Kosovo (14th century), followed by the songs about the period of the national hero Gjergj Kastrioti Skënderbeu (Skanderbeg, 15th century). More recent songs include

[11] Lambertz 1958: 184.

[12] See, for example, Mićović 1981: 5.

[13] Pjetër Budi (1566–1622), bishop of Sapa and Sarda in Northern Albania, was a writer who helped to inspire the uprising of Balkan populations against the Ottomans at the beginning of the seventeenth century. Pjetër Bogdani (1625–1659), bishop of Skopje, was an Albanian writer who helped to inspire the uprising against the Ottomans in 1689.

[14] Uçi 1986: 40.

[15] Shala 1985: 5.

[16] Katiçiq 1988: 1, 7.

examples related to historical events of the sixteenth and seventeenth century, figures like Ali Pasha Tepelena and Mahmut Pasha Bushatit (in the eighteenth and nineteenth centuries), the events of the League of Prizren (nineteenth century), the last period of uprising against the Ottoman Empire (at the beginning of the twentieth century), the period between the two World Wars, and finally the very last period related to the Independence of Kosovo at the beginning of the twenty-first century.

2. *Lahuta* and *Lahutarë*

The *kreshnike* songs are performed by *lahutarë*, rhapsodists distinguished for their voices, for their ability to move listeners, and for their skill in creating and performing traditional verses. The best singers have great ability in narrating; they employ comparisons and hyperbolic descriptions of the heroes, sketching for the listeners the fantastic aspects of the characters. They are expert at weaving dialogues and at describing duels and natural beauty. The best singers have repertoires of songs that, when performed, might collectively exceed 10,000 verses.[17] *Lahutarë* are almost always men;[18] traditionally they were shepherds, and the majority were born in the mountains or in the hills. All the singers documented by Lord belong to this type.

The *lahutarë* usually accompany their songs on the *lahuta*, a one-stringed instrument played with a bow and known among the Slavic population as the *gusle*. The songs can also be sung with other instruments belonging to the family of the long-necked lute with plucked strings: the *çifteli*, a two-stringed instrument very often present among Albanians, or the *sharki*, which can have three or more strings.

The *lahuta* belongs to an ancient type of bowed string instrument.[19] Its role is not only musical, but also symbolic and ritual. Significantly, the *lahuta* is typically decorated with symbolic figures, especially with the head of a goat, or a serpent.[20] In Albanian families a great respect is paid to this instrument, as well as to the *kreshnike* songs; in a traditional Albanian house, the usual place to keep the *lahuta* is in the men's room (that is, the room in which guests are received and the men of the household gather), in front of the fireplace.[21]

---

[17] In the region of Rugova, as of the end of the last century, the singers who have such large repertoires are Isuf Selmani-Kuklecaj, Haxhi Meta-Nilaj, Shaban Groshi, and Isë Elezi-Lekëgjekaj (Isë Muriqi in civil records).

[18] Gërcaliu 1986: 302.

[19] Miso 1987: 27–42.

[20] Sokoli and Miso 1991: 214; Tirta 2004: 62, 157, 158.

[21] Sinani 2006: 89.

Geographically, the distribution of the *lahuta* corresponds to the distribution of the epic songs. The primary areas for both in Northern Albania and in the border region between Kosovo and Montenegro are the following: Malësia e Madhe, Shala, Shosh, Nikajt-Mërtur, Malësia e Vogël, Plava, Gucia [Gusinje], Rugova, Peshter; many of these areas were visited by Lord during his trip in 1937. Other relevant areas are: Rrafshi i Dukagjinit, Drenica, Shala e Bajgorës, Llap, Gallap, Karadak. Marginal areas of presence of the *lahuta* are: Kurbin, Puka, Mirdita, Has. It is interesting to note the presence of *kreshnike* songs even in other areas, where today the *lahuta* is absent: they span from Rrafshi i Kosovës to Luginën e Vardarit, in Macedonia.[22]

Lahutarë usually perform the songs during weddings, feasts, moments of joy, as well as in the evening during the winter season. Listeners have a unique respect for the *lahutarë*, especially when they are singing, and they pay deep attention during the performance of a song. The silence is absolute, and when the *lahutarë* ends the song, the listeners offer benedictions and congratulations with traditional expressions such as "blessed mouth!" (*goja të lumtë!*) or "May your son inherit it!" (*djalit ia laç!*). For the singer, this is the greatest remuneration.[23]

3. The Songs in the Lord Collection: Characters and Contents

The Lord Collection includes in total twelve notebooks (thirteen, if one includes the notebook containing the first song in the Collection, described below). The first eight contain songs collected under dictation during Lord's trip; three more were sent to Lord in Cambridge a few months after his return by the local collectors Qamil Hoxha and Murat Paçi. The last one is the index of the songs. All told, the songs in Lord's collection amount to 22,645 lines; 20,445 of these belong to the *kreshnike* songs. Of the seventy-seven songs in the Collection, fifty-three are *kreshnike* songs, four are ballads, eighteen are historical songs, and two are lyric songs. Lord also made an incomplete transcription of one additional song, in a separate notebook. This song, dictated by the singer Kolë Marku and titled *Kanga e Zuku Bajraktarit* ("The Song of Zuk Bajraktari") (LAN 1), is catalogued as the first song of the Collection. The Collection includes also 38 song inventories (that is, individual singers' repertoires as they reported them to Lord) and information about the singers.

---

[22] Xhaferi 1996, Osmani 1999, Murati 2000.
[23] Sako and Haxhihasani 1966: 24–25.

Lord collected songs from many famous performers of *kreshnike* epics: Fran Pali and Pjetër Leka (Kelmend); Nikë Toma (Shkrel); Gjok[ë] Pjetri (Pjetroshan, Kastrat); Adem Brahimi and Musa Alushi (Vuthaj, Gusinje); Rizë Zymeri-Lucëgjekaj (Koshutan, Rugova); Ali Meta (Isniq) and Rexhep Zeneli (Trestenik, Peja); Ali Hyseni (Geghysen) and Alush Alija (Kolgecaj, Krasniq); Shaban Kadria (Kolmekshajve, Gash); Ukshin Smajli (Vishoqit, Bytyç); Sokol Martini (Brisa, Mërtur); Marash Nika (Pecaj) and Gjergj Pllumi (Theth, Shala); Ded Keçi (Gurrëz, Kurbin).

The songs of the Lord Collection exhibit interesting elements in their characterizations of the principal heroes of the *kreshnike*. Together with other variants of the songs (from the oldest, collected by Gustav Meyer, until the most recently collected), this collection offers us the possibility to have a rich portrait of the heroes.

Çeto Basho Muji is the leader of the *kreshnike* in the Albanian Epics; he is the first in the group of thirty heroes, the Thirty Agas. Muji is the older brother of the other leader, Sokol Halil Aga, and is the center of the family, which includes Muji's mother, brother, wife, and son. Muji makes arrangements for his brother's marriage, respects the authority of his mother, lives in the family tower, and takes care of the family; he hosts friends, companions, and relatives according to the Albanian rules of hospitality. During gatherings with the men, he speaks deliberately and with weighted words. In conversation, he respects the opinions of others, but when necessary he also corrects them. He is the leader of his friends and of the region where he lives. He honors promises and the *besa*. With his enemies he is prudent as well as severe; he never avoids combat in duels, in which he is usually victorious. He is the symbol of heroism, audacity, and valorous endurance. His mythological strength derives from the milk of the *zana* of the mountains; he is a friend to the *ora* and the *zana*; his body is of hyperbolic dimensions. He meets kings and heroes, and fights to preserve the unity and the freedom of his region. His band (*çeta*) is composed of thirty young heroes, selected from the inhabitants of the free villages; they are a defense against the Slavs (*shkjetë*), who threaten their possessions. He and the members of the *çeta* consider death in battle as the most worthy deed.

Sokol Halil Aga likewise appears as a protagonist in the Albanian cycle of *kreshnike*. He is the youngest brother of Muji. He participates in fights and follows Muji's instructions in doing so. He is one of the "seven Halils," Muji's seven younger brothers, all of whom but the youngest were killed by enemies. (The name 'Halil' was given to each brother in turn when his sibling was killed.) He is a hero, incomparably audacious and strong. Halil respects his brother and his brother's words, his mother and her authority, and his sister. He cherishes Muji's family. He is a beautiful young man, and the daughters of kings fall in love with him. He is a symbol of grace and heroism. He honors all the maidens of his region as if they were sisters. He is a friend of supernatural beings, the *zana* and *ora*, who protect him from danger; when necessary, even the moon and the sun take care of him. He is agile, slim, and smart. Faced with his enemies, he is shrewd as well as fierce. He often takes part in duels, and is usually the winner. He is concerned for honor—his own, that of his family, and that of his region. He respects the *besa*, and his behavior follows ethical principles that distinguish him from his enemies.

The songs of the Lord Collection help also in fleshing out a picture of the enemies of the *kreshnike*. In these songs they are heroic, with fantastic strength. They have as friends the *ora* and the *zana*. They are smart and agile, but without *besa*. They attack the livestock in the pastures, steal them, and kill the shepherds; they bring their sheep to the pastures without permission and without paying. They attack and burn towers. They threaten the honor of the families of the *kreshnike*, and kidnap their sisters and wives. They break the engagements and block the marriages of beautiful girls; they beguile the sweethearts of the *kreshnike* into friendship. They give the *besa* but do not respect it. They fight duels according to the same rules and use the same weapons (mace, club, sword, knife) as the *kreshnike*; their horses also help them during the fight. They are courageous, ready to start battles, and so on.

The language of the songs of *kreshnike* exhibits specific poetic devices. These include the personification of mythological elements, which occur side by side with depictions of natural elements and situations that range from the mundane level of the domestic hearth to the cosmic level, including fountains, springs, hills, valleys, mountains, horses, birds, the moon, the stars, the sun, the sky. Time is treated in a seductively fantastic way: for example, the hero Halil sleeps for one hundred years, and, when he awakes, declares that he has slept only for a short time[24]; the sentencing of Muji to two thousand years in prison is narrated in a single line of verse.[25] Similarly, space can be handled relatively freely: for example, in a single line the hero may travel from Judbina (Udbina) to Moscow.[26] As has been pointed out by scholars of these epics, the use of time and space turns upside down the rules of narration, in accordance with a tendency that is common and even necessary in legendary poetry.[27]

---

[24] Kadare 1987: 328, 329.

[25] Adem Salihi (singer), *Muja zëhet rop nga krali* (manuscript in the author's personal collection), line 25.

[26] Neziri 2003: 142, line 133.

[27] Shaban Sinani, for example, writes about the exceptional temporality of the *kreshnike* songs (Sinani 2006: 108).

The main narrative themes present in the *kreshnike* songs are: the defense of territory (woods and plains), the defense of livestock (sheep, goats, horses), the defense of the tower (or the courtyard, wealth, and material possessions), and the defense of the family (mother, wife, sister). In addition, one sometimes encounters the theme of opposition to the levying of taxes. Also common is the theme of the origins of the heroes, who were shepherds or orphans, and who receive their strength from the mythological figure of the *zana* and remain on friendly terms with her. Very prominent is the theme of the wedding of the heroes, who can obtain a bride in a variety of manners: in friendship, on conditions, as a prize in a competition, by force. The themes of kidnapping, imprisonment, and release from imprisonment are also very common in the repertories of many singers. In many songs one finds jealous, envious, or angry heroes engaged in rivalries, as well as the theme of the blood feud. The theme of betrayal by a woman (mother, wife, sister) is also present, and the theme of the desecration of graves by an enemy. Other important motifs include the *besa*; the love between brother and sister, and the death of brother and sister on the same day; dreams; animal helpers; a mother who loves the enemy (the Orestes and Clytemnestra motif); acts of charity; changes of dress; meals, especially the morning meal; and demonstrations of cleverness. Typical motivations for the initiation of a song's action are vengeance; the desire to kidnap or capture a woman, a horse, or a tower; or simply the desire for adventure.[28]

The singers from whom Lord collected shared themes and motifs with other Albanian singers active in the '30s. A complete thematic index for Albanian epic does not yet exist. Such an index would have to take into account all of the material collected by scholars in Tirana and Prishtina. This material, in combination with the material from Lord's collection, amounts to some four hundred thousand lines, many of them still unpublished. The themes and motifs of the *kreshnike* songs, which belong to a tradition that may go back to a time before the arrival of Ottoman power, provide an important source of information about Albanian culture. The study of these themes and motifs may also reveal connections with the historical period when viewed in relation to the period of conflicts between Albanians and Slavs in the second half of the last millennium, or at the beginning of the new one.

---

[28] For examples of work on the motifs of Albanian epic, see Shala 1985: 45–86, Panajoti 1986: 215, and especially Lambertz 1958: 25–76.

4. The Singers and Their Regions

Many of the singers from whom Albert Lord collected songs were well-known in the 1930s. They came from different ethnographic areas. Lord's research reveals two important features of the Albanian epic tradition. The first is the wide extent of the territory over which epic songs are performed in Northern Albania; the second is the fact that the epics of *kreshnike* are performed by both Roman Catholic and Muslim singers.

In the territory of Malësia e Madhe, Lord collected from singers of Kelmend, Kastrat and Shkrel.[29] From Kelmend, Lord collected five songs of the *kreshnike*, dictated by five singers, and recorded a repertoire of about fifty titles of songs belonging to the legendary cycle.[30] Mark Miri, from Nikç, was a forty eight-year-old captain in the army of King Zog. Fourteen out of the twenty-one songs in his repertory belonged to the cycle of *kreshnike*. He dictated *Kanga e Nande Jovanavet* ("The Song of Nande Jovanave," LAN 86, at 635 lines, the longest of the songs of *kreshnike* collected in the region of Kelmend). Fran Pali, a thirty three-year-old from Vukël, knew nineteen epic songs, sixteen of them belonging to the *kreshnike*; he dictated *Muja e Halili me Veshoviç Krajli* ("Muji, Halil and Veshoviç Krajli," LAN 17). Of the eleven songs in the repertoire of Zef Xharri, a thirty three-year-old from Nikç, 7 belonged to the *kreshnike* cycle. Xharri dictated *Kanga e Mujes me Filip Maxharin* ("The Song of Muj and Filip Maxhari," LAN 24, at 89 lines, the shortest song collected in Malësia e Madhe). The twenty seven-year-old Pjetër Leka, from Boga, had in his repertoire six *kreshnike* songs, and dictated *Kanga e Mujes me Millosh Kapitanin* ("The Song of Muji and Milosh Kapitan," LAN 99). Gjekë Miri, a young singer of twenty-four years, knew ten epic songs, six of them belonging to the *kreshnike* cycle; he dictated *Kanga e Kapitan Mark Sulo Markes* ("The Song of Kapitan Sulo Marko," LAN 89), which, though short, is very well-composed. In connection with the material collected in Malësia e Madhe should also be mentioned Ded Keçi, a thirty three-year-old singer born in the village of Gurrëz, in the region of Kurbin, but with family origins in Kelmend. Keçi dictated *Kanga e Mujes qi kerkoj Januken per Halilin* ("The Song of Muji Who Sought Januka for Halil," LAN 92), which, with 1,754 lines, is among the longest and most beautiful songs in the Collection.[31]

---

[29] Kelmend, Kastrat, and Shkrel designate both tribes and mountains in the Malësia e Madhe region. This region includes other mountains: Triesh, Piper, Kuç, Vasojeviq, Hot, and Gruda. For more details see Zojzi 1962: 41.

[30] For details see Neziri 2004: 101–111.

[31] I learned of Keçi's Kelmend origins in September 2006, in Gurrëz, with the help of Zef and Kolë Nishit.

The material collected by Lord in this region offers scholars comparative perspectives in connection with two other bodies of material. First, there are the songs transcribed from other singers from Kelmend in the same period. The monumental collection *Visaret e Kombit*[32] includes texts dictated by Dodë Nikollë Loshi, from Vukël, Pal Buli, from Selca, and Lekë Vuksani and Gjo Deda, both from Vukël. In addition to these famous singers, other singers from Kelmend were documented during the period between the two wars. A second corpus relevant to Lord's material is the body of about eighty songs of *kreshnike* collected from singers from Kelmend in the period 1953-1986. These singers include Fran Sokoli, Ndue Marku, Nikollë Sokol Çekaj, Martin Llesh Smajlaj, Prenk Gjon Naçaj, Dodë Llesh Smajlaj, and Palok Tomë Pllumaj.[33] Comparisons could also be made with the repertoires of singers active in the Kelmend area in recent years, including Januz Delaj, Martin Lleshi, Pretash Nilaj, Vera Qosaj, Tonin Mitaj, Kolë Kumaj, and Frederik Naçaj.[34] The songs from Kelmend are interesting for scholars both because of their content (their use of mythical beings, numerical symbolism, battles, and formulas), and because singers like Pjetër Leka are really masters in epic narration.

From the region of Kastrat come the singers Gjok Pjetri and Llukë Rroku. Gjok Pjetri was a thirty four-year-old from Pjetroshan; from his repertory of six songs of *kreshnike*, he dictated the songs *Kanga e Dragishes Vojvod* and *Kanga e Ali Bajraktarit* ("The Song of Dragisha Vojvod" and "The Song of Ali Bajraktari," LAN 13 and 14), each having about five hundred verses. Llukë Rroku, from Bajza, was ten years younger than Pjetri. He dictated *Kanga e Omeri Mujës* ("The Song of Omer son of Muji," LAN 19, seventy-eight lines) from a repertoire of five songs.

Nikë Toma, aged twenty-seven, came from the region of Shkrel. Having attended school, he was among the few literate singers Lord worked with. He knew nineteen songs, and dictated two: *Kanga e Mujes kur u zue rrob prej mbretit Sulejman* ("The Song of Muji Captured by Sultan Sulejman," LAN 21, 324 lines), and *Kanga e Sajane Ivanit* (LAN 22, 103 lines).

To the region of Plav and Gusinje belonged one of the most famous singers encountered by Lord, Adem Brahimi, who came from Vuthaj. Brahimi was fifty-seven in 1937. His repertoire included eighteen *kreshnike* songs. He dictated the longest song in Lord's collection: *Kanga e Sirotin Alis* ("The Song of Sirotin Ali," LAN 60), with 2,163 verses. This song is distinguished not just by its length but

---

[32] *Visaret e Kombit* is the title of a series of volumes published between 1937 and 1944, containing folkloric, ethnographic, and linguistic materials. The songs of the *kreshnike* are published in volumes I, II, and IV; volume II, edited by Bernardin Palaj and Donat Kurti, is particularly relevant.

[33] See Xhagolli 1999: 163–166.

[34] See Progni 2000: 224.

also by its aesthetic refinement and its unique poetic features. The traits of the heroes and their enemies are depicted with great ability. The song has rich and impressive descriptions, especially with regard to duels between warriors. The use of formulas and numerical symbolism add to the song's attractiveness. The other song dictated by Brahimi, *Kanga e Ali Bajraktarit* ("The Song of Ali Bajraktari," LAN 43, 1041 lines), is also of high quality; it is not inferior to the first so far as epic narration and poetic construction are concerned.

Another talented singer represented in Lord's collection, Musa Alushi [Musë Lushti], also came from Vuthaj (Gusinje). Thirty years old at the time of his encounter with Lord, he had in his repertory ten *kreshnike* songs. He dictated two songs about the deeds of Muji and his enemies (LAN 97 and 100).[35] The young, nineteen-year-old singer Brahim Haxhija likewise came from Plav and Gusinje; more precisely, from the village of Martinaj. He dictated a song about Muji and Sojan Ivan (LAN 94).

From the Rugova region Lord collected songs from the famous singer Rizë Zymeri-Lucëgjekaj (Riza Luz Gjekaj in the manuscript). When Lord met him in Kolgecaj, in Krasniq, he was thirty years old; he was born in the village of Koshutan (today Gjekaj). He knew twenty *kreshnike* songs and dictated two, totaling some 1,600 verses, about the wedding of Halil (LAN 50 and 51). Apart from their aesthetic value, these songs have historical significance as the first songs collected in a region that is now known to be especially important for the epic tradition. Rizë Zymeri-Lucëgjekaj became well known as a singer in the border region of Rugova and Montenegro during World War II; he was shot, together with his son, by the Yugoslavs in 1947. The important Rugova tradition remains fertile, with active singers up to the present day: other famous singers from the region are Haxhi Meta-Nilaj from Shtupeqi i Vogël,[36] Shaban Groshi-Husaj from Shkrel,[37] Isë Elezi-Lekëgjekaj from Koshutan / Gjekaj.[38]

The region of Rrafshi i Dukagjinit is represented in Lord's collection by two singers, one of whom, Ali Meta (1871-1956), ranks as one of the greatest singers encountered by Lord. Meta was born in the village of Isniq, in the area of Peja. Meta dictated historic epics, (including a song about the Battle of Kosovo [LAN 53, included in this volume]) as well as two *kreshnike* songs about Ali Bajraktari (LAN 57 and 58). The narrative style, poetic figures, formulas, and mythological elements employed by this singer make his songs both aesthetically pleasing

---

[35] Research I conducted in Kurbin in September, 2006, revealed that the name Musa Alushi, as recorded by Lord, should more properly be transcribed as Musë Lushti.

[36] On Haxhi Meta-Nilaj (1912–1994) see Neziri 1997.

[37] Shaban Groshi-Husaj (1923–1997) was among the best singers of Albanian epics.

[38] On Isë Elezi-Lekëgjekaj (b. 1947), see Neziri 2002.

and interesting for scholars.[39] Notable singers who learned material from Meta are Halil Beka (Turbuhoc)[40] and Zenel Sadria (Prejlep).[41] Unfortunately, Lord was not in touch with Mehmet Brahimi-Prelëvukaj, another significant singer who learned from Meta, and who, in 1937, was in the region of Kurbin.[42] A noteworthy fact about Meta is that he related to Lord information about the famous singer Qorr Hyso (Ćor Huso), about whom Parry and Lord had heard tales during their earlier fieldwork in Yugoslavia.[43]

The other singer from Rrafshi i Dukagjini is Rexhep Zeneli, from the village of Trestenik, outside Peja. He was fifty-five years old when Lord met him, and knew eleven *kreshnike* songs. He dictated just one song—*Kanga e Halilit qi ka nxanë Jovan Kapidanin* ("The Song of Halil Who Seized Jovan Kapitan," LAN 79, included in this volume), with a little more than 400 verses—but this song alone, which he claimed to have learned from Qorr Hysa, provides evidence of his ability and importance as a singer. Lord's biographical notes, which indicate that Zeneli owned property in Plava near Peja, suggest the possibility that he may have been in contact with other singers of the Rugova region.

Lord worked also with several singers from the region of Malësia e Gjakovës (Malësia e Vogël). Four of these came from the area of Krasniq: Ali Hyseni (aged sixty), from Geghysen (Tropoja), dictated two songs out of a repertoire of nineteen *kreshnike* songs; Ibish Bajrami (fifty years old), from Shipshan, dictated a song of more than three hundred lines; Myftar Hasani (thirty-five years old), also from Geghysen, dictated one song from a repertoire of eleven; and Ukë Salihi (twenty-seven), from Tropoja, dictated two songs from a repertoire of mainly historical songs. Three other singers were from the area of Bytyç. Ukshin Smajli, from Vishoq, was, at eighty years of age, one of the oldest singers contacted by Lord. Of the thirteen *kreshnike* songs he knew, he dictated *Kanga e Ali Bajraktarit qi me Begije Devojka lufton me Kulshedrat* ("The Song of Ali Bajraktari and Begjie Devoika Fighting the Dragon, LAN 81) with around six hundred verses. Mustafa Jusufi (aged seventy), from Kam, dictated from a repertoire of ten *kreshnike* songs

---

[39] See Neziri 2005.

[40] Neziri 2005: 19.

[41] "Epika legjendare e Rekës: lahutari Zenel Sadria" (1988), manuscript collected by the author, held in the archive of the Instituti Albanologjik, Prishtina.

[42] This information about Brahimi-Prelëvukaj, given to me by his granddaughter, Trashe Prelëvukaj from Martinaj, now resident in Prishtina, is recorded in field-notes held in the archive of the Instituti Albanologjik, Prishtina, under the title "Lahutari Mehmet Brahimi-Prelëvukaj" (April 24, 2007).

[43] Parry took the name of this legendary singer as the title for his unpublished notes and commentaries (*Ćor Huso: A Study of Southslavic Song*), extracts from which are printed in Parry 1971: 437–464. The manuscript of Parry's *Ćor Huso* is in the MPCOL.

a song of around four hundred verses about Halil and his deeds. Lord attributes a repertoire of eighteen songs of *kreshnike* to the sixty-five-year-old Lush Hoxha, but did not collect anything from him.

Another famous singer, Sokol Martini, came from the village of Brisa, in the Mërturi region. Martini was thirty-eight years old in 1937, and boasted a repertoire of thirty-three *kreshnike* songs—the most extensive repertoire recorded by Lord. He dictated five songs: *Kanga e marteses Muji* ("The Song of Muji's Wedding," LAN 38), *Kanga e Halili kur asht martue* ("The Song of Halil's Wedding," LAN 39), *Kanga e Muse Qesexhisë* ("The Song of Musa Qesexhi," LAN 40), *Kanga e Vojkoviq Alies* (The Song of Vojkoviq Ali," LAN 41), and *Kanga e Ivan Kapidanit* ("The Song of Ivan Kapidani," LAN 42). The shortest of these has eighty-two verses, while the longest has 310. Martini's repertoire attracted the attention of many other researchers after the Second World War. Qemal Haxhihasani, a well known scholar at the *Instituti i Kulturës Popullore* in Tirana, and someone well-versed in the *kreshnike* epics, communicated with Martini and held him in high regard.

Three other singers come from the Shala area. Of these, Marash Nika ranks among the great singers of the period; he was from the village of Pecaj and was sixty years old. He knew thirteen *kreshnike* songs and dictated three, about the heroes Budaline Tali and Arnaut Osmani, and their enemy Milosh Kapitan. He dictated also the song of Ali Pasha of Gusinje included in this volume (LAN 34). Gjergj Pllumi [Pllumbi], too, was an important singer, appreciated by important scholars like Ernest Koliqi and Anton Çetta. Forty years old at the time of Lord's expedition, he had fifteen *kreshnike* songs in his repertoire, and dictated for Lord a song about Musa Qesexhia (LAN 28). Kolë Marku (aged forty-nine) dictated a song about Muji and Halil (LAN 11a).

Two last singers round out this catalogue. From the thirty-five-year-old Hysen Halili, born in Va Spas, Lord collected a song of 492 lines about Halil and Pavlan Kapetani (LAN 70). Hyseni had a repertoire of ten songs of *kreshnike*. Finally, Dalip Ramadani, from Bicaj, represented the region of Luma; he dictated a single short song of *kresnhike* (LAN 66).

5. New Data About the Singers

Biographical details about the ends of the singers' lives present a certain interest because of the varied circumstances of their deaths: some died of natural causes, others violently; some met their end in the Second World War, others were killed for ideological reasons. The Miri family, from Kelmend, provides a striking example of ideologically-motivated violence resulting from opposition to the Hoxha regime by several members of the family. The singer Mark Miri was shot for ideological reasons in 1947.[44] Nue Gjergj Miri, a singer from the same family, was killed in 1946, while Mark Miri's grandsons Pal Gjoka and Gjelosh Gjoka, active as singers until recent years, were persecuted by the Hoxha regime: Pal spent ten years in prison.[45]

The singer Fran Pali, from Kelmend, died during the war in 1945, in Deçiq. His son, Zef Pali, was a well-respected singer in the region.[46] His daughter, Marë Pali, was also a singer—an almost unique example of a female performer of epics—based in Shën Gjin (Lezha); she participated in many folklore festivals.[47]

The famous singer Gjergj Pllumi was the son of Pllum Lulash Shytanit, and had a very hard life during the period of King Zog.[48] After the Second World War, he moved to the region of Plav and Gusinje in Yugoslavia, where he died, because it was risky for him to remain in Albania under the Hoxha regime; a part of his family emigrated to the United States of America. Pllumi had three sons, who were also singers: Nue Gjergj Pllumi, who lived in Shkodra; Lulash Gjergj Pllumi, based in Lezha; and Nikë Gjergj Pllumi, who moved to New York City and preserved one of his father's instruments.[49]

Rizë Zymeri, from Koshutan (Rugova), became a bandit after the end of the Second World War, while his family was confined in Gjilan. He was killed by Yugoslavs in 1947, together with his son Hasani, then twenty years old.[50] A number of singers died as emigrants to other lands, deprived of the support of family and friends at home. This was the case for Adem Brahimi, from Brahim

---

[44] Field-notes taken down by Lush Culaj on September 17, 2005, detailing information given by Pal Gjokë Miri from Gurrëz, Kurbin, then seventy years old. These notes can be found in "Lahutari Mark Miri" (manuscript in the archive of the Instituti Albanologjik, Prishtina).

[45] Field-notes taken down by the author on September 12, 2006, recording information collected from Zef Nishi, then seventy years old, from Gurrëz, Kurbin. These notes can be found in "Lahutari Mark Miri" (manuscript in the archive of the Instituti Albanologjik, Prishtina).

[46] Field-notes taken down by the author on September 12, 2006, recording information collected from Zef Nishi, then seventy years old, from Gurrëz, Kurbin. These notes can be found in "Lahutari Zef Pali" (manuscript in the archive of the Instituti Albanologjik, Prishtina).

[47] Field-notes taken down by the author on September 12, 2006, recording information collected from Zef Nishi, then seventy years old, from Gurrëz, Kurbin. These notes can be found in "Lahutari Marë Pali" (manuscript in the archive of the Instituti Albanologjik, Prishtina).

[48] Field-notes taken down by the author on March 4, 2006, recording information collected from Sadik Çelaj, then seventy-eight years old, from Vuthaj (Gusinje), then residing in New York City. These notes can be found in "Lahutari Gjergj Pllumi" (manuscript in the archive of the Instituti Albanologjik, Prishtina).

[49] Field-notes taken down by the author on March 24 and 25, 2007, recording information collected from Nikë Gjergj Pllumi, then sixty-nine years old, from Theth (Shala), then residing in New York City. These notes can be found in "Lahutari Gjergj Pllumi dhe pasardhësit e tij" (manuscript in the archive of the Instituti Albanologjik, Prishtina).

[50] Field-notes taken down by Ali Muriqi in September 2000. These notes can be found in "Zymerajt e Koshutanit dhe Zhuj Selmani" (manuscript in the archive of the Instituti Albanologjik, Prishtina).

Delisë, Mehmetkurtaj,[51] and Musë Lushti (whose name is given in Lord's collection as Musa Alushi), from the village of Vuthaj.[52]

6. The Local Collectors

Two local collectors, Qamil Hoxha (1908-1989) and Murat Paçi (1918-1943), sent material to Lord after his return to Cambridge. Hoxha was from the village of Bicaj, in the region of Luma (today in Kukës District). He completed his studies in Elbasan and worked as a teacher in Bicaj, in other villages, and in Gjakova. Hoxha sent Lord two notebooks containing 6 *kreshnike* songs collected in Gash and Mërtur in 1937.[53] The songs were dictated by two singers. Shaban Kadria was a twenty-one-year-old from Kolmekshaj in Gash; the first song attributed to him is *Muja e gjen babën e vet*, a rare song about Muji's father. The other four songs dictated by Kadria have as their protagonists Halil and Galan Kapetani, Halil and Dylber Gjelina, Muji and Milosh Kapitan, and Ymer Aga, liberator of Muji and Halil. The other singer was Mark Jetishi from Mërtur, who was twenty years old; he dictated a song about a duel between Muji and Rado that lasted for seven days. Evidence suggests that Hoxha continued to collect folkloric material, including songs of the *kreshnike*, after 1937, although there are no indications of further contact between him and Lord.[54]

Murat Paçi was based in Shkodra, although he came originally from the village of Pac in the region of Bytyç, Malësia e Gjakovës (today in Tropoja District). When he met Lord, he was a student in the State Gymnasium in Shkodra. He sent eight songs to Lord: four songs of *kreshnike* collected in Malësia e Gjakovës in the years 1934-1935, as well as two ballads, one historical epic song, and one lyric song collected in 1937.[55] These materials were dictated to Paci by two singers. Alush Alia (aged forty-five), from the village of Kolgecaj, dictated *Imer Aga i Ri*, which concludes with a seldom-narrated event: the disappearance of the *kreshnike* from this world. Rexhep Ahmeti, a forty-two-year-old from the

[51] Gjonbalaj 1986, figures 2 and 3; field-notes taken down by the author on April 27 and May 1, 2007, recording information collected from Hasan Gjonbalaj, from Vuthaj (Gusinje). These notes can be found in "Lahutari Adem Brahimi" (manuscript in the archive of the Instituti Albanologjik, Prishtina).

[52] Field-notes taken down by the author on March 4, 2006, recording information collected from Sadik Çelaj and Elez M. Çelaj. These notes can be found in "Lahutari Musë Lushti" (manuscript in the archive of the Instituti Albanologjik, Prishtina).

[53] Notebooks 9 and 10 in the Lord Collection. The first page of Notebook 10 is inscribed "Qamil Hoxha, Bicaj (Kosovë), Albania, Europe, 10.12.1937."

[54] Personal communication from Hoxha's son, Shefqet Hoxha, a scholar and collector of folkloric materials, in Tirana, February 2, 2003.

[55] Notebook 11 in the Lord Collection.

village of Shipshan, dictated three *kreshnike* songs distinguished by their length, focusing on the figures of Ali Bajraktari, Talime Devojka, and Kune Devojka. The notebook sent by Paçi bears the title *Teli i lahutës* ("The String of the *Lahuta*"), and on the first page Paçi has written this admonition: "From the string of the Albanian *lahuta* do not expect anything other than three sounds: honor, faith, and heroism, virtues belonging only to the Albanians." Paçi was an activist in the National Liberation Movement (*Lëvizja Nacionalçlirimtare*) during the Second World War; he was shot in Prishtina in 1943.

Qamil Hoxha and Murat Paçi did considerable service for the *kreshnike* songs; their names deserve to be included among those of other collectors of Albanian epics in the period between the two World Wars, collectors such as Bernardin Palaj, Donat Kurti, Karl Gurakuqi, Filip Fishta, and Hasan Reçi. Also worthy of mention is L. Lukaj. This name, inserted in pencil in the notebook containing the first, incomplete song collected by Lord, identifies the individual who took down the song by dictation from Kolë Marku. (Marku, originally from Shkrel, Malësia e Madhe, was then residing in Shtoj të Poshtëm, Ulqin.) The fragment was written in Dubrovnik, and is accompanied by a translation into Croatian.

3

Text, Music, Performance

Nicola Scaldaferri

Translated By Gregory Mellen

1. From the Collection of Texts to the Study of Music

THE YEAR 1937, as we saw in the introduction to this volume, proved to be of fundamental importance for the study of epic song in Albania. For one thing, this year saw the publication of the collection *Visaret e Kombit*, which represented the culmination of many years of research undertaken by the Franciscan brothers of Shkodër and in particular by Bernardin Palaj. The purpose of this collection was to categorize and to set down in writing—and at the same time to monumentalize—the tradition of Albanian epic song, within the broader context of local politics and the formation of Albanian national identity.

The same year also saw Albert Lord's trip to Albania and his collection of epic materials. The purpose of Lord's research was to document and to study the repertoires of Albanian singers by means of ethnographic fieldwork, the salient characteristics of which emerge in no small part thanks to the secondary documentation that was produced along the way (such as letters, photos, and notebooks). Lord's experience in Albania, though it was to a certain degree marginal with respect to his central line of research interests, constituted an expansion of the work he had undertaken a few years beforehand with Milman Parry; and when working on his own Lord would remain faithful to the goals and the research methods developed previously alongside his teacher and colleague. Thus, even if Lord did not have at his disposal the necessary technology for recording songs during his trip to Albania, his research always placed at the center of its attention the concrete experiences of the singers themselves along with the complexity and articulation of their poetic repertoires; and it always viewed these repertoires in a comparative perspective, in relation to the poetic practices employed in nearby Slavic areas.

The results of *Visaret e Kombit* and Lord's research, therefore, present us with a comparison between two contemporaneous but distinct approaches. On the one hand, the older view, which had its origins in Romanticism and is evident in the work of the Franciscans, tended to privilege the textual component of epic song and aimed to set down in written form the content of epics arranged by narrative cycles. On the other hand, Parry and Lord's work followed in the footsteps of a research paradigm that was just then being developed and would later result in new approaches in the study of the practice of epic song; this kind of research would shift the attention toward aspects of performance and toward the "voice" of the singer, and its goal would be to illuminate the structural components of singers' repertoires and to rethink the concept of the "oral text" by viewing such texts as dynamic and multiform.[1] This new direction in research was intimately bound up with contemporaneous technological developments, which played a key role not only in shaping the concrete actions of the researchers themselves but also in the formation of the conceptual categories by which researchers referred to the objects of their study. Indeed, the emergence of a notion like *performance philology*—which previously would have amounted to a contradiction in terms—is in effect the reflection of a paradigm shift, which has had important implications both at a practical level and at an epistemological level.[2] As time goes on, in fact, researchers continue to acquire greater and greater awareness that they ought not to limit themselves to the documentation of practices, but that they ought instead to play an active role in the processes of textualization.

In this reinvigorated framework for research, the musical elements of epic song have been accorded particular attention, both from the point of view of the structural components of the music itself and from the point of view of the cultural meanings that such music expresses. By extending scholarly interest beyond the simple descriptions that accompanied the older collections of texts, this new approach has strongly influenced, among other areas, studies

---

[1] See Saussy 2016: 63, and in general the treatment presented in Honko 2000.

[2] For a recent example of *performance philology*, which also includes an attempt to offer a theoretical account of the approach, see Arps 2016.

of Albanian epic song performed with the *lahuta*.[3] The musical aspect—a funda-
mental ingredient of epic song—thus had to wait a long time before receiving
its due space in scholarly work; and even in those studies that constantly
mentioned it, for a long time it amounted effectively to a secondary element of
the research.

Such a situation is inevitable, by the nature of things, for the study of forms
of ancient epic that have been transmitted only in writing. In these cases, the
extant testimonies that address singing practices are sometimes noteworthy
to a certain extent;[4] and yet they are not sufficient for a full understanding or
reconstruction of those practices, at least not beyond the realm of hypothetical
proposals concerning different types of performance. And this situation holds
true not only for the epic songs of the ancients: for instance, of ancient Greek
music in general we now have, of course, a deep awareness of the contempo-
rary theoretical issues and philosophical debates, alongside important pieces of
information at the level of iconography and instrumentation; but the pieces of
evidence that can illuminate ancient Greek musical practices in a concrete way
are few and far between.

The long delay in bringing attention to bear upon musical aspects has,
however, held true for a long time even in the case of epic traditions that are
still active. Before the rise of audio recording, this was due in part, of course, to
the lack of systems of documentation that could adequately allow for a musical
analysis in satisfactory terms. But it is certainly also true that a continued influ-
ence was exerted by the older research paradigm, which directed attention prin-
cipally to the texts alone and to their narrative content, even if these texts were
always nonetheless identified in the research as songs. This identification has
taken place in various linguistic traditions, and in many cases it has left its mark
upon literary works too: one may mention as a prime example, for instance, the
'songs' (It. *canti*) into which the principal poems in Italian are divided, starting
with the work of Dante in the early fourteenth century. Such an identification

---

[3] For a discussion of musical issues in epic, see the essays collected in Reichl 2000 and, for Balkan
epic, Bohlman and Petković 2012. For a detailed overview as it pertains to Albania in particular,
see in particular Ardian Ahmedaja's recent work (Ahmedaja 2012), which surveys the whole
field of research from the early, pioneering reflections of scholars like Ramadan Sokoli to the
anthology compiled by Ferial Daja (Daja 1983), which contains musical transcriptions. One
should also point out that in 1903, far in advance of his time, Paul Traeger recorded on phono-
graph a performance of the *lahuta* instrument alone (Ahmedaja 2012b). Absent from Ahmedaja's
overview, of course, are the materials collected by Parry and Lord. Also of note is the work of
Minna Skafte Jensen, who in 1974, inspired by the work of Parry and Lord, made recordings of
the singer Mirash Ndou at Shkodër, with the collaboration of Gjovalin Shkurtaj. Jensen recorded
materials that were both sung and recited under dictation, and these were made available online
in 2016: http://albanian-tales.net (accessed February 2021).
[4] See the discussion in Nagy 2000.

has resulted in a certain ambiguity; or rather, one might say that, by means of a kind of synecdoche, the identification has given the impression that the mere verbal text by itself could stand for an epic song as a whole.

In the correspondence that Lord had with the Serbian Academy of Sciences in preparation for his trip in 1950, the ambivalent sense of the Serbo-Croatian word *pjesma*—which means both 'song' and 'epic poem'—would be the source of a certain misunderstanding concerning the primary object of Lord's research interests: in fact, when Lord requested the help of a local assistant, he was directed to a musicologist, Miloš Velimirović. In the Albanian language, too, the term *kanga* possesses both of the meanings 'song' and 'epic poem'. And in the Geg dialect the term *kendim* refers at one and the same time to the action of singing and to that of reading (more precisely, reading aloud, in a high voice); moreover, it is precisely with this second meaning that the term appears with great frequency in Lord's manuscripts from his 1937 trip whenever it was necessary to indicate that some singers were unable to read: for example, in the biographical notes on Gjergj Pllumbi (LAN 26), there appears the note "*Nuk din shkrim e kendim, as shkollë nuk ka bâ*" ("he does not know how to read or write and has not attended school").[5]

For many years the collection of texts under dictation represented the fundamental step in the textualization of traditional oral epic. As has been emphasized by Honko, this amounts to nothing less than an intersemiotic translation, which moves from the living dimension of performance to a textual object recorded on sheets of paper by means of writing.[6] Even though it comes at the cost of a change of function, dictation does nonetheless constitute an effective method for the collection of verbal texts; but it is not adequate to the task of documenting and analyzing phenomena that are by nature rhythmic and melodic and that, therefore, remained understudied up until the advent of adequate systems of audio recording.

Nevertheless, it is also true that certain intrinsic characteristics of epic song have led scholars to consider the musical component as an element of only secondary importance. For example, the repetitive quality of the melodies can, at first hearing, suggest that the music plays only a supporting role compared to the role played by the text. But the advent of audio recording technologies, and subsequently audio-visual technologies, combined with a scholarly approach that has shifted attention toward performance, has opened up new possibilities of documentation and analysis; and these new forms of documentation and analysis have revealed a complexity in the musical components of epic song that

---

[5] See McMurray 2020 on the correspondence between Lord and the Serbian Academy of Sciences; LAN 26 is found in Appendix 3 of this volume.

[6] See Honko 2000: 13.

is not dissimilar to the most sophisticated techniques involved in the deployment of verbal formulae.

The research carried out by Milman Parry and the system he employed in order to record entire performances marked a turning point in research. It is therefore not surprising that precisely these recordings would be the object of close attention for their musical aspects in the work of individuals such as George Herzog and Béla Bartók; and in the future these recordings would continue to be at the center of important initiatives of transcription and analysis, as for instance Stephen Erdely's complete transcription of the music of three Bosnian epic poems contained in the MPCOL, H. Wakefield Foster's analysis of a performance recorded by Parry in 1935 and presented in a multimedia format by John Miles Foley, or Anna Bonifazi and David F. Elmer's studies of the relation between vocal melody and verbal text in a performance by the singer Alija Fjuljanin.[7]

On more than one occasion Béla Bartók expressed his admiration for the recordings Parry and Lord had made, both for their content and for the creative technical solutions the two scholars had come up with. In a letter written in December 1941 to his friend and colleague Zoltán Kodály, Bartók addresses in detail the musical components involved in the execution of an epic poem, and he clarifies that the sense of simplicity and musical monotony these works seem to exhibit is actually true only at a very superficial level and only to those who listen with haste and with untrained ears:

> But I would like to revert to the *Parry Collection*. He chose his singers exceptionally well; nearly all of them sing in a peasant style. . . . The notation of the heroic poems makes an awfully monotonous impression at first, but the more time one devotes to them the more one becomes familiar with them. Thus I am now already searching with great pleasure the lesser and greater individual or some other divergences amidst the uniformity. One could write a whole book on this way of making music. It is almost incredible that up to now I hardly had an idea that this last vestige of folk minstrelsy still flourishes in our neighborhood.[8]

Bartók's transcription and analysis of the song *The Captivity of Đulić Ibrahim*, performed in the Bosnian language by Ugljanin and published in an appendix to SCHS I, is a considerable achievement, the goal of which was to understand the musical characteristics of an epic song in all their complexity by taking down in

---

[7]   Erdely 1995; Foster 2004a; Bonifazi and Elmer 2012a, 2012b.
[8]   Bartók 1978, v. 1: xxiv.

staff notation every single aspect of Ugljanin's voice and instrument, down to the smallest melodic inflection.[9] In this case, too, one is faced with a process of intersemiotic translation, which moves from the audio recording to the musical notation that accompanies the transcription of the song's text; by means of this process the melodic inflections, which the singer effected spontaneously in the course of the performance and which can be appreciated by listening to the recording, become visualized in all their volatility and are rendered visually perceptible as one reads the notes of the sheet music. Of course, Bartók's ear and his felicitous creative touch played a central role, during the course of this "translation" from recording to musical notation, in rendering the transcription so attractive from a musical point of view, since Bartók brought out in particular those elements that fascinated him as a composer, above all the shifting and kaleidoscopic play of variations. It is worth recalling that it was precisely this transcription, due to the notable richness of variations it presents (despite the fact that these variations play out in a melodic range that is highly restricted), that recently exerted a notable degree of fascination upon the Italian composer Fabio Vacchi (b. 1949); Bartók's transcription, in fact, inspired part of Vacchi's *Concerto* for cello and orchestra (2018), even though Vacchi was not familiar with the narrative content of the text sung by Ugljanin. But this just goes to show that the musical element of an epic song can present grounds of interest that are autonomous and independent of the narrative and the textual element of the very same song. Vacchi was attracted to the richness of the melodic ornamentation that Ugljanin introduces in every verse, and for his refined ear the idea of monotony or simplicity simply does not exist as far as this work is concerned; to the contrary, what stands out for him is above all the complexity of the variations and the subtle contrapuntal relationship that is created between voice and instrument, however restricted the melodic range of the song may be: the repetitive structure of the verbal phrases constitutes merely a skeleton upon which the rest of the work is constructed.[10]

In a brief but important article published in 1951 and concerned with the epic materials of the MPCOL, George Herzog identified several key elements in the relationship between text and music. For one thing, the melodic line and the instrument play a supporting role vis-à-vis the song itself; for another, only a few melodies are used, but these melodies take on different functions in the course of the performance. Herzog in fact outlined the following typology of melodies: "(*a*) an introductory musical line, (*b*) one or more 'lines of continuity', (*c*) one

---

[9]   The transcription appears in print in SCHS I: 437–467. The original manuscripts are conserved in the MPCOL.

[10]   The above information is owed to personal communication with Vacchi. Other composers who have received inspiration from the MPCOL materials are mentioned in McMurray 2020.

or more 'dramatic lines', (*d*) a final line." At the same time Herzog proposed an explanation of how the musical structure reveals itself to be of crucial importance in providing the performance with a formal framework:

> Perhaps the most challenging point here lies in the possibility that through the musical performance itself, and through the disposition of the various musical motifs, the song attains—and at the same time reveals—a structure which the poem as a text does not have.[11]

2. Salih Ugljanin: *Muji and Gavran Kapetan*

Herzog's observation—namely, that the music can provide the performance with a formal component in the form of an overall structure that is not possessed by the text alone—finds clear confirmation in an examination of the song *Muji and Gavran Kapetan* (PN 679), performed by Ugljanin in Albanian. As has already been mentioned, this was the first recording of an entire epic song in the Albanian language, and a full transcription of the text is included in the anthology that forms part of the present volume.

In the course of the song, which consists of 236 verses, the singer makes use of only three brief melodies (or, more precisely, melodic patterns), each of which has its own precise position and function. Every single verse is sung in accordance with one of these three patterns, which are repeated numerous times and are continually varied. These melodic patterns fit into the categories identified by Herzog: we find, therefore, a specific melody that serves to open the song (and close it as well), and we find melodies that have a narrative function and vary in their intensity according to the narrative phase in which they are employed. These melodies are confined to an interval range that extends no further than a fifth; rhythmically, they present themselves in forms that are naturally related to the structure of the versification.

Sung to the first verse we find the *opening melody*. This melody covers an interval range of a fifth, beginning with the highest note and arriving at the lowest one, which is also the song's principal pitch (the tonic). The *opening melody* is the only melodic pattern in the song that covers all the notes contained in the interval of a fifth. The *opening melody* also returns two further times in the course of the song: once at an intermediate point, where it functions as a kind of caesura before the introduction of a new melodic pattern; and once at the very end of the song, where it coincides with the concluding verse:

---

[11] Herzog 1951: 62–63.

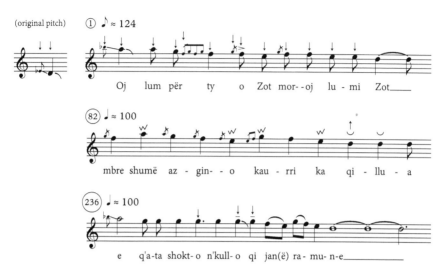

Glory to the Lord the blessed Lord (1)
very fiercely has the infidel struck (82)
these friends arrived at the tower (236)

The second pattern is articulated within the interval range of a fourth. It is repeated from verse 2 to verse 81, with melodic variations, but within the context of a rigorous rhythmic pattern that can be divided into ten units:

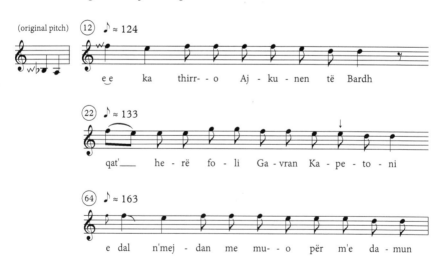

she called Ajkuna the Fair (12)
then spoke Gavran Kapetan (22)
come to the battlefield with me for a duel (64)

The third melodic pattern occupies the greatest space in the performance of the song, being employed from verse 83 to verse 235. It too presents melodic variations within the context of a rigorous rhythmic pattern that can be divided into 10 units:

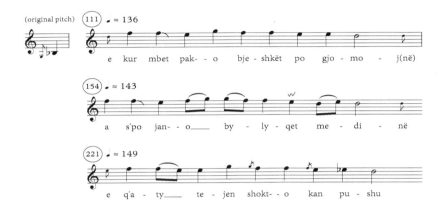

shortly afterwards the mountains trembled (111)
they are not soldiers of the town (154)
then the friends took some rest (221)

The rhythmic character and the tempo of the three melodic patterns are distinct: the first is quite free; the second is more marked in its articulation; and the third is the fastest. The shift from the second pattern to the third takes place at the point when the narrative enters into a phase that is highly intense and characterized by a series of duels between the two protagonists (as can be seen if one reads the text of the song in the anthology included in this volume).

Although the three melodic patterns have distinct rhythmic characters, over the course of the entire song one may note a gradual and constant increase in tempo, which is evident especially during the last part based on the third melodic pattern. This gradual increase in tempo gives the performance an intense feeling of drive and directionality, constantly pushing the song "further ahead" and leading the narrative to its conclusion. It is not possible to establish with precise certainty the metronomic indication (the exact tempo indication in beats per minute) because of certain irregularities in the audio recordings owed to the type of apparatus employed (in addition, during the switch from one disc to another there can be some oscillation in pitch due to some irregularities in the speed of each disc). Nonetheless, it is undeniable that, over the course of the performance of the song as a whole, there is a clear sense of acceleration and a strong feeling of forward movement:

The constant repetition of a few distinct patterns creates the frame upon which the singer inscribes his continual variations, both in terms of melody and in terms of tempo. The musical part of the song, considered as a whole, acts as a kind of structure into which is inserted the textual component, which in this particular case is itself fashioned out of a set of formulae. In addition, there is also the well-known and well-studied support function played by the instrument, which can intervene autonomously in the creation of interludes and variations; such interludes and variations make the play of ornamentation all the more attractive and interesting, and on top of this they may also function as a kind of aide-mémoire, both by acting as gestural reinforcement and by filling up any moments in which the singing comes to a stop. In sum, therefore, while from a certain point of view the music plays an ancillary role vis-à-vis the text, from another point of view the music proves to be crucial in the creation of a dramaturgy of performance that is founded upon features that the text itself does not possess; and in so doing, the music proves to be of vital importance in the way it provides a sense of development as the song unfolds temporally.

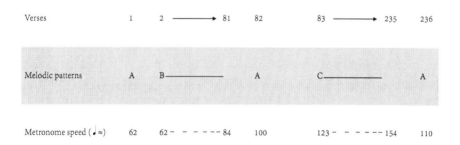

3. The Movement of Rhythm and Writing of the Body

Studying the recorded version of a performance offers the chance to perform an analysis focused on rhythmic aspects, which create effects at various levels, from the organization of the melodies to the structure of the versification and, more generally, the structure of the narrative.

To use the terminology proposed by Honko, the narrative elements, which are present in the "pool" the singer possesses in his or her memory, are organized into a sort of "mental text" that constitutes a preliminary phase in the process of textualization.[12] These elements, in a manner that is more or less extemporaneous during the course of a performance, are then "composed" in narrative discourse at the moment in which they are inserted into a rhythmic and temporal structure. Once established, a rhythmic pattern sets in motion a kind of repetitive automatism: it opens up a formal path that is constantly projected forward in time, and in this way it comes to constitute the basic structure into which the single verses of text are inscribed as the narrative of the song unfolds. The rhythm in fact functions as a kind of temporal writing instrument, in which the very composition of the text takes place through the use of specific metrical structures along with the melodic component of the song.

As far as Albanian meter is concerned, past studies, based in large part upon the analysis of texts collected under dictation, have identified an eight-syllable line as the most common verse-form in the oral tradition; the repertory of epic song in the northern parts of the country, however, and in particular the *këngë kreshnikësh* are characterized by the use of a ten-syllable line (though this presents various exceptions). And yet when we study the recorded materials (both sung and recited) a different picture emerges, one that is more fluid and should be explained on the basis of principles that are rhythmic rather than merely prosodic. It is by means of rhythmic principles, in fact, that singers are able to organize not only the single verses of any given song but also the concatenation of said verses into sequences of broader scope. Moreover, in those cases for which are documented practices that allow for more than one possible realization of the same text (that is, in cases where the text has a kind of multiform quality in that it may be both sung and recited) an organizational criterion based on rhythmic principles can provide a more adequate framework for an analysis of both types of realization.[13]

The materials collected by Milman Parry are highly noteworthy precisely in the way that they reveal the multiform quality of these songs, especially since his working methodology involved the recording of numerous distinct versions of the same text (recited, sung, and taken down under dictation). Even more interestingly, in the materials in Albanian performed by Ugljanin and in particular in the song *Marko and Musa* (PN 659, included in the anthology), there emerges a situation that is particularly unique insofar as both song and recitation are present in one and the same performance: in the shift from the one to the other there is at the same time a change in versification, with the singer

---

[12] Honko 2000: viii.

[13] For the debate over the metrical aspects of the epic songs, see Skendi 1953, Skendi 1954, Pipa 1978, Sokoli 1954, Zheji 1987. For a discussion of the switch in one and the same text between a spoken and a sung realization (and the respective rhythmic transformations), see Neziri and Scaldaferri 2016.

switching from the ten-syllable line of song to the eight-syllable line of recitation. Ugljanin in fact begins by singing, without an instrument; but after singing the first six verses, without missing a beat he continues by merely reciting, with rhythmic articulation, the rest of the song (below, and facing page):

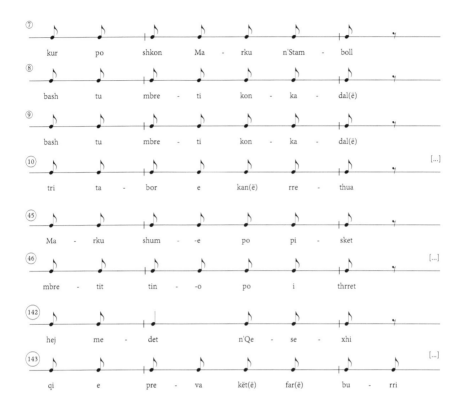

Praise be to God
 Kralieviç Marko arose
and Marko rose to his feet
he mounted onto the back of Sharan
and Marko set out mounted on Sharan
Marko went toward Stambol
when Marko was on his way to Stambol
to appear before the Emperor
to appear before the Emperor
three battalions surrounded him (1-10)

Marko is shouting a great deal
calling out to the king (45-46)

woe be to Qesexhi
that I have cut down such a man (142-143)

This example amounts to proof of the possibility that different generic conventions can co-exist in the course of one and the same performance; and it also shows that it is possible in both cases to analyze the versification by employing a descriptive system that is based not upon the number of syllables but rather upon rhythmic structures, such as the repetition of patterns that are based upon isochronous stress accents.

Furthermore, a system of isochronous stress accents seems to be the basis not only for the verses of epic song but in general for other metrical structures in the Albanian language as well. In any case, as far as epic versification is concerned, as has already been discussed in numerous scholarly contributions, each verse is organized like a bar of music, whose rhythm is established at the beginning of the song and repeated consistently and regularly; and within each verse oscillations are permitted in the number and the duration of syllables.[14]

The element, however, that I would like to highlight here concerns above all the physical and bodily implications of the song's rhythm. Such implications have long been present in reflections upon versification, as is evident not least from ancient metrical terms such as the metrical 'foot.' In modern scholarship this aspect of meter has been the subject of discussions that have sought to elucidate the gestural components of meter (for instance in Jousse 1969); it has also been re-examined recently by Haun Saussy (in Saussy 2016) and has been incorporated into a wide-ranging theoretical discussion that takes into account the intense debates over issues of the body and its relationship to technology.

The rhythmical-corporeal element of epic song emerges—both from the singers' direct testimony and from ethnographic accounts of the practice—as a central element in the discourse concerning the performance of epic songs. Nowadays this element is easy to document and to analyze thanks to the use of audio-visual technologies that permit more detailed analysis than was hitherto possible; in recent years, moreover, bodily experience has become the subject of scholarly discussion in ways that are increasingly more refined and better informed, thanks to a series of intense theoretical reflections and

---

[14] On the multiform nature of the song *Marko and Musa* and the switch from singing to recitation, see the discussion in Neziri and Scaldaferri 2016. One may note, moreover, that analogous studies of the meter of texts of the Arbëresh (the Albanian-speaking communities that established themselves in southern Italy in the fifteenth century CE) reveal an additional area of research in Albanian versification and also concern the written verse insofar as it shows points of contact with the oral tradition (see Scaldaferri 2008). Of particular note is the work of Francesco Altimari, who has recently re-examined the *Songs of Milosao* by the Arbëresh poet Girolamo De Rada; this is one of the central works of Albanian literature and is famous for the difficulty it presents in the analysis of its metrical structures (difficulties which have been pointed out by Pipa as well). Altimari offers a convincing reading of the metrical structure of this work and argues for a system based upon rhythmic principles that have been modeled upon the type of versification found in the oral tradition (see De Rada 2017).

anthropological discussions that go from Mauss to Merleau-Ponty, from Csordas to Jackson.[15]

In the practice of epic song, the singer is always accompanied by a musical instrument. In the case of Albanian epic, the instrument is the *lahuta*, the single-stringed instrument that is played with a bow and held by the singer in a vertical position. The singer's left hand presses down upon the single string using the interior, palm-side of the fingers and thereby produces the individual pitches, which are contained within the range of a fifth; the right hand holds the bow and draws it across the string in such a way as to produce the sound. The testimonies both of singers and of scholars who have analyzed this kind of performance all concur in stating that it is extremely difficult for singers to perform verses of epic song without the help of the instrument. When performances are attempted without the instrument, the central element that seems to be lacking is not so much the musical melody that combines with the song and supports it formally, but rather the rhythmic movement performed by the singer with the bow: numerous testimonies relate, in fact, that in the absence of the instrument or the bow singers will imitate the gesture of drawing the bow across the string, sometimes even employing a piece of wood or another object as a substitute. The role of the accompaniment performed with the instrument, therefore, does not only consist in the melody that backs up and supports the voice, but also—and above all—in the physical movement performed by the arm that supports the bow: with the regularity of its motion this movement establishes a rhythmic pattern that is of fundamental importance in supporting the performance overall.[16]

Taking its inspiration from the multiform quality of the Ugljanin materials, an investigation was undertaken of the performance practices of the singer Isa Elezi-Lekëgjekaj (in civil records Isa Muriqi, born 1947), who is in fact the principal performer now active in the area of Rugova in Kosovo. As has already been documented in other contributions, the research undertaken with Isa confirmed the importance of the rhythmic pattern as a fundamental basis for performance practices. Moreover, it revealed in addition a very peculiar performance practice that Isa has used in private as a kind of exercise: namely, the practice of reciting a text while walking and accompanying oneself with the regular alternation of footfalls, which track and mark the isochronous accents of the text.

---

[15] For an overview of the state of the field, see Ferrarini 2011.

[16] I myself have observed this phenomenon directly, during a rehearsal with a few singers during the Festival of Gjirokaster in September of 2009. A young singer, without his *lahuta*, sang to the accompaniment of the instrument of a second singer, with whom he alternated the singing portion of the text of a work recently composed by Shaban Lajci. The young singer imitated the movement of the bow with his hands, thus realizing a rhythmic or gestural accompaniment. The video is available at http://leavlab.com/portfolio/epic-songs-balkans/ (accessed February 2021).

This practice amounts to a sort of rhythmic pre-textualization, employed by Isa from time to time as he walks in the mountains with his flock of sheep; and it allows him to practice composing formulaic verses with the rigorous rhythmic basis established by the regularity of his footsteps. One can note the way the accents are marked by the footsteps in the verses below, which were recited by Isa as he walked and are given with rhythmic transcription:[17]

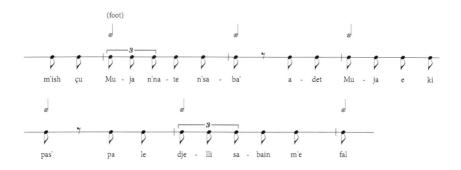

Muji arose in the morning
he washed up before praying
he greeted the sun of the morning

This episode certainly suggests the necessity of more detailed investigation into the connection between poetic rhythm and bodily movement, beginning with the concept of the metrical foot, which now seems to have not only a metaphorical meaning but also concrete significance in terms of the action performed by the body. Such an investigation could benefit from an increasingly interdisciplinary approach, which would also consider the role played by forms of technology in relation to the human body. And last but not least, one cannot leave out consideration of the singer's voice, not only at the level of its physical components and the complex relationships that tie the voice to the individual of whom it is the sonic representation, but also at the level of the cultural meanings that the voice assumes when it is disembodied and entrusted to an external apparatus—a new body—through the process of recording.

[17] These issues are touched upon in Scaldaferri 2011, Neziri and Scaldaferri 2016.

4

The Epic Admirative in Albanian

Victor A. Friedman

IN THIS CHAPTER I wish to discuss an element of Albanian epic poetry that is both unique to it in a Balkan context and not translatable, namely the use of admirative forms. The Albanian admirative is a set of verb paradigms that, in ordinary usage, convey surprise, disbelief, or the unwillingness of the speaker to confirm a report—without, however, casting any doubt upon it, but rather simply emphasizing that the information is second hand. When translating these forms into English, the surprise meaning is often equivalent to 'oh, look!' or old-fashioned colloquial 'lookee there!' (from 'look ye there!'), 'to my surprise'; the disbelief meaning is conveyed by post-posed 'indeed!' (with ironic or indignant intonation); and the neutral reported meaning is rendered by English 'apparently'. It should be emphasized that these English meanings, which must be expressed by a lexical item and/or intonation, are expressed grammatically in Albanian by the choice of an admirative form of a verb. Thus, Albanian has at its disposal a grammatical category that can be deployed to stylistic effect for which there is no grammatical equivalent in English, nor, for that matter, in the language formerly known as Serbo-Croatian.[1] Moreover, precisely in Albanian epic poetry there are uses of the admirative that are specific to epic poetic

---

[1] Turkish, which arguably influenced the development of the semantics of the Albanian admirative (Friedman 2010) sometimes uses its own perfect (the miş-past) in similar ways, and Macedonian, Bulgarian, and Meglenormanian all have perfect-based verb paradigms that are involved in conveying similar meanings (Friedman 2003). These are overlapping usages however, and Albanian usually uses the admirative where the other languages do not or cannot use their partially corresponding forms (see Friedman 1982 and 2012b for details). This is especially the case in the narrative or epic admirative discussed here.

diction. In this contribution, therefore, I will examine how the admirative is used in Albanian epic poetry as a stylistic device. My main concern will be to give a sense of the various types of nuances that can occur.

Before turning to the analysis, however, it will be useful to give the reader some general orientation regarding the history of the admirative and its use in everyday speech. The Albanian perfect, much like the English, is usually formed by means of 'have' plus a participle, e.g. Standard Albanian *unë kam pasur* 'I have had', *ti ke pasur*, 'you have had', *ai ka pasur* 'he has had', etc.[2] These examples also illustrate the fact that 'have' is an irregular verb, and the present and the participle have different stems. There is also a short participle, which for 'have' is *pasë* in the standard language, although its position in the standard is quite marginal, and most short participles are dialectal. At some point, it became possible to put the auxiliary after the participle (which is still the case today, albeit a rare one). Subsequently, the postposed auxiliary fused with the short participle into what became a new set of paradigms, the admirative. For example: *ka pasë* 's/he has had' > *paska* 's/he has [to my surprise / apparently / indeed [ironic]!]'. This admirative, which has a present meaning, can be used as an auxiliary to form a perfect admirative, e.g. *paska pasur* 's/he has had [to my surprise / apparently / indeed!]'. In Geg, the short participle is more frequent, e.g. *ka pas* and *paska pas*. Note that the perfect with postposed auxiliary became a true present tense, which then served to form a new, admirative perfect using the present admirative of 'have'.[3] For the verb 'be', the 3sg perfect in Standard Albanian is *ka qenë* 'I have been', which gave a present admirative *qenka* and a perfect admirative *paska qenë*. In the Geg dialects of most of the epics published here, however, the verb 'be' came to be used as the auxiliary for intransitive verbs, and so the present admirative of 'be', standard and some dialects *qenka* (also Tosk *qënka* in some older publications), in other dialects *kanka, kenka, konka*, is more common as an auxiliary in the epic than it would be in standard language publications.

In everyday usage, the admirative is used much more in speech than in writing. In speech, it is used most frequently to express surprise, more rarely

---

[2] The Albanian medio-passive perfect is formed using the auxiliary *jam* 'be' rather than *kam* 'have' plus participle. In many Geg dialects, including some of the ones in which these epics are sung, the verb 'be' also forms the active perfect of some intransitive verbs. This can be compared to the French rule that requires *être* instead of *avoir* to from the so-called *passé composé* of certain intransitive verbs, mostly verbs of motion. The admirative, however, was formed before this rule developed in the Geg dialects that have it, and only the verb 'have' is involved in forming admiratives, even when the verb is an intransitive that takes 'be' as the perfect auxiliary.

[3] This same process affected the pluperfect and imperfect, e.g. (using Standard Albanian) imperfect *kishte* 's/he had', pluperfect *kish(te) pasur* 's/he had had', imperfect admirative *paskësh*, pluperfect admirative *paskësh pasur*, but these forms are extremely rare and, moreover, the imperfect and pluperfect admirative do not occur in the epics published here.

to express sarcasm (dubitative), and, perhaps with a frequency between these two usages, to express a neutral report. Thus, for example, a typical expression of surprise would be *Ti kërcyeke shumë mirë!* 'You dance very well!' (I was not expecting you to know Albanian folk dances, since you are American) or *Ku paskeni mësuar shqip?* 'Where did you learn Albanian?' (I am surprised to meet an American who speaks Albanian). An example of a neutral report example is *Ai paska një letër* 'He says he has a letter' (someone told him he has a letter and he asked me to tell you). An expression of doubt or sarcasm would be, for example, if someone says *S'kam faj* 'It's not my fault', and another person says, *S'paske faj!* 'It's not your fault, indeed!' (i.e., it most certainly is your fault). In writing, precisely owing to the colloquial nature of the admirative, it is quite rare except in literary reproductions of reported speech. When it is used in formal writing, the most common usage is dubitative, i.e. the writer is purposefully casting doubt on the claim or report, although in some instances an admirative will be used to emphasize that, while the writer does not doubt the report, nevertheless s/he is or was not in a position to verify it. Thus, for example, during the period in the 1990s leading up to the 1999 NATO war in Kosovo, Kosovar electronic news sources would sometimes use admiratives in their dubitative meaning for reporting claims from Serbian news sources. During the war itself, the admirative occasionally appeared in these same sources with a neutral reported meeting, and after the war, while Kosovo was being administered by KFOR under UNSCR 1244, admiratives would again appear in their dubitative meanings, but this time when reporting disputed claims made by KFOR (see Friedman 2012a). Similarly, in scholarly articles, on rare occasion an author will use an admirative to report a claim or hypothesis that the author doubts (Friedman 2012b).

Turning now to the use of admiratives in Albanian epics, we shall begin with Table 1, which gives the numbers and percentages of admirative occurrences, and discuss their significance before turning to stylistic analysis.

Even with this relatively small sample, the patterns that emerge are striking. First we can note that there are no admiratives at all in the songs by Fatima Biberović. These are not epic songs, so epic style is not expected, but admiratives do sometimes occur in Albanian lyric songs in the same sorts of usage as in ordinary conversation. Their absence may be a matter of coincidence, of Fatima's personal style, or possibly a characteristic of Sanjak Albanian or the style of bilingual Sanjak singers. These last two speculations come into play when examining the songs of Salih Ugljanin, which have the lowest percentages of admiratives in the entire corpus of epics published here. What would be necessary for a definitive answer, however, would be a thorough analysis of as many Sanjak texts as possible, preferably with data identifying the singer's home language.

Song #	Singer	Title	Translation
PN 672	Salih Ugljanin	*Muji e Gavran Kapetani*	Muji and Gavran Kapetan
PN 659	Salih Ugljanin	*Mark e Musa*	Marko and Musa
LAN 28	Gjergj Pllumbi	*Musa Qeshexhi dhe vlla Bergjanine Gjemi*	Musa Qeshexhi and His Brother Bergjanine Gjemi
LAN 34	Marash Nika	*Kanga e Ali Pashë Gusinjes*	The Song of Ali Pasha of Gusinje
LAN 39	Sokol Martini	*Kanga e Halilit kur asht martue*	The Song of the Wedding of Halil
LAN 53	Ali Meta	*Kanga e Sultan Muratit*	The Song of Sultan Murad (The Battle of Kosovo)
LAN 57	Ali Meta	*Kanga e Ali Bajraktarit me Krajlicen e Inglizit*	The Song of Ali Bajraktari and the Queen of England
LAN 60	Adem Brahimi	*Kanga e Sirotin Alis*	The Song of Sirotin Ali
LAN 79	Rexhep Zeneli	*Kanga e Halilit qi e ka nxane Jovan Kapidanin*	The Song of Halil who Seized Jovan Kapidani

Table 1: Admiratives in the Albanian Epics published in this volume

Moving on to the texts from Northern Albania, the variation in percentage of admiratives is striking. Of particular significance here is the comparison of the songs by Ali Meta and the one by Adem Brahimi. Both are from the same Northeastern Geg dialect, and thus the fact that Ali has more than 20% admiratives in both his songs and Adem less than 10% in his suggests that admirative usage is, at least to some extent, a matter of personal style. Also worth noting here is that Sokol Martini, who is also from a Northeast Geg area, has the lowest percentage (5%) of all the North Albanian texts, while Ali has the highest. The fact that individual singers have individual styles is well attested for the South Slavic epics, and it would appear that admirative usage has a connection to

adm/total lines	%	song type	location	Dialect
1/236 lines	.04%	legendary	Novi Pazar/Sanjak	Geg
4/154 lines	2.5%	legendary	Novi Pazar/Sanjak	Geg
70/729 lines	10%	legendary	Theth, Shala	NW Geg
2/19 lines	10%	historical	Abat, Shala	NW Geg
16/310 lines	5%	legendary	Palç, Nikaj-Mërtur	NE Geg
61/250 lines	24%	historical	Tropoja	NE Geg
65/289 lines	22%	legendary	Tropoja	NE Geg
190/2163 lines	9%	legendary	Tropoja	NE Geg
51/425 lines	12%	legendary	Puka	NE Geg

personal style in the Albanian epics. We can also note here two other significant differences between the South Slavic and Albanian epic style. As is well known, the South Slavic epic has a strict ten-syllable line with a caesura after the fourth syllable, whereas the Albanian epic, while tending to such a model, has a free syllable count. It is thus the case that one cannot argue that admirative perfects are used to supply an extra syllable where required by the text, e.g. *ka pas* 's/ he has had' vs *paska pas* 's/he has had (admirative)'. The second difference is in the deployment and position of verbs. In the Albanian epic, the majority of lines end in a verb, and the overwhelming majority of lines contain a verb, and only one verb. In the South Slavic epic, however, verbless lines are by far more common than in Albanian, and lines frequently end in other parts of speech. The exact statistics require further study, but even a cursory examination of the texts makes these facts clear. Moreover, of a total of 453 lines with admiratives (of a total of 4576 lines), only 2 lines contain 2 admiratives. Thus the identification of verb count with line count is much more consistent for Albanian than for South Slavic.

One other feature of the North Albanian epic in particular is the use of the various tense forms. Albanian has a more complex system of verbal paradigms than the former Serbo-Croatian, and while the South Slavic epic is relatively conservative in its deployment of aorists and imperfects, it is nonetheless the case that the descendant of the Common Slavic perfect has become the general past, as is the case in the colloquial language. Perfects are much less frequent in colloquial Albanian than in the former Serbo-Croatian, but they occur with greater frequency in the epic. Here we can note that it would appear that Salih Ugljanin appears to use fewer perfects than the singers in Northern Albania, and thus the predominance of perfects in the North Albanian epic may be a matter of internal development. The details of these generalities require further study, and we only note them here in passing. Of relevance here is the fact that while most of the verb forms being studied here are perfects, their translations are simple pasts.[4]

In terms of admirative usage, we can distinguish two broad types in the Albanian epic song: 1) use in quoted speech that is consistent with admirative usage in ordinary colloquial Albanian, and 2) what I call the Albanian epic admirative. The epic admirative, in turn, tends to occur in two contexts: 1) introducing some significant action, and 2) describing a highlighted episode. In the remainder of this article, I shall illustrate these points.

Colloquial admirative usage in the Albanian epic occurs in direct quotation within the epic. The only examples of 2nd person admiratives (9 out of 26 lines) are in direct quotation. Present admiratives are always colloquial rather than epic. Here it is worth noting that while the progressive marker *po* plus ordinary present tense is used occasionally (albeit rarely) to heighten the action of the narrative, *po* never occurs in the epics with a present admirative. The epic admirative is always a 3rd person perfect, although 3rd person perfect also occurs as colloquial in direct quotation.

---

[4]   It could also be argued that the perfect is being used in Albanian for stylistic vividness, much like an historical present. Be that as it may, the problem of tense form usage in the Albanian epic is worthy of further investigation.

The present admiratives are exclusively quotational, and, moreover, 2nd person singular with one 3sg exception.[5] The effect in the 2nd person is to express surprise of some sort, i.e. an observation of something unusual or unexpected. The 3rd singular present is a quotation of a dream interpretation, and could plausibly be analyzed as an inferential. The examples are given here below (the numbers identify each verse by song and line number):[6]

2 sg

LAN 28/336	*qenke* i ri e shum marri me dek	*you are* young and it is sheer madness for you to die
LAN 28/496	se ti *paske* pushken me vedi	you *do have* your rifle with you
LAN 60/591	mysafir dhe hiri qi po i *paske*	even if *you have* a well-wishing guest
LAN 60/592	edhe mbrama kurrnjo nuk po i *lashke*	even in the evening *you* don't *let* anyone in.
LAN 60/597	mik permbrenda kurrnjo nuk po *lashke*	*you* do not *let* a single friend inside.

3sg

LAN 57/17	qare s'*kanka* ne Kossove pa dal	that *it is* not to his advantage not to go to Kosovo

---

[5] Although *kenka* appears to be a 3rd sg form, the meaning is clearly 2 sg. There are four occurrences of what appear to be 2nd person present admiratives with apparent 3rd person perfect admirative meaning. The data are these:

39/33	q'there *ndije ke* Sokol Halili	Just then Sokol Halili hears
60/1357	Muja i *çelke* dyert te kallas	Muji opens the doors of the fortress
79/46	Muja i *thojke* Beg Alaj Begut	Muji says to Beg Alaj Beg
79/52	Muja i *thojke* Beg Alaj Begut	Muji says to Beg Alaj Beg

These examples are deviations that may represent peculiar dialectal archaisms (i.e., participle + 'have' as past), a phenomenon known from the Albanian dialects of Ukraine, in which case the meaning would be past rather than present (see Friedman 2010).

[6] A note on translations in this article: In some places, the translation differs slightly from the one in the body of this book. The translation here is sometimes more literal, whereas in the translations in the body of the book it is sometimes the case that English stylistic devices will replace the epic diction for the sake of readability and flow. The epic makes very little use of gerundive constructions and other forms of hypotaxis, preferring sequences of short main clauses. While this works well when the epic is performed orally, it does not read well on the page, and therefore the decision was made to use more subordination in the translations. Other differences are also related to citing the lines outside of the larger text for the specific purposes of this article.

There are also 4 occurrences of 2sg perfect admiratives and a single 1sg perfect admirative, all quotational and also of the 'surprise' sort:

1st sg

LAN 60/705	çyqe jam taksirat *paskam pas*	I am all alone, I've had bad luck

2 sg

LAN 28/397	shka keshtu Muso qi *qenke lodhë*	how is it, Musa, that you *have become tired?*
LAN 60/1105	kurve e madhe ti e *kenka kan*	you *are* such a bitch![7]
LAN 60/1250	qi me gjak e çike ti *kanke mblue*	that you *have covered* me with blood, girl
LAN 60/1252	qi per ishane faqet i *paske bamë*	that *you have put* a scar on my face

In addition to these examples, there are also 15 quotational 3rd person perfect admiratives, of which 3 refer to the addressee (LAN 28/310, 28/656, 60/1083), 6 refer to the speaker himself, and these latter are all more or less the same formula (LAN 5/202, 5/210, 39/202, 39/210, 39/250, 60/671):

LAN 5/202	ky hyzmet zoti qysh e *paska bamë*	how could God *allot* me a fate such as this?
LAN 5/210	kyzmet Zoti nuk i *paska bâ*	God *did* not *grant* [me] good fortune
LAN 28/310	a thue ty mendja te *paska lan*	*have* you by chance *lost* your mind?
LAN 28/656	me tamam tue te *paska goditë* Zoti	God *has created* you just right

---

[7] The form *kenka kan* is 3rd singular, but the reference is clearly 2nd singular. This is, moreover, the one example of a perfect admirative with present meaning, indicating surprise at a pre-existing state, corresponding to admirative usages of perfects in other Balkan languages (see Friedman 2003).

LAN 39/202	ky hyzmet zoti qysh e *paska bamë*	how could God *allot* me a fate such as this?
LAN 39/210	kyzmet Zoti nuk i *paska bâ*	God *did* not *grant* [me] good fortune
LAN 39/250	e kyzmet zoti nuk e *paska bâ*	and God *did* not *grant* [me] good fortune
LAN 57/18	se Zot në enderr *paska kalzue*	because God *had* so *revealed* in the dream
LAN 57/86	tridhete çadra i *paska çue*	he *raised* thirty tents for him
LAN 60/489	se q'ashtu shkrue e kysmet *kanka kan*	as it is written thus *has* fate *decreed*
LAN 60/671	po rreziku Ali m'*paska ardh*	misfortune has befallen me, Ali [Muji speaking]
LAN 60/1083	fuqi të madhe Zoti të *paska dhan*	God *has indeed given* you great strength
LAN 60/1219	si gjumi dekun baben e *paska marre*	for a deep sleep *has overtaken* father
LAN 60/1265	*paska pre* aj Sirotin Alia	Sirotin Ali *has killed* him
LAN 60/1478	ndonji luft o shok qi e *paska nise*	he *has started* a battle, my friends

It is also worth noting that the non-3rd person colloquial admiratives occur in only two of the epics—LAN 28 and 60—one NE Geg and the other NW Geg, and both singers are in the middle range in terms of their percentage of admirative lines (10% and 9% respectively). From this it can be deduced that non-3rd person admiratives are not limited to NE or NW Geg, and, moreover, they occur in epics by singers whose style is in the middle range vis-à-vis the use of admiratives.

The remaining 427 admiratives are all 3rd person perfects and are of the narrative type, with one or the other function as noted above, i.e. either introductory highlighting or episodic highlighting. The following examples illustrate these two functions. In each example, I cite only the lines with admiratives to focus on the epic admirative effects.

The admiratives in PN 659 and 672, i.e., those of Salih Ugljanin, the bilingual singer in this collection, are all of the type that introduces an episode or a heightened moment (PN 659/126), although in the case of PN 659/8 and 9 we have the repetition of a line.

PN 659

2	*Konka çua* Kraleviçu Marka	Kralević Marko *arose*
8	bash tu mbreti *konka dalë*	he *headed* straight for the Emperor
9	bash tu mbreti *konka dalë*	he *headed* straight for the Emperor
126	n'hanxhar e *paska ngulë*	he *took out* a dagger

PN 672

6	e *koka dal*-o e shoqeja e Mujes	then *came out* the wife of Muji

The closing episodes (lines 695-739) of LAN 28 also illustrate the introductory or transitional function of the epic admirative. Out of 45 lines, 6 are admirative, i.e. 13% in an epic where the total admirative percentage was 10%, so just slightly above the average. The usages are both in direct quotation and in introducing transitional moments:

LAN 28

695	*Kenka nise* Marku per vatan	Marko *set off* for the homeland
711	fill ne ode te Gjemi *paska shkue*	he *went* straight to Gjemi's room
718	*paska qi* Gjemi e i ka than	Gjemi *addressed* him and said
722	*paska qit* Marku i ka than	Marko *addressed* him and said
728	*paska qit* Gjemi i ka than	Gjemi *addressed* him and said
736	Me te shpejt Marku e *paska leshue*	Marko quickly *released* him

For LAN 39, whose singer is the most parsimonious of the North Albanian singers in terms of admiratives, we give all 16 admiratives, and these give a good sense of the introductory/transitional epic usage. These include the 3 quotative usages that are cited above.

LAN 39

33	q'there *ndije ke* Sokol Halili	just then Sokol Halil *heard*
71	n'shefi të krajlit q'there *kenka hi*	and then he *entered* the border-lands of the King
77	shpejt ne mejhan djali *kenka hi*	the boy soon *entered* the tavern
127	e asht nise n'mik *kenka shkue*	he set out and *went* to his friend
135	ne saraj te krajlit prap djali *kenka hi*	the boy *went* back into the palace of the King
141	fillë ne atë odë me te shpejt *kenka hi*	she *went* immediately into a room
147	e n'oborr djali *kenka ra*	the boy *went out* into the courtyard
154	e ne pazar djali *kenka ra*	the boy *rushed* into the market place
176	shpejt ne pazar çika *kenka dal*	the girl quickly *came* to the market place
201	unë i mjeri vete *paska than*	"woe is me," he *said* to himself
202	ky hyzmet zoti qysh e *paska bamë*	how could God *allot* me a fate such as this
210	kyzmet Zoti nuk i *paska bâ*	God did not *grant* [me] good fortune
230	edhe shpejt n'shpie krajli *kenka ardhe*	the King *came* home at once
231	fill në sarraj te djali *kenka hi*	[he] *went* straight to the palace to see the boy
250	e kyzmet zoti nuk e *paska bâ*	and God has not *granted* me good fortune
288	e n'sarraje tu krajli *kenkan hi*	they entered the palace of the King

LAN 53 provides a good example of epic admiratives as framing an episode:

LAN 53

232	atherë Miloshi nji fjal e *paska fol*	then Milosh *spoke* a few words
242	pa pike shpirt babina *kenka ra*	the old woman *fell down* stone dead

In the episode itself, Milosh uses his last wish to trick the old woman who had betrayed him into leaning close to him; he bites off her nose and thereby kills her.

The following example from LAN 57 provides a good example of admiratives used for heightened effect in a single episode. As can be seen from the line numbering, out of 15 lines, 9 are admiratives, and the non-admirative lines are superfluous to the flow.

LAN 57

65	nusja e Alies kur *paska ndije*	when Ali's bride *learned*
66	ne Stamboll Alia *paska shkue*	that Ali *had gone* to Stambol
67	nusja e Alies *kanka shtrengue*	Ali's bride *girded* herself
70	dymdhjete nishana i *paska vënue*	she *put* her hair inside the headpiece
71	e *paska vesh* shpaten prej dukati	and *strapped* on a golden sword
73	*kenka bâ* sikur ma i miri Zotori	she *looked like* the finest of noblemen
74	gjokun pllakut ja *paska marrë*	she *took* her father's grey-white horse
78	se n'Stamboll kur *kakan shkue*	and *went* to Stambol
79	nji hotel kur *kenka shkue*	and when she *went* into a hotel

As I hope to have shown in this brief study, the admirative verb forms in the Albanian epic perform functions that are specific both to the Albanian language and to the Albanian epic style. First, the Albanian admiratives are unique among the verbal paradigms of the Balkan languages in their usage and distribution.[8]

---

[8] As noted above, there is some overlap with perfects in other Balkan languages, but roughly 90% of the time there is not (Friedman 1982). See also Friedman 1994.

Second, whereas in spoken and written Albanian prose the admirative is used to express surprise, disbelief, or a neutral report, in the Albanian epic, in addition to these three colloquial functions in direct speech, the admirative is deployed in the narrative itself either 1) to highlight beginnings, endings, and points of transition, for which it is most often used with verbs of speaking or motion, and is generally preceded and/or followed by non-admiratives or 2) to highlight a particular episode, in which case a series of admiratives will be used in succes-sive or near-successive lines. These functions are both specific to the epic and do not occur in ordinary speech or prose writing. Moreover, owing to the speci-ficity of the admirative in its epic usage, it represents an untranslatable stylistic effect.

PART TWO

CATALOGUES

Albanian Recordings in the Milman Parry Collection of Oral Literature

The catalogue includes the catalogue number, prefixed by PN (Parry Number) or LN (Lord Number); the singer's name; the place and date of recording; the title of the song, generic classification (where appropriate), and number of verses; the first line of the text; the number(s) assigned to the relevant phonograph disc(s) or wire spool(s); and biographical information about the singer.

The legendary songs included in the following recordings belong also to the cycle of *këngë kreshnikësh*: PN 659, 655, 656, 659, 972, 682.

Recordings on Aluminum Disc, 1934–1935

PN 473. Hasanović, Etem [Alb: Hasani, Et-hem]. Alexandrovo (Macedonia). September 7, 1934. *Arnautska pjesma / Dem-ahmeti (Demë Ahmeti)*. Historical song. 96 lines. *Ej kokan mledhe treqin haranbashe*. Discs 381–384.
Biographical note: age 22; Muslim, farmer, illiterate, from Gjilani (Kosovo).

PN 474. Hasanović, Etem. Alexandrovo (Macedonia). September 7, 1934. *Arnautska pjesma / Sinan binaki 1-2*. Historical song. 38 lines. *Ej, Arif Sinani, ej, Arif, bre djalë*. Discs 392–393.

PN 654. Ugljanin, Salih [Alb: Uglla, Sali]. Novi Pazar (Serbia). November 16, 1934. Pričanje II (Conversation II).
Ali paša od Gusinja. Historical song. 91 lines. *Ali Pasha fjalë ka çua*. Discs 907–908.
Ženska pjesma. Lyric song. 10 lines. *Shkurte Hakli shkurt e trash*. Disc 915.
Marko Kraljević i Đerđelez Alija. Legendary song. 144 lines. *P'e vetë nana Kraleviq Markun*. Discs 916–917.
Emin Halaći. Historical song. 26 lines. *Emin Halaçi djalë i ri*. Disc 919.
Biographical note: age 85 (?); Muslim. Born in Ugao, a district of Senica. His parents were Albanians, the father from the district of Shkodra. He learned to sing in Albanian; started to sing in Bosnian at the age of 30. M. Murko and A. Schmaus, among others, also collected and recorded songs from him.

More information about him, as well as English translations of his Bosnian songs, can be found in SCHS, vol. 1: 53–223, 329–400, and in Kolsti 1990. These Albanian texts were experimental 'translations' of Bosnian songs, which were also recorded. The song included in PN 672 is entirely sung; other sung fragments are included in PN 656 and PN 659; the other texts were recited.

PN 655. Ugljanin, Salih. Novi Pazar (Serbia). November 17, 1934. Pričanje III (Conversation III).
Marko Kraljević i Bajramaga. Legendary song. 58 lines. *Po i hipë Marku kalit Sharan.* Discs 954–955.
Examples of formulas. *Po pin ven-o Kraloviq-o Marko.* Discs 957–958.
Marko Kraljević i trideset kapetana. Legendary song. 84 lines. *Këqyre, Marku u çua n'kamë.* Discs 960–961.

PN 656. Ugljanin, Salih. Novi Pazar (Serbia). November 18, 1934. Pričanje IV (Conversation IV).
Emin Halaći. Historical song. 77 lines. *Jashar Pasha, mjekërr bardhë.* Discs 978–979.
Ramo Kovaçi. Legendary song. 25 lines. *Lum për ty, more, i lumi Zot.* Discs 980–981.
Includes a sung version of part of the text.

PN 658. Ugljanin, Salih. Novi Pazar (Serbia). November 19, 1934. Pričanje V (Conversation 5).
Emin Halaći. Historical song. 142 lines. *Emin Hallaçi, tha, djalë i ri.* Discs 1015–1017.

PN 659 Ugljanin, Salih. Novi Pazar, (Serbia). November 20, 1934. Pričanje VI (Conversation VI).
Marko Kraljević i Musa Keserdžija [Mark e Musa]. Legendary song. 156 lines. *E lum për ty-o moro j-lumi Zojote.* Discs 1056–1058. The first 6 lines are sung, the others recited.

PN 672 Ugljanin, Salih. Novi Pazar (Serbia). November 24, 1934. *Hrnjičić Mujo i Gavran Kapetan [Muji e Gavran Kapetani].* Legendary song. 236 lines. *Oj lum për ty o Zot mor-oj lumi Zot.* Discs 1205–1210. Sung with *gusle;* followed by the Bosnian version on discs 1211–1219.

PN 682. Zogić, Đemo [Alb: Zogu, Xhemajl]. Novi Pazar (Serbia). November 25, 1934. Pričanje (Conversation). Untitled fragment. 22 lines. *Hej, ni nat-to mor-o ish djehun.* Disc 1327. Sung with *gusle.*
Biographical note: age 38; Muslim. Zogić was born in Glogovik, Serbia and lived there for 20 years before settling in Novi Pazar, where he ran a coffee house. In his home village there were Albanians who came from Rugova. His

parents spoke Albanian. He reported to Parry that some Albanian singers could translate Bosnian songs into Albanian. For more on Zogić, see SCHS, vol. 1: 235–245.

PN 6327. Biberović, Fatima [Alb: Arifi, Fatime]. Gacko (Bosnia-Hercegovina). April, 22, 1935.
Esad paša. Historical song. 36 lines. *Esat Pasha nji zog bylbyli*. Discs 3045–3046.
Biographical note: Biberović was born in Prizren, and was 33 years old at the time the recording was made. Her mother was from Prishtina, her father from Kosovo. She was married four times (the first time at age 15). Her maiden name Arifović; her current husband was Meho Biberović, a gypsy then jailed in Dubrovnik for having stabbed one of his fellows. Biberović sang in Albanian and Turkish. Much information about her can be found in PN 6546, which includes a long conversation about her life. Other information and materials have been published in Bartók and Lord 1951: 251–252, 367.

PN 6332. Biberović, Fatima. Gacko (Bosnia-Hercegovina). April, 22, 1935. *Kunjam Kam Elbasan*. Lyric song. 41 lines. *Oh, ti je e keqe, dilber-o, more bac*. Discs 3054–3055.

PN 6361. Biberović, Fatima. Gacko (Bosnia-Hercegovina). April, 23, 1935. *Husni Cura i Bajramberg* [*Hysni Curri e Bajram Begu*]. Military song. 129 lines. *Hej, se kam uri se Shen Meria pret*. Discs 3118–3120.

PN 6371. Biberović, Fatima. Gacko (Bosnia-Hercegovina). April, 24, 1935. *Cikazuri dukati me bist*. Lyric song. 57 lines. *Çika e Zhurit dukatin me bisht*. Discs 3145–3146.

PN 6386. Biberović, Fatima. Gacko (Bosnia-Hercegovina). April, 24, 1935. *Ej, Elbasan, medet, koftë farue*. Lyric song. 21 lines. *Haj, Shkurte Hakli, he, more, n'atë Gjakove*. Disc 3172.

PN 6409. Biberović, Fatima. Gacko (Bosnia-Hercegovina). April, 27, 1935. *O nizami nizami te grate*. Emigration song. 57 lines. *Oj, nizamt-e, oj, nizamtë e grat-e*. Discs 3227–3229.

PN 6451. Biberović, Fatima. Gacko (Bosnia-Hercegovina). May 20, 1935. *Esad paša*. Historical song. 41 lines. *Esat Pasha nji zog bylbyli*. Discs 3494–3495. Another version of PN 6327.

PN 6454. Biberović, Fatima. Gacko (Bosnia-Hercegovina). May 20, 1935. *Husni Cura i Bajrambeg* [*Hysni Curri e Bajram Begu*]. Military song. 76 lines. *Hej, se kam uri se Shen Meria pret*. Discs 3503–3504. Another version of PN 6361.

PN 6456. Biberović, Fatima. Gacko (Bosnia-Hercegovina). May 20, 1935. *Hifan furi*. Lyric song. 59 lines. *I kam hip pamporit*. Discs 3507–3508.

PN 6467. Biberović, Fatima. Gacko (Bosnia-Hercegovina). May 20, 1935. *Pjesma o kolačima*. ["The song of the Turkish cakes"]. 84 lines. *Kur ka thane gazda jone*. Discs 3534–3535. For the background to this song, see Bartók and Lord 1951: 367.

PN 6473. Biberović, Fatima. Gacko (Bosnia-Hercegovina). May 21, 1935. *Curja more nane*. Lyric song. 51 lines. *Kqyre more nane dreqin te xhamija*. Discs 3545–3546.

PN 6502. Biberović, Fatima. Gacko (Bosnia-Hercegovina). May 21, 1935. *Kambana dije mome*. Lyric song. 13 lines. *Kambane bije mome ca gurabije*. Disc 3598.

PN 6503. Biberović, Fatima. Gacko (Bosnia-Hercegovina). May 21, 1935. *Dü darda meni dard* [*Dy dardha me ni dardhë*]. Lyric song. 60 lines. *Dy molla me ni mollë*. Discs 3599–3600.

PN 6523a. Biberović, Fatima. Gacko (Bosnia-Hercegovina). May 23, 1935. *Mrtvačka pjesma i pričanje*. Lament and conversation. 120 lines. *E mjera une*. Discs 3777–3779.

PN 6555. Biberović, Fatima. Gacko (Bosnia-Hercegovina). May 25, 1935. *Faćfacene card*. Lament. 42 lines. *Mjera une*. Discs 3928–3929.

PN 6830. Nuhodžić, Šaban [Alb: Nuhoxha, Shaban]. Bijelo Polje (Montenegro). July 2, 1935. *Arnautske pjesme i pričanje*. Song and conversation. *Kanga e Gani Begut*. Historical song. 100 lines. Discs 5391–5395.
Biographical note: Age 39, Muslim, "literate only in Turkish [*pismen samo Turski*]."
The inventory of his repertoire contains the following note from Nikola Vujnović: "Šaban says that he heard these songs in Albania, and there he learned to speak Turkish and Albanian and that he heard and sang these songs with others in his company [*sa društvom*]. He says that he cannot say exactly from whom he learned [these songs], because he heard many singers who sang them."

PN 6835. Nuhodžić, Šaban. Bijelo Polje (Montenegro). July 2, 1935. *Arnautske pjesme i pričanje*. Lyric song and conversation. 64 lines. *Gu gu gu gu ban gugashi*. Discs 5425–5427.

Recordings On Wire Spools, 1951

Recordings are of low quality because of frequent changes in recording speed.

LN 196. Kadrija, Murati. Kažani (Macedonia). August 8, 1951. *Ljubavna pesma*. Lyric song. 30 lines. *E-ej, xhamadani-o oj me-e kapak-o me kapak*. Wire spool 5, min. 30–33.

LN 197. Kadrija, Murati. Kažani (Macedonia). August 8, 1951. *Pečalbarska pesma*. Emigration song. 36 lines. *Hej moj çele moj balaxhufe*. Wire spool 5, min. 33–38.

Albert B. Lord Collection of Epics From Northern Albania, 1937

The collection comprises 13 notebooks, collectively titled *Heroic Ballads and Folksongs from Albania.*

10 notebooks contain materials collected by Albert Lord:

Notebook "Kânge N. 1: Kol Marku," Dubrovnik, before August 25, 1937.

Notebooks 1–8, Northern Albania, September 4–October 13, 1937.

Notebook 12 (a catalogue of songs included in Notebooks 1–8).

3 notebooks contain materials sent to Lord by local collectors:

Notebook 9, received on December 20, 1937, and sent by Qamil Hoxha, a teacher from Bicaj, Kukës.

Notebook 10, dated December 10, 1937 and received on January 17, 1938, sent by Qamil Hoxha.

Notebook 11, titled "Teli i lahutës," received on January 26, 1938, and sent by Murat Paçi, a student from Shkodër. This notebook contains some material Paçi had collected several years before meeting Lord in 1937.

The following catalogue includes the catalogue number, prefixed by LAN (Lord Albanian Number) and corresponding to the "manuscript" (*dorëshkrim*) number assigned by Lord; the singer's name; the place and date of dictation; the title of the song; generic classification (where appropriate), and number of verses; the notebook and pages in which the song is recorded; and additional information, as appropriate, about the singer and his repertoire.

Albanian terms have been maintained in their original forms, although the term *kanga / kangen* has been regularized as *kanga*. Corrections or supplements to the information recorded by Lord are given in square brackets.

Places are designated with reference also to the new administrative denominations introduced in 2015. See the map on p. 385.

The following legendary songs belong also to the cycle of *këngë kreshnikësh*: LAN 1, 11a, 13, 14, 17, 19, 21, 22, 24, 28, 32, 33, 35, 38, 39, 40, 41, 42, 43, 46, 47, 50, 51, 55, 56, 57, 58, 60, 63, 66, 70, 73, 74, 79, 81, 83, 86, 89, 92, 94, 97, 99, 100, 101, 102, 103, 104, 105, 106, 107, 108, 109, 110.

LAN 1. Marku, Kol. Dubrovnik. S.d. (before August 25). *Kanga e Zuku Bajraktarit*. Legendary song. 25 lines. Notebook "Kânge N. 1. Kol Marku." The fragmentary text includes also a translation into Serbo-Croatian.
Biographical note: Marku was from Shkrel and residing in Ulcinj.

LAN 2. Trepshi, Pjeter. Shkodër. September 4, 1937. *Kanga e Zek Jakinit*. Historical song. 23 lines. Notebook 1: 1–3. The text includes also a short biography of the singer.
Biographical note: age 14, Catholic, from Shkodër. Trepshi had some formal education. He began playing the *çifteli* at age 4 or 5; he learned to sing from Gjergj Pllumbi, from Theth, and from singers who visited the hotel owned by his father.

LAN 3. Trepshi, Pjeter. Shkodër. September 4, 1937. *Moj e mira nen folet*. Lyric songs. 20 lines. Notebook 1: 3–4.

LAN 4. Preni, Martin. Shkodër. September 4, 1937. Biography and repertoire (3 songs). Notebook 1: 5.
Biographical note: age 60; Catholic; born in Dushman (Dukagjin), residing in Shkodër; illiterate.

LAN 5. Prendushi, Dod. Shkodër. September 5, 1937. Biography and repertoire (25 songs). Notebook 1: 6–7.
Biographical note: age 34; Catholic; born in Mërturi i Gurit (Puka), residing in Shkodër; illiterate.

LAN 6. Prendushi, Dod. Shkodër. September 5, 1937. *Kanga e Bajram Beg Currit*. Historical song. 38 lines. Notebook 1: 8–10. Prendushi learned this song from Prendush Gega.

LAN 7. Prendushi, Dod. Shkodër. September 5, 1937. *Kanga e Shaqir Grishes*. Historical song. 68 lines. Notebook 1: 10–14.

LAN 8. Lleshi, Mark. Shkodër. September 5, 1937. Biography and repertoire (16 songs). Notebook 1: 14, 19.

Biographical note: age 34; born in Temali-Dushman (Dukagjin), and residing in Shkodra; illiterate.

LAN 9. Trepshi, Pjeter. Shkodër. September 5, 1937. *Shaqir Grisha*. Historical song. 28 lines. Notebook 1: 15–16. Song written down by Pjeter Trepshi; learned from Fran Pali, age 30, from Gryk Lugjiat (Boga).

LAN 10. Trepshi, Pjeter. Shkodër. September 5, 1937. *Tradhtija e mikut*. Historical song. 41 lines. Notebook 1: 16–18. Song written down by Pjeter Trepshi; learned from Fran Pali.

LAN 11. Kol, Mark. Shkodër. September 5, 1937. Biography and repertoire (3 songs). Notebook 1: 20, 34–35.
Biographical note: age 49; born in Shala, residing in Shkodër; Catholic; illiterate. Kol began to play the *lahuta* at the age of 10, having learned by listening to his father. He traveled widely in Yugoslavia, including in parts of Bosnia-Hercegovina, Kosovo, and Montenegro (where stayed for several years). He claimed to be able to learn a song after hearing it three times. He stated that the *lahuta* is older than the *çifteli*.

LAN 11a. Kol, Mark. Shkodër. September 5, 1937. *Kanga e Mujes e Halilit*. Legendary song. 255 lines. Notebook 1: 20–34.

LAN 12. Pjetri, Gjok. Bajza (Kastrat) [today Malësia e Madhe, Bashkia Koplik]. September 6, 1937. Biography and repertoire (8 songs). Notebook 1: 35–36.
Biographical note: age 34; Catholic, born in Pjetroshan (Kastrat) [today Malësia e Madhe, Bashkia Koplik]; illiterate. Pjetri began to sing at age 14 or 15 years, having learned to sing from his father. He composed a song about King Zog's departure from Albania.

LAN 13. Pjetri, Gjok. Bajza (Kastrat) [today Malësia e Madhe, Bashkia Koplik]. September 7, 1937. *Kanga e Dragishes Vojvod*. Legendary song. 476 lines. Notebook 1: 36–61.

LAN 14. Pjetri, Gjok. Bajza (Kastrat) [today Malësia e Madhe, Bashkia Koplik]. September 7, 1937. *Kanga e Ali Bajraktarit*. Legendary song. 573 lines. Notebook 1: 62–90.

LAN 15. Pjetri, Gjok. Pjetroshan (Kastrat) [today Malësia e Madhe, Bashkia Koplik]. September 8, 1937. *Kanga e ikjes e Mbretit Zog I në Jugoslavi*. Historical song. 213 lines. Notebook 1: 91–101. The text concludes with the following note: "This song was composed by Gjok Pjetri on the occasion of the return of King Zog I to power. His reason for the song is because he was not able to be with the King in exile; therefore, to show his appreciation for the King's return, he composed this song (101)."

LAN 16. Pali, Fran. Boga (Shkrel) [today Malësia e Madhe, Bashkia Koplik]. September 9, 1937. Biography and repertoire (19 songs). Notebook 1: 102–103, 122.
Biographical note: age 33; Catholic; illiterate; born in Vukël (Kelmend) [today Bashkia Shkodër], then residing in Breg i Matit (Lezhë), but spending summer months at Boga. Pali had relatives who were singers.

LAN 17. Pali, Fran. Boga (Shkrel) [today Malësia e Madhe, Bashkia Koplik]. September 9, 1937. *Muja e Halili me Veshoviç Krajli*. Legendary song. 349 lines. Notebook 1: 103–122.

LAN 18. Rroku, Lluk. Boga (Shkrel) [today Malësia e Madhe, Bashkia Koplik]. September 10, 1937. Biography and repertoire (9 songs). Notebook 1: 123.
Biographical note: age 24; illiterate; born in Bajza (Kastrat) [today Malësia e Madhe, Bashkia Koplik]. Rroku began to sing at age 10; he learned from other singers, including his brother.

LAN 19. Rroku, Lluk. Boga (Shkrel) [today Malësia e Madhe, Bashkia Koplik]. September 10, 1937. *Kanga e Omerit të Mujës kur ka qenë 7 vjeç dhe dha provat e trimerisë*. Legendary song. 78 lines. Notebook 1: 124–128.

LAN 20. Toma, Nik[ë]. Boga (Shkrel) [today Malësia e Madhe, Bashkia Koplik]. September 10, 1937. Biography and repertoire (24 songs). Notebook 1: 129–131.
Biographical note: age 27, born in Boga. Toma had some schooling, including at the military school. He began to sing at age 13, having learned from his father; he collected songs from other singers.

LAN 21. Toma, Nik[ë]. Boga (Shkrel) [today Malësia e Madhe, Bashkia Koplik]. September 10, 1937. *Kanga e Mujës kur u zue rrob prei Mbretit Sulejman*. Legendary song. 324 lines. Notebook 1: 131–148.

LAN 22. Toma, Nik[ë]. Boga (Shkrel) [today Malësia e Madhe, Bashkia Koplik]. September 10, 1937. *Kanga e Sojane Ivanit*. Legendary song. 103 lines. Notebook 1: 148–153.

LAN 23. Xharri, Zef. Boga (Shkrel) [today Malësia e Madhe, Bashkia Koplik]. September 11, 1937. Biography and repertoire (11 songs). Notebook 1: 154.

Biographical note: age 33, born in Nikç (Kelmend) [today Bashkia Shkodër], residing in Gurrëz (Kurbin); illiterate. Xharri learned to sing from his father and others.

LAN 24. Xharri, Zef. Boga (Shkrel) [today Malësia e Madhe, Bashkia Koplik]. September 11, 1937. *Kanga e Mujes me Filip Maxharin.* Legendary song. 89 lines. Notebook 1: 155–159.

LAN 25. Xharri, Zef. September 11. *Kanga e Riza Pashes.* Historical song. 219 lines. Notebook 1: 160, Notebook 2: 171.

LAN 26. Pl[l]umbi, Gjergj. Theth (Shala) [today Bashkia Shkodër]. September 12, 1937. Biography and repertoire (22 songs). Notebook 2: 172–174.
Biographical note: age 40; born in Theth; illiterate; began to sing at the age of 5, learning from Mark Kola and other elders in Theth. Pllumbi had traveled to Kolašin, Andrijevica, Plav, Podgorica. He also played the *çifteli*, but not so well as the *lahuta*. He learned the song of Musa Qesexhies from an old singer in Montenegro who knew Albanian and Bosnian.

LAN 27. Kola, Zef. Theth (Shala) [today Bashkia Shkodër]. September 12, 1937. Biography and repertoire (1 song). Notebook 2: 175. Biographical note: age 50; born in Theth (Shala); illiterate; began to sing at age 12, having learned from his father, uncle, and others.

LAN 28. Pl[l]umbi, Gjergj. Theth (Shala) [today Bashkia Shkodër]. September 12, 1937. *Musa Qeshexhi dhe Vllau Bergjanine Gjemi.* Legendary song. 729 lines. Notebook 2: 176–214.

LAN 29. Prela, Martin. Abat (Shala) [today Bashkia Shkodër]. September 14, 1937. Biography and repertoire (2 songs). Notebook 2: 215.
Biographical note: age 33; born in Abat; illiterate; learned to sing from his father. Prela had traveled to Gucinje.

LAN 30. Prela, Martin. Abat (Shala) [today Bashkia Shkodër]. September 14, 1937. *Kanga e Hysen Fukaraja.* Legendary song. 28 lines. Notebook 2: 215–216.

LAN 31. Nika, Marash. Abat (Shala) [today Bashkia Shkodër]. September 15, 1937. Biography and repertoire (13 songs). Notebook 2: 217–218.
Biographical note: age 60; born in Pecaj (Shala); illiterate; began to sing at age 15, having learned from his father, grandfather, and other elders. Nika had been to Gjakova and Prizren under Ottoman rule, but did not otherwise travel outside of Albania.

LAN 32. Nika, Marash. Abat (Shala, today Bashkia Shkodër). September 15, 1937. *Kanga e Budalija Tali*. Legendary song. 175 lines. Notebook 2: 218–227.

LAN 33. Nika, Marash. Abat (Shala) [today Bashkia Shkodër]. September 15, 1937. *Kanga e Milosh Kapitanit*. Legendary song. 205 lines. Notebook 2: 227–238.

LAN 34. Nika, Marash. Abat (Shala) [today Bashkia Shkodër]. September 15, 1937. *Kanga e Ali Pashë Gusinjes*. Historical song. 87 lines. Notebook 2: 238–243.

LAN 35. Nika, Marash. Abat (Shala) [today Bashkia Shkodër]. September 15, 1937. *Kanga e Arnaut Osmanit*. Legendary song. 114 lines. Notebook 2: 243–249.

LAN 36. Brahimi, Adem. Palc (Nikaj-Mërtur) [today Bashkia Puka]. September 16, 1937. Biography and repertoire (19 songs). Notebook 2: 249–250.
Biographical note: age 57; born in Vuthaj (Gucinje, Montenegro); began to sing at age 16, having learned from his father and others. Brahimi learned some of his songs (included the song of Sirotin Ali) from Sadri Ademi, a bilingual singer of Vuthaj. Brahimi was travelling with Lord; his two songs (*Kanga e Ali Bajraktarit*, LAN 43, and *Kanga e Sirotin Alis*, LAN 60), were taken down at different times and places.

LAN 37. Martini, Sokol. Palc (Nikaj-Mërtur) [today Bashkia Puka]. September 16, 1937. Biography and repertoire (42 songs). Notebook 2: 251–253, 300.
Biographical note: age 38; born in Brisa (Nikaj-Mërtur) [today Bashkia Puka]; illiterate; began to sing at age 8, having learned from his father, grandfather, and others, including Bosnians. Martini had travelled near Ferizaj.

LAN 38. Martini, Sokol. Palc (Nikaj-Mërtur) [today Bashkia Puka]. September 16, 1937. *Kanga e Marteses Mujit*. Legendary song. 144 lines. Notebook 2: 253–261.

LAN 39. Martini, Sokol. Palc (Nikaj-Mërtur) [today Bashkia Puka]. September 17, 1937. *Kanga e Halilit kur asht martue*. Legendary song. 310 lines. Notebook 2: 261–277.

LAN 40. Martini, Sokol. Palc (Nikaj-Mërtur) [today Bashkia Puka]. September 17, 1937. *Kanga e Muse Qesexhisë*. Legendary song. 170 lines. Notebook 2: 277–286.

LAN 41. Martini, Sokol. Palc (Nikaj-Mërtur) [today Bashkia Puka]. September 17, 1937. *Kanga e Vojkoviç Alies*. Legendary song. 170 lines. Notebook 2: 287–296.

LAN 42. Martini, Sokol. Palc (Nikaj-Mërtur) [today Bashkia Puka]. September 17, 1937. *Kanga e Ivan Kapidanit*. Legendary song. 82 lines. Notebook 2: 296–300.

LAN 43. Brahimi, Adem. *Kanga e Ali Bajraktarit.* 1041 lines. Notebooks 2–3: 301–321, Palc (Nikaj-Mërtur) [today Bashkia Puka], September 17, 1937; 356–366, Geghysen [today Bashkia Shkodër], September 20, 1937; 424–426 Kolgecaj (Tropoja), September 21, 1937; 445–453 Tropoja, September 22, 1937; 458–469 Tropoja, September 22, 1937.

LAN 44. Hysen, Ali. Geghysen [today Bashkia Shkodër]. September 19, 1937. Biography and repertoire (18 songs). Notebook 3: 322–323.
Biographical note: age 60; illiterate; began singing at age 7, having learned from his father and Sjaf Qerimi. Hysen had served in the Ottoman Army. He had performed before Riza Beg Gjakovës and Bajram Beg Curri.

LAN 45. Hysen, Ali. Geghysen [today Bashkia Shkodër]. September 19, 1937. *Kanga e Ymer Agës.* Legendary song. 41 lines. Notebook 3: 324–326.

LAN 46. Hysen, Ali. Geghysen [today Bashkia Shkodër]. September 19, 1937. *Kanga e Bani Zadralise.* Legendary song. 319 lines. Notebook 3: 326–343.

LAN 47. Hysen, Ali. Geghysen [today Bashkia Shkodër]. September 19. *Kanga e Mujes me Krajlin e Kotorrit.* Legendary song. 141 lines. Notebook 3: 343–348, 351–352.

LAN 48. Abdulla, Mustafa. Geghysen [today Bashkia Shkodër]. September 19, 1937. *Kanga e ikjes dhe këthimit Mbretit.* Historical song. 52 lines. Notebook 3: 353–355.

LAN 49. Gjekaj, Riza Luz [Zymeri-Lucëgjekaj, Rizë]. Kolgecaj (Tropoja). September 20, 1937. Biography and repertoire (21 songs). Notebook 3: 367–369.
Biographical note: age 30; born in Peja [Koshutan] (Kosovo); could write a little; began to sing at age 12, having learned from his father and others, including from Rusvan Berica. He had traveled to many places, including Gjakova, Prizren, and Novi Pazar.

LAN 50. Gjekaj, Riza Luz [Zymeri-Lucëgjekaj, Rizë]. Kolgecaj (Tropoja). September 20, 1937. *Kanga e marteses se Halilit kur asht martue me çikën e Haxhi Beg Garbeni.* Legendary song. 796 lines. Notebook 3: 369–413.

LAN 51. Gjekaj, Riza Luz [Zymeri-Lucëgjekaj, Rizë]. Kolgecaj (Tropoja). September 20, 1937. *Kanga e Marteses se Halilit me çikën e Krajlit Xhevar.* Legendary song. 544 lines. Notebook 3: 413–423, 427–445.

LAN 52. Meta, Ali. Tropoja. September 22, 1937. Biography and repertoire (23 songs). Notebook 3: 454–457.

Biographical note: age 60; born in Isniq, Peja (Kosovo); illiterate; began to sing with *lahuta* and *çifteli* at age 20; learned to sing from his father, Zymer Selmani, who knew Serbian, and Fazli Aziri. Lived in Nikšić, Cetinje, Podgorica. Meta had met Qor Hysa in Nikšić and listened to Bosnian songs. Meta stated that he dictated two songs to Muji Boletini, a bilingual speaker from Mitrovica, who transcribed them and translated them, line by line, to Qor Hysa; Hysa learned them after two or three hearings. These were the songs of Ali Pasha Gusinje and of Sultan Murad (that is, the song of the Battle of Kosovo, which Meta learned from his father).

LAN 53. Meta, Ali. Tropoja, September 23, 1937. *Kanga e Sultan Muratit.* Historical song. 251 lines. Notebooks 3–4: 470–483.

LAN 54. Bajrami, Ibish. Tropoja. September 23, 1937. Biography and repertoire (9 songs). Notebook 4: 484.
Biographical note: age 50; born in Shipshan, Krasniq (Gash); illiterate; began to sing at age 12, having learned from his father and Haxhi Ismail, who lived to be 110. Bajrami had traveled to Bjelina, Podgorica, Novi Pazar, Gjakova, Prizren, Peja, Mitrovica, Skopje, and Senalik (where he sang for Turks). In Cetinje he heard songs in Albanian and Serbian. He played the *çifteli* only.

LAN 55. Bajrami, Ibish. Tropoja. September 23, 1937. *Kanga e Osman Agës.* Legendary song. 337 lines. Notebook 4: 485–502.

LAN 56. Meta, Ali. Tropoja, September 23, 1937. *Kanga e Ali Bajraktarit me Krajlicen e Inglizit.* Legendary song. 74 lines (unfinished). Notebook 4: 503–507.

LAN 57. Meta, Ali. Tropoja, September 23, 1937. *Kanga e Ali Bajraktarit me Krajlicen e Inglizit.* Legendary song. 289 lines. Notebook 4: 508–523.

LAN 58. Meta, Ali. Tropoja. September 24, 1937. *Kanga e Ali Bajraktarit qi ka marre nusen e Rustem Kapitanit.* Legendary song. 900 lines. Notebook 4: 523–572.

LAN 59. Meta, Ali. Tropoja. September 24, 1937. *Kanga e Isa Boletinit.* Historical song. 149 lines. Notebook 4: 572–580.

LAN 60. Brahimi, Adem. Tropoja. September 24, 1937 (begun). *Kanga e Sirotin Alis.* Legendary song. 2163 lines. Notebook 5: 642–756.

LAN 61. Hoxha, Lush. Paç, Bytyç [today Bashkia Kukës]. September 26, 1937. Biography and repertoire (9 songs). Notebook 4: 581.
Biographical note: age 65; born in Paç, Bytyç; illiterate; began to sing at age 15, having learned from his grandfather and others.

LAN 62. Jusufi, Mustafa. Kam, Bytyç [today Bashkia Kukës]. September 26, 1937.
Biography and repertoire (19 songs). Notebook 4: 582–583.
Biographical note: age 70; born in Kam; illiterate; began to sing at 17. Jusufi
had traveled to Skopje, Peja, Prizren, Gjavoka, Pristhina. He had heard songs
in Albanian and in Serbian.

LAN 63. Jusufi, Mustafa. Kam, Bytyç [today Bashkia Kukës]. September 26, 1937.
Kanga e Halilit qi e zuni çikën e Agan Kapitanit. Legendary song. 434 lines.
Notebook 4: 584–606.

LAN 64. Ramadan, Dalip. Bicaj, Diber [today Bashkia Kukës]. October 1, 1937.
Biography and repertoire (11 songs). Notebook 4: 607.
Biographical note: age 38; illiterate; began to sing at 15, having learned
from his father and others. Ramadan could also play the *çifteli.*

LAN 65. Ramadan, Dalip. Bicaj, Diber [today Bashkia Kukës]. October 1, 1937.
Kanga e Osman Pashes. Historical song. 20 lines. Notebook 4: 608–609.

LAN 66. Ramadan, Dalip. Bicaj, Diber [today Bashkia Kukës]. October 1, 1937.
Kanga e çikes se Ferhat Pashes. Legendary song. 57 lines. Notebook 4: 609–612.

LAN 67. Ramadan, Dalip. Bicaj, Diber [today Bashkia Kukës]. October 1, 1937.
Kanga e Isa Boletinit. Historical song. 8 lines. Notebook 4: 613.

LAN 68. Ramadan, Dalip. Bicaj, Diber [today Bashkia Kukës]. October 1, 1937.
Kanga e Selman Hasanit. Historical song. 45 lines. Notebook 4: 613–616.

LAN 69. Halili, Hysen. Va Spas, Dukagjin [today Bashkia Kukës]. October 3, 1937.
Biography and repertoire (11 songs). Notebook 4: 617.
Biographical note: age 35; born in Va Spas; illiterate; began to sing and play
the *çifteli* at 7, having learned from his brother (who had learned from their
father). Halili had been to Peja, Gjakova, and Prizren, where he learned
some songs. He had heard singers able to sing in Albanian and Serbian.

LAN 70. Halili, Hysen. Va Spas (Dukagjin) [today Bashkia Kukës]. October 3, 1937.
Kanga e Mujes dhe Halilit qi janë pre me Pavlan Kapitanin. Legendary song. 492
lines. Notebook 4: 618–641; notebook 5: 757–758.

LAN 71. Zeneli, Rexhep. Spaç (Orosh) [today Bashkia Mirdita]. October 4, 1937.
Biography and repertoire (11 songs). Notebook 5: 759–760.
Biographical note: age 55; born in Trestenik, Peja (Kosovo); illiterate; began to
sing at age 25, having learned from his father and others. Zeneli had traveled

in Kosovo and Montenegro. When he was 27 or 28 years old, he heard Qor Hysa sing in "Albanian and Serbian." He learned some songs from Qor Hysa.

LAN 72. Salihi, Ukë. Puka. October 5, 1937. Biography and repertoire (12 songs). Notebook 5: 761.

Biographical note: age 27; born in Tropoja; illiterate; began to sing and play the *çifteli* at 10, having learned from his father and others. Salihi had been to Gjakova and Peja.

LAN 73. Salihi, Ukë. Puka. October 5, 1937. *Kanga e Zuk Bajraktarit qi bani luft me Ali Bajraktarin.* Legendary song. 232 lines. Notebook 5: 762–774.

LAN 74. Salihi, Ukë. Puka. October 5, 1937. *Kanga e Tale Budalinit.* Legendary song. 171 lines. Notebook 5: 775–784.

LAN 75. Salihi, Ukë. Puka. October 5–6, 1937. *Lista e kangave te reja* ("List of new songs," 31 songs). Notebook 5: 785, 788.

LAN 76. Pjetri, Gjok. Puka. October 5, 1937. Biography and repertoire (1 song). Notebook 5: 786.

Biographical note: age 40; born in Parave (Puka); Catholic; illiterate; learned to sing as a child from friends.

LAN 77. Pjetri, Gjok. Puka. October 5, 1937. *Kanga e Fetah Hyses e Shales.* Historical song. 34 lines. Notebook 5: 786–788.

LAN 78. Salihi, Ukë. Puka. October 6, 1937. *Kanga e Azem Bejtes.* Historical song. 189 lines. Notebook 5: 789–799.

LAN 79. Zeneli, Rexhep. Puka. October 6, 1937. *Kanga e Halilit qi ka nxane Jovan Kapidanin.* Legendary song. 425 lines. Notebooks 5–6: 800–827. Zeneli learned the song from Qor Hysa (822).

LAN 80. Ismajli [Smajli], Ukshin. Puka. October 6, 1937. Biography and repertoire (13 songs). Notebook 6: 823–824.

Biographical note: age 80; born in Vishoq (Bytyç) [today Bashkia Kukës]; illiterate; began to sing at age 15, having learned from various singers in inns and villages. Smajli had traveled throughout Kosovo and learned songs there.

LAN 81. Ismajli [Smajli], Ukshin. Puka. October 6, 1937. *Kanga e Ali Bajraktarit qi me Begije Devojka lufton me Kulshedrat.* Legendary song. 617 lines. Notebook 6: 825–857.

LAN 82. Hasani, Myftar. Puka. October 7, 1937. Biography and repertoire (11 songs). Notebook 6: 858–859.
Biographical note: age 35; born in Geghysen [today Bashkia Shkodër], residing in Plav. Hasani could write a little. He began to sing at 16, having learned from his father, Hasan Hoxha, and others. He had traveled to the cities of Kosovo and could sing to the *çifteli*.

LAN 83. Hasani, Myftar. Puka. October 7, 1937. *Kanga e Lito Bajraktarit qi u kërkue në mejdan prej Markelute Sllavit.* Legendary song. 168 lines (unfinished). Notebook 6: 860–868.

LAN 84. Gega, Prendush. Puka. October 7, 1937. Biography and repertoire (4 songs). Notebook 6: 869.
Biographical note: age 85; born in Kabash (Puka); illiterate; began to sing at age 25, having learned from various singers, and at age 60 began to compose his own songs; Gega called himself a "poet." He had been in Kosovo where learned *kange kreshnike.* He played the *çifteli* a little. He provided songs to other collectors as well.

LAN 85. Miri, Mark. Gu[r]rëz (Kurbin) [today Bashkia Laç]. October 10, 1937. Biography and repertoire (21 songs). Notebook 6: 870–871.
Biographical note: age 48; captain in the Albanian army; born in Nikç (Kelmend) [today Bashkia Shkodër], residing in Gurrëz; could write a little; began to sing at age 12, having learned from his father and others. Mark Miri had been once to Cetinje.

LAN 86. Miri, Mark. Gu[r]rëz (Kurbin) [today Bashkia Laç]. October 10, 1937. *Kanga e Nande Jovanave.* Legendary song. 635 lines. Notebook 6: 872–905.

LAN 87. Miri, Kolë Mark. Gur[r]ëz (Kurbin) [today Bashkia Laç]. October 11, 1937. Biography and repertoire (4 songs). Notebook 6: 906.
Biographical note: age 25; son of Mark Miri; born in Mirditë; had attended primary school and could write; began to sing at age 12, having learned from his father and others. Kolë Mark Miri also played the *çifteli*.

LAN 88. Miri, Gjekë. Gur[r]ëz (Kurbin) [today Bashkia Laç]. October 11, 1937. Biography and repertoire (10 songs). Notebook 6: 907.
Biographical note: age 24; nephew of Mark Miri; born in Gur[r]ëz (Kurbin); had attended primary school; began to sing at age 12, having learned from his uncle and others, including Gjergj Pllumbi and Arif Dines.

LAN 89. Miri, Gjekë. Gur[r]ëz (Kurbin) [today Bashkia Laç]. October 11, 1937. *Kanga e Kapiten Mark Sulo Markes.* Legendary song. 95 lines. Notebook 6: 908–913.

LAN 90. Miri, Gjekë. Gur[r]ëz (Kurbin) [today Bashkia Laç]. October 11, 1937. *Kanga Kanga e Ali Pashë Gusinjes.* Historical song. 98 lines. Notebook 6: 913–918.

LAN 91. Keçi. Ded. Gur[r]ëz (Kurbin) [today Bashkia Laç]. October 11, 1937. Biography and repertoire (4 songs). Notebook 6: 919.
Biographical note: age 33; born in Gur[r]ëz (Kurbin) [today Bashkia Laç]; illiterate; began to sing at age 10, having learned from his father and others. Keçi had traveled to Plav and Podgorica.

LAN 92. Keçi. Ded. Gur[r]ëz (Kurbin) [today Bashkia Laç]. October 11, 1937. *Kanga e Mujes qi kerkoi Januken per Halilin.* Legendary song. 1754 lines. Notebooks 6–7: 920–992, 995–1014.
[NB: the materials from Gurrëz, especially those included in Notebooks 7 and 8, were evidently taken down by multiple people working more or less simultaneously. The songs are not in order, many pages are blank, and the writing is in different hands.]

LAN 93. Haxhija, Brahim. Gur[r]ëz (Kurbin) [today Bashkia Laç]. October 12, 1937. Biography and repertoire (5 songs). Notebook 8: 1119.
Biographical note: age 19; born in Martinaj (Montenegro); illiterate; began to sing at age 10, having learned from his father and others. Haxhija had traveled with his father in Montenegro and Kosovo.

LAN 94. Haxhija, Brahim. Gur[r]ëz (Kurbin) [today Bashkia Laç]. October 12 and 13, 1937. *Kanga e Mujes dhe Sojane Ivanit.* Legendary song. 376 lines. Notebook 8: 1120–1131, 1154–1162.

LAN 95. Oruqi, Man. Gur[r]ëz (Kurbin) [today Bashkia Laç]. October 12, 1937. Biography and repertoire (9 songs). Notebook 7: 993.
Biographical note: age 60; born in Vuthaj (Gucinje, Montenegro), residing in Gurrëz (Kurbin); illiterate; began to sing at age 15, having learned from his father and others. Oruqi had traveled in Yugoslavia, including in Kosovo.

LAN 96. Alushi, Musa [Lushti, Musë]. Gur[r]ëz (Kurbin) [today Bashkia Laç]. October 12, 1937.
Biography and repertoire (10 songs). Notebook 7: 994.

Biographical note: age 30; born in Vuthaj (Gucinje, Montenegro), residing in Gurëz; illiterate; began to sing at age 15, having learned from his father. Lushti had traveled to a few places in Kosovo.

LAN 97. Alushi, Musa [Lushti, Musë]. Gur[r]ëz (Kurbin) [today Bashkia Laç]. October 13, 1937. *Kanga e Mujës qi a pre me Behul Kapitanin*. Legendary song. 309 lines. Notebook 7: 1015–1031.

LAN 98. Leka, Pjeter. Gur[r]ëz (Kurbin) [today Bashkia Laç]. October 13, 1937. Biography and repertoire (6 songs). Notebook 8: 1133.
Biographical note: age 27; born in Boga; illiterate; began to sing at age 13, having learned from his father, brother, and others. Leka played the *lahuta* and the *çifteli*. He had traveled with his father to Peja, Plav, and other places.

LAN 99. Leka, Pjeter. Gur[r]ëz (Kurbin) [today Bashkia Laç]. October 13, 1937. *Kanga e Mujës me Millosh Kapitanin*. Legendary song. 374 lines. Notebook 8: 1134–1153.

LAN 100. Alushi, Musa [Lushti, Musë]. Gur[r]ëz (Kurbin) [today Bashkia Laç]. October 13, 1937. *Kanga e Smilaliq Alisë qi ka grabit nusen e Mujës*. Legendary song. 282 lines. Notebook 7: 1032.

LAN 101. Kadria, Shaban. S.d. [*Halili e Galan Kapetani.*] Legendary song. 109 lines. Notebook 9: 1–6.
Biographical note: age 21, from Kolmekshaj (Malsi e Gjakovës); son of Kadri Ali Ukës.

LAN 102. Kadria, Shaban. S.d. [*Muja e gjen baben e vet.*] Legendary song. 195 lines. Notebook 9: 7–17.

LAN 103. Kadria, Shaban. S.d. [*Halili merr miqasisht Dylbere Gjelinën.*] Legendary song. 322 lines. Notebook 9: 17–34.

LAN 104. Fetishi, Mark. S.d. [*Muja e Rada shtatë ditë ndajnë mejdanin.*] Legendary song. 103 lines. Notebook 9: 35–40.
Biographical note: age 20, from Merturi (Malësia e Gjiakoves); illiterate.

LAN 105. Kadria, Shaban. S.d. [*Muja e ban hyzmeqare gruen e vet.*] Legendary song. 231 lines. Notebook 10: 1–13.

LAN 106. Kadria, Shaban. S.d. [*Ymer Aga i liron Mujen e Halilin.*] Legendary song. 166 lines. Notebook 10: 13–22.

LAN 107. Ahmeti, Rexhep. December 31, 1934. *1. Ali Bajraktari.* Legendary song. 524 lines. Notebook 11: 1–28.
Biographical note: age 42; born and residing in Shipshan (Malsi e Gjakovës).

LAN 108. Ahmeti, Rexhep. S.d. *2. Talime Devojka.* Legendary song. 475 lines. Notebook 11: 29–54.

LAN 109. Ahmeti, Rexhep. December 31, 1934, and January 1, 1935. *3. Grabitja e Kune Devojkës.* Legendary song. 541 lines. Notebook 11: 55–83.

LAN 110. Alija, Alush. December 27, 1937. *4. Imer Aga i Ri.* Legendary song. 305 lines. Notebook 11: 84–100.
Biographical note: age 45; born and residing in Kolgecaj (Malësi e Gjakovës).

LAN 111. Alija, Alush. S.d. *Ag'-e Hasan Aga.* Legendary song. 274 lines. Notebook 11: 101–115.

LAN 112. Alija, Alush. S.d. *Aga Imeri.* Legendary song. 81 lines. Notebook 11: 116–120.

LAN 113. Jusufi, Elez. S.d. *Rrustem Aga.* Historical song. 45 lines. Notebook 11: 121–123.

LAN 114. Sadria, Rrustem. S.d. *E bukura e i keqi.* Lyric song. 142 lines. Notebook 11: 124–131.
Biographical note: age 50; from Kolgecaj (Malësi e Gjakovës).

PART THREE

ANTHOLOGY

SECTION 1

FROM THE RECORDINGS OF
THE MILMAN PARRY COLLECTION
OF ORAL LITERATURE, 1934–1935

PN 659. Salih Ugljanin, *Marko Kraljević i Musa Keserdžija*

Salih Ugljanin [Sali Uglla]; Novi Pazar (Serbia); November 20, 1934
Marko Kraljević i Musa Keserdžija [*Mark e Musa*]
Marko and Musa
Discs 1056-1058
Legendary song. The first 6 lines are sung, the rest recited. See pp. 80–81.

[1056]

    E lum për ty-o moro j-lumi
       Zojote
    konka çua Kraleviçu Marka
    edhe Marku n'kôm-o çi o çua
    me Sharanin n'shpid-o m'i kish
       ra-me
5   e n'shpid Sharanit Marku çi i ka
       shkua
    e n'Stamboll-o Marku kish pa
       shkua
    Kur po shkon Marku n'Stamboll

    bash tu mbreti konka dalë

    bash tu mbreti konka dalë

10 tri tabor e kanë rrethua
    tri tabor e kanë rrethua
    edhe Markun e kanë ngujua
    qyre Markun n'Sharanin
    gjith rreth e rreth p'e rrethojnë
15 p'e rrethon asqeri mbret

    me martinë e me fishekë

[1056]

Praise be to God!

Marko Kraljević arose.
And Marko rose to his feet,
he mounted onto the back
    of Sharan
5 and Marko set out mounted on
    Sharan
and Marko went toward
    Stambol.
When Marko was on his way
    to Stambol
he headed straight for the
    Emperor;
he headed straight for the
    Emperor,
10 three battalions surrounded him.
Three battalions surrounded him
and they besieged Marko.
Behold Marko on Sharan
being entirely surrounded.
15 The soldiers of the Emperor are
    surrounding him
with single-shot rifles and
    cartridges,

me martinë e me fishekë

qyre Markun fort po qet
qyre Markun fort po qet
20 n'Sharanin po pisket
n'Sharanin po pisket
nuk lidhuan sal vet
nuk jam xha mo lidhun vet
po i kauzua bab's mbret
25 po i kauzua bab's mbret
Marku s'don me ra n'tô
nuk do Markun Mark Milani
se un jam i Kraleviç Marko
qat'er folin dy shqiptarë
30 kadal dar he Mark o djalë
kadal dal ti Mark o djalë
se ne mbreti na ka thirrë

mbreti ynë na ka pa çua
edhe Markun m'e rrethua
35 edhe Markun m'e rrethua
ai i gjallë për m'e shtrëngua
m'Sharanin për me e çua
mbretit t'im më ja kauzua
qat'here Markun e kan çua
40 mbreti Markun e ka mësua

with single-shot rifles and
cartridges.
Behold Marko shooting strongly,
behold Marko shooting strongly
20 shouting on Sharan,
shouting on Sharan.
"I won't be tied up all by myself,
I won't allow myself to be bound."
He told the father Emperor,
25 he told the father Emperor.
Marko will not to be taken
Marko, Mark Milani, will not:
"Because I am Marko Kraljević."
Then two Albanians spoke up:
30 "Be quite you young Marko,
be quite you young Marko
because the Emperor has called
us.
Our Emperor has sent us
and to surround Marko
35 and to surround Marko,
to take him alive
to send him on Sharan
to speak with our Emperor."
Then they sent Marko off.
40 The Emperor taught Marko
a lesson:

[1057]

n'zidan e ka ngujuar
tri vjet Marku qi ka ndajë

bash tri vjet o ne zidan

fort piske tha Marku fort

45 Marku shum-e po pisket

[1057]

he threw him into the prison.
Marko remained there three
years,
precisely three years was he in
prison.
Marko—he said—is shouting
very loudly;
45 Marko is shouting a great deal

	mbretit tin-o po i thrret		calling out to the our Emperor:
	amon mbret pash jeten tonde		"Aman Emperor—may you live long—
	qitem ktyj pej hapsâne		get me out of this prison;
	qitem ktyj tha pej hapsâne		get me out—he said—of this prison.
50	se un me Marku tha nuk po del	50	Marko—he said—does not want to suffer more."
	kadal Marko he djal-i ri		"Be quiet you Young Marko,
	mos u tut as mos u gut		don't be afraid and don't become anxious;
	mos u tut as mos u gut		don't be afraid and don't become anxious
	s'e ka vakt me ndej aty		there's plenty of time for you to remain there,
55	ka vakt shumë me ndejë me ndejë	55	much time to stay and stay.
	nal kadal he Marku i ri		Be quite you young Marko,
	nal kadal he Marku i ri		be quite you young Marko."
	teligraf po i bjen mbretit		A telegram the Emperor is sent.
	po i bje mbretit teligrafi		The Emperor receives a telegram,
60	prej Kosove qi po i thonë	60	from Kosovo speaking to him.
	prej Kosove ja kanë çua		From Kosovo they send word:
	Musa neve na shtrëngua		"Musa is harassing us!
	shum ne Musa na ka shtrëngua		Musa has been harassing us greatly,
	çona dikâ me na ngujua		send us someone to lay a siege for us.
65	lype mirë o Musën tone	65	We beg you for Musa,
	Qesexhinë për m'e na nxanë		to capture Musa Qesexhi,
	Qesexhinë për m'e na nxanë		to capture Musa Qesexhi.
	tana rrugët i ka shkurtua		He has cut off our roads,
	tana rrugët i ka shkurtua		he has cut off our roads,
70	tanë tuxharet qi po na i bashkon	70	he is uniting the merchants
	tanë tuxharet i ka padishë		he has filed suit against all our merchants
	tanve hakun po ja u merr		taking revenge upon them

127

	e haraçin po ja u mbledh		and collecting our land-tax,
	me dukat qi po i rrethon		surrounding himself with ducats;
75	por dukatet po ja u merr	75	he is taking ducats from them
	armët e grita po ja u ep		and giving them arms for an uprising
	armët e grita po ja u ep		and giving them arms for an uprising."
	qat'herë Marku k'i pisket		Then was Marko shouting,
	qat'herë Marku k'i pa folë		then was Marko saying:
80	unë mbret ma kon ta zâ	80	"Emperor, I will seize him!
	ta zâ Musën n'allati		I will seize Musa in this trouble,
	sall t'm'lshosh pej hapsane		just release me from prison.
	sall t'del nesra pej hapsane		Just let me go tomorrow from prison,
	am mâ mir-o për me hanger		give me good food to eat
85	mbamnu mirë tha tre muej ditë	85	treat me well—he said—for three whole months
	qat'herë Musën kam me ta ngjite		and then I will take Musa,
	qat'herë mbretin te ndihmoni		then I will help the Emperor!"
	mban'je Markun bash si nânë		He kept Marko just like a mother,
	mban'je Markun bash si nânë		he kept Marko just like a mother
90	qe ai Musën për m'na e zanë	90	so that he will seize Musa:
	po don Musën me na e zanë		"Yes, he will seize Musa for us,
	n'Kaçanik po don m'e hanë		in Kaçanik he will enter,
	n'Kaçanik n'mejdan me dale		in Kaçanik he comes to the battle field
	Qesexhinë për m'e bashkua		to encounter Qesexhi,
95	Qesexhinë për m'e na e nxanë	95	to seize Qesexhi for us
	hajde Musën me na e pre		hey—to cut down Musa,
	kryet e Musës me na e pru		to bring us back the head of Musa
	Markun djalë për m'e qorru		and then blind the boy Marko."
	qat'erë Musa po na folë		Then Musa said:
100	po ti Marko je budall	100	"You Mark are a fool,
	qishme Musën me liftua		how can you fight with Musa?
	pobratima kem qillua		We have met as blood brothers
	pobratima kem qillua		we have met as blood brothers
	âsht jazek për me liftua		it is a shame for us to fight!"
105	qat'erë foli Marku i ri	105	Then Young Marko said:

mbau ti Musë qare z'del

mbau Musa se mbarre s'âsht
mos thuaj te vona qi t'mashtroi

s'ka mashtrime Qeshexi
110 po mbau mire me jatagan
qat'herë bâne dal jurish

qiti Musa me topuz
qiti Musa me topuz
për nder Markun topuzin ja shtje
115 nën Sharanin ja ka çua
jurish bâne u barua
kanë bâ jurish e janë kapë

fyt për fyt-e qi jan rrokë
për ledinë burrat jan qitë
120 qat'herë Musa ki pa qitë
e rrxoi Musa Mark Milani
e n'ledinë i ki pa hipë
bash në qjyks e ki pa shkelë
që shka bâni Marku keq
125 don me shti n'qizme t'Musës

n'hanxhar e paska ngulë
i ra Musës tha t'hollë të djathtë

deri n'fyt ja ki pa çua

[1058]

e çpërtheu tha Qesexhinë

130 dekun Musa n'ledinë
qat'herë Marku keq e çpërtheu
kur ni seri qi e ka par
tre gjerponj Marku ja gjet
gjithë rreth zêbrave jan pilqetë

"Hold on Musa to see what will
happen!
Hold on Musa this isn't right,
don't say that I have come to
cheat you;
there will be no cheating Qesexhi
110 but hold in to your sword well!"
Then they came and rushed at
one another:
Musa took this spiked mace,
Musa took this spiked mace
and hurled the mace at Marko
115 sending it over Sharan.
They finished their attack;
in the attack they had seized
one another
battling hand to hand.
The heroes come onto the field,
120 then Musa overcame him
and Musa toppled Mark Milani
jumping onto him on ground
stepping right onto his chest.
What did poor Marko do?
125 he put his hand into Musa's
boots,
he took out a dagger,
he hit Musa—he said—in his
right side
penetrating right up to his
throat

[1058]

and he ran—he said—through
Qesexhi.
130 Musa fell to the ground dead!
Then Marko felt very bad;
when he saw a chance
Marko found three snakes
entwined all around his hearts,

135 te tri zêbra Marku i ka
Musa n'bark i kish pa pasë
te tre gjarpna rreth zêbrave

njâni sallte çi â çua
dy tha flejnë haber nuk kanë

140 qat'herë Marku shi ç'po bân

po pisket tha Marku i ri

hej medet n'Qesexhi
qi e preva këtë farë burri
shumë mâ t'mirë se veten sot
145 shumë mâ t'mirë se Markun vet

qat'herë hipi në Sharan
n'shpinë Sharanit i ka ra
e në shpellë qi ka ngujua
n'shpellë të Sharës kur ha hi

150 kurrë mâ Marku mos me dale
kurrë s'â dale mâ shumë
n'jashtë
qat'herë Marku ki pa çkapë

shumë bre n'hallkun po e ka
lypë
kurkun Markun s'po na e gjâjnë
155 Marku mbet n'shpellë të madhe
qat'herë mâ shumë nuk â dale

135 for three hearts Marko he has
Musa had them in his stomach
the three snakes around the
hearts
only one awoke
two—he said—were sleeping
and had no idea.
140 Then Marko—you see—what he
did?
Young Marko—he said—was
wailing:
"Woe be to Qesexhi
that I have cut down such a man
who was much better than myself
145 who was much better than
Marko himself."
Then Marko mounted Sharan,
he landed on Sharan's back
and retired into a cave.
And when he entered the cave
of Shara
150 never again did Marko emerge.
Never again did he venture
outside
from then on Marko fought no
more.
People sought him much

they could never find Marko.
155 Marko remained in this great
cave
from that time coming out no
more.

PN 672. Salih Ugljanin, *Hrnjičić Mujo i Gavran Kapetan*

Salih Ugljanin [Sali Uglla]; Novi Pazar (Serbia); November 24, 1934
Hrnjičić Mujo i Gavran Kapetan [Muji e Gavran Kapetani]
Muji and Gavran Kapetan
Discs 1205–1210
Legendary song. Sung with *gusle*.

[1205]

    Oj lum për ty o Zot mor-oj lumi
        Zot
    e qi ç'ka bâni-o çure ne po fal
    e n'kulla t'Muj's o thiu e kish pa
        ran
    e kur â ardh-o tu dera-u e kulles

5   e qyre Muj's-o i ka cokatë në der

    e koka dal-o e shoqeja e Mujes
    e kush je ti-oj qi cokatë n'der

    e o at'herë foli Gavran Kapetani
    e unë jam-oj pobratim-o i Mujes
10   e m'ka marr malli n'Mujn o për
       me u tesh
    e qyre grueja derën s'ja ka çel

    e e ka thirr-o Ajkunen të
       Bardh[ë]
    e kur â ardh-o Ajkuneja e Bardh
    e kush je ti-oj qi cokat në der

15   e qat'herë foli Gavran Kapetani
    e çilma deren Ajkuneja e Bardh

[1205]

Glory to the Lord the blessed
    Lord,
it is He Whom we praise.
At the tower of Muji the tough
    guy arrived;
when he was at the door of the
    tower

5   behold, he knocked at the door
    of Muji.
Then came out the wife of Muji:
"Who are you who knocks on
    the door?"
Then spoke Gavran Kapetan:
"I am the sworn brother of Muji
10 I have a longing to visit Muji."

Behold, the woman did not open
    the door!
She called Ajkuna the Fair.

When Ajkuna the Fair arrived:
"Who are you who knocks on
    the door?"
15 Then spoke Gavran Kapetan:
"Open up the door Ajkuna the
    Fair

e se un jam-oj probatim-o i
Mujes
e m'ka marrë malli n'Muj'n-o
për më u piek
e qat'herë foli Ajkuneja e Bardh
20 e nuk â ktu-o Muj-oj as Halili
e n'teferiq-o n'do bjeshk-o të
nelta
qat'herë foli Gavran Kapetoni
e çilma deren Ajkuneja e Bardh

e un e duo Mujen për m'e prite
25 e dej t'um vjen-o n'kull-o ne
oxha-i
e qat'herë çik-o derën ja ka
çilun
e kur â hi-o Gavran Kapetoni
e me Galanin kâlin të mejdanit
e sa mbas grushtit çikës ja ka
ngjitun
30 e ka çua n'vithe të Galanit
e tri her-o çiken qi e ka
ngjeshun
t'katërtën-o rrypin ja ka
ngjytun
ka marrë fushen për me votë
prapun
e krism po bân-o e shoqeja e
Mujës

because I am the sworn brother
of Muji,
I have a desire to meet Muji."

Then spoke Ajkuna the Fair:
20 "Neither Muji nor Halil is here
they went to a feast in the high
mountains."
Then spoke Gavran Kapetan:
"Open up the door Ajkuna the
Fair;
I want to wait for Muji,
25 he will come to the fireplace of
the tower."
Then the girl opened the door.

When Gavran Kapetan came in
with Galan the battle horse,
he struck the girl with his fist
30 and tied her to Galan's back.
Three times he wrapped it
around the girl,
four times he wrapped the rope

and ran away back across the
plain.
The wife of Muji is screaming,

[1206]

35 e koka hip-o në beden të kullës

e ka çpraz-o pushkën habertare
e dha haber-o Çeto Bashe Mujës

e Muja nelt-o bjeshk-o ka çillua
e me te vëllau Halilin të Ri

[1206]

35 she climbed at the top of the
tower
and fired with the signal rifle:
gave the alarm signal to Çeto
Basho Muji.
Muji was gone in the mountains
with his brother the Young
Halil.

40 e qat'herë Muja Halilit po i
    thot-o
  e ti bre djal-o Halili-o i Ri
  e krisi breshka n'kull-o në
    beden
  e neve kaurri n'kulla na ka ram

  e na e nxu rop-o Ajkunen të
    Bardh
45 hait me ret-o bjeshkëve ke me
    votun
  e në hudut-o rrugën të m'ja
    nxashë
  e se tu kulla djal-o dua me shkua

  e me pa-o kullën me avlitë

  e çka-o bâ-o n'kull-oj â mbarue
50 e kush Hajkunën rop-o na e ka
    nxanun
  e qat'her Muja n'shpit gjogut
    m'i ra
  eu teposht-o bjeshkëve tym-o
    dredhun
  e qyr Halili bjeshkëve për me
    rendun
  o të shohësh-o Gavran
    Kapetanin
55 e se n'hudut Gavrani qi â dalë

  ani kalit burri qi i ka zhdripun
  e o n'dal-o ven-o qi po pin
  gjth po i qet-o Hajkuneja e
    Bardh
  â mbet pak-o bjeshket po
    gjemojnë
60 e tash â dal-o Ali Bajraktari
  ndal po i thot-o Gavran
    Kapetani

40 Then Muji said to Halil:

  "O you children Young Halil
  the signal shot from the top of
    the tower,
  the infidel has attacked our
    tower
  he has stolen our Fair Ajukuna!

45 You will go across the
    mountains
  to the border to find the way for
    me
  because o youth I will go to the
    tower
  to see the tower with its
    courtyards
  what they did in the tower
50 who has stolen our Ajkuna."

  Then Muji quickly got on his
    grey-white horse
  and turned him down the
    mountains.
  Behold, Halil go quickly through
    the mountains
  to see Gavran Kapetan,

55 for Gavran had gone to the
    border:
  the man has gotten off his horse
  and was drinking wine,
  the Fair Ajkuna was serving
    him.
  Shortly afterwards the moun-
    tains trembled
60 and Ali Bajraktar appeared:
  "Stop—he says—Gavran
    Kapetan

o t'kujën motër rop-o qi e ke
nxânë
a për kendi-o Ali Bajraktarin
e dal n'mejdan me mu-o për m'e
damun
65 e jyrish ban-o shpatat i kan
nxierrë
ka nji her-o shpatat qi janë ram

e fyt për fyt me Alin qi janë
rrokë
m'për ledin-o trimat qi jam
shtrim
e ma rrxoj shkau-o Ali
Bajraktarin
70 ja kish lidh-o duert për mbas
shpinë
an-o mbet-o ven-o qi po pinë
e qi po i qet-o Hajkuneja e
Bardh
kur mbet pak-o bjeshket po
gjumojnë
e kur ish dal-o Arrnaut Osmani
75 e në krah-o breshkën qi e kish
qityun
e jurish bâni piskam qi po
bânun
ndal po i thot-o kaurri i
palamun

who has stolen our sister!

have you heard of Ali Bajraktar?
come to the battlefield with me
for a duel!"
65 They attacked, they have pulled
out their swords
immediately the swords
clashed.
Hand by hand he fought with
Ali
to the ground the heroes have
fallen.
The Slav captured Ali Bajraktar,

70 tied his hands behind his back

and sat to drink wine,
the Fair Ajkuna served him.

Shortly afterward the moun-
tains trembled
and Arrnaut Osman appeared
75 carrying the rifle on his
shoulder.
They rushed at each other
yelling.
"Stop—he says—you unclean
infidel

[1207]

e t'kujën motër rrop-o qi e ke
nxanun
k'at'herë foli Ali Bajraktari
80 e mo Osman-o kaurri azgin
âshtun
e shumë azgin-o kaurri ka qillua

[1207]

who has taken our sister
captive!"
Then said Ali Bajraktar:
80 "O Osman, the infidel is fierce!

very fiercely has the infidel
struck

mbre shumë azgin-o kaurri ka
    qillua
e jyrish bâni-o Arrnaut Osmani
gjyth me breshkës zjarmin ja
    kish dhanun
85   e kurkun shej-o kaurrit-o po i
    banun
e jyrish ban-o fytas qi janë
    rrokun

e fyt për fyt me kaurrin qi janë
    rrokun
e n'ven n'ledin-o trimat qi janë
    shtimun
e ma rrxoj kaurri Arrnaut
    Osmanin
90   e pas shpin-e duert ja kish
    lidhun
e prapë o ndej-o ven-o qi po
    pinun
e po pin-o ven-e dhe raki-je
e i po jep-o Ajkuneja e Bardh
e mbet-o pak-o bjeshkt-o po
    gjomojnë
95   e tash po vjen-o Imeri-o i Ri
djali Mujs-o Omeri-o i Ri
e dymdhet' vjeç-o djali ky qillue
e dy pishtol-oj djali qi i ki
    ngrehun
e po pisket-o Imeri-o i Muj's
100 e ndal kadal o kaurr-o i palam
e t'kujën motër rrop-o qi e ke
    nxanë
e vegeli o Imerin të Mujës

e kurku vendin kaurr-o nuk ta
    lân
e jyrish bâni zjarmin ja u kish
    dhezë

very fiercely has the infidel
    struck."
Then Arrnaut Osman attacked,
he fired his rifle
85   he missed the infidel.

They rushed at each other and
    grabbed each other by the
    throat
hand to hand he fought with
    the infidel
to the ground the heroes fell.

The infidel captured Arrnaut
    Osman,
90   tied his hands behind his back

and once again he sits and is
    drinking wine.
He is drinking wine and raki
and Fair Ajkuna serves him.
Shortly afterwards the moun-
    tains are trembling:
95   now Young Imer is coming
the son of Muji, Young Imer.
The boy is twelve years old,
the boy was carrying two
    pistols.
Imer Muji's son is shouting:
100 "Stop you unclean infidel
who has stolen our sister.

Have you heard of Imer son of
    Muji?
I will never let you go, O
    infidel!"
And he attacked and fired.

105 e dy pishtole burri qi i kish
    çprazun
  e kurku shej-o kaurrit nuk po i
    bâjnë
  në po n'qil-o kaurri-o ka qillu
  e sa me-j dor-o duert ja kish
    lidhën
  e prap-o ndej-o ven-o qi po pin

110 e-u po pin-o ven-o edhe raki
  e ku mbet pak-o bjeshkt-o po
    gjomojnë
  e tash po vjen-o Budaline Tali
  e ka çua topuzin në krah

  e ndal po i thot-o kaurr-o i
    palamë
115 e t'kujën motër rrop-o qi e ke
    nxânë
  vë ke tij-o Tale Budalinën

  e besa Tales kaurri nuk po i
    tutet
  e topuzit vendit qi po lëkundet

  e ja mrriu shpejt-o Tale
    Budaline
120 me topuz-o kaurri qi i kish ramu

  shejë të mir-o n'krah-o ja kish
    dhanun
  o mbet pak-o kaurri n'kam â çue

[1208]

  e Sharanin kalin p'e
    shtërngonun
  e mbas veti Ajkunen të Bardh

---

105 The hero emptied his two
    pistols
  he couldn't hit the infidel at all.

  The infidel seized him,
  using one hand he tied the boy's
    hands
  and once again he sat and was
    drinking wine
110 he was drinking wine and raki.
  Shortly afterwards the moun-
    tains trembled:
  now Budaline Tali is coming,
  he has his spiked mace on his
    shoulder.
  "Stop—he said—you unclean
    infidel
115 who has stolen our sister,

  Here is Tale Budaline before
    you! "
  The *besa* of Tale did not worry
    the infidel
  and he swings the mace at the
    place.
  He quickly reached Tale
    Budaline
120 the infidel hit him with the
    mace
  he wounded him well on the
    shoulder.
  The infidel stayed for a bit on
    his feet,

[1208]

  he spurred the horse Sharan

  and with him the Fair Ajkuna

125 e muer rrugën kaurri-o për me shku	125 and the infidel took to the road
e gjith me rrend-o kaurri qi â ndalë	and the infidel set out at a run.
e mbet-o pak-o bjeshka po gjomon	Shortly after the mountains are trembling:
e tash-o dal-o Halili-o i Muj's	now Halil of Muji goes out.
po pisket-o Halili-o i Mujt	Halil of Muji is shouting:
130 e ndal po i thot-o kaurr-o i palamë	130 "Stop—he says—you unclean infidel
e t'kujën motër rrop-o jo qi e ke nxânë	who has stolen our sister,
vë ke tij-o Halilin të Muj's	here is Halil of Muji before you
e si kurkun-o vendin nuk ta lâ	I will not give way to anyone!"
e jyrish bânte kalit qi i ka shtripun	And he rushed to the attack and jumped off his horse.
135 e fyt për fyt me Halilin janë rrokë	135 Hand by hand he fought with Halil
n'për ledin-o trimat qi jan shty	to the ground the heroes fell.
e ma rrxo kaurri Halilin të Muj's	The infidel captured Halil of Muji
e për mbas shpind-o duert ja kish lidhë	and tied his hands at his back,
e prap-â ndej-o kalit n'shpindë po i bjenë	and again mounted his horse.
140 e n'shpind Sharanit kaurri qi-i ki ra	140 The infidel jumped on Sharan's back
e përmbas veti Ajkunën të Bardh	and with the Fair Ajkuna after him
e muarr rrugën kaurri-o për me shku	and the infidel took to the road.
e mbet-o pak-o bjeshket po gjomojnë	Shortly after the mountains are trembling,
e gjâmë e madhe tokës qi po i bjenë	a great noise shakes the earth
145 e mjegull bjeshka tim-o qi â mbushë	145 and the mountain is covered with fog.
e qat'herë foli Gavran Kapetani	Then said Gavran Kapetan:
e pa po ndij-e Ajkunëja e Bardh	"Listen Fair Ajkuna

e ç'â kjo gjam-o tokës qi po i
    bjenë
thot a jan-oj bylyqe medinë

150 e thot a janë tallazet në deti

e thot a janë topat në Klladushë

e qat'herë foli Aikunëja e Bardh
nal kadal-o Gavran Kapetani
a s'po jan-o bylyqet medinë
155 a s'po jan-oj tallazet në deti
a s'nuk jan-oj topat në
    Klladushë
e tash po vjen-o Çeto Bashë Muja
ndal të shohsh-o Çeto Bashë Muj
e fjalt vonojn-o Muja nuk
    vononë
160 e kur ka dal-o n'gjog-o të
    mejdanit
e ndal po i thot o kaurr-o i
    palamë
e t'kujën motër rrop-o qi e ke
    nxanun
e vë ke li-o Çeto Bashe Mujen

qi n'krali-o vendin nuk ta lânë

165 e jyrish bâni Çeto Bashe Muja

e bân jurish-o kualve m'u kanë
    shtripun

[1209]

e fyt për fyt me Mujën qi janë
    rrokun
kur-e Muja duert ja ka ngjeshun
e për mbas shpind-o duert ja ka
    shtimun

---

what is the great noise that
    shakes the earth?
he said—are they soldiers of the
    town?
150 he said—are they the waves of
    the sea?
he said—are they the cannons
    of Klladusha?"
Then spoke the Fair Ajkuna:
"Stop you o Gavran Kapetan!
they are not soldiers of the town,
155 they are not the waves of the sea,
they are not the cannons of
    Klladusha:
now Çeto Basho Muji is coming,
stop to see Çeto Basho Muji."
The words delay, Muji does not
    delay
160 when he comes out on his battle
    horse.
He said: "Stop you unclean
    infidel
who has taken our sister
    captive!
Here is Çeto Basho Muji before
    you,
not to leave you a place in the
    kingdom."
165 And Çeto Basho Muji rushed to
    the attack.
They attacked and spurred their
    horses;

[1209]

hand to hand with Muji he
    fought,
when Muji took his hands
and put his hands to his back.

170 e p'e shtrëngon-o Çeto Bashe
    Mujën
  e bytym eshtnit llom-o ja kish bâ
  e rrxoi Muja kaurrin të palamun
  e ja kish lidh-o duert për mbas
    shpinë
  me Sharanin Hajkunën të Bardh

175 vet në shpind-o gjogut m'i ka
    ramu
  e lidhun Muja kaurrin e ka
    kthyer
  e kur e gjet-o Halilin të Ri

  e qy Halilit duert për mbas
    shpine
  e po po i lutet Halili o-i Ri

180 e Baça Mujo mua do t'ma falesh
  e do t'ma falesh kryet t'ja
    shkurtoj
  e qat'herë fole Çeto Bashe Muja
  e ku janë shokt-o t'lidhun
    n'bjeshkë me ren
  e n'at bjeshkën mbas-o qi janë
    shku
185 e qaty ish-o Ali Bajraktari
  e prë nga tyne Arrnaut Osmani
  e nga tyne Omeri-o i Ri
  don m'e lidhun duert përmbas
    shpinun
  për nga tyne Tale Budaline
190 e mbrrini Muja duert ja ka
    zglidhun
  e fort po i lutet Tale Budalina
  falme Muj-o kryet t'ja shkurtoj
  e shumë zullumin Mujo ma ka
    bamun
  shplak mas qafe kaurri qi m'ka
    ramun

170 Çeto Basho Muji tied him up

  and he broke all his bones.
  Muji seized the unclean infidel
  tied up his hands in his back;

  with Sharan [and] the Fair
    Ajkuna,
175 he mounted on the back of the
    horse
  and brought the infidel back
    tied up.
  And when he found the Young
    Halil
  he untied his hands from his
    back.
  The Young Halil is begging of
    him:
180 "Brother Muji, grant me,
  grant me to cut his head off!"

  Then said Çeto Basho Muji:
  "Where are the friends tied up
    in the mountain?"
  And to that mountain they
    went.
185 There was Ali Bajraktar
  and next to him Arrnaut Osman
  and next to them the Young Imer,
  all with their hands tied up
    behind their backs;
  next to them Tale Budaline.
190 Muji untied their hands.

  Tale Budaline begged him:
  "Grant me to cut off his head!
  A great damage he did to me,
    Muji
  the infidel slapped me on the
    back of the neck

195 ne ledin-o dhombt-o m'i ka
    qitun
    s'muj ha Tali ... [*molleçka*
    çemakun]
    e fort po keshet Klladushane
    Muja
    tanëve Muja duert ja u ka
    zglidhun
    e fort po i lutet Imeri o i Ri
200 e falma bab-o kryet t'ja shkurtoj

    a sall me nj'dorë ai duert m'i ka
    lidhun
    s'at her foli-o Çeto Bashe Muji
    e dua m'e lshua kaurrin të
    palamun
    bisi e bjel o vashe kush e
    nxanun
205 kush përpjet-o kaurrin ka me
    nxanun
    falë i koft-o kryet ja shkurton

    qat'herë Muja kaurrin qi e ka
    lshua
    e muar fushën malit për me
    ikun
    e përmbas tina turqit qi janë
    nisun

[1210]

210 e gjithë me me rend-o bjeshkës
    qi e përzunë
    kurkun ngat-o kaurrit s'po i
    afrohen
    e sill sall pak-o Halili o i Mujs
    e pa Muja kaurrin don me shkua
    n'shpindë gjogatit Muja m'i ka
    ra

195 he tossed my teeth onto the
    field
    I can't eat ... [unintelligible]"

    Klladushane Muji laughed
    aloud!
    Muji has untied everybody's
    hands.
    The Young Imer begged him:
200 "Grant me, father, to cut off his
    head
    using one hand he tied up my
    hands!"
    Then said Çeto Basho Muji:
    "I will release the unclean
    infidel:
    anyone who seizes him, man or
    woman,
205 who succeeds in seizing the
    infidel
    let it be granted to him to cut
    off his head!"
    Then Muji released the infidel.

    He took to the fields to go to the
    mountains
    and after him the turks set out,

[1210]

210 and they all went running to the
    highland to hunt him down
    but they couldn't get near to
    the infidel,
    Halil of Muji just hung around.
    Muji saw the infidel was escaping!
    Muji jumped on the back of his
    horse,

215 e përmbas tina Muja tym e nga
e n'gjogat-o Muja qi e ka nxanun
e opet Muja duert ja ka lidhun
e ja pru Tale Talit ja ka falun

e ja fali Tali Budalines
220 e Tali shpeit-o kryet ja shkurtoi
e q'aty tejen shokt-o kan pushu
e shumë pushim-o tre sahat po
rrinë
e qat'here Muja shokve m'u kish
thanun
hajde shok-o n'kulla për me
shku
225 e n'shpind kualve burrat qi ju
kan ra
eu teposht-o bjeshkëve-o tye oi
shkelen
n'vithe t'kalit kryet ja kanë
vjerrun
në Sharanin Ajkunen të Bardh

para Ajkune Omerin të Ri

230 e tre shok-o n'kâm-o qi kanë
votë
Tali kâm-o bjeshkëve tye-o
zvjetë
kur janë ra-o n'fush-o të
Klladushës
qaty shum-o shok-o qi janë
mbledhë
pesqin shok-o n'bajrak qi ja
mbledhë
235 bash në kull-o t'Çeto Basho
Muj's
e q'ata shokt-o n'kull-o qi janë
ramun-e

215 and Muji reached him
and took him on the horse
and again tied up his hands
and he brought him to Tale and
granted him to Tale,
he granted him to Tale Budaline.
220 Tale immediately cut his head.
Then the friends took some rest,
they rested a lot, for three
hours.
Then Muji said to his friends:

"Come on friends let us go to
the tower! "
225 And the heroes jumped on their
horses
and went down the mountains.

They hung the head on the
horse's rump
and on Sharan [he put] the Fair
Ajkuna
in front of Ajukuna the Young
Imer
230 and three friends went on foot

Tale on foot coming down from
the mountains.
When they got to the plain of
Klladusha
there many friends gathered
together:
five hundred friends gathered
around the banner
235 right at the tower of Çeto Basho
Muji,
these friends arrived at the
tower.

PN 6467. Fatima Biberović, *Pjesma o Kolačima*[1]

Fatima Biberović [Fatime Arifi]; Gacko (Bosnia-Hercegovina); May 20, 1935
The Song of the Turkish Cakes
Discs 3534–3535

[3534]

Kur ka thane gazda jone
a po dish se sa Fatime
un po dije gospodine
gji ke bone mua-lle

une kam zallëm zotnija jone
per ma pare unë do të bleje

Fatima tija i ka thane
a po dish me bon kulaçe

un po dije zotnija jone
10   do t'boj per ty per qefin tane

do t'boj per ty per qefin tane

[3534]

When our master said:
Do you know how, O Fatima?
Yes I know, sir.
What a thing you have done me,
   oh dear.

I have a disaster, sir.
I'll buy it for more money.

He said to Fatima:
Do you know how to make sweet
   cakes?

Yes I know, sir.
10   I'll do it for you for your
     pleasure
I'll do it for you for your
   pleasure.

[1] Lord described the context for this song in a note appended to his translation of PN 6464, a song composed in response to the same incident by another singer, Almasa Zvizdić (Bartók and Lord 1951: 367): "While we were recording at Salih Zvizdić's house, Professor Parry asked Fatima Biberović to make us some Turkish cakes. The pastry was prepared with fond care, as his request was felt to be a great honor, a compliment to Fatima's ability as a cook. But after the cakes had been placed in the oven, Fatima became absorbed in the singing and recording, and forgot her cooking until it was too late. The cakes were burned to a crisp. Fata [sic] burst into tears of bitter humiliation. Our hostess, Almasa, deftly turned this tragic situation into an amusing incident by making up a song about it. . . . Fatima retaliated later the same day with a song of her own in Albanian, which has not yet been transcribed (No. 6467)."

Une shkova bleva sheqer
i tlyni mir n'u me bone

shkova n'muftak me gatuve
kolaçin me bone

Ka dal gozojami i jon
çka ka thane mue
zi po vdel maca jone

gji po bon ti mue
20 zi po bone maca jone
gji ke bone ti mue

Une shkova vune saçin
se kam dite qysh me pjek
une vune saçin zije
se kom dit se qysh me pjek

Une korbo qysh me bon
kur kam kqyre saçin mire
e kom gjete shkrum krejte
kur kom kqyre saçin zije
30 e kom bone shkrum krejte

Gji kom bone ku ku për mu
nuk po m'bon me kqyr zotni
gji kom bone ku ku per mu
gji kom djege gurabije

Ka ardh dhe mira jone

une po qaj shume
ka ardh Almasa çatje poshte
une po lshoj lote shume

I went and bought sugar,
and good butter in order to
   make them.
I went to the kitchen to cook,
to make the cake.

Our master came out.
What has he said to me:
our cat [andiron] is coming out
   black
the thing you are doing for me.
20 Our cat is being made black
the thing you are doing for me.

I went and put on the griddle
for I knew how to cook,
I made the griddle red hot
for I knew how to cook.

Woe is me, what to do!
When I saw the griddle well
I found it burnt to a crisp.
When I saw the red hot griddle
30 I had burned it to a crisp.

What have I done, woe is me!
It is not for the master to see,
what have I done, woe is me!
I have burned the cake.

There also arrived our good
   woman,
I am crying a lot
Almasa came down
I am shedding many tears.

[3535]

          Mjera une gji po bone
40   Sarko po thot mos kaj shume
          mjera une gji po bone
          Sarko po thot mos kaj shume

          Una erdha lart e nalte
          po thres zotnin tane
          le ta kqyri gurabijen
          shka ka bone Fatime
          une e ta kqyri nalte
          po thot gazdi çka ka bone

          Ka ardh Sarku hajde po thot
50   hajde atje nalte
          ka mar n'sobe kraj aginisu
          une po qaj shume
          ka marr po kra[j] aginisu
          po kjaj une shume

          Ka ardh Nikolla ka çukare

          ka marr meu pri dore
          ka ardh Nikolla kraj meja
          ka marr-e pri dore

          Do t'i flasin shnetin tane
60   sikur vllajin teme
          do t'i lashe shnetin Nikolles
          po sikur vllajit teme

          Gjith po bojni ju mue
          e kom troshit pare shume
          Zoti dhash ga *dhizhindë*
          qi ja bone mue
          o marofshe Fatimat-je

[3535]

          Poor me what did I do!
40   Sarko says: don't cry a lot.
          Poor me what did I do!
          Sarko says: don't cry a lot.

          I came up there
          I call our master
          let him look at the cake
          What Fatima has done!
          I was looking upstairs
          the master said what has she
                  done.

          Sarko came, come he said
50   come up here
          there's a disaster in the room
          I am crying a lot.
          There's a disaster
          I am crying a lot.

          Nikola has come, has knocked
                  [i.e., scolded lightly]
          he took my hand,
          Nikola came up to me
          he took my hand.

          They will speak for our health
60   as if for my brother,
          I would leave health to Nikola
          as if to my brother.

          You are doing everything for me
          I have spent a lot of money
          God gives [unintelligible]
          ...that did for me?
          O for shame Fatima

qi ke bone shum sete

you have sifted a lot.

Une kom bo se kom dite
70   me pjek ktu në saçe
une e kom dite
me çë pjeker me pjek mire
gosnoshe ju shume
gji jon bone per mue

I did what I knew
70   to cook it here on the griddle.
I did know
to cook it to cook well.
I was regaling you a lot
things were done for me.

Me ka dite une ku ku
nuk po marshe doste me
kafarrofte emni eme
qi kom bone shum sete
kafarrofte emni eme
80   qi kom bone shum sete

I knew how, woe is me!
I wasn't taking enough
[unintelligible] my name
I did a lot of sifting.
[unintelligible] my name
80   I did a lot of sifting.

Po thot Nikolla nuk ka çartun
mos kije Fatime derte
kur gja nuk ke çartun gji ke bo

But Nikolla said it isn't spoiled
Fatima don't be in pain,
you haven't spoiled anything at
    all

shume mire asht e pjeke

it is very well cooked.

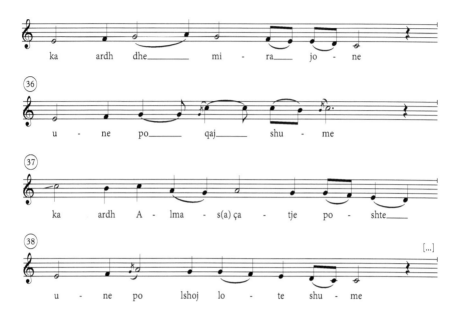

PN 6503. Fatima Biberović, *Dü Darda meni Dard* [*Dy Dardha me ni Dardhë*]

Fatima Biberović [Fatime Arifi]; Gacko (Bosnia-Hercegovina); May 21, 1935
Two Pears with One Pear
Discs 3599–3600
Lyric song

[3599]

    Dy molla me ni moll
    dy molla me ni moll
    mor je mir e lales o
    po kanga fort e holl
5 mor je mir e lales o
    po kanga fort e holl

    Dy dardha me ni dardh
    dy dardha me ni dardh
    mor je mir e lales o
10 po kanga fort e bardh
    mor je mir e lalës o
    po kanga fort e bardh

    Dy ftue me ni ftue
    dy ftue me ni ftue
15 mor je mir e lales o
    po kanga pa martuve
    mor je mir e lales o
    po kanga pa martuve

    Dy kumlla me ni kumll
20 dy kullma me ni kumll
    mor je mir e lalas o

[3599]

    Two apples with one apple
    two apples with one apple.
    Hey, you are daddy's darling
    but the song very high pitched.
5 Hey, you are daddy's darling
    but the song very high pitched.

    Two pears with one pear
    two pears with one pear.
    Hey you are daddy's darling
10 but the song very fair.
    Hey you are daddy's darling
    but the song very fair.

    Two quinces with one quince
    two quinces with one quince
15 Hey you are daddy's darling
    but the song unmarried.
    Hey you are daddy's darling
    but the song unmarried.

    Two plums with one plum
20 two plums with one plum.
    Hey you are daddy's darling

po kanga pa ku[m]
mor je mir e lalës o
po kanga pa ku[m]

but the song unfulfilled.
Hey you are daddy's darling
but the song unfulfilled.

25 Dy dardha marin o
dy dardha marin o
kush asht ç'ajo kush po bone
more djal i ri
kush asht ç'ajo çi [gji] po bone
30 more djal i ri

25 Two pears they took
two pears they took.
who is she, what's she doing
Hey young man!
who is she, what's she doing
30 Hey young man!

Dy ftue pa more
dy ftue pa more
mor je mir e lales o
po gji nuk ke bone
35 mor je mir e lales o
po pse nuk ke bone

Two quinces not taken
two quinces not taken.
Hey you are daddy's darling
But you haven't done a thing?
35 Hey you are daddy's darling
But why did you not do it?

Dy arra me ni arr
dy arra me ni arr
mor je mir e lalës o
40 po pse nuk je vra
mor je mir e lalës o
po pse nuk je vra

Two walnuts with one walnut
two walnuts with one walnut.
Hey you are daddy's darling
40 why didn't you crack it?
Hey you are daddy's darling
why didn't you crack it?

[3600]

Dy malla me ni mall

dy malla me ni mall

45 morje mir e lales o
po pse nuk ke marr
mor je mir e lales o
po pse je nuk ke marr

Dy malsore me ni malsor

50 dy malsore me ni malsor

[3600]

Two loads of goods with one
load of goods
two loads of goods with one
load of goods.

45 Hey you are daddy's darling
But why did you not take it?
Hey you are daddy's darling
But why did you not take it?

Two highlanders with one
highlander
50 Two highlanders with one
highlander.

150

	mor je mir e lales o		Hey you are daddy's darling
	po qish a e ki bon		But how did you do it?
	mor je mir e lales o		Hey you are daddy's darling
	po pse nuk ke bon		But why didn't you do it?
55	Dy molla me ni moll	55	Two apples with one apple
	dy molla me ni moll		two apples with one apple.
	mor je mir e lales o		Hey you are daddy's darling
	po pse je nuk ke lan		why did you not leave it?
	mor je mir e lales o		Hey you are daddy's darling
60	po pse je nuk ke lan	60	why did you not leave it?

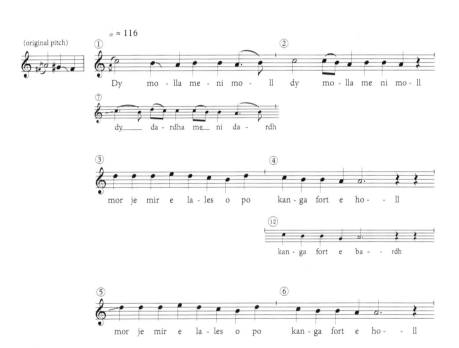

PN 6523a. Fatima Biberović, *Mrtvačka Pjesma i Pricanje*[1]

Fatima Biberović [Fatime Arifi]; Gacko (Bosnia-Hercegovina); May 23, 1935
Mourning Song and Conversation
Discs 3777–3779
Lament

[3777]

    E mjera une
    nan oj loçko-je ime
    ku-r m'ke lane
    bijen tane

5   Mjera u-h-ne
    a gjithmone
    nano je loçk-o jeme
    a po dish une çi ke lane

    Mi ke lan ori nane
10   zi për mue
    pse nuk m'ke myte ori nan

    kur kam pa xhe-h-nazin ton
    pse nuk (m')ke myt mu mori
      nane
    kur e kam pa xhenazin ton

[3777]

    O poor me,
    mother, O my darling,
    when you left me,
    your daughter!

5   Poor me,
    ah, forever
    O mother, you are my darling
    do you know how you have left
      me?

    You left for me, O mother,
10   mourning for me
    why did you not drown me
      mother
    when I saw your funeral?
    why did not you drown me
      mother
    when I saw your funeral?

---

[1] The singer's mother died when she was 6 or 7. She had fallen asleep by her mother. Her older brother came and told her that her mother was dead. She didn't understand anything. Her siblings had to deal with the tragedy and with their little sister as well.

15 Mi ke lan ori nane
    mo jetime
    kam harrue nane
    dertin teme

    A ke harrue nan
20 qysh ke lane
    bijen tane ori nane
    shum zi se ka bone

    Vllaj i jeme nane
    mu mi ka lane
25 shum prej krejes tane
    nane mi ka shkue

    Nuk e harroj nane
    sisen tane
    gji kam pi ori nane
30 mjera une

    Ti (m')ke lane
    mu ma jo
    e m'ke lane
    faq e zije

35 Kur kam shkuve
    te vllaj i jeme
    vllaj i jeme
    me grush mi ka myte

    Po bon hallvën
40 nanes teme
    un po qaje
    me lot shume

[3778]

    Un po qaje
    me lot shume

154

15 You left me, O mother,
    me an orphan
    I have forgotten, mother,
    my pain.

    Have you forgotten, mother?
20 Since you have left
    your daughter, O mother,
    much misery it has caused.

    My brother, O mother,
    has left me,
25 close to your head
    mother I stayed.

    I don't forget, mother,
    your breast,
    I drank breast milk, O mother
30 poor me!

    You have left me,
    for me no more
    and you have left me
    deep mourning.

35 When I went
    to my brother
    my brother hit me
    with his fist.

    He's making *halva*
40 for my mother,
    I am weeping
    with many tears

[3778]

    I am weeping
    with many tears.

45	Mos me vra-e		45	Don't hit me,
	vllaj i jeme			my brother
	un jam jetime			I am an orphan
	pa kërkane			without anyone
	un kam jetime			I am an orphan
50	ah pa kërkane		50	ah, without anyone.

Ka ardh nusja
mu me m'kqyre
nanes teme
xhenazi po lane

My sister-in-law
came to see me,
my mother's funeral
she is leaving.

55 Motra jeme
mu po m'kqyr i zije
ah lot nuk po dalin

55 My sister
sees me in mourning,
Ah, the tears are not coming out,

e mjera une

poor me!

Une po mys vehten
60 krai nanes teme
e ka dek nana
zi per mue

I'm beating myself,
60 beside my mother,
my mother has died,
woe is me!

Ka flet mjera
kraj mames vete
65 kur ka than e mjera
nana ka vdeke
kur ka than e mjera
nana ka vdeke

The poor thing was sleeping
beside mother herself
65 when he said, you poor thing
mother has died!
When he said, you poor thing
mother has died!

Ka ardh hoxha
70 me laj nanen
ka than nana
me kenue
ka than nana
me kenue

The *hodja* came
70 to wash mother,
for mother
he recited prayers
for mother
he recited prayers.

75 Po laj hoxha
nanes teme
e kan çuve

75 The *hodja* is washing
my mother,
they have put her

155

	te mezare		to the grave.
	Ah e kan çuve		Ah, they have put her
80	a mezare	80	in the grave,
	mi kan mlue		they have buried
	nanën e zije		my poor mother.
	Kuku nane		O woe, mother,
	ku m'ke lane		where have you left me!
85	ka lan bije	85	You have left your daughter
	kuku vete		O woe, alone.
	Nana jeme		The grave has covered
	ka mlu mezare		my mother,
	ka ardh vllaji		my brother came
90	me shkel n'kame(n)	90	stepped on my foot,
	ka ardh vllaji		my brother came
	me shkel n'kame(n)		stepped on my foot.
	E kqyr nanen		And look, mother,
	çka po m'bone		what he is doing to me.
95	mos vllaj i jeme	95	Don't, O my brother,
	asht ah jetime		she is an orphan,
	mos bre vllaj i jeme		don't, hey, my brother,
	jam jetime		I am an orphan.
	E ka mshel deren		My brother
100	vllaj i jeme	100	has closed the door,
	motra jeme		my sister
	qi po k'qyre		is watching.

[3779]

[3779]

	Kur po dal n'avlije		When I go into the courtyard,
	po kqyr lule		I see a flower
105	nanen teme	105	I don't have
	kurkun s'e kam-e		my mother anywhere,
	nanen teme		I don't have
	kurkun s'e kam-e		my mother anywhere.

Pse nuk ke bon
110 nana, gur per mu
pse nuk ke mlue
zi mu n'toke

Mi ke lane
dhet vllazen kam pa-e
115 une njo
kam me zije

Kur kam dale
ullezi
ah mori nane
120 mjera une kam thane

[Conversation]

Why did you not make
110 a stone for me, mother?
Why did you not bury
poor me in the ground?

You have left me,
ten brothers I had,
115 I have only one
in mourning.

When I went out
wailing,
ah, O mother,
120 poor me I have withered away.

SECTION 2

FROM THE TRANSCRIPTIONS OF THE ALBERT B. LORD COLLECTION, 1937

LAN 28. Gjergj Pllumbi, *Musa Qeshexhi dhe Vlla Bergjanine Gjemi*

Gjergj Pllumbi; Theth (Shala); September 13, 1937
Musa Qeshexhi dhe Vlla Bergjanine Gjemi
Musa Qesexhi and His Brother Bergjanine Gjemi
Legendary song

Lum per ty more i lumi Zot

May You be praised, O blessed God.

e sjem kan e Zoti na ka dhan

We would not be but for God's grace,

e te pa nafak ishalla s'na ka lan

and He has not left us, God willing, without good fortune.

kur jan qenë burrat prej vaktit

When in times gone by there were real men,

5 gjith i cilli ma i mire se i shoqi

5 each and every one better than the next,

e m'ish qenë Musa Arbanasi
ne hyzmet Mbretit Musa ish pa kan

there lived Musa Arbanasi.
Musa was in the service of the Emperor.

nji dit ka hi ne lakant per me pi

One day he entered an inn to have a drink,

e asht mbledhë Musa me shoqni

and Musa got together with his friends.

10 e kan shtrue pijen tue pi

10 They were casually sitting and drinking,

deri ne qef Zotniet jan bâ
pashka fol Musa Qeshexhija
pa ndijoni more shoqët e mi
tri vjet Mbretit ne hyzmet qi po
    i ri

and got into a good mood.
Then Musa Qesexhi spoke:
"Listen up, my friends,
the three years I have been in the service of the Emperor

15   nuk po me del me ngran as me
         pi
      as po me del me u vesh as me u
         mbath
      e tybe kjoft ne hyzmet ma me i
         ndej
      se vendin t'em ishalla e kom
         gjet
      kur te me vine vera e prendvera
20   due me i mbledhe treqind
         ustalar
      ne Mexh te Primores due per
         me i çue
      aty sarrajet due me i fillue

      me uzdaj te Zotit gjitha me i
         punue
      rrugë e vjeter aty ka qillue
25   e shum dunja per at rruge tue
         ullue
      drum njasajt me s'due me lan

      njer gjiallë s'due me lan pa pré

      due me pre frat dhe ipeshkevë
      kan me çue krajlat mejdanxhi
30   me uzdai te Zotit tanë kam pe i
         pre
      kom pre prë hoxhë dhe haxhi
      shoket e vet gjith tue ndigjue
      e me aq te gjith jan çue
      kur po del prendvera e bardhë
35   e po nisë vera per me dal

      shka po ban Musa Qesexhia
      fjal te dimnit trimi s'po i harron

      e ka dal trimi e po shetitë

15   I have not had enough to eat or
         to drink,
      nor have I had enough clothes
         or footwear to put on.
      No longer will I stay in his
         service,
      because, God willing, I have
         found my calling.
      When summer and spring come
20   I will assemble three hundred
         craftsmen.
      I will send them to the Border
         of Primore,
      there I will begin building my
         castles
      and complete them trusting in
         God.
      There is an ancient road there,
25   and many people travel along
         that road.
      I will not allow anyone on that
         highway,
      I will not leave a living soul
         unscathed.
      I will cut down friars and bishops.
      The kings will send out fighters,
30   trusting in God I will cut them
         all down.
      I will cut down *hodjas* and *hadjis*."
      His friends, ever listening to him,
      all together arose to a man.
      When a mild spring arrived
35   and summer was starting to
         follow,
      what did Musa Qesexhi do?
      The hero did not forget his
         words of winter.
      The hero went outside and
         strolled about,

	e po i zgedhe mjeshtrat ma te mirët		and assembled the best artisans,
40	e i ploteson treqind ushtalar	40	and supplemented them with three hundred craftsmen.
	ne Mexh te Primores trimi pashka çue		The hero sent them to the Border of Primore.
	kan fillue punë me punue		They began to do their job,
	plotë tri vjet ne atë punë tue vazhdue		staying on the job a full three years.
	allamet sarraja ka punue		What wondrous castles he built!
45	dymdhete pode perpjete i ka çue	45	He raised them twelve stories high,
	treqind oda mbrend i paska lan		he laid out three hundred rooms inside them.
	kçyre shka ban Musa Qesexhija		Consider what Musa Qesexhi did:
	tana paret mjestret jan pague		he paid all the money due the artisans,
	e kurkuej hakut s'jau ka hanger		he did not hold back anyone's pay.
50	atherë nise Musa me u forcue	50	Then Musa began to reinforce himself,
	shum djelt te fort zabte paska shkrue		he enlisted many tough youths as armed policemen.
	atherë nise drumin e ka ndalue		Then he began to block the highway,
	atherë nise halkun e po i pret		next he began to cut down people.
	paska pre frat edhe ipeshk		He cut down friars and bishops,
55	e ne dynja zani i paska dal	55	and word spread across the world
	ma lugat Musa Qesexhi		that Musa Qesexhi was a werewolf!
	paskan çue krajlat mejdanxhi		The kings sent out fighters,
	tonë Musa i paska pre		Musa cut down all of them.
	paska pre hoxhë dhe haxhi		He cut down *hodjas* and *hadjis*,
60	e kenka prish me Mbretin ne Turki	60	and he severed ties with the Emperor in Turkey.
	paska çue Mbreti mejdanxhi		The Emperor sent out fighters,
	tanë Musa ja paska pre		Musa cut down all of them.

	shka po ban Mbreti ne Stamboll		What did the Emperor in Stambol do?
	tanë po i mbledh amiret e vet		He assembled all his emirs,
65	paska mbledh Pashë e Kadi	65	he assembled pashas and cadis,
	paska mbledh Beglerr e Vizir		he assembled beys and viziers,
	paska mbledh argë e zotni		he assembled agas and lords,
	e kuvend Mbreti me ta tuej bâ		and the Emperor held council with them.
	pa ndigjoni amirat e mi		"Listen, my emirs,
70	si te ja bajmë Muses Qesexhi	70	how are we to deal with Musa Qesexhi
	qi kand mbi vedi s'don me lau		who won't tolerate anyone over him?
	ne Mexh te Primores sarrajet i ka bâ		He has built castles on the Border of Primore,
	krajl as Mbret ma te mira nuk i kem		neither king nor emperor has better ones.
	dymbdhete pode perpjetë i ka çue		He has raised them twelve stories high,
75	treqind oda mbrend jau ka lan	75	he laid out three hundred rooms inside them.
	gjith rreth tyne avllin prej çelikut		All around them is a wall of steel,
	rreth avlis hendekun e ka çilë		around the wall he has dug a ditch,
	e ka shte at vredhun ne te		and has diverted a spring into it
	qi gja e gjalle at vredhun mos e kecye		so that nothing can cross the spring alive.
80	shum djelt te fort zaptie ka shkrue	80	He has enlisted many tough youths as armed policemen,
	e ka nise gjaden e ka keput		he has begun to block the main road,
	njery gjalle nuk po lau pa pre		he does not leave a living soul unscathed,
	e ka pre frat dhe ipeshkev		he has cut down friars and bishops.
	kan çue krajlat mejdanxhi		The kings have sent out fighters
85	e tan Musa i ka pre	85	and Musa has cut them all down.

tash ka pre hoxhë dhe haxhi

e asht prish Musa me Turkië

kam çue me Musen Mejdanxhi

e te tane Musa i ka pre

90 e kam thirr Mujen e Halilin
e s'kan ndigjue ne mejdan me i
dal
se s'jan kan te zot per me i bâ
ballë
si te ja bajme burra i paska than

mejdanxhi per Musen ku me
marrë
95 me te fol Chuperli Viziri
pa ndigjove ti more Mbreti jonë
mejdanxhi vet ta kam gjet
por nuk e di asht gjalle a ka dek

kçyre ku e ke Krajleviçe Markun

100 qi pe shtate vjet ne burg i ke lan

e ke lan ne at burg shum t'keq

tu po me asht kalm e knet
tu po jan gyrpaj e haqrep

e gjith gyrpajt gjakun tuej ja pi

105 e gjith haqrept mishin tuej ja gri

e nuk e di a asht gjall a ka dek

ne kjoft i gjalle Krajleviçe Marku

Now he has cut down *hodjas* and
hadjis,
and Musa has severed ties with
Turkey.
I have sent out fighters against
Musa,
and Musa has cut down all of
them.
90 I have summoned Muji and Halil
but they do not dare to go out
to the battle ground,
because they are not strong
enough to confront him.
What are we to do with him,
men?—he said to them—
Where can I get a fighter to face
Musa?"
95 Çuperli the Vizier spoke up:
"Hear me out, O Emperor of ours.
I myself I found a fighter for you,
but I do not know if he is alive
or has died.
See where you are holding
Marko Kraljević
100 whom you have left in a
dungeon for seven years.
You have left him in that most
foul dungeon
where there is rot and bog,
where there are snakes and
scorpions,
with all the snakes drinking his
blood
105 and all the scorpions consuming
his flesh.
I do not know if he is alive or
has died.
If Marko Kraljević is alive,

ndo e qart njaj Musen Qesexhi

ndo ne dynja s'di kur per me
gjet
110 i thotë Mbreti Vezir goja te
lumit
se mua prej menç Mark ka pa dal
se shum i zot imen ka pa kan
Mbreti urdhen ne burg e paska
çue
e prej burgut Markut per me i
leshue
115 si do te jetë Mbreti e ka kerkue

sa me te shpejt Markun e kan
leshue
hukubet Zoti e kish ba
floket e krës sa fort ju kishin
rrite
para e mbrapa ne toke ju kishin
râ
120 kur ja çojne Mbretit e ka pâ

e shyqyrim Mbreti ja ka bâ

por falenderimin hiç s'ja ka
dredh
per te mire teme Mbret nuk me
ke leshue
por ndoj nevojë te randë e ke
pasë
125 si dikush me gjase paska ngutse

e per mue atë sherr don me e
vesh
mire po e dini e goja te lumit

por po drue se i Zoti s'ke me kan

either he will handle Musa
Qesexhi
or I do not know where in the
world to find one who can."
110 The Emperor said: "May your
mouth be blessed, Vizier,
for Marko has slipped my mind,
And was a very capable man."
The Emperor sent an order to
the dungeon
to release Marko from the
dungeon.
115 The Emperor was curious about
how he was.
They released Marko as quickly
as they could:
God made him like a monster!
The hair on his head had grown
so long,
it had fallen to the ground in
front and behind him.
120 When they delivered him to the
Emperor,
the Emperor warmly thanked
him.
But he did not return his thanks
at all:
"You have not released me,
Emperor, for my own good,
but you find yourself in dire
need,
125 as if someone is making trouble
for you,
and you want me to end the
mischief."
"You know me full well, may
your mouth be blessed.
But I am afraid you are not up to
it."

e ne makin Mbreti e paska çue

130 e berberat mire i ka urdhnue

per me e qeth e ma mire e me
 rrue
per me e lâ e mire per me e limue
e ne terzi Mbreti e paska çue

e sa mire petkat ja kan mat

135 ja kan qep petkat krejt boj gjak

si gjithmon ashtu Marku i kish
 mbajtë
atherë Mbreti po i thrret ne
 palat
e kan nise po bajne muhabet

per gjithe shka Mbreti e ka vet

140 ç'far sefajet Mark don me lypë

shka te pelqen me pi dhe me
 ngran
me u bâ i fort ti Mark si je qenë

due thotë Marku mish kaut dhe
 vin
e gjashte muej per me ndej
145 e ishalla bahem Mbret si jam
 qenë
e per Musen Mbreti po i kuvend

qi i ka bâ sarrajet shum binê

deri sot mbi vedi kon s'ka lan

ne Mexh te Primores drumin e
 ka keput

And the Emperor sent him off to
 a barbershop,
130 and strongly ordered the
 barbers
to trim his hair and shave him
 even better,
to wash him and comb him well.
And the Emperor sent him to a
 tailor shop.
How well did they measure his
 clothes!
135 They hemmed all his blood-
 colored clothes
as Marko had always worn them
 that way.
Then the Emperor summoned
 him to his palace
and they struck up a
 conversation.
The Emperor questioned him
 about everything:
140 "What favors would you like to
 request?
What would you like to drink
 and to eat
to become as strong as you used
 to be, Marko?"
"I would like—said Marko—beef
 and wine
and to recuperate for six months,
145 and, God willing, Emperor, I will
 become as I used to be."
And the Emperor discusses
 Musa with him,
that he has built enormous
 castles,
and today won't tolerate anyone
 over him.
"On the Border of Primore he
 has cut the main road,

150 e njerz gjallë a'ka lan pa pre

e ka pre frat dhe ipeshkev

e s'ka lan pa pre mejdanxhi

e ka pre hoxhë dhe haxhi
e ka bâ dunjanë jeremi
155 tash ja peshtet more Mark mi ty

e me aq trimat jan çue

shka po bon Krajleviçe Marku
shka ka lypi me ngran dhe me pi

shum sefa per gjashtë muej ka bâ
160 bajgi Marku asht forcue
trupi ne vend Markut i ka shkue
kur gjashte muej Markun i ka
     plotësue
fill te Mbreti atherë ka shkue

ja lipe Mbretit nji drynin prej
     thanes
165 qi tri vjet druni të jete i thamë

e me te shpejt Mbreti ja ka prue

me dore te djatht Marku e ka
     shtregue
miell ne grusht Marku e ka bâ

e ka qit Mbreti i ka than

170 edhe dy muej due pushim me
     ndej
se nuk me ka shkue hala fuqija
     nevend
edhe dy muej pushim paska
     ndej

150 he does not leave a living soul
     unscathed,
he has cut down friars and
     bishops,
and has not left unscathed any
     fighters.
He has cut down *hodjas* and *hadjis*,
he has made the world a desert.
155 Right now, Marko I am relying
     on you."
And with that the heroes stood
     up.
What did Marko Kraljević do?
What he requested to eat and to
     drink
he savored for six months.
160 Marko became quite stronger,
Marko's body recovered.
When Marko completed his six
     months
he then went straight to the
     Emperor.
He asked the Emperor for wood
     from the cherry tree
165 whose wood had dried out for
     three years.
And the Emperor hastily
     provided it for him.
Marko squeezed it in his right
     hand
and turned it into powder in his
     fist.
He stood up and said to the
     Emperor:
170 "I want to rest and recuperate
     two more months
because my strength has not yet
     recovered."
And he recuperated for two
     months.

e per s'dytit tu Mbreti ka shkue

ja ka lip Mbretit drunin e thanes

175 me dore te djatht ka marre e me
        shtrengue
    i leshon ne tokë tri pikla prej
        ujit
    athere ka qesh Krajleviçe Marku
    e i ka qit Mbretit e i ka than

    tash per se dytit Mbret kam le

180 se me ka shkue fuqja ne vend
    e me ka bâ dora si ka qene
    po i thote Mbreti Mark shka po
        lype
    i ka lype Mark peseqind okë
        çelik
    e me të shpejt Mbreti ja ka dhan

185 e çelikun Marku e paska marre
    e ka çue ne Novane Kovaçi
    e ka qitë Kovaçit e i thanë
    ne kullen shenjte nji bê ma bâ

    qi shpate ma te mire kurr ka
        s'po punon
190 e Kovaçi bên ja paska bâ
    qi shpatë ma te mire kurr ma
        s'po punoj
    ndihmo Zot Kovaçi ja fillon
    e sa mire çelikun e ka shkri
    e sa mire çelikun e ka zi
195 e sa mire çelikun po e kullon
    ndihmo Zot kurr shpaten e ka
        punue
    e e ka marrë spaten e ka peshue

And for the second time he
        went to the Emperor,
he asked the Emperor for wood
        from the cherry tree.

175 He took it in his right hand and
        squeezed it
and lets loose three drops of
        water on the ground.
Then Marko Kraljević laughed.
He stood up and said to the
        Emperor:
"Now I have been born for the
        second time,

180 for my strength has recovered.
and my arm is as it used to be."
The Emperor said to him: "Marko,
        what else do you want?"
Marko asked him for five
        hundred *okas* of steel,
and the Emperor hastily
        provided it for him.

185 Marko took the steel
and sent it to Novane Kovaçi.
He addressed Kovaçi and said:
"Give me your *besa* on your
        sacred tower
that you will never make a
        better sword."

190 Kovaçi gave him his *besa*
that he would never make a
        better sword.
God help him, Kovaçi started in:
how well he smelted the steel,
how well he purified the steel,
195 how well he poured the steel.
God help him, when he finished
        the sword,
he took the sword and weighed
        it.

tridhete oke shpata i ka dal
çon e thrret Krajleviçe Markun

200 e me të shpejt Mark kur ka
shkue
e ka marrë shpaten e ka shikue

e ka qit Kovaçi e i ka than
te lumit dora mire e ki punue

due edhe nji herë Kovaç per me
te betue
205 qi shpate ma te mire ndoj herë a
ki punue
be ka bâ Novane Kovaçi
edhe nji herë nji shpate e kam
punue
i kam bâ i shpate Muses Qesexhi
mi ka prue pesëqind oke çeliku

210 e si ketê s'kam muejte me e
kullue
edhe pesë oksh ma rande me ka
dal
kur e muer Musa ne dorë
e i ka ra kulles me te
kull e çung Musa i ka pre

215 e i ka ra shpata per dhe
e nji meter ne dhe i ka shkue

pa ndigjove Krajleviçe Marku
shpaten tande mundesh me bâ
provë
e ka marrë shpaten me dorë
220 ndihmo Zot e kulles i ka râ
kull e çung me te shpejt e ka pre

e i ka shkue maja per dhe

The sword came to thirty *okas*.
He stood up and summoned
Marko Kraljević.

200 When Marko arrived as quickly
as he could,
he took the sword and looked at
it.

He addressed Kovaçi and said:
"Well done! You have done good
work.
I would like you, Kovaçi, one
more time to swear to me
205 that you have never before
made a better sword."
Novane Kovaçi gave him his *besa*:
"One other time have I made a
sword,
I made a sword for Musa Qesexhi.
He provided me with five
hundred *okas* of steel

210 and I was unable to pour it like
this one:
it came out five *okas* heavier.

When Musa took it in his hand
he struck the anvil with it.
Musa cut through the anvil and
the block.

215 The sword struck the ground
and went one meter into the
ground.
But listen, Marko Kraljević,
You can test your own sword."

He took the sword in his hand.
220 God help him, he struck the anvil.
He quickly cut through the anvil
and the block,
and the tip went into the ground,

maja shpates Marku ka ra

ndihmo Zot ne kamb a çue
225 e kun mat deri ku ka shkue

nji meter e gjyse ne dhe kish
    kallue
e sa fort ne qef Marku a bâ
qi me than mendja don me
    fliturue
doren e djatht Kovaçit ja ka kap
230 shpat mbas grushtit Kovaçit i ka
    râ
doren e djatht ja paska keput
ne mal te thatë Kovaçi ka bertit
me more ne qaf ti Krajleviçe
    Marku
si me la rrobet e mi mem dek

235 qi jam qene ka i mbaj me kete
    zanat
ka qit Marku e i ka than
kurr ma mire rrobt nuk i ke pas

se ty e rrobt zotni kam per te
    mbajt
por shpate si temen ma
    smundesh me bâ
240 e ka shti Markun doren ne xhep
e ja ka falë peseqinda duket

e ja ka lidhe buken opet
e ja ka dhan Marku me dekret
ndihmo Zot Marku asht fillue
245 fill te Mbreti pashka shkue
e ka qit Mbretit e i ka than

sod shtate vjet Mbret kur me ke
    zan

Marko struck it with the tip of
    the sword.
God help him, he rose to his feet,
225 and he measured how far it had
    gone in.
He had plunged it a meter and a
    half into the ground.
Marko was so overcome with joy
that one might say he was half
    out of his mind.
He seized Kovaçi's right hand
230 and struck Kovaçi above his fist.

He cut off his right hand.
Kovaçi cried out in great pain:
"You have hurt me badly, Marko
    Kraljević!
You have left my family
    members to die,
235 for I am the one supporting
    them through my trade."
Marko addressed him and said:
"Worry no more about your
    family members,
for I am man enough to support
    you and your family members.
But a sword like mine you will
    not be able to make."
240 Marko put his hand in his pocket
and offered him five hundred
    ducats.
He gave him back his livelihood,
Marko did this by a decree.
God help him, Marko set out,
245 he went straight to the Emperor.
He addressed the Emperor and
    said:
"It is now seven years, Emperor,
    since you seized me.

a din gja per atë gjokun ku e
    kam

paska qit Mbreti e i ka than

250 gjokun tande Vidke Bedevine
    te kam çue te kadija ne Kapi
    e kan çue me shpejt jau kan
      prue
    e kerkush atë gjok se kish
      mundue
    e ka marrë Marku me e shillue
255 fren florinit ja paska vnue

ja ka vënue fren prej florinit

ja ka qit at shalë telatinit
ja merthen me kater kollana
dy brishimit dy prej telatinit

260 ja ka vue dy gurë xhevahirit

bajshin drit si flaka prej kandilit

Ndihmo Zot arm e shpatë po i
    ngjesh
e halal me Mbretim qenka bâ

ndoshta se shihena Mbret per
    atë dynja
265 e halal per gjith shka kan bâ

e lot per faqet te dyve po
    shkojne
e jan puth me Mbretin gojë per
    gojë
e me aqë e Mark a fillue
shka po bon ai Krajleviçe Marku
270 i bjen ne shpine Vidke Bedevisë

Do you know anything about
    where my grey-white horse
    is?"
The Emperor addressed him and
    said:
250 "Your horse, Vidke Bedouin?
    I sent it to the *kadi* in Kapi."
They quickly sent for the horse
    and brought it to him.
No one had tormented the grey-
    white horse.
Marko took it to saddle it,
255 he put gold embroidered reins
    on it,
even putting on reins embroidered
    with gold.
He threw a leather saddle on it
and fastened it with four girths,
two of fine thread and two of
    leather.
260 He placed two precious stones
    on it,
they emitted light like the flame
    of a candle.
God help him, he strapped on
    his sword,
and asked for the Emperor's
    forgiveness:
"Perhaps, Emperor, we will see
    each other in the other world."
265 And they forgave everything
    they had done,
and tears ran down both their
    faces,
and he and the Emperor kissed
    mouth to mouth.
With that Marko set off.
What did Marko Kraljević do?
270 He mounted on the back of
    Vidke Bedouin.

ne fushë te mbretit trimi ka dal

sa fort dizginat ja shtrengon

kryet perpjet gjokut po ja çon

Ndihmo Zot harrushlek po luen

275 gjith parë llojnash Marku po ban
e ne sarraje Mbreti po e shikjon

kçyre me e pa Krajleviçe Markun
Ndihmo Zot kur e paska marre vrapin
vrap te fort gjokut i ka dhan

280 qi ska muejt Mbretit ma per me e pâ
tym e mjegull gjokun e ka bâ

po kalon bjeshk e kasaba

po kalon shehera e katunde
ne Mexh te Primores trimi paska dal
285 kundra kullat Muses Qesexhi

ka nisë i herë zemra i ka therr

e ka nisë nji herë e a dridh
por me te shpejt Marku asht trimnue
e ka kjek at setren të Maxharit

290 Ndihmo Zot Marku e va vesh
e i ka mblue petkat prej boj gjakut
e tevdil Marku a bâ

The hero came out on the Emperor's plain.

He pulled so tightly on the bridal strap,

he yanked the grey-white horse's head up.

God help him, it danced like a bear!

275 Marko let it prance all about.
The Emperor was watching from the palace
looking to see Marko Kraljević.
God help him, when it broke into a gallop,
he made the grey-white horse speed away

280 so that the Emperor could not see him.
He spurred the grey-white horse on,

he crossed mountain pastures and towns,

he crossed cities and villages.
The hero came to the Border of Primore,

285 opposite the towers of Musa Qesexhi.

All at once his heart began to pound

and all at once he started shaking.
But in an instant Marko took courage,
and pulled out his woolen Magyar jacket.

290 God help him, Marko put it on
and covered his blood-colored clothes.
Marko put on a disguise

e a nise gjades tue shkue

kur sarrajet Marku asht afrue

295 rroja e parë para i ka dal

me i zane te idht Markut i
bertasin
a thue mendja ty djal paska lan

a ke ndija s'don per me e ndije

qi rrugen njesajt ma nuk ka

300 se ketu rrin Musa Qesexhi
shka ka ba Krajleviçe Marku
hiç ma ta nuk ka folë
e ka shti doren ne xhep
e ka nxjerre nje mezdrak te hollë
305 rrojen e parë sa idht i ka gjue

tre kun qene e gjashte i ka bâ

e ka qa e ka shkue
rroja e dytë para i paska dal

ku don djal rroja i paska than

310 a thue ty mendja te paska lan

qi rrugen njesajt ma nuk ka
mbet
hiç me ta Marku nuk ka folë

e ka nxjerre at mezdrakun e dyte
e sa idht rrojen e ka gjue

and continued traveling along
the highway.

When Marko approached the
castles,

295 the first patrol came out and
met him.

They shouted at Marko in an
angry voice:
"Have you by chance lost your
mind, youth?

Do you know, or don't you want
to know,

that this very road no longer is
open?

300 For Musa Qesexhi lives here."
See what Marko Kraljević did.
He did not speak to them at all:
he put his hand into his pocket
and pulled out a sharp mace.

305 He hurled it at the first patrol so
angrily,
where there were three he
made six.

He grumbled and went on.
The second patrol came out and
met him.

"Where do you think you are
going, youth?—the patrol
said—

310 Have you by chance lost your
mind?
This very road no longer is
open."

Marko did not speak to them at
all.
He pulled out a second mace.
He hurled it at the patrol so
angrily,

315 kater jan qene e tetë i ka bâ	315 where there were four he made eight.
e ka qa trimi e ka shkue	The hero grumbled and went on.
rroja e tretë shpejt e kan hetue	A third patrol quickly spotted him,
hiç s'po duen Markun me ndalue	but in no way did they want to block Marko.
te kausha Marku kur ka shkue	When Marko approached their barracks
320 lajm mbrenda Muses i ka shkue	320 news reached Musa inside.
Ndihmo Zot Musa ne kamb a çue	God help him, Musa rose to his feet!
e zaptia Muses po i kuvend	The armed policemen reported to Musa
qi na ka ra nji serhatli i ri	that a young border hero has arrived,
qi s'ja kem pa kurr shoqin me syë	the likes of whom they have never set eyes on,
325 qi dy rroje na i ka coptue	325 and who has cut to pieces two of the patrols.
e ka ditë Musa Qesexhi	Musa Qesexhi knew
se do te jete ndoj azgon Zoti	that he had to be a bold nobleman.
armë e shpate Musa i pashka ngjesh	Musa put on his weapons and sword.
ne shpine gjokut zi i ka râ	He jumped on the back of his ominous black horse.
330 gjith haletet me vedi i ka marrë	330 He took all his paraphernalia with him.
o dal ne dru sherbez po rrin	He came out on the highway, waiting contemptuously.
kur ja mbrini Krajleviçe Marku	When Marko Kraljević reached him
tek e pau Musa Qesexhi	Musa Qesexhi caught sight of him.
me i zan te idhun Markut po i bertet	He yelled to Marko in an angry voice:
335 Zoti te vraft o serhatli i shkret	335 "May God strike you dead, you pitiable border hero!

qenke i ri e shum marri me dek

ku ke qene e djal a te kan kalzue

se njisajt kjo rruga asht ndalue
sa daije ketu qi asht damtue

340 e hala Musa s'asht ligshtue

paska qitet Marku e i ka than
ta lutem Muso kesaj rruget mem
lan
se nuk kam qef per mejdan

nji amanet nana me ka lan
345 fjalet te mija kurr mos me e ngran
as kujte rrugen mos me ja
leshue
me i zâ te idhët Musa i asht
germue
ka don djal me dal ti permbi
mue
paska qit Marku e i paska than
350 mos te vin çudë Muso Qesexhi

se me ka fal Zoti mejdanxhi
a thua zanin ti nuk ma ki ndi

qi mua me thone Krajleviçe
Marku
qi boll shum herrna kam dal ne
mejdan
355 qi deri sod ska mujet kush me
ma lan
paska fol atherna Musë Shqiptari
ti nuk je Krajleviçë Marku
se aj ka pa mbajte petkat prej
boje gjakut
nji as dy Marku nuk ka bâ

You are young and it is sheer
madness for you to die.
Where have you been, youth,
and have they told you
that this very road is not open,
and how many brave men have
perished here,
340 and that Musa still is not
intimidated."
Marko addressed him and said:
"I implore you, Musa, to let me
pass along this road
Because I have no desire for a
fight.
My mother left me a mandate:
345 Never to eat my own words
And never to yield the road to
anyone."
Musa thundered in an angry
voice:
"You dare, youth, to ride over
me?"
Marko addressed him and said:
350 "Do not be surprised, Musa
Qesexhi,
For God has made me a fighter.
Haven't you by any chance
heard of my fame?
I am called Marko Kraljević.

I have come out to duel many a
time,
355 yet to this day no one has been
able to defeat me."
Then Musa the Albanian spoke:
"You are not Marko Kraljević,
because he wears clothes the
color of blood."
Marko did not hesitate a second:

360 e ka hjek setren maxharesh
e i kan dal petkat prej boj gjakut

athere e pau Musa Qesexhi
se u perpoq trimin mejdanxhi

me i za te idht Musa i ka berit

365 njetash besa Mark nau ka prish

Musa doren ne xhep e paska shti
e ka nxjerre nji topuzin e randë
fort me krah prej Markut e ka dhan
shka po bon aj Krajleviçe Marku
370 me dorë shmbajti topuzin ja dobit
ton cope cope ne sokak ja ka bâ

e ka nxjerre Marku nji topuz
e sa idht Musen e paska gjue
me dore te djatht Muso e ka dobitë
375 ton copë copë ne sokak ja ka bâ

Ndihmo Zot e trimat bajne jurruq
ballë per ballë gjokat i kan ndesh
dy per i herë shpatat i kan hjek

dy ne shoj shojni per i herë kun sjelle
380 të per të shpatat i kun ndesh

ngatsat te ndezuna në tokë kun qitë
copa mishit shoj shojni tue pre

dy gjokat me gjak i kun lâ

360 he took off his Magyar jacket
and his clothes the color of blood began to show.
Then Musa Qesexhi realized
that he had encountered a courageous fighter.
Musa thundered in an angry voice:
365 "Our besa, Marko, as of now is broken!"
Musa put his hand in his pocket
and took out a heavy mace.
He aimed it with great force at Marko.
What did Marko Kraljević do?
370 He caught the mace in his left hand
and dashed it to pieces on the cobblestone alley.
Marko took out a mace,
he hurled it angrily at Musa.
Musa caught it in his right hand,
375 and dashed it to pieces on the cobblestone alley.
God help them, the heroes charged!
Their horses met head to head,
the two drew their swords at the same time.
The two struck at each other at the same time,
380 their swords met blade against blade
and sent flaming chunks to the ground.
Cutting to pieces each other's flesh,
they drenched their two horses in blood.

ndihmo Zot e qe paskan bân luftë
385 deri ne grusht shpatat i kun
    keputë
e prej gjokash n'tokë jan ulë

fytë per fytë trimat jan dobitë

tre sahat jan dredh e jan
    shperdredh
deri ka bâ nata per me u err
390 me te foli Krajliviçe Marku
shpetyë ne tokë Musa Qesexhi

se me jarg ja kam ndue
kopilan Marku paska ndodhë
kur ne tokë Musa ka shpetye
395 copa gjakut per gojet ka qit

pashka qit Marku i ka than
shka keshtu Muso qi qenke
    lodhë
kur u shpetye ne tokë Krajleviçe
    Marko
bardhë si bora shpetymen e ka
    qitë
400 Me te foli Krajli Viçe Marko
shtrengoj kambët Musa Qesexhi
se njitash zemren ta kam shkye

athere Musen kambet e kun
    leshue
e nen vedi Marku e ka shti
405 edhe ne fyt Marku e ka
    shtrengue
dekun ne tokë Musen e paska bâ

shka ka bâ Krajleviçe Marku
e ka marrë nji shpaten te keputun
edhe ne bark Musen e ka cile
410 edhe zemren e paska nxjerre

God help them for battling!
385 To the point they shattered
    their swords at the hilt.
They dropped to the ground off
    their horses,
the heroes grappled hand to
    hand.
For three hours they turned and
    twisted
even until night was about to fall.
390 When Marko Kraljević spoke:
"Spit on the ground, Musa
    Qesexhi,
for I am covered with saliva!"
Marko proved to be clever indeed.
When Musa spit on the ground
395 he let fly drops of blood from
    his mouth.
Marko addressed him and said:
"How is it, Musa, that you are
    tired?"
When Marko Kraljević spit on
    the ground,
he let fly spittle as white as
    snow.
400 Then Marko Kraljević spoke,
"Brace your legs, Musa Qesexhi,
Because I am now going to cut
    your heart out."
Then Musa's legs let go,

and Marko threw him under him.
405 And Marko tightened his grip
    on his throat
and strangled Musa to death on
    the ground.
What did Marko Kraljević do?
He took a shattered sword
and struck Musa in the stomach.
410 And he took out his heart,

e per gjyse me shpate e paska da	He divided it in half with the sword.
tre gjiarpi mbren ja paska gjet	He found three snakes inside it:
dy te voglit çue jan qene	the two small ones were awake,
nji aj ma i madhi ne gjumë paska qene	the largest one was asleep.
415 me pa bâ tre gjarpinat per me u çue	415 Had the three snakes been alert
kurr s'kish muejt Marku me e pre	Marko would never have been able to slay him.
i ka marrë kryte Muses Qesexhi	He took the head of Musa Qesexhi
e i ka ra gjokut ne shpine	and jumped on the back of his grey-white horse.
ne vrap e leshon Vidke Bedevine	He let Vidke Bedouin run at a gallop,
420 fill te Mbrete kish nise me shkue	420 he set off heading straight for the Emperor,
kryte e Muses mbretit ja ka çue	he delivered Musa's head to the Emperor.
e sa fort Mbreti atherë a gezue	How delighted the Emperor was then!
Ndihmo Zoti Mbrete shka ka bamë	God help him, what did the Emperor do?
u nep haber krajlave te tanë	He sent a message to all the kings
425 per me bâ gjith bota nji denom	425 for the whole world to celebrate.
po shprazë Mbreti top e havan	The Emperor fired his cannons and mortars,
dymbdhete dit dasmen po e ban	making the celebration last twelve days,
i ban shyqyrin Muses Qesexhise	expressing gratitude for the death of Musa Qesexhi.
ashtu bajne gjith krajlat e krajlisë	All the kings of the kingdom do the same.
430 lavdrim muer Kraileviçe Marku	430 Marko Kraljević accepted their praise,
i vetmi ky qi kete luft e bani	he alone fought the battle.
po shtetit Marku po ban qef	Marko strolled about and did as he pleased,
po ma thrasin Krajla per meret	the Kings invited him to receptions

e i kan dhan lavderim e gajret

435 po i vjen Markut nata e emnit
vet

e ju çon lajme miq e probatina

qi per emen te gjith per me i
ardhë

kokra kokra kan nise tue ju
mbledhë

treqind vetë e ma teper jan bâ

440 jau fillon per nder dhe qirom

mjaft nder te bukur Marku pe ju
ban

nanes vet Marku i paska than

due ne pazar nanë nji herë me
ra

disa sende me lypet per me i
marrë

445 nana vet ka qit e i ka thanë

pash nji Zot Mark qi te ka dhanë

te ka fal Zoti shum rrezikqar

pushkë me vedi te lutem mos
me marrë

pse gjith sa herë pushken qi po
merrë

450 pa vra gjin ti Mark kurr nuk
vjen

sod me e marre pushken me vedi

mire po e di qi diko ke me vra

naten e emnit sod po e kena

sod s'asht haku kon me i idhnue

455 a s'asht haku kon me i damtue

and gave him fervent praise.

435 As the eve of Marko's name day
approached,

he sent news to his friends and
blood brothers

that they all come for his name
day.

When they began assembling
little by little

there were more than three
hundred of them.

440 He welcomed them with honor
and praise,

Marko honored them quite
beautifully.

Marko said to his mother:

"Mother, before anything else I
want to go to the market place

to get a few things I need."

445 His mother addressed him and
said:

"For the love of God who gave
you life, Marko,

God has made you a dangerous
person.

I beg you not to take your rifle
with you,

for whenever you do take your
rifle

450 you never come back without
having killed someone.

If you take your rifle today,

I know full well you will kill
someone.

Today is the eve of your name day,
it is not right to get angry.

455 it is not right to injure anyone,

sa kjo miqesi per gezim jan
bashkue

nanen e vet Marku e ka ndigjue
pushkë me vedi Markun nuk ka
marrë
e ka ra Marku ne pazar

460 ka krye pune e ka desht per me
dal
ne skele te detit Marku kur ka
dal
e ka ndih nji ushtimë tue ardh

ka prite pak se ka desht per me
pamë
kçyre po vjen nji djal si duhi

465 kishte hipe djali ne vrash t'zi

edhe i del Marku para tij
tungatjeta i thotë More Zotni

ka je nise keshtu per me shkue

a prej ka je emnit shka te thonë

470 ka zane vend aj djali e po e
shikjon
ne paçë qef ti djal per me e ditë
prej Stambollit fisin po e kam
e prej vakthit Shqiptar po jam
per emen me thone Bergjanine
Gjemi
475 jam i vllau i Muses Qesexhi
nuk kam pas tjeter veç njat vlla

ma ka pre Krajleviçe Marku
due me shkue ne oxhak per me i
ra

because your friends and rela-
tives have gathered for a
celebration."
Marko obeyed his mother,
he did not take his rifle with
him.
Marko quickly entered the
market place,
460 he finished his business and
wanted to get out.
When Marko got out on a pier
by the sea
he heard a distant rumble
approaching.
He waited a while because he
wanted to see it:
he saw a youth riding like a
windstorm.
465 The youth was mounted on an
ominous black horse,
and Marko went out before him.
"Long life to you, my lord!—he
says to him—
Where do you think you are
going like this?
Where are you from and what is
your name?"
470 The youth came to a stop and
looked at him.
"If it pleases you to know, youth,
my family is from Stambol
and I am an Albanian by blood.
My name is Bergjanine Gjemi,
475 I am the brother of Musa Qesexhi.
I had no other brother but that
one,
Marko Kraljević killed him.
I want to go and attack his
family.

edhe emnin kam ndie se e ka

480 e i ka mbledhe miq e probatina

e i ka mbledhe ilakët gjith ka i
ka
rrafsh me tokë due per me i bâ

me ja prish robnien e miqesinë

e me e nzanë Krajleviçe Markun
485 e ne Stamboll due per me e çue
e nji send hyçmet due ne to me
bâ
e per se gjallit due per me e rrjepe
gjalle ne dhe kam per me e shti
e me marre gjiakun Muses
Qesexhi
490 Me te fol Kraileviçe Marku
kadalë djal ma andej ske se
shkon
se kurr ma i lireshem s'em
kishte gjet
e me ke gjet ma pushke e pa
thike
e nana ema sod me past ne qafë

495 qi s'em la sod pushken per me e
marrë
se ti paske pushken me vedi
pat me krye Bergjanine Gjemi

tash bje djal e ty ta dasht Zoti

se un jam Krajleviçe Marku
500 qi ta kam pre Musen Qesexhi
e ja kam marrë vet kryte e tij
e ja kam çue Mbretit ne Turki

athere Gjemi bani jurruq prej tij

And I have heard he has a name
day
480 and has gathered his friends
and blood brothers.
He has gathered all the relatives
he has.
I want to flatten them to the
ground,
to ruin his close family and
friends,
and to capture Marko Kraljević,
485 and send him off to Stambol.
I want to pass judgment on
them
and I want to skin him alive.
I will bury him in the ground alive
and avenge the blood of Musa
Qesexhi."
490 Marko Kraljević spoke up:
"Calm down, youth, you do not
have to go any farther,
for you could never find me
more exposed.
You have found me without a
rifle and without a knife.
Today my mother pleaded with
me
495 and kept me from taking my
rifle with me.
You do have your rifle with you
so you have the advantage,
Bergjanine Gjemi.
God has now granted you your
wish, young man,
for I am Marko Kraljević
500 who killed Musa Qesexhi.
I took his head
And sent it to the Emperor in
Turkey."
Then Gjemi lunged at him.

kamb te para i çoj ka vrançi i zi

505 dy patkoj ne gjokse ja ka vue
e nen vedi vrançi e ka zaptue

kçyre me pâ Gjemin qe ka punue
kamsh e duersh Markun e ka
lidhe
edhe ne vrançç Markun e ka vue

510 per Stamboll athere asht fillue
kur ka ra ne i pazar kaurit

shum zotni para i kan dal

i kan dal vojvode e bajraktar

shum rigja Gjemit po i bajne

515 me na fal Krajleviçe Markun

po ti napim tri mushka me pare

pashka qit Gjemi ju ka thanë
due hatrin ju me jau kecyre
bim ni paret se njerin po jau
leshoj

520 ja kau prue tri mushka me pare

ka marrë parat njerin se leshon

kur ka ra ne atë shelerin e
keshtanimit
jan mbledhe pari e Zotni

e po shikjojne Krajleviçen
Markun
525 qi po shikjojne taksirat i zi qi
kish i mri

His ominous black horse raised
its forelegs,

505 it planted two hoofs on his chest,
and the black horse pinned him
under itself.
Consider seeing what Gjemi did.
He bound Marko by his legs and
arms
and he placed Marko on the
black horse.

510 Then he set out for Stambol.
When he entered an infidel
market place
any lords came outside to see
him.
Chieftains and standard-bearers
came out,
they made many entreaties to
Gjemi:

515 "If you turn over Marko
Kraljević to us
we will give you three mule-
loads with money."
Gjemi addressed them and said:
"I want to see your appreciation.
Bring the money and I will
release the man."

520 They brought him three mule-
loads with money.
He took the money but would
not release the man.
When he entered the Christian
city
the leading dignitaries and lords
gathered
and were looking at Marko
Kraljević,
525 even looking at the great misfor-
tune that had befallen him.

i bajne regja Bergjanine Gjemit

me na u fal Krajleviçe Markun

po te napim tri mushka me pare

paska qit Gjemi jau ka thonë
530 bimni paret se njeriu po ja
    leshoj
ja kan prue tri mushka me para

ka marre paret njeriu s'ja leshon

e ju ka bâ gjashte mushka me
    para
ka marrë rrugen Gjemi e po
    shkon
535 e me ka ra ne pazarin e Turkisë

shum pari perpara ju ka dal
po e rrethojne Beglerr e
    Pashalar
po e shikjojne Krajleviçin Markun
qi i kish mri aj taksirat i zi

540 shum gajret me goj i kau dhanë

rrigja te madhe me goj i kau
    bamë
pash i Zot Bergjanine Gjemi
me na u fal Krajleviçe Markun
ton e kena mik e dashmirë
545 ne besin tonin ku iman nuk asht

por noj te keqe prej tij nuk e
    dimë
po ti napim tri mushka me pare

bimni paret se po jau fali

They made entreaties to
    Bergjanine Gjemi:
"If you turn Marko Kraljević
    over to us
we will give you three mule-
    loads with money."
Gjemi addressed them and said:
530 "Bring me the money and I will
    release the man."
They brought him three mule-
    loads with money.
He took the money but would
    not release the man,
which gave him six mule-loads
    with money.
Gjemi took to the road and went
    on.
535 He came to a Turkish market
    place,
many dignitaries came out.
Beys and pashas were
    surrounding him
and looking at Marko Kraljević
whom—ay!—great misfortune
    had befallen.
540 Many words of support came
    from their mouths,
They made strong entreaties to
    Gjemi.
"For God's sake, Bergjanine Gjemi,
turn Marko Kraljević over to us.
He is a benevolent friend of ours,
545 even though he does not believe
    in our faith in Allah.
We know of no trouble coming
    from him,
we will give you three mule-
    loads with money."
"Bring me the money and I will
    release him to you."

ja kun prue tri mushka me para

550 ka marre parat njeriun s'jau
    leshon
i ka bâ nandë mushka me pare

e i ka marre bjeshkët perpjetë
ne qjyse bjeskvet kur ka dal

kun zanë vend aty e po
    pushojne
555 paska qite Gjemi e ka fol
pa ndigjiove Krajleviçe Marku
a din kund ndoj gure me uje

se rrezi ilet jam bâ
ti mos dijsh kund ndoj gurë me
    uje
560 shpate ne qafe due me te pre

ne kapzer tand gjakun do ta pri

paska qite Markun i ka thanë
me kso fjalshë e korritë Turkinë

djali mire e prej oxhakut mirë
565 gjake kaurit si the me pi

tue qene vllau i Muses shum
    daji
edhe i sahat në muejsh me
    qindrue
nji lakant ne bjeshk na ka qillue

asht nji çik mbrend ne lakant
570 mjaft e bukur çika per me e pâ
pasunie Zoti i ka dhan
e ka laukanten si mali me borë

They brought him three mule-
    loads with money.
550 He took the money but would
    not release the man,
which gave him nine mule-loads
    with money.
He set out for the highlands.
When he came halfway up the
    highlands,
he found a spot there and
    rested.
555 Gjemi addressed him and said:
"Listen to me, Marko Kraljević,
Do you know of any spring with
    water anywhere,
for I am dying of thirst?
If you do not know of any spring
    with water
560 I will cut your neck with my
    sword:
I will drink the blood from your
    throat!"
Marko addressed him and said:
"With these words you have
    shamed Turkey!
A fine boy from a fine family,
565 how can you think of drinking
    the blood of an infidel,
you being the brother of the
    noble Musa?
If you can hold up for one more
    hour
We will make it to an inn in the
    highlands.
There is a girl inside the inn,
570 A girl quite beautiful to behold.
God has given her means,
she keeps an inn as clean as
    mountain snow,

si ne qytet zotni ska do te
    kerkojsh
nuk ka pasë tjeter veç i vlla

575 me pushk teme vetë ja kam vra
driten e djellit çikes ja kam tha

bashk katili sajna vet po jam
kur te me çojsh ti mue aty rob
    zan
çikat para ty ka me te dal
580 ka me than kjoft kjo dit e
    bardhe
ka me pritë e ka me te prefarit

se ka çika shoqen ne shtate
    krajlit
ka me te dhan faqet dhe sytë

ka me te dhan me hanger edhe
    me pi
585 edhe gjith sa duesh ti me marrë
    flori
se hazmi saj vet kam qillue
me te shpejt Gjemi e ka hutue
sum merak ne krye ju ka gujue
skan vonue dhe jan fillue
590 ne majet bjeshkes kur kun
    shkue
bash lakanta ne vend ka qillue
kur i dalin lakantes per ballë

Marku Gjemiti ka qit e i ka than
bezaj nje herë oj Danusha e
    bardhë
595 del nji herë me mue me u pamë

me te shpejt Gjemi çikes i ka
    bezâ

you will not find the likes of it
    among the lords in the city.
She did not have anyone besides
    one brother,
575 I killed him myself with my rifle.
I have taken away the light of
    the girl's sun,
I am her murderer as well.
When you take me there as a
    captive
the girl will come out to meet you.
580 She will say 'May this be my
    lucky day!'
She will receive you and wait on
    you,
for the girl has no equal in the
    Seven Kingdoms,
she will give you her face and
    eyes,
she will give you something to
    eat and to drink,
585 and all the florins you want to
    take
because I am her blood-enemy."
He quickly confused Gjemi,
great concern entered his head.
They did not delay, but set out.
590 When they reached the top of
    the highlands
the inn was right on the spot.
When they came in front of the
    inn
Marko addressed Gjemi and said:
"Call out at once: 'O Danusha
    the White,
595 come out at once so I can see
    you.'"
Gjemi quickly called out to the
    girl:

del nji herë moj Danusha e
    bardhe
se ta kom prue gjaksin e vllaut

se ty e mua te dyve na ka fikë

600 e Zoti e vraft ketë kaurr e kjo
    ditë
me te shpejt çika jashte paska dal
ka hapt syt çika e i ka pamë

ja ka nise çika e po kjan
ty te ruejte i madhi Zot bre djal

605 bash nji ky mue me vra vllan

driten e diellit mua ma ka
    thamë
urdhno mbrend daije Zotni
shka urdhnon me ngran e me pi

muhabetin e kun marrë mahi

610 te dy bashk mbrend paskan hi
shka ka bâ kjo Danusha e bardhe

ja ka qit rakies nji barr
e perpare Gjemit ja ka vue
se te pini gjumi per me e marrë

615 ne dore e meri Bergjanine Gjemi

tu vrite ndera çikë e lezeti

dyvet sod nau ka kryë qefti

ka pi goten e ka çue deri ne
    gjyse

"Come out at once, O Danusha
    the White,
for I have brought you your
    brother's killer.
For he has brought ruin to you
    and me both.

600 May God this day strike this
    infidel dead!"
The girl quickly came outside,
she opened her eyes and saw
    them,
The girl started to cry.
"May almighty God watch over
    you, oh boy,
605 this is the very one who killed
    my brother.
He has blotted out my light of
    the sun!
Please come inside, noble lord.
What does it please you to eat
    and to drink?"
They struck up a playful
    conversation,
610 the two went inside together.
What did this Danusha the
    White do?
She put an herb into some raki
and set it before Gjemi
so that sleep would overcome
    him when he drank it.
615 Bergjanine Gjemi took it in his
    hand:
"May your honor and looks
    increase, girl.
both our wishes have been
    fulfilled today!"
He drank the glass halfway
    down,

po i vjen gjum e po i voglohen syt	sleep was coming over him and his eyes were getting smaller.
620 paska qit e i ka than mori çikë	620 He addressed the girl and said: "Oh, girl,
due me fjet se me gjasë jam i ligë	I want to sleep because it appears I am ill."
me te shpejt çika shtratin ja ka shtrue	The girl quickly made his bed.
sa po ulet Gjemi me pushue	As soon as Gjemi lay down to rest
atherë gjumi nise me ju rendue	His sleep there and then began to get deeper.
625 gjumi randë atherna e ka kap	625 Then a deep sleep overtook him,
ja ka nise Gjemi po kerrhat	Gjemi started to snore.
nisi çika atherë me u halakat	The girl then began to become distracted.
me i zanë te madh çika po vikat	In a loud voice the girl cried out:
o ku je ti Krajleviçe Marku	"Hey, where are you, Marko Kraljević?
630 po ti e ke nji miknesh te marre	630 You sure do have one deranged lady friend!"
te baft mire ty Danush e bardhë	"Good luck to you, O Danush the White!"
mire te vuna në gjum ketë budall	"I have put this fool to sleep!"
me te shpejt çika jasht ka dal	The girl quickly came outside,
ka hap syte Marku e ka pamë	Marko opened his eyes and saw her.
635 Marku qesh e çika nisë e kjam	635 Marko laughs and the girl starts to cry,
njatherë çikes ka nise e i ka ra mallë	compassion suddenly overcame the girl.
e sheh Markun lidhe ne dorë e kamb	She saw Marko bound hand and foot.
me te shpejt limen çika paska marre	The girl quickly picked up a file,
tre fije hekura me limë i ka premë	she cut through three bands of iron with the file,
640 njathere Markun me shpejt e ka zgidhe	640 then quickly set Marko free.
shka ka bâ Krajleviçe Marku	What did Marko Kraljević do?

paska hi tu çika ne atë lakant
e i ka gjet hekura prej fabrikes
kambash e duersh Gjemin e ka
lidhë
645 trup te dekun ne dyshek e ka
lan
qef te bukur me çiken athere po
bon
shka kun desht me pi e me
ngran
dy sahat pushim qi kun bamë
athere gjumi Gkemit i ka dal
650 a ska mujet me luejt kamb as
dorë
ka hap syt e te dy bashk i ka pa

ndihmo Zot te madhë qef tue bâ

pashka qit Gjemi e jau ka thanë
boft mire tue pi e tuej ngran
655 pa ndigjove more Mark Sokoli
me taman tue te paska godite Zoti
kush asht i zoti kjoft i bardh
moti
atherë a çue Krajleviçi Marku
ka shtrengue nandë mushka me
pare
660 ka marrë lidhun Bergjanine
Gjemin
e halal me çik a bâ

e a dredh Marku per me ardhe
kur ka ra ne ate sheherin e
Turkisë
tan Zotnit perpara i kan dal
665 kur me sye Markun e kun pamë

jan çudite shum seri ju ka ardhë

He entered the girl's inn,
he found factory-finished irons.
He bound Gjemi by his legs and
arm
645 and left his dead weight body
on the mat.
Then he enjoyed himself with
the girl,
He drank and ate what he
wanted,
taking a rest for two hours.
Then Gjemi woke up,
650 he was not able to move his legs
or arms.
He opened his eyes and saw the
two of them together,
God help them, having a great
time.
Gjemi addressed them and said,
"Enjoy your drinking and eating!
655 Listen to me, O Mark Sokoli:
God has created you just right,
Good luck follows the clever
man."
Then Marko Kraljević stood up.
He harnessed the nine mule-
loads with money,
660 he took Bergjanine Gjemi
tightly bound
and said his fond farewells to
the girl.
Marko turned away to return.
When he came to that Turkish
city,
all the lords came out.
665 When they saw Marko with
their own eyes
they were amazed, quite over-
come with surprise.

u falet nderes Krajleviçe Marku	Marko Kraljević thanked them,
jau ka dhan tri mushkat me pare	he gave them three mule-loads with money.
e bajn kabull Markut me ja fal	They agreed to offer them to Marko,
670 se pranon Marku si ka marrë	670 Marko refuses to accept them.
kur ka ra ne ate sheherin e keshtanimit	When Marko entered the Christian city
ton parija para i paskan dal	all the nobles came out,
jau serit per Markun kur e panë	They were surprised when they saw Marko.
tonvet nderes Marku kenka fal	Marko thanked them all,
675 jau ka dhan tri mushka me pare	675 he gave them three mule-loads with money.
kan desht paret mos me i marrë	They did not want to take the money,
por me zorr Marku jau ka lanë	but Marko with difficulty left it for them.
e kun percjell me qef e me mallë	They saw him off with joy and compassion.
kur ka ra ne at sheherin e kaurit	When he entered the infidel city,
680 e rrethojne vojvode e Bajraktar	680 chieftains and standard-bearers surrounded him.
jan serit kur Markun e panë	They were astonished when they saw Marko,
u falet nderes e paret jau ka lanë	he thanked them and gave the money to them.
kun pas qef te tona me jau fal	They were all happy to offer it to him,
hiç kabull se ka bë me i marrë	Marko did not agree at all to take it.
685 kenka nise Marku per vatan	685 Marko set off for the homeland:
e ne vend vet Marku kur ka mbri	And when he reached his own place
i ka pa sarrajet me sy	he saw his palaces with his own eyes,
kishin ngul tonë bajraket te zi	they had raised all the black standards.
me te shpejt lajmin Markun jau ka çue	Marko quickly sent a message,

690 shpejt bajraket ka than per me i
    ndrrue
    se bash zote mue me ka ndihmue
    gjaksin lidhun e vet ka peshtue

    kçyre familje vet shka kun punue
    shpejt me gezim bajraket i kun
    ndrrue
695 e çon ne nji ode Gjemin e kan
    gujue
    atherë per se dytit emnin e ka
    fillue
    don e me lute e mire e don me e
    gezue
    shum dunjaja ma kishin pas
    rrethue
    mrekulli ti Mark ki punue
700 kçyre me i pâ krajlin shka ka bâ

    fill ne ode te Gjemi pashka
    shkue
    e i ka çue me pi e me ngran

    e muhabet ka nise me to po ban

    nji rigja me ty Gjemi po e kam

705 shum te lutem vllan per me ma
    fal
    e probatina bashk po duem men
    bamë
    e ne vend te vllaut gjithmonë ke
    mem pas
    pashka qi Gjemi e i ka than
    Pash ai Zot qi shpirtin ma ka
    dhane
710 krejt dunjaja bashk per me u
    bamë
    gjak me ty kush me pi s'me ban

690 He told them: "Change the stan-
    dards at once!
    For God himself has helped me,
    He saved me and have the
    avenger tightly bound."
    Consider what his family did.
    At once they joyfully changed
    the standards,
695 they put Gjemi in a room and
    locked him.
    Then for the second time he
    began his name day,
    wanting to celebrate it well and
    to enjoy it.
    A great multitude surrounded
    him:
    "You have done wonders, Marko!"
700 Consider seeing what the prince
    did:
    he went straight to Gjemi's
    room,
    he took him something to drink
    and to eat
    and started making conversa-
    tion with him.
    "I have one request for you,
    Gjemi.
705 I very much beg you to forgive
    me over your brother,
    and that together we become
    blood brothers,
    and I forever more take your
    brother's place."
    Gjemi addressed him and said:
    "For the sake of God who has
    given me life,
710 if the whole world were to try,

    it could never make me drink
    blood with you!"

pashka qit Marku i ka than	Marko addressed him and said:
nem pranofsh une gadi jam	"If you accept me I am ready,
ne mos ndigjove un skom shka baj	but if you won't hear of it, there is nothing I can do.
715 edhi nji herena due me te fal	715 I want to ask you once and for all to forgive me.
ty keso herët sdue me te damtue	I do not want to harm you at a time like this.
edhe njiherna due me te leshue	I want to release you once and for all."
paska qit Gjemi i ka than	Gjemi addressed him and said:
n'daç me e hjek vesvezin te ton	"If you want to remove all melancholy
720 sod mem pre dhe mem vorrue	720 kill me and bury me today,
skena punë pse me e sgjatue	there is no reason to prolong it.
se pasha Zotin qi kjoft lavdue	For the sake of God who must be praised,
e pasha letrat qi i kam shkrue	and for the sake of the letters that I have written,
e tridhete dite qi ka agjinue	and the thirty days that I have fasted,
725 ja vrasë ty ja vretë ti mue	725 either I will kill you or you will kill me!"
me te shpejt Marku e paska leshue	Marko quickly released him,
e ka percjelle e a nise me shkue	He saw him off and started to leave.
keshtu me kun than kun bamun motit	This is the way they acted, I have been told, in bygone times.
na koft e paçim ndihmen prej Zotit	May we ever have God's help.

LAN 34. Marash Nika, *Kanga e Ali Pashë Gusinjes*

Marash Nika; Abat (Shala); September 15, 1937
Kanga e Ali Pashë Gusinjes
The Song of Ali Pasha of Gusinje
Historical song

	Shka ka bâ Knazi i Malit zi	What did the Prince of Montenegro do?
	çoj e thirri Knazi Pop Ilia	The prince rose and summoned the priest Ilia,
	çoj e thirri Markun e Milanit	he rose and summoned Mark Milani,
	çoj e thirri Todore Milanin	he rose and summoned Todore Milani:
5	a ndigjoni burra per nji fjalë	5 "Listen, men, to my words.
	si tja bajme thote Plaves e Gusinjes	What are we going to do—he says—about Plav and Gusinje?
	si tja bajme thote Pejes e Djakoves	What are we going to do—he says—about Peja and Gjakova?
	qajre Zoti mue nuk me ban	God leaves me no choice
	per pa i marrë nen hyqem me i shi	but to take them and place them under my power."
10	keçyre e ç'foli Todore Milani	10 Consider what Todore Milani said:
	tungatjeta Knaze Gospodari	"Long life to you, Prince and Master!
	fjalen tande bytheprap smun ta dredhi	I can not turn back your words,
	po si te na thujsh duhet me te ndigjue	for we must heed what you tell us."
	kish pa fol q'athere Pop Ilia	Then the priest Ilia said:
15	tungatjeta Knaze Gospodari	15 "Long life to you, Prince and Master!

	mem ndigjue ma mire ty te bjen	You had better heed me.
	se s'mund i marrim Pejen as Djakoven	We can not take Peja and Gjakova,
	se s'mund i marrim Plaven as Gusinje	we can not take Plav and Gusinje,
	se ka e ka hyçmin mbreti si sundon	because the Emperor has the power to control them.
20	shefëtar ma te fort kerkund nuk ka	20 Stronger border guards are nowhere to be had."
	q'atherë foli trimi Mark Milani	The hero Mark Milani spoke:
	tungatjeta thotë Knaze Gospodari	"Long life to you, Prince and Master!
	mem i dhan dymedhete mij asqer	If you give me twelve thousand soldiers
	bukë e pushk sa te due me marre	and all the food and guns I want to take,
25	un ti marrë Pejen e Djakoven	25 I will take Peja and Gjakova,
	un ti marre Plaven e Gusinjen	I will take Plav and Gusinje."
	n'jathere Knazi ne kamb kenka çue	Thereupon the Prince rose to his feet,
	ne dy faqe tha Marku e k'i puth	he kissed Mark on both cheeks:
	ta pashe hajrin Marku i Milanit	"May good fortune be yours, Mark Milani,
30	se bash si djalit ti mue me dhimesh	30 for I care for you like a son.
	nuk ti jap dymedhete mij asqer	I will not give you twelve thousand soldiers,
	por un ti jap njezet mij asqer	but I will give you twenty thousand soldiers.
	bukë e pushkë sa duesh me marrë	and all the food and guns you want to take."
	Mark Miiani nji leter e ka shkrue	Mark Milani wrote a letter,
35	ndoj tartarit ne dore ja ka dhan	35 he put it in the hand of a rider:
	shko ja ço Ali Pashe Gusinjes	"Go and deliver it to Ali Pasha of Gusinje!"
	ti si je i thote Komandar Gusinje	"You who are—he says—the commander of Gusinje,

fal me shndet thote Marku i
  Milanit
nji kafshat bukë thotë gadit me
  ma bâ
40 se neser mbrama ne konak ti me
  kije
p'e merre Pasha letren e p'e
  kendon
çon e thirri Begleret te tone

çoj e thirri arg e bajraktar

çoj e thirri esnafet e sheherit

45 çoj e thirri djelt e mire k'a jan

a me ndigjoni burra u ka than
Mark Milani nji leter na ka çue
fal me shndet Ali Pashë Gusinjes

nji kafshat bukë gadi mem a bâ
50 se neser mbrama ne konak t'im
  e ke
a doni me e leshue trima a me
  qindrue
bese te madhe te tone i kin dhan
qi per pa dek nu' gjegjena me
  leshue
Ali Pasha gjokut i ki hip

55 te Begolli tha ne Peje kerka râ
çoj e thirri Haxhi Zek Byberri

çoi e thirri trimin Bajram Begun

çoj e thirri trimin Hasan Begun
çoj e thirri begleret te tane

Mark Milani—he says—sends
  greetings.
Make ready for me, he says, a
  modest meal,
40 for tomorrow evening you will
  be entertaining me."
The Pasha takes the letter and
  reads it.
He rose and summoned all the
  beys,
he rose and summoned the agas
  and standard-bearers,
he rose and summoned the
  guildsmen of the town,
45 he rose and summoned the
  finest lads anywhere.
"Listen to me, men—he said —
Mark Milani has sent us a letter:
'Greetings to Ali Pasha of
  Gusinje—he says —
make ready for me a modest meal,
50 for tomorrow evening you will
  be entertaining me.'
Do you want to give in to him,
  my heroes, or to stop him?"
They all swore a binding *besa*
to resist giving in to him as long
  as they are alive.
Ali Pasha mounted his white
  horse,
55 he rose to Begolli in Peja.
He rose and summoned Haxhi
  Zek Byberri,
he rose and summoned the hero
  Bajram Beg,
he rose and summoned the hero
  Hasan Beg,
he rose and summoned all the
  beys,

60	çoj e thirri Arg e Bajraktar
	o sa mire tha trimave ju kallzon
	Mark Milani leter nau ka çuem
	dojne me e marrë Pejen e Djakoven
	dojne me e marre Plaven e Gusinjen
65	a doni trima ju per mem ndihmue
	a mem kallzue se due per me e leshue
	gjith te ton tha besen ja kan dhanë
	Amon Zotit ushtries qi kan bâ
	po aj tre muej bashkim qi kan bâ
70	Mark Milani tha i Malit Zi
	drek ne Plave dark ne Gusinje
	mos u ngut i thote moj Çerngore
	se pot avitem me vapore
	ka i martine ne kamb n' dore
75	Mark Milani thotë po ban seri
	n'ate Noksiç qe em ka nxane sherri
	Mark Milani thote po ban bê
	ne ksi trimash kurr s'jam pre
	Mark Milani tha Mark Milica
80	nuk jam Shkodra e Podgoritza
	nuk jam Shkodra me fistana

60	he rose and summoned agas and standard-bearers.
	Oh, how well he reports to the heroes:
	"Mark Milani has sent us a letter.
	They want to take Peja and Gjakova,
	They want to take Plav and Gusinje,
65	do you want to help me, my heroes?
	Tell me if I need to surrender them."
	All of them gave him their *besa*.
	Good God, what an army they mustered,
	organizing it, hey, in three months!
70	"Mark Milani of Montenegro— he said —
	lunch in Plav, dinner in Gusinje?
	Do not act in haste, dear Montenegro,
	for we are approaching by boat,
	on the double, armed to the teeth."
75	Mark Milani was seeing
	that he was outfoxed at Novšiće.
	Mark Milani swore a *besa*:
	"I have never fought with such heroes!"
	"Mark Milani—he said—Mark Milica,
80	I am not Shkodra or Podgorica,
	I am not Shkodra wearing skirts

po jam Rogova me tagana

pa pevete Kuçin qa ti bana

shka ka Limi qi po shkon gjak

85   nuk po i çon trupat fort larg
     por ne Taslice e ne Vishegrad

but I am Rugova carrying
      yataghans!
Just ask the Kuçi what we have
      done,
and why the Lim is running
      blood red.

85   It is not carrying bodies very far
     just to Taslice and Visegrad."

LAN 39. Sokol Martini, *Kanga e Halilit kur asht martue*

Sokol Martini; Palc (Nikaj-Mërtur); September 17, 1937
Kanga e Halilit kur asht martue
The Song of the Wedding of Halil
Legendary song

	Lum per ty Zot kjofshim fal	Blessings on You, Lord, may we give thanks to You.
	kurr s'jam kan e Zoti nau ka dhanë	We would not be if God had not made us.
	shka ka ba aj Çeto Basho Muja	What did Çeto Basho Muji do?
	tridhetë argët ne gost mi ka mbledhun	He gathered the thirty Agas at a banquet,
5	mire po qet me ngran e me pi	he served them much to eat and to drink,
	po'm jau pjek ka i kafe sheqerli	he roasted them coffee with sugar,
	po'm jau qet venen me raki	he served them wine and raki,
	e i kan kap lafet po lafojne	and they got down to talking.
	kan qitë Mujit argët i kan thanë	The Agas addressed Muji and said:
10	Pash nji Zot Muji si t'ka dhanë	"For the sake of God who made you, Muji,
	pa martue Halilin pse e ki lan	why have you let Halil go unmarried?
	a e ke lan para se ske pas	Have you let him go because you have no money?
	a e ke lan se dazem s'muej ke bâ	Have you let him go because you cannot afford a wedding celebration?"
	q'athere Mujo shokevet u ka thanë	Then Muji said to his friends:

15   Pash aj Zot shokët si me ka
          dhanë
      se kam lan per pare si skam pas

      se kam lan dazem si smund kam
          bâ

      por kam shetitë dunjan rreth e
          rreth
      çike per to tha shoket s'mund
          kam gjet
20   se ku gjêj çiken miku s'me
          pelqen
      e ku gjêj mikun çika nuk vjenë
          gja
      q'atehere shoket Mujit i kan than
      Mik e çike tue ti gjême vet

      ne mundsh me votë te krajli i
          Maxharise
25   kerkun shoqin krajli nuk e kâ
      as kerkun shoqen çika nuk e kâ

      q'athere shokevet Muja ju ka than
      shuheni shoke juve Zoti ju vraft

      ju ç'aq fjal Halili me jau ndije
30   ndon krajlijë kryët ka me lan

      ndonse çiken krajlit me ja marrë

      mue pa vlla shokët doni m'em
          lan
      q'athere ndije ke Sokol Halili
      ish çue djali m'ish vesh e m'ish
          mbath
35   e m'ka marre at thiken
          helmatore
      e m'ka marre at shpaten
          xhaverdare

15   "For the sake of God who made
          me, my friends,
      I have not let him go because I
          do not have money,
      I have not let him go because
          I cannot afford a wedding
          celebration.
      But I have traveled all around
          the world,
      I have not been able, friends, to
          find a girl for him—he said—
20   for wherever I find the girl, I do
          not like the in-law,
      and wherever I find the in-law,
          the girl is not suitable."
      Then his friends said to Muji:
      "We will find you a girl and an
          in-law.
      If you can go to the King of
          Hungary.
25   The King has no equal anywhere,
          nor has the girl an equal
          anywhere."
      Then Muji said to his friends:
      "Be quiet, friends, may God
          strike you dead!
      If Halil were to hear such words,
30   either he would lose his life in
          the Kingdom
      or he would marry the King's
          daughter.
      You would leave me, friends,
          without a brother."
      Just then Sokol Halil heard that,
      the boy stood up and put on his
          clothes and shoes,
35   and he took his poisoned knife

      and his flintlock's bayonet.

q'athere Muja djalin ma ka pa
ka qit djalit Muja m'i ka than
e per frenit gjokun m'ja ka kap

40 ndal Sokol ty Zotit vraft

se kan shoket ty per me te rrêjte
se nuk ka çike krajli i Maxharisë

amon Zot si djali nuk me ish ndal
e tridhete argët perpara i k'in
dal
45 e bet n'Zotit djalit i k'in bâ

si ken pas ty per me të rrêjte
se nuk ka çike krajli i Maxharisë

be po ban aj Sokole Halili
si ne shtate krajli çiken ne mos
koft
50 ndo krajli kryët kam me e lan

ndo të kulla krajlit kam me e ra

nana e vet perpara i ka dal
Pash nji Zot nanes i ka than

Ti me fjal nane mos m'lig

55 e mos m'thuej nane per me u
ndal
hiç me e ndal nana nuk po i
thotë
veç kçyre qa qiti nana e ka bâ

Maxharisht djalin e ka vesh

e nji shishak skijesh ja ka venuë
60 kur të vejsh të krajli i Maxharisë

Just then Muji saw the boy.
He addressed the boy and said,
grabbing the reins of the white
horse:
40 "Stop, Sokol, may God strike you
dead!
For my friends have lied to you,
because the King of Hungary
has no daughter!"
By God, the boy did not stop.
The thirty Agas stepped out in
front of him,
45 and swore a *besa* to God to the
youth:
"We have indeed lied to you,
Because the King of Hungary
does not have a daughter."
Sokol Halil swears a *besa*:
"If I do not find the girl in the
Seven Kingdoms,
50 I will either lose my life in the
Kingdom,
or I will attack the tower of the
King."
His own mother came forward.
"For the sake of God—he said to
his mother—
do not make me angry, mother,
with your words,
55 and do not tell me to stop,
mother."
His mother does not tell him to
stop at all.
But consider what his mother
went and did:
she dressed the boy
Magyar-style,
and placed a Slavic cap on him.
60 "When you go to the King of
Hungary,

	mire pomozhe krajlit ke me i than	you will greet the King well.
	e të pevete krajli prej ka je	Should the King ask you where you are from,
	thuej jam i biri i Ladishe Pazhanit	Tell him 'I am the son of Ladishe Pazhani,
	mik të moçëm thuej babe të ka pas	you—tell him—were an old friend of my father.
65	e un kam ardh me ty per me ndej	65 I have come to stay with you.
	edhe me thonë per emen Gjuro Harambashi	And they call me by the name Gjuro Harambashi.'"
	atherë halalin nanes m'ja ka marrë	Then Halil received his mother's farewell blessing
	e per krajlije gjokun e ka shti	and urged his grey-white horse on towards the Kingdom.
	tim e mjegull gjokun po ma ban	· The grey-white horse raised a cloud of dust,
70	shtate parë bjeshk mrapa mi ka lan	70 it left seven highland meadows far behind
	n'shefi të krajlit q'atherë kenka hi	and then entered the border-lands of the King.
	e ne mejhan krajhli ish pa kan	The King was in a tavern.
	tridhetë shkije ne mejhan i kish pas	He had with him in the tavern thirty Slavs,
	me turbija djalin ma k'in pa	they had seen the boy through their field glasses.
75	ka qit krajli i Shkijevet e jau ka than	75 The King addressed the Slavs and said:
	nji musafir ne derë po na vjen	"A guest is coming to our door,
	si kurr me sy shoqin s'ja kem pa	I have never seen his equal."
	shpejt ne mejhan djali kenka hi	The boy quickly entered the tavern
	e mire pomozhe shkijet jau ka than	and he greeted the Slavs well.
80	sa mirë djali aty m'ja kau dredh	80 How well the boy tricked them!
	e në karrig djalin e kan ulë	They seated the boy on a chair
	edhe gjokun djalit ja kan mbajte	And took care of the boy's grey-white horse.
	m'i kan qit duhan kadaif	They offered him finely shredded tobacco,

e ja kan pjek kafen me sheqer

85 ja kan qit vênen e rakinë
q'atherë krajli e ka qit e po
    pevetë
a m'kallzon djal prej ka je

a m'kallzon emnit qysh te thonë

a ç'far tizaja ne krajli ty te ka
    prue
90 q'athere djali i ka nise e i kalzon
jam i biri i Ladishe Pazhanit
e m'thonë per emen Gjuro
    Harambashi
mik te moçëm baba të ka pas

e kam ardhë me ty per me ndej
95 q'atherë qiti krajli e i ka thanë

mik të moçem imand e kam pas
por ka dek aj Ladishe Pazhani
e kond n'oxhak m'ka than nuk
    ka lan
sa mire djali fjalen po m'ja
    kethen
100 imant baba mua m'ka dekë
e në barkut nanes baba mue
    m'ka lan
dyervet hallkut Zoti më ka fal

q'ather qiti krajli po mi thotë

mire se vjen thotë Gjuro
    Harambashi
105 gjith sa duesh me mue me ndej
ty ma të parin mas vedit kam
    me të vue
gjith shka t'duesh me ngran e
    me pi

---

they roasted him coffee with
    sugar

85 and offered him wine and raki.
Then the King addressed him
    and asked:
"Might you tell me, my boy,
    where you are from?
Might you tell me by what name
    they call you?
What matter has brought you to
    the Kingdom?"
90 Then the boy started to tell him:
"I am the son of Ladishe Pazhani,
They call me by name Gjuro
    Harambashi.
You were an old friend of my
    father,
I have come to stay with you."
95 Then the King addressed him
    and said:
"In truth he was my old friend,
but Ladishe Pazhani has died,
and he told me he had left no
    heir in his family."
How well the boy responded to
    these words:
100 "In truth my father has died,
but my father left me in my
    mother's womb,
God opened people's homes to
    me."
The King then spoke and said to
    him:
"It is good—he said—that you
    have come, Gjuro Harambashi,
105 stay with me as long as you want.
I will seat you first next to me,

to eat and drink as much as you
    want,

gjith shka t'duesh me vesh e me mbath	to put on as much clothing and footwear as you want."
malli i çikes atë djalin nuk e lan	Longing for the girl does not leave the boy.
110 i shikon kullat Krajli kapidanit	110 He keeps looking at the towers of the courageous King,
aj shtat katësh kullen ma k'i pas	he had a seven-story tower.
e në ma teprin çiken ma k'i shti	He put his daughter inside the highest one,
e shtate parë rroji çiken tuej rruejte	with seven guards guarding her.
q'ateherë djalin krajli m'ka marrë	Then the King took the boy,
115 e në sarraj me të qi ka shkue	115 and went to the palace with him.
e ka qit krajli nuses e i ka than	The King addressed his wife and said:
nji musafir mori nusa na i ka ardhë	"O bride, a guest has arrived,
kurr me sy shoqin s'ja kem pa	I have never seen his equal.
veç mue nji mik sonte me kan thirr	But a friend has called me away this evening,
120 e un ne vend t'em këta due me lan	120 and I want to leave him in my stead.
veç a merr vesh nuses i ka than	But do understand—he said to his wife—
mos le djalin ne Pazar per me dal	do not let the boy go out into the market place,
se ka dal nej harap prej detit	for an Arap has come out of the sea.
aj me sy djalin per me e pa	Should he set eyes on the boy,
125 ton copë copë djalin ka me e bâ	125 he would tear the boy to pieces."
q'atherë doren djalit po m'ja nep	Then he extends his hand to the boy,
e asht nise n'mik kenka shkue[1]	he set out to go see his friend,
e tu shpija djalin ma ka lan	and left the boy in his house.
kçyre qa qiti Halili e ka bamë	Consider what Halil went and did.

---

[1] A note added in the margin to the left of this line indicates that Martini "Has paused here to think about the rest of the song."

130 tri herë rrotull kulles mi ka
      ardhe
   hiç me sy at çiken nuk e sheh

   zemra ne bark djalit don me
      plasë
   e ment prej kreje djalit vinë me
      i dal
   se kund per xhamash çiken nuk
      e sheh

135 ne sarraj te Krajlit prap djali
      kenka hi
   e i ka qit krajlices e i ka than
   Pash nje Zot krajlices qi te ka
      dhanë
   petka argësh ketu ate qillojne

   se me ka ra qef mua per me i
      vesh
140 keçyre qa qiti krajlica e ka bâ

   fillë me atë ode me te shpejt
      kenka hi
   nji pal petka djalit ja ka çue

   si m'ishin kan t'argëvet
      t'Judbines
   bash si argë djalin m'ka vesh

145 e nji tanuz n'krye ja ka vue
   si ne dy krah tufa m'ka ra

   e n'oborr djali kenka dal

   e tri herë rrotull kulles mi ka
      ardh
   hiç me sy çika nuk e sheh

130 He walked around the tower
      three times,
   he did not set eyes on the girl at
      all.
   The boy's heart was about to
      burst in his belly,
   and the boy's senses came close
      to leaving him,
   because he could not see the
      girl anywhere through the
      windows.

135 The boy went back into the
      palace of the King.
   He addressed the Queen and said:
   "For the sake of God who made
      you, Queen,
   let them bring the clothes of
      Agas here
   for a desire to put them on has
      overcome me."
140 Consider what the Queen went
      and did.
   She went immediately into a
      room.
   She brought the boy an outfit of
      clothes
   that belonged to the Agas of
      Judbina.
   She dressed the boy just like an
      Aga
145 and placed a cap on his head,
   in such a way that tassels fell on
      both his shoulders.
   The boy went out into the
      courtyard
   and walked around the tower
      three times.
   The girl did not set eyes on him
      at all.

150 sa merak tha djali kenka bâ	150 How worried the youth became!
prej Pazarit syt mi ka leshue	He fixed his eyes on the market place
aj me sy arapin e ka pa	and with his own eyes saw the Arap.
n'drejte pazarit djali e ka m'sye	The boy ran straight for the market place,
e ne pazar djali kenka ra	the boy rushed into the market place.
155 ma kish pa aj arapi i detit	155 The Arap of the Sea saw him
e perpara djalit i ka dal	and came out in front of the boy.
ndal kadal tha Zoti të vraft	"Slow down—he said—may God strike you dead.
prej Judbine ty ç'ka pruë	What has brought you here from Judbina?"
shpatë per shpatë trimat qi ka sjellun	The heroes struck sword against sword
160 kater copash shpatat i kan bâ	160 and broke them into four pieces.
fyt per fyt n'atë kaldram si jan kap	They grabbed each other on the cobblestones by the throat,
kamben mrapa Sokoli ja qet	Sokol put his leg behind him
e perfundi arapin e ka vue	and threw the Arap down.
e ka nxirre thiken helmatore	He took out his poisoned knife
165 e ne bri harapit ja ka ngul	165 and plunged it into the Arap's ribs,
edhe dekun ne sakak e ka qitë	and he dropped him dead on the street.
tridhete pushka djalin e k'in gjue	Thirty rifles fired at the boy,
e pesë pushke at djalin ma k'in marrë	and five rifles struck the boy,
e pak gjalle djali m'ish kan mbet	and the boy was left barely alive.
170 nusja e krajlit q'athere kish pa ndije	170 The King's wife then learned of it.
tridhete shkije me vedi i ka marrë	She took thirty Slavs with her
edhe rrethin djalit m'ja ka qitë	And sent them to surround the boy.
e perdore djalit ja kan ngite	They raised the boy up in their arms,
tridhete vete vendit s'une luejn	thirty people could not budge him from the spot.

175 q'athere çika prej xhamesh ma
    k'i pa
   shpejt ne pazar çika kenka dal

   e perdore djalit ja ka ngit
   edhe ne kambë djalin ja ka çue
   e ne sarraje djalin e ka çue
180 e kish hip atë djalin ku rrin vetë

   sa hyzmetin djalit m'ja ka nise

   e ne minerë djalin po ma vënon
   shum heçima ne varrë po m'ja
    bjen
   e sa t'mira baret po m'ja vënon
185 e ka qit djalit e i ka than
   mos ki dert Gjuro Harambashi
   se besen e Zotit ty po ta ape
   si ne shtate Krajlije heçima gje
    kut jene
   kam me i prue ne varre me ti
    vënue
190 edhe baret ku te jenë ma të
    miret
   edhe ne koft kyzmet shpirti per
    me t'ë dal
   kur i fije vedja mos të dhimet

   se me gajret ty dekja po të vjen

   si e ke pre atë arapin e detit

195 e besen e Zotit ty po ta ape
   si n'kishë vorrin po ta bajme

   edhe prej florinit vorrin ta
    punojme
   edhe treqind popa te kryet po ti
    bimë

175 Then the girl saw him from the
    window.
   The girl quickly came to the
    market place.
   She raised the boy by the arm
   and lifted the boy to his feet.
   She sent the boy to the palace,
180 and moved the boy up to where
    she herself stayed.
   How much care she started
    showing the boy!
   She placed the boy on a sofa,
   she sought out many physicians
    to attend to his wounds.
   What fine herbs she put on them.
185 She addressed the boy and said:
   "Do not fear, Gjuro Harambashi,
   for I give you my *besa* to God,
   that wherever there are physi-
    cians in the Seven Kingdoms,
   I will get them to place on your
    wounds,
190 Also the best herbs, wherever
    they are.
   And if it be *kismet* that your
    spirit will leave you,
   never feel the least bit sorry for
    yourself
   for you will face death with
    courage,
   as you have killed the Arap of
    the Sea.
195 I give you my *besa* to God
   we will build you a tomb as in a
    church
   and decorate the tomb in gold.

   And we will get put three
    hundred priests at your head,

ty ne dhê popa me te vue	and the priests will bury you in the ground."
200 veç mendon Halil arga i ri	200 But Halil the Young Aga thinks it over:
une i mjeri vete paska than	"Woe is me—he said to himself—
ky hyzmet Zoti qysh e paska bamë	how could God allot me a fate such as this,
mue ne krajli shpirti per mem dal	that my spirit should leave me in the Kingdom,
e nde kishi vorrim me ma bâ	and my grave be built under a church,
205 mue me popa ne dhet mem vue	205 and priests bury me in the ground?"
q'atherë qiti çikes e i kalzon	Then he addressed the girl and informed her:
mue s'me thone Gjuro Harambashi	"They do not call me Gjuro Harambashi
po mue m'thone Halil arga i ri	but they do call me the young Aga Halil.
e ju kam ardhë ty kesh me te marrë	I have come to you to marry you.
210 kyzmet Zoti nuk e paska bâ	210 God did not grant me *kismet*."
q'athere qiti çika m'i ka than	Then the girl addressed him and said:
mos ki dert Sokole Halili	"Do not fear, Sokol Halil,
se besen e Zotit ty po te ape	for I give you my *besa* to God,
si ne shtatë krajli heçimet gjikund t'jen	that wherever there are physicians in the Seven Kingdoms,
215 e ku te jen baret ma te mirat	215 and wherever the best herbs are,
kam me i prue ne varët me ti vënue	I will get them to place on your wounds.
e per kyzmet keq skam me te lan	I will not leave you to bad fortune.
e ne koft kyzmet shpirti per me të dal	If it be the case that your spirit leaves you,
kur i fije vedja mos të dhimet	never feel the least bit sorry for yourself
220 se me gajret ty deka po të vjen	220 for you will face death with courage,

si ke pre atë Arapin e detit

edhe besen e Zotit ty po te api
si ne xhami vorrin po ta bajme

treqind hoxhe te kryet po t'i
    bimë
225 e me hoxhe ne dhêt po të
    vënojnë
prej florinit vorrin ta marojme
e ne koft kyz[m]et Zoti me te
    peshtue
une per burr ty due me te marrë
q'athere ndije aj Krajli ne
    Krajlije
230 edhe shpejt n'shpie krajli kenka
    ardhe
fill në sarraj te djali kenka hi

edhe djalit q'atehere mi ka than
mos ki dert o Gjuro Harambashi
se per hyzmet keq s'kam me të
    lan
235 ne shtate krajli heçimet gjikund
    jene
e gjikund t'jene baret ma të
    mirat
kam me i marre ne varë me ti
    vënue
ne koft kyzmet shpirti per me të
    dal
me gajret ty deka po te vjen
240 si ke pre atë Arapin e detit

besen e Zotit ty po ta api
si ne kish vorrin ta punoj

treqind popa te kryet po ti bije

as you have killed the Arap of
    the Sea.
And I give you my *besa* to God
we will build you a tomb as in a
    mosque,
and I will put three hundred
    hodjas at your head,
225 the *hodjas* will bury you in the
    ground,
we will finish the tomb in gold.
If it be the case God spares you,

I want to take you for a husband."
Then the King heard of this in
    the Kingdom.
230 The King came home at once,

and went straight to palace to
    see the boy.
And then said to the boy:
"Do not fear, O Gjuro Harambashi,
For I will not leave you in bad
    care.
235 Wherever there are physicians
    in the Seven Kingdoms,
and wherever the best herbs
    are,
I will get them to place on your
    wounds.
If it be the case that your spirit
    leaves you,
you will face death with courage
240 as you have killed the Arap of
    the Sea.
I give you my *besa* to God,
I will make you a tomb as in a
    church.
I will get you three hundred
    priests,

e me popa ne dhët kam me te vënue
245 prej florinit vorrin ta punoj
q'athere qiti djali e i ka than

unë nuk jam Gjuro Harambashi
po un jam Sokole Halili
e un kam ardh çiken me ta lyp

250 e kyzmet Zoti nuk e paska bâ

çiken tande unë per me e marrë
sa mire foli krajli kapidani

mos ki dert Sokole Halili
besen e Zotit ty po ta api
255 në shtate krajli heçimet gjikund t'jen
e gjikund t'jene barat ma te mirat
kam me i prue ne vare me ti vënue
e per hyzmet keq skam me te lan
koft kismet shpirti per me te dal

260 une ne xhami vorrin ta punoj

treqind hoxhe te krye po ti vënoj
e me hoxhe ne dhet kam me te vënue
koft kismet Zoti me te shpetue

edhe çiken vet po ta fali
265 sa hyzmet krajli po mi ban

e nji leter krajli e ka shkrue
ne Judbine Mujit po m'ja çon
ne daç sokolin me ardhë per me e pâ

and the priests and I will bury you in the ground.
245 I will decorate the tomb in gold."
Then the youth addressed him and said:
"I am not Gjuro Harambashi, but I am Sokol Halil.
I have come to ask for your daughter's hand,
250 And God has not granted me good kismet
to take your daughter away."
How well the courageous King spoke:
"Do not fear, Sokol Halil.
I give you my *besa* to God
255 wherever there are physicians in the Seven Kingdoms,
and wherever the best herbs are,
I will get them to place on your wounds.
I will not leave you in bad care.
If it be your lot that your spirit leaves you,
260 I will build you a tomb in a mosque.
I will put three hundred *hodjas* at your head
and the *hodjas* will bury you in the ground.
If it be your *kismet* that God spares you,
I will grant you my daughter."
265 How much care the King renders him:
The King writes a letter
and sends it to Judbina to Muji.
"If you like, come and see Sokol,

se pesë pushk djalin e kan
marrë

270 keçyre shka bani Çeto Basho
Muja

e ka shpraze aj pushken habertare

e kan ndije Judbine e krahina

tridhet Argaj aty m'ishin
mbledhun

e ka qit Argvet e ju ka than

275 Zoti ju vraft Arget qi jau ka
dhan

se fjala e juej pa vlla m'e ka lan

se në krajli djali me ka met

se pesë pushk djalin me kan
marrë

e me kan thirr me votë e me pa

280 e me vedi arget mi ka marrë

per krajli q'athere si m'jan nise

edhe ne rruge shokvet jau ka
than

bê t'Zotin Muja po m'u ban

si e ne Krajli mue mem korrit

285 tan cope cope me shpate kam
me u bâ

hiç per djal mos kini dert

kur te krajli q'athere ishin votë

e n'sarraje tu krajli kenkan hi

mire selam krajlit i kan dhan

290 mire selamin Krajli po m'jau
kethen

---

for five rifles have struck the
boy."

270 Consider what Çeto Basho Muji
did:

he fired his signaling rifle

and Judbina and the Borderland
heard it.

Thirty Agas assembled there.

He addressed the Agas and said:

275 "May God strike you dead—he
said to the Agas—

for your words have left me
without a brother.

For the boy has gotten stuck in
the Kingdom,

for five rifles have struck the
boy,

and they have summoned me to
go see him."

280 He took the Agas with him,

then they set out for the
Kingdom.

And on the road Muji said to his
friends,

Swearing a *besa* to God to them:

"If you disgrace me in the
Kingdom,

285 I will cut you all to pieces with
my sword.

Do not complain about the boy
at all."

Then when they arrived at the
King's

they entered the palace of the
King.

They warmly gave the King
greetings,

290 the King warmly returned their
greetings.

muhabetin krajli jan kan nise	The King started a conversation,
sa hyzmet tha krajli p'e mu ban	how much care he rendered them.
e n'ode te djali Argët kur kan hi	When the Agas entered the boy's room,
e n'miner atë djalin e kan gjet	they found the youth on a sofa.
295 ka qit Muja djalit e i ka than	295 Muji addressed the boy and said:
çou Sokol Zoti te vraft	"Get up, Sokol, may God strike you dead.
per pese pushk burri qysh me u ndej	How can a brave man stay down because of five rifles?
si ka dymdhete sa herë m'kan marre	The twelve times they have struck me
e kur per ta ne dyshek s'kam ra	I never took to my bed because of them?"
300 e dy jave q'athere kishin ndej	300 Then they stayed for two weeks,
edhe djali ma mire kishe bâ	and the boy got better.
prej dyshekut djali m'ish kan çue	And when the boy got up from the bed
edhe nusen krajli m'ja shtrengon	the King takes hold of the bride
edhe çiken djalit po m'ja nep	and gives his daughter to him.
305 miq nder vedi atherë ishin bâ	305 Then and there they became in-laws!
per Judbine argët ishin nisë	The Agas set out for Judbina,
shndosh e mire ne Judbine kishin votë	they arrived in Judbina safe and sound.
e sa te mira dazmet po mi bajne	How well they celebrated the wedding!
kangen e nise q'itash e mbarova	I have now finished the song I started.
310 vete jam lodh e juvet ju shurdhova	310 I myself am tired, and I have worn you out!

LAN 53. Ali Meta, *Kanga e Sultan Muratit*

Ali Meta; Tropoja; September 23, 1937
Kanga e Sultan Muratit
The Song of Sultan Murad [*The Battle of Kosovo*]
Historical song

	Sa me fjet davleti kenka ra	As soon as the Emperor went to sleep
	nje enderr te mire davleti kenka pa	the Emperor dreamed a good dream:
	se ne Kossove oredite ka qit	that he had sent his army to Kosovo
	me Syfarin luften e ka nise	and begun the battle with a campaign.
5	Sanxhaktaret shehit i kan metë	5 Standard-bearers were martyred,
	edhe sheh Isamit shehit i ka metë	and the Sheikh of Islam was left dead,
	edhe Sadriazemi me gjith te birin	and the Grand Vizier together with his son,
	edhe neferet zarar ju kan bâ	and his foot soldiers suffered losses.
	q'athere mbretit gjumi i ka dal	At that moment the Emperor's dream was gone.
10	rreth sabahit endrren e ka pa	10 He had the dream around dawn.
	imamin e vete davleti e ka thirr	The Emperor summoned his Imam,
	e Sandriazemi çoj e paska thirr	and he quickly summoned the Grand Vizier.
	mire se atë enderr mbreti jau kalzon	The Emperor related the dream to them in detail,
	Imami mbretit kryte i ka rudhë	the Emperor's Imam shook his head.

15 Sadriazemi ne kambe kenka çue
per hajr endrren mbretit ja ka
bâ
qare s'kanka ne Kossove pa dal

se Zot në enderr paska kalzue

shka paska bâ Sultan Murati
20 gjith miletit xhevap u ka dhan

baba mbret ne darsem u ka thirr

tri jave baba mylet don me u
dhan
fukaraja opangat sa ti bojne

kur si ka davuleti do te jau apin

25 pushk tu shpija q'ata qi ti kan
ton me vedi pushket do ti
marrin
kush si ka davleti do te jau apin

grosh tu shpija q'ata qi ta ka

mos tu dhunen me vedi me i
marrë
30 kush si ka babloku do jan apin

sod tri jave ne Brus me u
mbledh
ton turqnija gadi kenkan bâ
ne kryte tri jave ne Brus kenkan
mbledhe
lujti mbreti sanxhak e sherifin

35 duan mbreti luftes e paska bâ
ka fillue ne Kossove me dal

---

15 The Grand Vizier rose to his feet,
he interpreted the Emperor's
dream as a good omen:
that it was riot to his advantage
not to go to Kosovo
because God had so revealed in
the dream.
Consider what Sultan Murat did.
20 He sent a message to all his
people:
"Your father Emperor has
summoned you to a wedding
celebration.
He will give you three weeks
time
for the poor to make enough
footwear.
The Emperor will provide it to
whoever has none.
25 Those who have rifles at home
are to take their rifles with
them,
he will provide them to
whoever has none.
Let those who have money at
home
not be ashamed to take it with
them,
30 your old dad will provide it for
whoever has none.
Three weeks from today we
assemble in Brus."
All Turkdom made ready.
At the end of three weeks they
assembled in Brus.
The Emperor touched the noble
standard
35 and recited the battle prayer.
He set out for Kosovo.

ne breg te detit mbreti kur asht
   ardh
shka ka bâ Sultan Murati
e telal per hurdi paska shti

40 me pishman ketë darsem kush
    asht ardhe
pa hashlak rrobët kush i ka lan

ata let dredhin tu shpija let
   shikojne
se une me vedi hash nuk i kam
fort pak njeri q'atherë kenka
   kthye
45 hiç gjemi ne atë vakt nuk ka
    pasë
nji dua mbretit detit ja ka bâ

Zot'yn detit dyzash e ka da

neper det ordite e ka qit
kesaj kendej detit ordit kur i ka
   qit
50 opet telat per ordi i ka shti

qi me pishmon kete darsem
   kush asht ardh
edhe pa hashlak rrobët kush i ka
   lan
ata dredhun tu shpija let shkojne
se hala detit rrugen s'nau ka
   nxane
55 kurr nji njer q'atherë s'ju ka
    kethye
ka bâ dua deti asht perzije

ka fillue ne Kossove me dal
Mbreti he Shkup kur kenka ardh
ne anmikin luften ju pashka nise

When the Emperor came to the
   shore of the sea,
consider what Sultan Murat did.
He sent a rider throughout the
   army:
40 "Whoever has come to the
    wedding with regrets
 whoever has left his family
   without means,
let them turn back and go
   home,
because I have no funds for them."
Very few of them turned back
   then.
45 At that time there were no ships
    there.
The Emperor offered a prayer
   for the sea,
and God divided the sea into
   two parts.
He sent his army through the sea.
He sent his army to this side of
   the sea
50 and again sent a rider
   throughout the army:
"Whoever has come to the
   wedding with regrets
and has left his family without
   means,
let him turn back and go home,
because the passage through
   the sea is still not blocked."
55 Not one of them turned back
    then.
He said a prayer and the sea
   came together.
He set out for Kosovo.
When he came to Shkup
he joined battle with the enemy.

60 sanxhaktar shehit i paska mbet
edhe sheh islami shehit i paska
   mbet
edhe sandriazemi me gjith te
   birin
edhe shum nefert zarar ju
   paskan bâ
dhimta ne zemer mbretiti i
   kenka shkue
65 sa nji bet te madhe mbreti e
   pashka bâ
ne zenxhi t'atit gjaku pa shkue

skom dushmanit luften me ja da

komandarët çoj i paska thirr
qi ne kater çoshet luften me ja
   nise
70 kursun sod vllazni mos me bâ

ne te kater çoshet luften e
   paskan nise
nji sahat lufta kur po mbush

pushka a ndal topat paskan
   ndejt
sol n'singijat trimat po luftojne

75 luft kan bâ tri ditë e tri natë

hej singija malin per me e tha
kur jan mbush tri ditë e tri net

lufta marr mbretit i paska shkue

shufrak zoti dushmanit i paska
   dhan
80 gjaki vadë per Kossove po hec

Zot'yn shiu ne Kossove e ka fal

60 Standard-bearers were martyred,
and the High Priest of Islam was
   left dead,
along with the Grand Vizier
   together with his son.
And many foot soldiers suffered
   losses.
Pain struck at the heart of the
   Emperor.
65 How great an oath he swore:

"Not until blood reaches the
   stirrups of my steed
will I break off the battle with
   the enemy."
He called out to his commanders
to begin the battle on all four
   sides.
70 "Brothers, do not let me down
   today."
On all four sides they began the
   battle.
When the battle had gone on
   for one hour,
rifle fire stopped, cannon fire
   ceased.
The heroes were fighting only
   with bayonets,
75 they fought for three days and
   three nights.
Hey, even the mountains shook!
When three days and three
   nights had passed
. the battle turned in the
   Emperor's favor:
God put the enemy to flight [to
   retreat].
80 Blood flowed like water across
   Kosovo.
God sent rain on Kosovo,

gjak e shi bashk kenka bâ

gjith sa prosk ne Kossove qi jan kan

tan me gjak proskat kenkan mbush

85 sa me sarja n'ot s'un ti del

ne singji te atit gjoku i paska prek

bêja mbretit ne vend i paska votë

ka fillue ne Kossove kenka dak

se në Golosh ordite ka hyp

90 pika e ujit ne Kossove s'ish kan

muaser ordit ju kan bâ

po s'ka bâ aj Sultan Murati

kershi çizme mbreti i ka ra

Zotynë ujet q'aty e paska fal

95 ton orditi idare ju paska bâ

nji leter te bardhe mbreti po mbaron

ja paska çue Milosh Kopiliqit

ja te mi çojsh çilsat e kallave

ja te mi çojsh vergine e nandë vjetve

100 bê i ka bâ per posten e pigamerit

qi kurr s'ta daj luften e gazepin

as mbi tokë vendin nuk ta lâ

letra ne dorë Miloshit i paska ra

muer Miloshi letren p'e kendon

and blood and rain mixed together.

However many springs there were in Kosovo

were all filled up with blood,

85 which made them impossible to cross.

Blood reached the stirrups of the battle steed

and the *besa* of the Emperor was realized.

He set out for Kosovo,

and the army reached Golesh.

90 There was not a drop of water in Kosovo,

the army became thirsty.

But consider what Sultan Murat did:

he kicked some rocky soil with his boot,

and God delivered water from it,

95 providing relief for the whole army.

The Emperor wrote a well-writ letter

And sent it to Millosh Kopiliq [Miloš Obilić]:

"Send me the keys to your fortress,

and send me taxes for nine years,

100 I swear a *besa* on the throne of the Prophet

that I will never stop the battle and the fury

or leave you any land to stand on."

The letter landed in Millosh's hand,

he took the letter and read it.

105 sa në gazep Miloshi kenka ra
    me ja çue çilsat e kallas

    edhe me ja çue vergine per
        nande vjet
    shum gazep Miloshit po i vjen
    me ja ndal kyvetin s'ja ka

110 kenka hi krajlica e shoqja
    po shka kije Milosh i ka than

    qi ne njizet vjet mua me ke
        marre
    turrli letrash ne dorë të kau ra

    në kesij gazepi kurr nuk të kam
        pa
115 krajlices Miloshi i paska than
    qi keso letra kurr n'dorë s'em ka
        ra
    ma ka çue Sultan Murati
    mi ka lype çilsat e kallêvet

    ma ka lype vergin per nandë
        vjet
120 bê ka bâ per posten e pigamerit

    qi s'mi leshon çilsat e kallêvet

    kur s'ta daj luften as qazepin

    me ja çue inati po m'vjen
    me ja ndal kyvetin s'ja kom

125 sa fisnike krajlica kanka kan

    çoja çilsat Miloshit i kathan

    nuk a mare verginë me ja dhan

105 How furious Millosh became!
    Over sending him the keys to
        the fortress
    and sending him the taxes for
        nine years.
    Millosh became very furious,
    not having the strength to stop
        him.

110 His princess wife came in:
    "What is the matter, Millosh?—
        she said to him—
    Over the twenty years you have
        been my husband
    all sorts of letters have reached
        your hand,
    I have never seen you as
        troubled as this."

115 Millosh said to the princess:
    "A letter such as this has never
        reached my hand.
    Sultan Murat has sent it to me.
    He has asked me for the keys to
        the fortress,
    he has asked me for taxes for
        nine years.

120 He has sworn a *besa* on the
        throne of the Prophet
    that if I do not turn over the
        keys to the fortress
    he will not break off the battle
        or the fury.
    It galls me to send them,
    not having the strength to stop
        him."

125 What a noblewoman the prin-
        cess was:
    "Send him the keys—she said to
        Millosh—
    it is not shameful to pay him
        the taxes,

se aj asht baba i gjith dunjês

krejt e sosi çilsat me ja çue

130 edhe kreit e sosi verginëme ja
dhan
shka i ka than Avrame Begolli

mos u ngut çilsa me ja çue

as mos u ngut verginë me ja dhan
se nji tertip mbretit do të ja bajme
135 tridhet çika ne krajli due me i
zgjedh
ka i tepsi dukat due me ja
mbush
se ne Kossovë çikat due me i qitun
agjami po aj turku e qi ka
dal't naj turku çikat me i gezhat
140 a n'dal't ndoj turk parat me jau
marre
kurgja mbreti në dore nuk të ka
po i ngulimi kambët se nuk ka
shka na i ban
po mos të dal't turk çikat me i
qezhat
as mos të dal't turku parat me
jau marrë
145 mbreti pune të mira t'i ka

po ja çojme çilsat e kallas

e po ja çojme vergin per nande
vjet
se as mbi tokë vendin nuk a lan

tridhete çika ne krajlit i ka
zqedhë
150 ka i tepsi dukat jau kan mbush

because he is the father of the
whole world."
He was fully prepared to send
him the keys,
130 and fully prepared to pay the
taxes.
And what did Avrame Begolli
say to him?
"Do not rush to send him the
keys,
or rush to pay the taxes.
Let us test the Emperor.
135 I will select thirty girls in the
kingdom,
fill each one's tray with gold
ducats
and send the girls to Kosovo.
If the Turks are inexperienced,
and come out to tease the girls,
140 or come out to steal their coins,

the Emperor has nothing in hand:
we can stand our ground because
there is nothing he can do.
But if the Turks do not come out
to tease the girls,
or come out to steal their coins,
145 the Emperor has things under
control.
We will send him the keys to the
fortress,
and we will send him the taxes
for nine years,
because he will not leave us
land to stand on."
He selected the thirty girls in
the kingdom,
150 and filled each one's tray with
gold coins.

se në Kossove çikat kenkan dal
neper ordi çikat po siellen
kankan sjelle tri dit e tri net

ska dak turk çikat me i gezhat
155 as ka dal turk parat me jau
     marre
kankan lodh uni per me dek
ne Vuçitern çikat kankan ra
kenkan vatë te Gjioka
     Hekmekgjija
a kije buken ne vete me na dhan

160 e na jemi lodh uni per me dek

gjith sa duersh dukat kemi me't
     dhan
shka u ka thau Gjioka
     Hekmekgjija
gjith sa të doni buk kam me u
     dhan
kurrnji para s'guxhoj me jau
     marrë
165 se qysh se a dal Mbreti ne
     Kossove
gani Zoti buken nau ka bâ

gani zoti parat na i ka bâ

muasere per uje jemi kan
gani zoti ujit na ka bâ

170 sa kan dhesht bukë u paska
     dhan
kurrnji para Gjioka s'jau paska
     marrë
filluen çikat tek Miloshit kan
     votë
gjith si a kan Miloshit po i
     kalzojne

When the girls went to Kosovo
they strolled through the army,
even strolling three days and
     three nights.
No Turk came out to tease them,
155 no Turk came out to steal their
     coins.
Exhausted and starving to death
the girls went to Vuçitem,
Even going to Gjoka
     Hekmekgjija.
"Do you have any of your bread
     to give us?
160 We are exhausted and starving
     to death.
We will give you all the gold
     coins you want."
Consider what Gjoka
     Hekmekgjija said to them:
"I will give you all the bread you
     want.
I dare not take any money from
     you,
165 because ever since the Emperor
     came to Kosovo
God has provided us with an
     abundance of bread,
God has provided us with an
     abundance of money.
We were thirsting for water,
God provided us with an abun-
     dance of water."
170 Giving them as much bread as
     they wanted,
Gjoka took no money from
     them.
The girls set off and went to
     Millosh.
They relate to Millosh every-
     thing that happened:

na kemi ndejt tri dit e tri net

175 gjith ordit e mbretit kemi
trupue
nuk ka dal turk me ne me fol
as nuk ka dak turk parat me na i
marre
shka ka bâ Miloshi Kopiliqi
krejt miletin i paska mbledh
180 dert p'e bau tri dit e tri net

kursi qajren s'ja kan gjetun

mbi toke vendin Mbreti s'do të
na lan
besatue Milosh me milet kenka
kan
unë po shkoj tu Sultane Murati
185 ai ne u çoft doren me na dhan
shahadet q'aty due me ra
te ton mbarë turqit duem me u
bâ
mos e çoft doren me ma dhan
haxhar ne bark doren do të ja
shti
190 se në panzir Miloshin kenka vesh
edhe vrançin ne panzir e pashka
vesh
ne shpine vrançit Milloshi paska
ra
ka fillue në Kosove kanka dal
aj xhevap mbretit i paska votë
195 qi po vjen Miloshi Kopiliqi

mbreti mend q'aty e paska bâ

qi kur te vinë Milosh kopiliqi
jallah ne kamb vet due me çue
edhe doren Miloshit due me ja
dhan

"We stayed three days and three
nights,
175 cutting straight through the
Emperor's army.
No Turk came out to talk to us,
no Turk came out to take our
money."
What did Millosh Kopiliq do?
He assembled all the people,
180 haranguing them for three days
and three nights,
they could not come to any
decision.
"The Emperor will not leave us
land to stand on!"
Millosh swore a *besa* to the
people:
"I am going to Sultan Murat.
185 If he offers me his hand,
I will bear witness to Islam
that we all in due order will
become Turks.
If he does not offer me his hand,
I will plunge a dagger into his
belly."
190 Millosh put on coat of mail
and put coat of mail on his black
horse.
He jumped on the back of his
black horse
and set out to go to Kosovo.
Hey, news reached the Emperor
195 that Millosh Kopiliq was
coming.
Then the Emperor made up his
mind:
"As soon as Millosh comes,
I will at once rise to my feet
And extend my hand to
Millosh."

200 Munafiku q'aty qa i pashka than
    qysh Miloshit n'kamb me ju çue

    edhe atë mendim mbretit ja
        pashka prish
    fjalët vonojne Miloshi kenka
        ardh
    para çadra vrançit i ka zhryp

205 ka çue tsohen ne mbreti kenka
        hi
    hiç prej vendit Mbreti s'kenka
        luejt
    e ka ngat kamben Miloshit me ja
        dhan
    sa gazep Miloshit i ka ardh
    se aj hanxharin e ka nxjerre
210 dogri mbretit ne bark ja ka shti

    q'atherë mbreti jet paska
        ndrrue
    duel perjashta Milosh Kopiliqi
    dogri vrançit n'shpine i ka ra

    q'athere lufta Miloshi ju nise

215 te ton ordija rrethin ja ka qit
    pushk po i bijen po s'kan shka
        me i bâ
    shpata sjellin po s'kan shka me i
        bâ
    ngat asht rras ne hudud per me
        dal
    nji shkine moçme q'aty kenka kan
220 keçyre ordise shkina q'au paska
        than
    kurr qysh Miloshin s'mundi me
        e mbyt
    veç para vrançit kosat me ja qit

200 Then a schemer said:
    "How can you possibly rise for
        Millosh?"
    And he changed the Emperor's
        mind.
    While they were still talking
        Millosh arrived.
    He climbed off his black horse
        in front of the tent,
205 raised its flap and went over to
        the Emperor.
    The Emperor did not budge
        from his place,
    but stretched his leg out
        towards Millosh.
    Millosh became so furious
    that he took out his dagger
210 and plunged it right into the
        Emperor's stomach.
    Then and there the Emperor
        passed away.
    Millosh Kopiliq went outside
    and jumped right on the back of
        his black horse.
    Then and there Millosh started
        fighting,
215 the entire army surrounded him.
    They fired rifles at him, but
        they could do nothing.
    They swung swords at him, but
        they could do nothing.
    He was close to reaching the
        border.
    An old Slav woman was there.
220 Consider what the old Slav
        woman told the soldiers:
    "You will never be able to kill
        Millosh,
    unless you throw my scythes in
        front of the black horse

te kater kambët ne kopit me ja
  keput
se papanser ne kopit i ka

225 shpejt ordije kosat i kan marre

para vrançit kosat ja kan qit

te kater kambët ne kopit ja kan
  keput
q'ather vrançi ne tokë kenka
  rrezue
Miloshit sipri i paskan ra
230 ja kan desh kemishen prej
  papansirit
athëre po don krytë me ja pre

atherë Miloshi nji fjal e paska fol
nji mylet mua mem ma dhan
q'at shkinë ngat mue me na
  prue
235 nji fjal ne vesh shkines dua me
  ja than
shpejt ordija shkinen ja kau
  prue
keçyre Miloshi shkines shka i ka
  than
afroma veshina babina e
  Kossoves
q'athere shkina veshin ja ka
  afrue
240 dham ne hundë Milosh ja ka
  ngjite
nji çerek larg e ka gjue
pa pike shpirt babina kenka ra

athere Miloshit kryte ja kam pre

i vojte xhevapi Sultan Mehmetit

to cut off its four legs at the
  hoofs,
because at the hoofs there is no
  chain mail."

225 The soldiers quickly took her
  scythes
and threw them in front of the
  black horse.
They cut off its four legs at the
  hoofs,
then and there the black horse
  crashed to the ground.
They fell on top of Millosh
230 and took off his coat of mail.

Then they wanted to cut off his
  head.
Then Millosh spoke a few words:
"Grant me one request,
bring that Slav woman closer to
  me,
235 I want to speak a few words into
  her ear."
Soldiers quickly brought the
  Slav woman to him.
Consider what Millosh said to
  the Slav woman:
"Bring your ear closer to me,
  old woman of Kosovo."
The Slav woman then brought
  her ear closer to him.
240 Millosh sank his teeth into her
  nose
and flung it a mile away.
The old woman lay without an
  ounce of breath.
Then and there they cut off
  Millosh's head.
News reached Sultan Mehmet

245 qi ka ndrrue jet Sultan Murati

    ka fillue Sultan Mehmeti
    se ne Kossove dogri asht ardhe
    gjith si a kam ordija po i
      kalzojne
    shka ka bâ Sultan Mehmeti
250 per shpirt pllakes nji ure e ka
      mbarue
    sod i thonë ura e Babinosit

245 that Sultan Murat had passed
    away.
    Sultan Mehmet set out,
    and came straight to Kosovo.
    The soldiers related everything
      that had happened.
    What did Sultan Mehmet do?
250 He built a bridge in memory of
      the old woman.
    Today it is called the Old
      Woman's bridge.

LAN 57. Ali Meta, *Kanga e Ali Bajraktarit me Krajlicen e Inglizit*

Ali Meta; Tropoja; September 23, 1937
Kanga e Ali Bajraktarit me Krajlicen e Inglizit
The Song of Ali Bajraktari and the Queen of England
Legendary fantastic song

Lum per ty e per diten e sodit	Blessings on you and on this day!
kenka çue Ali Bajraktari	Ali Bajraktari arose,
ne shpine po i bjen gjokut mejdanit	jumped on the back of his grey-white battle horse
per kismet Alia asht dal	and set out to seek his fortune.
5 dogri shkoj tu pllaku Emin Aga	5 He went straight to old Emin Aga.
muhabet pllaku po i ban	The old man pleasantly chatted with him.
dikur foli Ali Bajraktari	Finally Ali Bajraktari said:
pse s'pom vet pllak perse jam ardhe	"Old man, why do you not ask me why I have come?"
shkaj i ka than pllaku Emin Aga	Consider what old Emin Aga said:
10 kurr adet vet se kom pas	10 "Never has it been my custom
mysafiret perpara me i vete	to ask guests first,
mysafiri vehten do ta kalzojne	before my guests tell me themselves.
	If I can, I make it easy for them."
ne kofsha i zoti una ja ndreqi	Then Ali Bajraktari said:
athere foli Ali Bajraktari	"I have come, old man, to ask
15 jam ardh pllak çiken me ta lyp	15 you for your daughter
	and that you not fault me as a friend."
edhe ti per mik mue mos mem sha	Consider what old Emin Aga said:
shka i ka than pllaku Emin Aga	"No one would fault you as a friend.
ty per mik kerkush nuk te shan	
tash me fjet na duem me ra	Now we should go to sleep.

<table>
<tr><td>20</td><td>kur ta fali Zotyn sabahin</td><td>20</td><td>As soon as God grants you morning's light</td></tr>
</table>

20 kur ta fali Zotyn sabahin

    q'ather çiken per hajr ta boj

    sa me qef Alia asht ra
    kur e fali Zotyn sabahin

    mire sabahin e paskan fal
25 xhezven ne zjarm pllaku ka shti

    mire po i mbaron kafet me sheqer
    ne ndor Alies kafen ja ip
    dhe per hajr çiken pllaku ja bani

    shka ka bâ Ali Bajraktari
30 dore ne xhep Alia ka shti
    njiqind duket pllaka ja ep

    per dy jave vaden e kan da

    a shtrengue Ali Bajraktari
    izë mem dhan pllaku Emin Aga

35 ra ne podrum gjokun po shtrengon
    ne shpine Alia gjokut po i bjen

    rruga e marr pllaku po i thote

    Lokes'ate selam te mi bojsh

    Ne kullat të veta Alia a shkue
40 Lokes vet myzhde po i merr

    nuse të bukur nane qi kam nxane
    tash per dasem gadi me u bâ

    se per dy jave vaden e kemi da

---

20 As soon as God grants you morning's light

    then I will betroth my daughter to you."
Ali went to sleep feeling pleased.
When God granted morning's light
they recited the morning prayer.
25 The old man placed the coffee pot on the fire;
he added sugar to the coffee
and handed the coffee to Ali,
And betrothed his daughter to him.
Consider what Ali Bajraktari did:
30 Ali put his hand in his pocket
and gave the old man one hundred gold ducats.
They set the wedding date for two weeks.
Ali Bajraktari girded himself.
"May I take leave of you, old Emin Aga?"
35 Ali went down to the cellar and saddled his grey-white horse.
He jumped on the back of his grey-white horse.
"May you have a safe journey— the old man said—
Give my greetings to your mother."
Ali returned to his own tower
40 bearing his mother the good news:
"I have taken a beautiful bride, mother.
Now we must get ready for the wedding,
because the date has been set for two weeks."

duem per darsem gadi me u bâ

45 prej Sultan Sulejmanit leter i ka
ardh
ti si je Ali Bajraktari

thresin [treqind] vete me vedi
me i marrë
nji orë ma pare ne Stamboll me
ardhe
fort Alia kanka gushtue
50 pllakut fjal i paska çue
ti q'at vade mos em prit mua

mua davleti m'ka thirr mua
qare skom ne Stamboll pa shkue

Zoti e din shka don me mua

55 treqind vetë i ka bashkue
prej Stambollit ka fillue
se n'Stamboll kur kankan shkue
babes Mbret i ka kallzue

babes Mbret i paska than
60 Ali Bajraktari ketu asht ardh
treqind vete me vedi i ka

urdhen Mbreti jau paska dhan
ne Stamboll Alien mos me e lan
ne fushë Stambollit çadrat ja çoj

65 nusja e Alies kur paska ndije
ne Stamboll Alia paska shkue
nusja e Alies kanka shtrengue
bash si beg teshat po i vesh
nder sullah floket po i shtjen

70 dymdhete nishana i paska vënue
e paska vesh shpaten prej dukati

"We will get ready immediately
for the wedding."

45 A letter arrived from Sultan
Sulejman:
"None other than you, Ali
Bajraktari,
are to take three hundred men

and come to Stambol as quickly
as possible."
Ali became very distressed!
50 He sent word to the old man:
"Do not expect me by the date
we set.
The Emperor has summoned me,
I have no choice but to go to
Stambol.
God knows what he wants from
me."

55 He assembled three hundred men
and set out for Stambol.
When they reached Stambol,
he reported to the Father
Emperor.
He said to the Father Emperor:
60 "Ali Bajraktari is here present
and has three hundred men
with him."
The Emperor gave the order
not to let Ali inside Stambol.
He raised tents for them on the
plain of Stambol.

65 When Ali's bride learned
that Ali had gone to Stambol,
she girded herself,
donning clothes just like a Bey.
She put her hair inside the
headpiece,
70 pinned on twelve medals,
and strapped on a golden sword.

bukuri Zoti i kish fal
kenka ba sikur ma i miri Zotori

gjokun pllakut ja paska marrë

75 sa gjok te mire pllaku kish pas

çiken n'shpine gjokut po i bjen

prej Stambollit ka fillue
se n'Stamboll kur kakau shkue
nje hotel kur kenka shkue
80 Hotexhinë e ka urdhnue

nji xhevap prej teje due
per Alien ti mem kalzue
ç'far konaqesh Mbreti e ka çue

hotelxhia i ka kalzue
85 në fushë Stambollit Mbreti e ka
       çue
tridhete çadra i paska çue
Begu n'kambe kanka çue
ne fushë Stambollit kankan
       shkue
çadren e Alies ja kan kallzue
90 dogri ne çader i paska shkue
Ali Bajraktari ne kamb asht çue
Alien Begu e ka nderue
muhabet shum Begut po i ban
dikur Begu Alies po i thote
95 çfar nevoja te ka qit ne Stamboll

Alia Begut i paska than
un kurrgja nuk di me të than
mue më ka thirr Sultan
       Sulejmani
qe tri dite ne Stamboll jam ardh
100 para Mbreti hala s'jam dal

God adorned her with beauty,
she looked like the finest of
       noblemen.
She took her father's grey-white
       horse,
75 and what a fine grey-white
       horse her father had!
The girl jumped on the back of
       the grey-white horse
and set out for Stambol.
When she reached Stambol,
and when she went into a hotel,
80 she gave an order to the hotel
       keeper:
"I want an answer from you.
Tell me about Ali,
what quarters has the Emperor
       made for him?"
The innkeeper reported:
85 "The Emperor has sent him to
       the plain of Stambol,
he raised thirty tents for him."
The Bey stood up
And set out for the plain of
       Stambol.
They pointed out Ali's tent
90 and she went straight to his tent.
Ali Bajraktari rose to his feet
and saluted the Bey,
They had a pleasant conversation.
Finally the Bey says to Ali:
95 "What need has brought you to
       Stambol?"
Ali said to the Bey:
"I do not know what to tell you.
Sultan Sulejman has summoned
       me.
I came to Stambol three days ago,
100 I have yet to appear before the
       Emperor.

nuk di Mbreti mua shka me
   thotë
mos ma qet ndoj pune qi sune
   baj
q'atherë Bega i paska than
n'dash tu Mbreti un po shkoj

105 ato punë po ti mbaroj
me ma dhan myhyrin tandë
se un po i thom Alia jom
besen e Zotit po ta api
hedije Mbretit shka te na bojne

110 të tona ty kam me ti dhan
çoj Alien Mbreti po i thrret
ne vend t'Alies Begu m'asht shkue
para Mbretit kur kanka shkue

muhabetin e ka fillue

115 Mbreti Alies i paska than
a din Ali për shka të kom thirr

prej Inglizit krajlica a çue
ne skelet te detit krajlica ka ardh
muhasere mua me ka bâ
120 po ma lyp vergin per nande vjet

do të ma nxjerrsh krajlicen prej
   detit
ndo krye t'at ka me shkue
qathere foli Ali Bajraktari
un ti due tri barr duket

125 me jau shkep qorrave sokatave

ata nji dua bajne per mua
athere jam i zoti myhyr me te
   dhan

I do not know what the Emperor
   is going to say to me."
I hope he will not assign me a
   task I cannot do."
Then the Bey said to him:
If you like, I will go to the
   Emperor
105 and carry out that task.
Give me your seal,
so I can tell him I am Ali.
I give you my *besa* to God,
whatever rewards the Emperor
   offers us
110 I will turn over to you."
The Emperor sent for Ali,
in Ali's place went the Bey.
When she appeared before the
   Emperor
the Emperor chatted pleasantly
   with her.
115 The Emperor said to Ali:
"Do you know, Ali, why I have
   sent for you?
The English Queen has appeared,
she has come to our port
and is besieging me.
120 She is demanding from me taxes
   for nine years.
Either you will drive the Queen
   out to sea
or you will lose your head."
Then Ali Bajraktari spoke:
"I want three loads of gold coins
   from you
125 to give to the blind and the
   crippled
for them to say a prayer for me.
Then I will be able to give you
   my seal.

ndo krajlicen prej detit ta
   nxjerri
ndo krytë tem ke me ma pre
130 ashtu myhyra Alia i ka dhan
tri barr duket Mbreti ja dha

ton jau shkepi qorrave sokatave

shum dua Alies po i bajne
puna mare gjithmon met votë
135 tu Alia Begu asht shkue
Alia Begu p'e pëvete
per shka m'kish thirr Sultan
   Sulejmani
Alies Begu po i kallzon
ty t'kish thirr Sultan Sulejmani
140 se prej Inglizit krajlica ish çue

ne skele te detit i paska ardhe
muhasere Mbretin e paska bâ
per nande vjet vargin ja lype

Mbreti urdhnat mi ka dhan

145 ndo krajlicen gjalle me e nxane

ndo krytë t'at ty po të shkon
un myhyr Mbretit i kam dhan

qi ndo krajlicen kam me e nxane
ndo kryte tem ndet em shkojnë
150 tri barr para mi ka dhan

fukarave jau kam dhan
e nji dua ma kan bâ

gjithmonë Zoti ty të ndihmoft
deshen Alien ment me e lan
155 fort Alie m'ish gushtue

Either I will drive the Queen out
   to sea,
or you will cut off my head."
130 Thus did Ali give him the seal.
The Emperor gave her three
   loads of gold coins.
She gave them all to the blind
   and the crippled.
They said many prayers for Ali:
"May your task ever end well!"
135 The bey returned to Ali,
Ali asks the Bey:
"Why has Sultan Sulejman
   called for me?"
The Bey explains to Ali:
"Sultan Sulejman has sent for you
140 because the English Queen has
   appeared.
She has come to our port,
she is besieging the Emperor,
she is demanding taxes for nine
   years.
The Emperor has given me
   orders:
145 either you will take the Queen
   alive
or you will lose your head.
I have given the Emperor your
   seal,
either to capture the Queen,
or to lose my head in the sea.
150 He has given me three loads of
   gold coins.
I have given them to the poor,
and they have said a prayer for
   me:
May God ever help you!"
Ali was about to lose his mind,
155 he was very distressed.

s'muej krajlicen per me e nxane
kryte tem em paska shkue
shum gajret Begu i ka dhan

si vet krajlicen kam me e nxane
160 ndo kryte tem ndet em shkojnë
q'ato lafe i kan mbarue

para sabahi Begu m'o çue
dogri ne det i ka fillue
gjoku ne det e paska leshue

165 tu gjemija e paska çue
n'derë gjemies ju ka afrue

per skêj gjemies kanka palue
adet kraljica paska pas
per dit dielli kur po le
170 deren e gjemies krajlica po e çel

po del diellin per me e pa
athere Begu gadi i ka ndej

dielli detit i paska ra
duel krajlica diellin me e pa

175 a habit diellin gjith tue keçyre

Begi zorr vedi i ka dhan

mire krajlicen e paska nxane
ne vithet gjokut e paska qit

ka fillue ne breg me dal

180 kambët e gjokut ju paskan ndal

fort kulshedra ja paska kap
nuk po e lan nji kamb me e bâ
sa fort Begu kanka ngushtue

"I can not capture the Queen,
my head is lost!"
The Bey offered him great
    comfort:
"I will capture the Queen myself
160 or lose my head in the sea."
With that they ended their
    conversation.
The Bey arose before dawn
and set out straight for the sea.
She plunged her grey-white
    horse into the sea,
165 sending it toward the ship.
She approached the hatchway
    of the ship
and hid alongside it.
The Queen had the habit
—when the sun rose each day—
170 upon opening the hatchway of
    the ship
and emerging to see the sunrise.
At that moment the Bey waited
    in readiness.
Sunlight fell across the sea.
The Queen came out to see the
    sunrise,
175 marveling all the while
    watching the sunrise.
The Bey, gathering all her
    strength,
easily captured the Queen.
She placed her on the croup of
    the grey-white horse
and started heading for the
    shore.
180 The legs of the grey-white horse
    stopped moving,
a *kulshedra* had grabbed them,
not letting a single leg kick.
How distressed the Bey became!

231

tash n'det pom mysin mua
185 ora e Begut i paska brit
shpejt ti shpaten per me nxjerre
ne deti shpaten per me e shti
ne dash kulshedren per me e pre
q'athere Begu shpaten e ka
    nxjerre
190 per skêj gjoku shpaten e ka shti

fort kulshedren e paska pre
me gjak deti kanka mbush
dogri kambët gjokut ju leshuen

prej Stambollit e ka fillue
195 ne breg te detit kur ka shkue
duel prej detit e kanka peshtue

xhevap Mbretit i paska çue

xhevap Mbretit i paskan dhan
gjalle krajlicen ta kom nxane

200 shum shejlek Mbreti po i ban
njiqind topa Mbreti po i qet
çoj Alien opet po i thrret
shum livdimin po ja ep
shkum bakshishin po ja jep
205 treqind veta qi kankan kan

te tonve hedije jau paska dhan
ize Alies i paska dhan
ti kur te duesh ne shpi me votë

ti kur te duesh ne shpi me shkue

210 se punen teme ma ki mbarue

tuk Alia Begu m'asht shkue
ton bakshishet ja paska çue

"Now it will drown me in the sea."
185 The Bey's *Ora* cried out:
"Draw your sword quickly!
Plunge your sword into the sea
if you want to kill the *kulshedra*."
Then the Bey drew her sword

190 and plunged it down beside the
    grey-white horse.
She wounded the *kulshedra* deeply
and the sea was filled with blood.
The legs of the grey-white horse
    were instantly freed.
She set out for Stambol.
195 When she made it to the shore
she came out of the sea safe and
    sound.
She sent a message to the
    Emperor,
and it was delivered to him:
"I have captured the Queen
    alive!"

200 The Emperor joyfully celebrates,
firing one hundred cannons.
Again he sent for Ali.
He showers much praise on him,
he showers many gifts on him.
205 As for the three hundred men
    assembled,
he gave gifts to all of them.
He gave Ali leave:
"You may head home whenever
    you want,
you may go home whenever you
    want,
210 for you have accomplished my
    task."
The Bey went to Ali.
She gave him all the gifts,

fjalet e Mbretit ja ka kalzue

tash kur te duesh ne shpi me
    shkue
215 kenkan çue paskan fillue
se ne Kladush po don me shkue

ne gjyse të rruges kur kankan
    shkue
e ka kap Begun per me u
    vllaznue
sa fort Begu kenka ngushtue
220 burr e grue qysh me u vllaznue

vet me vedi kanka krytue
amanet Baba ma ka lan mue
kurr per rruge mos me u
    vllaznue
Ali Begut besen ja lypi
225 qi sod nji jave kam me u martue

ne shpi teme bashk me shkue
Begu Alies i paska than
po t'ap besen e din e iman

sod nji jave un gjalle me kan
230 nuk e la ne darsem pa t'ardh

gryk ne gryk athere jan marre

q'athere rrugen e paskan da
çika rrugen e paska marre
se ne shpi te vet çika m'ish shkue
235 e po don per nuse me u gatue

ne shpi te vete Ali m'ish shkue
shoket e vet i ka bashkue
punen e Mbretit jau ka kalzue

and reported the Emperor's
    words:
"You may now go home when-
    ever you want."
215 They rose and set out,
for they wanted to go to
    Klladusha.
When they had gone halfway,

he asked the Bey to become his
    blood brother.
The Bey became very distressed:
220 how could a man and a woman
    become blood brothers?
She thought this over to herself:
"My father left me a last wish
that I never become a blood
    brother on the road."
Ali requested a *besa* from the Bey:
225 "One week from today I will be
    married,
come join me in my house."
The Bey said to Ali:
"I swear a *besa* to you on my
    religion and my faith,
if I am alive one week from today,
230 I will not fail to come to your
    wedding."
Then they embraced around the
    neck,
and went their separate ways.
The girl set out on the road,
and went to her house,
235 wanting to ready herself as a
    bride.
Ali went to his house,
and assembled his companions.
He told them about the
    Emperor's task,

per qita Mbreti em kish thirr mua
240 tash per dasem due me u gatue

peseqind vete krushq me i çue

dita dites java m'asht shkue
peseqind krushq ju kan bashkue

p'e pret Begu e si ka shkue

245 fort Alia kenka ngushtue
Begu besen qysh ma ka dhan mua
aj kanka dek ke paska mbarue
fort Alia kanka ngushtue
mos ma vënoni mendjen mua

250 se me nji Beg jam kan vllaznue

besen e Zotit ma ka dhan mue
qi sod nji jave ja gjalle mem nxane
nuk e la tu ti pa ardh
ne darsem Begu nuk m'erdh mue
255 tek a dek tek a mbarue
q'athere krushqit paskan fillue

bash te pllakuk kankan shkue
nusen e Alies ja paskan çue
asht ardh vakti ne gjerdek me shkue
260 ne gjerdek Alia s'po don me shkue
nuses Alies i kan kalzue
qi keshtu Alia a ngushtue
per nji probatim qi asht vllaznue
nusja Alies shka paska than
265 ne dere Alien me ma prue mue

"That is why the Emperor summoned me.
240 Now I need to get ready for the wedding,
to invite five hundred wedding guests."
Day by day the week went by,
five hundred wedding guests gathered.
He waited for the Bey but he did not come.
245 Ali was very hard distressed:
"Since the Bey gave me his *besa*
He must be dead and done for!"
Ali was very distressed.
"Do not trouble yourselves on account of me,
250 for I have become blood brother to a Bey.
He swore to me a *besa* to God
that if he should be alive after one week
he would not fail to come,
but the Bey has not come to my wedding,
255 he must be dead and done for."
At that time the wedding guests set out,
riding straight to the old man,
escorting Ali's bride to him.
The time came for him to enter the nuptial chamber,
260 Ali did not want to go inside.
They reported to Ali's bride
that Ali was distressed
over a blood brother that he had made.
Consider what Ali's bride said:
265 "Bring Ali to my door

se kam dy fjal me ja kalzue

shpejt Alies i kan kalzue
thotë ne derë nuses me i shkue

se kom dy fjal me ti kalzue

270 shpejt Alia në derë m'ish shkue
nuses vet ju kish germue
nji probatim m'paska mbarue
une ne Stamboll kur jam shkue
me q'at Beg jam besatue
275 une krajlicen kur e kam nxane
shume ndejn me at Beg kam bâ
q'atherë nusja i paska fol
vet q'aj Beg une jam
edhe krajlicen vet e kam nxane
280 ti m'ke kap me u vllaznue

burr e grue qysh me u vllaznue

q'athere Alia Asht rahatue
ne gjerdek të nuses i paska shkue
po pak i kuqun i paska shkue
285 per q'at lafe qi ka gabue
ka marr nusen asht rahatue

keshtu kan than atje s'jam kan

por pa kan nuk din me than

gjithmone Zoti neve na ndimoft

because I have a few words to
say to him!"
They quickly reported to Ali:
"She says, 'Come to the door of
the bride,
Because I have a few words to
say to you.'"

270 Ali quickly went to her door,
he thundered at his bride:
"My blood brother is done for!
When I went to Stambol,
I swore *besa* to that Bey.
275 When I captured the Queen
I spent a long time with him."
Then the bride spoke up:
"I myself am that Bey,
and I captured the Queen myself!
280 You asked me to become your
blood brother.
How can a man and woman
become blood brothers?"
Then and there Ali relaxed,
he entered her nuptial chamber,
even entering a little red-faced
285 over the mistake he had made.
He married his bride and was
relieved.
This is how they tell it, I was not
there.
But had it not happened, they
would not know how to tell it.
May God always help us!

LAN 60. Adem Brahimi, *Kanga e Sirotin Alis*

Adem Brahimi; Tropoja; dictation begun on September 24, 1937
Kanga e Sirotin Alis
The Song of Sirotin Ali
Legendary song

Lum të na për të lumin Prendi
qi s'jem kon e aj na ka falë

konka dalë sabah drites e bardhë

e prej gjumit Alija ish çue
5   nanes vet Alija i ha thirë
në oxhakli zjarmin me na dhezë
nana vet sa mirë e kish ndigjue
e n'oxhak zjarmin po ja dhezë

e xhygymat në zjarm e ka shti
10 po ja pjek kafen me sheqer

pin Alija në qeif tako bâ

n'mat nargile duhan qi ka dhezë
pak ka ndej e nuk ka vonue

se po dron qi sabahi don me i
    shkue
15 po mi mer ibrik e legen
po mer abdes të paçë
don sabahin Alija o moj falë

e me vakt sabahin poj falë

Blessed be our blessed God!
We would not be had He not
    granted us life.
The white light of morning
    appeared
and Ali woke from his sleep.
5   Ali summoned his mother
to kindle a fire in the fireplace.
How well his mother understood!
And she kindled a fire in the
    fireplace
and placed a kettle on the fire.
10 She made coffee with sugar for
    him.
Ali drank, it put him in a good
    mood,
he lit tobacco in his water pipe.
He remained seated for a short
    while, he did not linger,
for he feared that the morning
    would pass by.
15 He took a pitcher and basin,
made his ritual ablutions.
Ali wished to pray the morning
    prayer,
and he prayed the morning
    prayer on time.

i lutet Zotit me na dhon mbar

20 e prej sexhde Alija kenka çue
te dorija në podrum kenka ra

e shilue dorin shilue çi e ka

të mirë takamin në shpin ja ka
 çit
Frê prej arit në kry ja ka vnue

25 prej podrumit dorin e ka nxjer
e n'obor të avlis pashka çitë
e në kalltak dizginat ja ka çue

e n'avli dorin paska lshue

vet dorija avlis po shetitet

30 ghjith rreth kulles sa mirë po
 sidhet
e Alija shkallavet po hipë
n'odë të vet Alija konka shkue
po mi veshet teshat e Bajramit
kenka ngrie n'ar e në dukat

35 e ma gjesh shpaten me nishana

në kupaçe shpaten e ka çitë

dy koburet në sylah i ka shti

prej florinit armet i kish pasë
njanin sy tanuzin e ka çitë
40 xhyherdaren në dorë e ka marë

nana vet Aline pe pvete
ku po shkon more Ali e lum
 nana
nanës vet Alija poj kallzon

He beseeched God to grant him
 justice,
20 and Ali rose from his prayer rug.
He went to the stable to his bay
 horse
and he saddled the bay with its
 saddle:
he placed fine equipment on its
 back.
He put a golden bridle on its
 head.
25 He led the horse out of the stable
and sent it into the courtyard.
And he put the reins onto the
 pommel
and let the horse go freely in
 the courtyard.
The horse walked about the
 courtyard by itself.
30 How well it went all around the
 tower!
And Ali went up the steps:
Ali entered his own room
and put on his clothes for Bajram
embroidered with gold and with
 ducats,
35 and he girded on his sword with
 decorations.
He plunged the sword into its
 scabbard,
he tucked two pistols into his
 sash,
his weapons were of gold.
He cocked his cap over one eye.
40 He took his flintlock rifle in his
 hand.
Ali's mother asked him:
"Where are you going, O Ali,
 mother's darling?
Ali told his mother:

sot ô Loke dita e xhymos
45   du me ra thot dorise në shpind
e me dalë at xhymo mej falë
aty jane tridhet agallar
e në Llonxhe nanë janë bashkue

e te ta Loke du me shkue
50   me ta bashk nanë me kuvendue

ndoj krahin a mos po domë me
    shkue
qather djali prej odet ô dalë

Lokja vet poj thot udha mbar

teposht shkallave n'obor kenka
    dalë
55   e n'avli dorin e ka gjetë

tuj shtetit dorija ish konë
prej dizginash doris ja ka ngjitë
bismilahin në shpin i ka ra

Lokja vet doren po ja çelë

60   ja celë dyrt e kalas

e në fushe dorin paska çitë

tue lujt fushës e çue

rreth e rrotull fushen poj
    trupon
e ishkon vojt tu dera e xhamis

65   tridhet age aty i ka xhetë
e selam Alija paska dhanë
e ma mirë selamin ja kan marrë

"Today, O mother, is Friday.
45   I want to mount my horse
and to go to the mosque to pray.
The thirty Agas are there:
they have assembled, mother, in
    the place of council
and I want to go to them, mother;
50   I want to speak with them
    together, mother,
to see whether or not they want
    to go to the Borderland."
The youth thereupon went out
    of his room;
his mother wished him a good
    journey.
He went down the steps and
    into the courtyard
55   and in the courtyard he found
    his bay horse.
The bay had been strolling about.
He grabbed the horse's reins
with the name of Allah, he
    mounted the horse.
His mother opened the gate for
    him;
60   she opened the gates of the
    fortress
and he headed his bay horse
    into the plain
sending him galloping across
    the plain.
It cut straight across over the
    plain
and they came to the door of
    the mosque.
65   He found the thirty Agas there
and Ali gave them his greetings,
and received a better greeting
    in return.

shum ieram Alis paskan bâ
pak kan ndej e shum nuk kon
   vonue
70 ish ardhë vakti xhuman moj folë

e në xhami qatherë kênkan hi

e teçmil nemazin e kan bâ
prej xhamije athere janë dalë

e në Llonxh at herë kenan rá

75 muhabet shoj shojt poj bojnë

kan shtrê pijen aget e po pinë

çka po bone Sokol Halili aga
njonen dorë bardakun me raki

tjetren dorë goten e prarue
80 poj sllugon tridhet agallar
venë të kuqe e raki të bardhë
qatherë llafet aget i kan morë

poj qyrtojnë Syrotin Alin
Zoti të vraftmore Ali i kanë
   thanë
85 gjâ e madhe Zoti të ka falë

pa martue Ali qi ja mbetë

â po të dhimet malli me
   harxhitë
â ty nana s'po të len me u
   martue
se mocit tu Ali çi janë martue

90 djelm e çika Zoti i ka falë

They paid great respect to Ali.
They remained there for a short
   while, they did not linger.
70 The time had come to pray the
   Friday prayer,
and then they entered the
   mosque
and recited all the prayer.
Then they went out of the
   mosque
and then came to the place of
   council.
75 They conversed much with each
   other.
The Agas distributed the drinks
   and drank.
What did Aga Sokol Halil do?
In one hand he held a pitcher of
   raki,
in the other a gilded goblet.
80 He served the thirty Agas:
red wine and white raki.
Then the Agas took up the
   conversation,
they rebuked Sirotin Ali.
"May God strike you dead, Ali!—
   they said to him—
85 God has granted you great
   possessions,
but you have remained
   unmarried.
Either you don't want to spend
   them on a dowry,
or your mother will not let you
   marry.
For all your contemporaries are
   married,
90 God has granted them sons and
   daughters.

djelt e tyne ne Llangje jan dalun

per martese çikat qi jan bâ

pa u martue o Ali je mbetun

e Alija q'atherë ç'ka fol
95 bë Alija shokvet ju ka bâ
se kam lan as per gja as per mall

erdhe qi kur e kam gjet a mikun
per qef
aty çika nuk me u begenisë
ku e kam gjet çikun per qeft
100 miku i keq e nuk me u begenisë

çikë e mik nuk mhjeta me i
perpjeke
soj e mire kerkund s'mujeta per
me i gjet
e pa rodë nuk mujeta me u
martue
deri sot dhe kysmet s'kanka kan

105 sot nji nuse shoke qi due me e
nxane
nuse të mire e mikun ma të
mire
hajrli kjoft thotë Ali ku e ki gjiet

kam gjet mik Beg Osman Beg

burr te mirë Zoti e ka falë
110 gja e mall zoti i ka dhan

nji çikë të mire Zotyn ja ka fal

qi në botë unë shoqen nu ja di

Their sons have come out to the
place of council;
their daughters are ready for
marriage.
You, oh, Ali, have remained
unmarried."
And what did Ali then say?
95 Ali swore an oath to his friends:
"I do not stint on possessions or
goods.
Whenever I found suitable
in-laws,
I found no favor with the girl.
Whenever I found a suitable girl,
100 the in-laws were bad and I
found no favor with them.
I could not get both a girl and
in-laws at the same time.
Nowhere could I find a good
family
and I could not marry into an
ignoble family.
And until today I have had no
luck.
105 Today there is a bride, friends,
that I would like to take:
a good bride and better
in-laws."
"Good luck to you!—he says—
where did you find her?"
"I found an in-law, Beg Osman
Beg.
God has made him a good man;
110 God has given him wealth and
goods.
God has granted him a fine
daughter,
whose equal I do not know of in
the world.

evllad tjeter Begu qi nuk ka
veç q'ate çike Zotyn qi ja ka fal

115 per hazret çiken e ka mbajt
teri sot kerkuj nuk ja ka fal

sot mue çiken Begu ma ka dhan

tridhetë Agë me hajr ja kan bâ
shka me ja nji seri ju me sye

120 e shka foli Dezan Agë Osmani

O kopil Alies edhe i ka than
po n'mik tem ty shka të ka çue

po un per djal çiken e kam
   nxane
per te gjalle tyber me ta lan

125 sa Dezani këcyre shka ka bâ
e prej mille shpaten e ka nxjerre

jurish ban Alien per me e pre
ish tranue aj Sirotin Alia
si vetem ne kambe kenka çue

130 Zoti te vraft qafire Dezdar

as don me lan kerkon ti me u
   martue
e gëzon çiken e per te ngjalle
   nuk ta lan
prej mille shpaten e ka nxjerre

jurush ban Dezdarin me e pre
135 n'kamb u çue Çeto Basho Muji

e ndermjet aj Mujo qi ju ka hi
tridhetë Agët te gjitha jan çue

The Beg has no other children:
just the one daughter that God
   has granted him.

115 He has kept the girl chaste
until today he has given her to
   no one;
today the Beg has given me his
   daughter."
The thirty Agas rejoiced!
What strange sight was to be
   seen?

120 And what did Dezdar Aga
   Osman say?
"You sly bastard—he said to Ali—
what was it that sent you to my
   in-law?
For I have taken the girl for my
   son,
by my life I will not leave her to
   you."

125 See what Dezdar did:
he drew his sword from its
   sheath,
he rushed at Ali to kill him.
Sirotin Ali became angered
quick as lightning he just
   jumped to his feet.

130 "May God strike you dead, you
   infidel Dezdar
not only will you not leave her,
   you want to marry her,
I will not leave you alive to
   rejoice in the girl."
He drew his sword from its
   sheath;
he rushed at Dezdar to kill him.
135 Çeto Basha Muji jumped to his
   feet,
and Muji jumped between them.
All the thirty Agas rose

e ndermjet burave jau kan hi
edhe sa veshtirë pa pre i paskan da
140 ka qit Muja Agvet e jau ka than

Zoti te vraft more Dezdar Agë Osmani
shpije e pare e oxhak qi je kan

e murtak qitash ti nau ki bâ

prej krajlish ty mare per me të ardh
145 me shoket tu ne Llangje per me pre

per nji çikë ne kete grade me shkue
a u vjen mare he Zoti ju vraft

aj Alia ne mare kenka ra
edhe ka ugj kryte djali po mendon
150 hiq me goje Alia nuk flet
aj Dezdari fjalet nuk i ka lan
po bon bê ne din dhe iman

per te gjalle çiken tybe me ja lan

ka qit Muja trimeve e ju ka than

155 s'muej nder vedi me u pre e me ju lan
por nji pune e shoke duem me bâ
te shtergohesh ti Dezdar Osmani
edhe djalin mir ke me e shtrengue
e me vedi djalin e me e marrë
160 shka a dredh Alies edhe i ka than
ti ne shpi Alie per me shkue

and jumped between the heroes,
and with difficulty they separated them uninjured.
140 Muji spoke to the Agas and said to them:
"May God strike you dead, O Dezdar Aga Osman.
You are from one of the finest houses,
and now you have become a traitor to us.
Your shame will spread over the kingdom:
145 that you wanted to kill among your friends in the place of council
to go after a girl in this enclosure.
Aren't you ashamed, may God strike you dead!"
Ali, too, was overcome by shame;
and the youth lowered his head to think.
150 Ali did not utter any word at all
but words did not fail Dezdar:
he swore an oath on his faith and his belief,
he would make the girl regret her life.
Muji spoke to the heroes and said to them:
155 "I cannot allow you to kill among us;
instead, we fulfil a friendly task.
Gird yourself, Dezdar Osman,
and you will gird your son well
and take your son with you."
160 And then he turned to Ali and said to him:
"You go to your house Ali,

edhe gadi Ali ke me u bâ

na po çohem tridhete Agalar
e ne konaqet te gjitha pe
shkepem
165 edhe tridhete Age gadi duen me
u bâ
shokeve vet Muja jau kish kalzue
qi neser ndaje gjith me u
shtrengue
banu gadi ti Dezdar Age Osmani

banu gadi ti Sirotin Alia
170 e ne nadje dielli kur ka me ra

edhe te gjith ne llangje kemi me
u bashkue
se na begut mrenda domi me u
shkue
te cillet don ai mik ka me nxane

te cillet don aj çiken me ja dhan

175 q'aj bre nusen hajrin ja patë

fjalet per mrapa ma per mos me
pas
q'ashtu than edhe q'ashtu
paskan lan
edhe prej llangje Agêt kenkan
çue
ne shpijat veda te gjitha kankan
shkue
180 fjet kan naten driten kenka dal

e jan çue Agët e jan shtrengue

keçyre që bani aj Dezdar Agë
Osmani

and you too will make yourself
ready Ali.
We thirty Agas will rise
and all of us will go to our
homes,
165 and the thirty Agas will make
themselves ready."
Muji said to his friends
that all be girded on the
following evening.
"Make yourself ready Dezdar
Aga Osman,
make yourself ready Sirotin Ali.
170 And when the sun sets in the
evening,
all of us will assemble on the
place of council
because we will all go to the
Beg's.
He will choose whomever he
wants for an in-law
he will give his daughter to
whomever he wants
175 so that he may rejoice in the
bride,
he will not be able to take his
words back."
They left matters as they had
stated them.
And the Agas left the place of
council,
all of them went to their own
houses.
180 They slept through the night
and the day dawned,
and the Agas rose and girded
themselves.
See what Dezdar Aga Osman
did:

e ka vesh djalin e ka mbat

e prej arit teshat ja kish vesh
185 prej dukatit armet ja kish dhan

prej florinit shpaten ja ka
ngjesh
ne njanin sye tanuzin ja kish
vënue
ja shillon at gjokun tan pulle
pullë
prei arit shalen ja ka qit
190 prej dukatit frenen ja ka vënue

u shtrengue Dezan Age Osmani
ne shpine vrançit Dezdari i kish
ra
në at pullali djalin e kish hip

kan marrë rrugen ne llagjen jan
shkue
195 aty gjeten Mujin e Halilin
e selan Dezdari jau ka dhan

e selamin mire jau pashkan
marre
pak vonojne e shum vakt nuk ka
shkue
e u bashkuen tridhete agalar
200 qe po vjen aj Sirotin Alia
e ki ra dories ne shpine

tuej luejtë fushes tuej ardhe

n'qato tesha Alia qi kish qillue
as s'ish la as djali hiq s'ish ndrue

205 por Aget gjith e kan shikue
vjen selamvet Agvet ju ki dhan

---

he dressed his son and put
shoes on him,
and he put on clothes of gold.
185 He gave him weapons made
from golden ducats,
he girded him with a sword
made from golden florins,
he cocked his cap over one eye.

He saddled his dappled grey-
white horse,
the saddle he put on was of gold.
190 He placed on it a bridle made of
ducats.
Dezdar Aga Osman girded himself.
Dezdar mounted the back of his
black horse,
he sat his son on the dappled
horse.
They took to the road and went
to the place of council.
195 There they found Muji and Halil
and Dezdar gave them his
greetings.
And they received his greetings
well.
They lingered a short while
much time did not pass
before the thirty Agas assembled.
200 And Sirotin Ali came:
he had mounted the back of his
bay horse
and arrived prancing across the
plain.
What clothes Ali was dressed in!
He was not washed, neither had
the youth changed,
205 and all the Agas beheld him.
He came and gave his greetings
to the Agas

e ma mire Agët ja kan marre

e iqram Alies i paskan bâ

q'atherë Muja Agvet shka u ka
    than
210 çon ju shokë e vllazen me u
    shtrengue
se ne shpine atlarvet e po ju
    bjen
e ne shpine atlarve paskan ra

kan marre rruges fushes po
    shkojne
tuej ladrue atlaret e po i çojne
215 e sa shpejt e fushen po kalojne

ato bjeshke perpjete i kan marre
ja mesyne kullat e Bega Osman
    Beg
e sa shpejte bjeshket i kan
    trupue
n'ate fushë të Begut Aget i jan
    ra
220 gjith po çojne atlarer tuej luejte
sa gjimon e toka ka po shkojne

tre sahate e gjama per me u
    ndije
hajt me pa nji çude me sye

ne nadje çika e Begut ish kan
    çue
225 e kish marrë gjergjef e gjylpan

e ish hip ne at bedel te kallas

e ish ugj ne at miner deri ne gu

and the Agas received him even
    better,
and they paid their respects to
    Ali.
What did Muji then say to the
    Agas?
210 "Rise, friends and brothers, to
    gird yourselves
and to mount the backs of your
    horses."
And they jumped onto the backs
    of their horses.
They set off on the road going
    across the plain
letting the horses run freely.
215 How quickly they crossed the
    plain!
They started up the mountains,
they sallied forth the towers of
    Beg Osman Beg,
and how quickly they plunged
    through the mountains.
The Agas arrived at the plain of
    the Beg's
220 letting their horses run freely.
How the earth thundered where
    they passed,
the sound could be heard three
    hours away.
Come see a wonder with your
    own eyes:
the Beg's daughter rose in the
    night!
225 She took out her embroidery
    frame and needle
and she climbed on the battle-
    ments of the tower,
and she lowered herself to her
    knees on the divan.

me at gjergjef çika po qindise

tuej punue gjamen e ka ndije

230 kryte n'xham çika e ka dredh

larg ne fush Agët i ka pa

kalabllek e Agët tuej ardh
e sa trant atlaret tuej lujte

sa mjerue çika kenka kan
235 edhe punen q'athere e ka lan

fluturimi te baba kenka shkue
e çel deren e n'ode kenka hi

o bab-loke Begut i ka than
qe ç'kabahat e Bab ç'ke bâ

240 tubë asqer kullat na i ka mësye

Begu çikes q'athere i ka than

kabahat kerkun nuk kam bâ
por mysafirit e lum baba qi jan

kurr i fije çikë mos me u frigue

245 po del lum baba ne bedelt te
     kallas
keçyre a mundesh bije per me i
     njofte
çika baben sa mire p'e ndigjon

u dredh e shkoj n'at kalla ka hip

e me sy Agët qi po i kerçyre

The girl embroidered on the
     embroidery frame;
she heard the din while she was
     working.
230 The girl turned her head
     towards the window:
she saw the Agas far off in the
     plain,
the Agas coming in a crowd,
and how their horses galloped
     madly.
How wretched the girl became:
235 She immediately abandoned her
     work
and went flying to her father.
She opened his door and
     entered his room.
"Oh, father—she said to the Beg—
what sin have you committed,
     father?
240 A troop of soldiers has sallied
     forth against our towers."
The Beg thereupon said to his
     daughter:
"I have not committed any sin,
rather these are good guests of
     your father.
Do not be the least bit afraid,
     daughter.
245 But go out, daddy's darling, to the
     battlements of the fortress,
see if you can recognize them
     for me, daughter."
How well the girl obeyed her
     father:
she turned and went to climb
     the tower
and she observed the Agas with
     her eyes.

250 e fort kulles Agët ju kan afrue

e s'po mundet çika per me i
   njoft
prap te Begu n'sob kenka shkue

more babe s'po muej un me i
   njoft
veç se njo bab qi po pergitet

255 kujtoj asht ai Sirotin Alia
Begu çikes n'jathere e ka nam

Zoti te vraft mori Begzadie e
   bukur
ku e pa ti Alien e me e njoft

çika n'mare q'atherë ish ra
260 babes vet bê edhe po mi bon

po i bon bê n'at lumin perendi
se kam pa Alien kurr me sye
veç mas zanit djalit qi kom ndije

pom pergjet si Alia me kan
265 fjalët vonojne e Agët kerkan
   ardh
tu kulla Begut i kan ra
para Begu sa shpejt jau ka dal

hyzmetqarre Begu i ka brit
atlarët agve jau kan marre
270 selam Muja Begut ja ka dhan

e ma mirë selamin ja ka marrë

atlarët ne podrum jau ka çue

sa mire rahat jau ka bâ

250 The Agas had approached quite
   close to the tower
and the girl was unable to
   recognize them.
She went back into the Beg's
   room:
"O father, I was unable to recog-
   nize them.
I knew only the one who
   answered,
255 I think it was Sirotin Ali."
The Beg then cursed his
   daughter:
"May God strike you dead, beau-
   tiful Begzadje.
Where have you seen Ali to be
   able to recognize him?"
The girl then became distraught
260 and she swore an oath to her
   father.
She swore by blessed God:
"I have never set eyes upon Ali;
It was just by the lad's voice
   that I recognized him.
I guessed that he was Ali."
265 Words lingered, and the Agas
   arrived.
They came to the Beg's tower.
How quickly the Beg went out
   to meet them.
The Beg shouted for the servants,
they took the Agas' horses.
270 Muji gave his greetings to the
   Beg,
and received even better
   greetings.
He sent their horses into the
   stable,
how well he set them at their
   ease.

athere Agvet Begu u paska pri

275 e po hip shkalleve perpjete
e ne atë kulle nalt kankan shkue
n'ode te vet Begu i paska shti

sa iqrom Agve qi po i bon

edhe armet q'athere jau ka vjerr
280 e ne minere te tona jan ugj

mire duhane Begu pom u qet

sheqerlije kafe pom u piek
e me kafe n'qef i ka bâ

prap ish dredh Begu shka kish ba
285 jau ka prue vênen me raki
edhe Agët sa mire po jau shkep

shkoj edhe Mujes goten me ja dhan
p'e merr Muja para e ka vënue

ish dredh Begut e me goj i ka than
290 a ndigjon more Begu Osman Beg
pse s'na vete Agë shka ju ka qitë

kallablleke na qi te kem ardh

q'atherë Begu Mujes shka i ka than
amanete Baba m'ka lan

295 mysafiret brenda kur te vinë

mos i pi vete ka shkon e ku je kan

Then the Beg led the way for
the Agas:
275 he climbed up the steps
and they went up into the tower.
The Beg escorted them to his
own room.
How much respect he showed
the Agas:
he then hung up their weapons,
280 and all of them sat down on the
divan.
The Beg offered them fine
tobacco;
he boiled sweet coffee for them
and his coffee gave them
pleasure.
The Beg turned back—what did
he do?
285 He offered them wine and raki,
and how well did he relax the
Agas.
He went and gave even Muji a
tumbler.
Muji received it and put it in
front of himself.
He turned and said to the beg:
290 "Listen to me, O Beg Osman Beg.
Why don't you ask us what
sends us Agas to you,
as we have come to you in a
crowd."
Then what did the Beg say to
Muji?
"My father has left me a last
request:
295 'When guests come inside the
house
do not ask where they are going
and whence have they come,

se mysafirvet edhe q'ju vjen
   rand

por po s'po muej iqram me u ba

nji motmot qitu per me ndej

300 nuk ju vetë ç'bevoje ju ka prue

me te foli Çeto Basha Muji

nji nevoje të madhe ketu Beg na
   ka prue

jan marrë Agët nder vedi me u
   pre

per çike tande kan desht e me u
   pre

305 të ka ndie zanin Sirotin Alia

miku burr i mire e çiken ma
   t'mire

edhe thotë Alia e kam nxane

fat per vedi thotë dhe me e
   marre

edhe trodhete Agë me hajre ja
   kem bâ

310 veç s'ja bani aj Dezdar Agë
   Osmani

heçyr more beg ai Dezdari shka
   ka bâ

Zoti të vraft thotë Sirotin Alia

qi n'mik têmin ty shka të ka çue

i thotë per djal un çiken e kam
   xane

315 edhe per gjallet un çiken nuk ta
   la

edhe jalla bon e shpaten e ka
   nxjerre

mësye Alien e me shpat don me
   e pre

e Alia fort qi u idhnue

for that will be difficult for both
   guests and you.'

Whether I can or not I must pay
   you due respect

even if you are to remain here a
   whole year,

300 I do not ask you what misfor-
   tune has brought you here."

Çeto Basha Muji spoke up:

"A great need has brought us
   here, Beg.

The Agas have started to kill
   each other.

They wanted to kill each other
   over your daughter.

305 Sirotin Ali learned of your
   reputation:

a good man for an in-law and
   for the girl even better.

And he says 'I have taken her:

I want to take—he says—a
   consort for myself.'

And the thirty Agas rejoiced,

310 only Dezdar Aga Osman did not.

Look, O Beg, at what Dezdar did:

'May God strike you dead,
   Sirotin Ali—he said—

what made you go to my in-law?

—he said to him—I have taken
   the girl for my son

315 and by my life I will not let you
   have the girl.'

And he cried out 'Allah' and
   drew his sword.

He attacked Ali and wanted to
   cut him down with his sword.

And Ali became very angered,

si vetim n'kamb edhe a çue

320 prej mille shpaten e ka nxjerre

hurrysh ban nder vedi me u pre
e tridhete Aget sa vështir i kem
da
por ti fjalet Agë ki me jau
keputë
na t'kem mesye edhe n'xhak
t'kem ra
325 cillin duesh mike per me e
nxane
cillin duesh çiken me ja dhan

çikes hajrin q'aj edhe ja patë

fjalët per nrapa ma edhe nuk ka
keçyre c'foli Begu Osman Beg
330 pa ndigjoni e tridhete more Agë
evllad tjeter e Zoti nuk m'ka fal

fort per qef at çiken e kam pas
bê kam bâ ne din edhe iman

kuj vetë çiken me goj me ja
dhan
335 vet ka te don çika ka me marrë

athere ç'bani Begu Osman Beg

ne tjetren ode te Fatime a shkue

per fillue çikes begu i ka kalzue

të ka lyp bije ty Sirotin Alia

340 fat per vedi Ali per me të marre

edhe me hajr Agët qi t'kan bâ

and he jumped to his feet like
lightning

320 and drew his sword out of its
sheath.
He attacked to kill him among us
and the thirty Agas separated
them with difficulty.
But you, Aga, will settle the
matter:
we have sallied forth to you and
come upon your house
325 to learn which one you want to
take as an in-law;
which one you want to give
your daughter to.
Which one is to have the good
fortune of the girl,
your decision will be unchanged."
See what Beg Osman Beg said:
330 "Listen to me, O thirty Agas.
God has granted me no other
children,
I have loved my daughter greatly.
I have sworn an oath by my
faith and my belief
to give my consent for my
daughter to the one
335 that my daughter herself wants
to take."
What did Beg Osman Beg then
do?
He went into another room to
Fatima.
He related everything in detail
to the girl:
"Daughter, Sirotin Ali has asked
for you,
340 Ali wants to take you for his
consort,
and the Agas were happy for him.

e ka lyp aj Dezdar Agë Osmani

e per djali don aj Dezdari me të
    marrë
e jau hjek nder vedi per me u
    pre
345 qajre s'asht bije jeme njanin per
    me e marre
ban bê Begu ne din edhe iman

ty me goje çike kurre skam me
    të dhan
as kund mike me ty skam me
    nxane
por ku te duesh ti vet per me u
    martue
350 keçyre çika q'athere q'kish punue
u vesh e u mbath e mire kenka
    shtrengue
e me havajle mire qi kanka
    mblue
e ne xhep nji mollë e paska gjue

per mbas babes n'ode kenka
    shkue
355 n'ode nder Age çika kur a hi

tridhete Age kryt e kan ugj

po u vjen mare çiken me shikue

pak vonon e çike q'ka punue

tridhete Age me rend po i
    shikon
360 e keçyre per seri at Bylyk Basha
    Mujin
sa t'mershem Zoti qi kish fal
pak vonoj e çika kenka dredh

And Dezdar Aga Osman has
    asked for you:
Dezdar wants to take you for his
    son.
And they have refrained from
    killing each other.
345 It is not difficult, my daughter,
    to select one of them."
The Beg swears an oath by his
    faith and his belief:
"I will never give my consent,
    daughter,
nor will I take any in-law for
    you,
but you will marry whomever
    you desire yourself."
350 See what the girl then did:
she put on clothes and shoes
    and girded herself well,
she covered herself well with
    her mantle,
and she put an apple into her
    pocket.
She went into the room behind
    her father.
355 When the girl entered the room
    among the Agas
the thirty Agas lowered their
    heads:
they were ashamed to look at
    the girl.
A short time passed, and what
    did the girl do?
She looked at the thirty Agas
    one by one.
360 She looked in wonder at Bylyk
    Basha Muji:
how terrible God had made him!
A short time passed and the girl
    turned around.

ja lëshoj syt Sirotin Alies
edhe doren n'xhep e paska çue

365 e prej xhepit mollen e ka
nxjerre
e me molle Alien e paska gjue
e ne gjykse Alies qi i paska ra
molla ne prehen Alies i ka met
n'xhep Alia e paska shti
370 q'athere çika ish dredh e kenka
dal
me hajre çiken Begu ja kish bâ

e po ja bajne tridhete agalar
hajt e hajt nji seri per me pa

e shka bani Dezdar Age Osmani
375 per hajr çika Ali mos te koft

per te gjalle çiken mos ta la

e per djal u nusen due me e
marre
fort Alie q'atherë ish idhnue
fjalët vonoje e shpaten e ka
nxjerre
380 jurrush ban e Dezdarin per me e
pre
hjeke e madhe n'at ode kenka bâ

Begun deren Agve jau gujoj

Zoti ju vraft e tridhete more Age

po a jeni ardh miq e per me u
nxane
385 miqasisht çiken me jau dhan

She let her eyes fall on Sirotin Ali,
and she put her hand into her
pocket,
365 and she took the apple out of
her pocket,
and aimed the apple at Ali.
It fell on Ali's chest:
the apple remained in Ali's lap.
Ali then put it into his pocket.
370 Thereupon the girl turned away
and went out.
The Beg was happy for his
daughter,
the thirty Agas also rejoiced
but wait and behold a wondrous
sight.
What did Dezdar Aga Osman do?
375 "May you not succeed with the
girl, Ali,
by my life I will not let you have
the girl
and I will take her as a bride for
my son."
Then Ali became very angered.
After the words were spoken he
took out his sword,
380 he rushed at Dezdar in order to
kill him.
A great uproar arose in the
room.
The Beg closed the door on the
Agas.
"May God strike you dead, oh,
thirty Agas!
Have you come to take me as an
in-law,
385 for me to give away my daughter
in a friendly manner,

po a jeni ardhe e mejdan e mem
    lyp
nuk muej tanve n'oxhak e me u
    pre
nji aj qi të doni ne mejdan kish
    mu dal
si me krajla me ju per me u pre
390 ma kabul Agve e kish bâ
se kete pune n'sob nder vedi me
    u pre

po sa veshtir ne miner i ka ugj

qysh oxhakun ju per me ma
    korrit
n'kullat mija miqët e qish me u
    pre
395 tjeter mare mue s'mu kish desht

fort idhnue Begu kenka kan
prap te çika s'sob kenka shkue
prej idhnimit çiken qi p'e nam

Zoti te vraft thotë Fatime
    Turkija
400 djal as çike tjeter nuk kam

per hazret edhe çike te kam
    mbajt
kenka shkrue sherrin me ta pa

miqët nder vedi mbrenda mem
    u pre
shtate krajlit në veshe per me u
    marre
405 qe zez dita tu Begu kenka bâ

per sherr ton bije Agët don me
    u pre

or you have come to ask me to
    duel?
I cannot kill all of you at my
    hearth;
let the one that you choose
    come out to duel me,
to fight with you as kings do."
390 He answered them more:
"Why don't you settle this
    matter among yourselves in
    this room?
—How heavily he lowered
    himself to the divan—
Which of you will dishonor my
    hearth?
In my tower, friends, whom will
    you kill?
395 You could not wish me any
    other shame."
The Beg was very angered,
he went back to the girl's room.
Out of anger he cursed his
    daughter:
"May God strike you dead,
    Fatima Turkija!—he said—
400 I have no son nor another
    daughter.
And I have kept you respected,
    my daughter.
It was fated for us to witness
    discord,
for our best friends to quarrel,

so the Seven Kings would find
    out
405 that a dark day had befallen the
    Beg.
The Agas will fight over our
    discord, my daughter.

unë nuk dije mori çike shka me
   bâ
çika babes q'atherë i ka thanê
mos ki dert more bab i ka brit

410 se ishalla sherrin mua nuk ma
     sheh
se q'ato pune vet kam me i da

si ish kan çika vet ne minere tue
   ndej
jalla bani edhe n'kamb kenka çue
as s'asht vesh as hiq s'kenka
   shtrengue

415 q'ata tesha n'vesh qi i kan qillue
pa havajle nder Agë kenka
   shkue
prej idhnimit çika qi ish gushtue

fort me goje Agët qi po mi nam

Zoti të vraft o Bylyk Basha Muji

420 e pa u vra Zoti Agë mos ju lasht

po a jeni ardh miqet per me na
   nxane
po a jeni ardh ketu nder vedi me
   u pre
per imij vjete oxhakun me na
   fliqe
u dredh çika Agvet e ju k'i than

425 po ban bê ne din e iman
un dunjaja burre skam me
   marrë
veç n'past bâ nana ndonji djal

me perkun motra ndonji vlla

I do not know, daughter, what to
   do."
The girl then said to her father:
"O father, do not worry—she
   cried—

410 for no discord, God willing, will
     come to pass,
because I will settle the matter
   myself."
As the girl was sitting by herself
   on the cushions,
by Allah, she rose to her feet,
she was neither dressed nor at
   all girded

415 wearing what clothes she had on.
She went out among the Agas
   without her mantle,
the girl was hard pressed out of
   anger.

She loudly curses the Agas
   directly:
"May God strike you dead, Çeto
   Basha Muji,

420 may God not leave you alive, O
     Agas.
Have you come to take us as
   in-laws,
or have you come here to kill
   each other
and to defiling our house for a
   thousand years?"
The girl turned and said to the
   Agas:

425 "I swear by my faith in God
there is no man on earth I will
   take,
unless a mother gives birth to a
   hero,
or a sister proffers any brother,

e ne past ba pela ndonji mase
t'mire
430 qi mi bjen djali ne shpine
ne ato bjeshke djali per me e dal

se n'bjeshk a dal aj Milosh
Kapitani
edhe treqind shkije me vedi i ka
marre
e çardakun n'ate bjeshk e ka bâ

435 e zidanin me bjeshk e ka
mbarue
kur i nxane turqit ne mal e per
bjeshk
çetanikt n'bjeshkt kur po
kerkojne
e po i nxane e ne zidan po i
shtin
e gjejtarvet bjeshkvet kah
gjejtojne
440 po i nxan e ne zidan po i shtin

e çobata me gja ka po shkojn

n'ato bjeshke dalin e verojne

kerku te mjeret nuk guxojne me
shkue
e bjeshkët Miloshi te tona i ka
zapue
445 as lan kon travinen per me i
marre
per muhasere dunjan e ka bâ
kush te djalin Miloshin rrob me
e nxanë
te kulla s'gjallit me na prue

e ne zidone vetem per me e shti

or a mare gives birth to a fine
steed,
430 for the boy to mount on its back
and for the boy to ride into the
mountains.
For Captain Milosh has ridden
into the mountains,
he has taken three hundred
Slavs with him
and built a manor house in the
mountains
435 and has completed a prison in
the mountains.
When he captures Turks in the
highlands and mountains,
when they were raiding in
raiding parties,
he seizes them and throws them
into the prison.
And when hunters were
hunting in the mountains,
440 he seizes them and throws them
into the prison.
And when shepherds were
herding their flocks,
coming out to spend the
summer in the mountains,
the wretches dared not go
anywhere.
Milosh has taken over all the
mountains,
445 without stopping to seize the
grassy meadows.
He has laid siege to our lands.
Whoever goes out to take
Milosh prisoner,
and to bring him back to the
tower alive,
and to simply throw him into
the prison,

450	e treqind shkije Miloshit me ja pre		450	and to cut down Milosh's three hundred Slavs,
	e prej zidanit turqit por me i nxjerre			and to release the Turks from his dungeon,
	rrofsh me token çardakun me ja djeg			razing his manor house to the ground,
	q'at fat per burr per vedi kom me e marrë			that is the groom I will take for myself.
	ndo tybe koft kurr shkom e me u martue			Otherwise I will never marry."
455	u dredh çika prej odet a dal		455	The girl turned away and left the room,
	edhe hiq nuk foli Begja tjeter fjal			and the Beg did not utter another word.
	tridhete Agë ne mare kenkar ra			The thirty Agas became embarrassed,
	edhe e kan ugj kryte per tokë			and they lowered their heads to the ground.
	e duhani a pre e s'muej e pinë			They stopped smoking and could not drink,
460	as nji lafe per vedi s'p'e bajne		460	nor did they speak one word to each other.
	Begu ish met n'kamb e tue keçyre			They Beg remained on his feet, watching them.
	pak kan ndej e shum fort s'kan vonue			They sat for a while and did not wait long.
	aj Dezdari me djal hiq s'po lua			Dezdar and his son did not stir at all.
	jalla u çue Sirotin Alia			By Allah, Sirotin Ali rose,
465	si vetima n'kamb kenka çue		465	he rose like lightning to his feet.
	arme e shpata Alia i paska ngjesh			Ali put on his weapons and sword.
	tymyrmeqi shokë i paska than			"Farewell my friends—he said—
	tymyrmeqi u pjeshim na me hajr			farewell may we meet again in good times:
	se unë per bjeshk e rrugen due me u marrë			because I want to get on my way to the mountains,
470	nuk muej fytyren shoke me ju marrë		470	I cannot lose face my friends.

ndo Miloshin shoke kam me e
nxanë
ndo ne bjeske kryte due me e
lan
ka qit Begu Alia e i ka than
pash nji Zot more Ali qi të ka
dhan
475 per çiken t'eme krytë mos me e
lan
hiq dobiri rixhaja nuk ban
por a djerg shkallave te posht
prej podrumit dorien e ka
nxjerre
në telqit kalit bisargjet i kish
pas
480 shpejt e shpejt Alia i paska çel
nande kollana prej tyne i ka
nxjerre
e te nandë dories ja ka vënue

edhe frenin mire ja pashka
ndrrue
nji gjem te vogel ne goj ja ka qit

485 sa nandë oksh ne kandare me
ardh
edhe ne shpine dories i paska ra

Begun doren q'athere ja paska
dhan
tymyrmeq u pjekshim na me hajr
se q'ahstu shkrue e kysmet
kanka kan
490 e n'fushë dorien e paska qit

sa idhnue Alia ish kan
krejt n'hava dorien qi po ma çon

sa idhnue dorien e kish pas

Either I will take Milosh, my
friends,
or I will leave my head in the
mountains."
The Bey addressed Ali and said:
"For the love of God who made
you, Ali,
475 do not lose your head over my
daughter."
His plea was to no avail.
Ali climbed down the stairs,
he led his bay horse from the
stable,
he had saddle bags on the
horse's saddle.
480 In a second he opened them.
He took nine belts out of them

and placed all nine on the bay
horse,
and deftly changed reins.

Into its mouth he placed a small
bit
485 weighing nine *okas* on the scale.

And he jumped on the back of
his bay horse,
and them extended his had to
the Beg.
"Farewell! I hope we meet again.
As it is written will be my fate."

490 And he sent his bay horse into
the plain.
How angered Ali was!
He sent the bay horse straight
into the air.
How angered the bay horse
became!

shkum te bardha dorja po
gjuhet
495 gjith ka shkon fushen se Begut

gjith po doken si copa me borë

e sa shpejt atë fushen e kaloj
me shpejt ne bjeshken kenka
hip
po shetit tha bjeshk edhe ne
bjeshk
500 a asht mymqym Miloshin me
zatet
kish kerkue tri dit e tri net

e çardakun kerkue se ka gjet

kur ish dal nji bjeshk e te nalt

nji maxhar n'ate bjeshk ish
zatet
505 sa serbez aj maxhari m'ish kan
arm e shpatat mira qi i kish pas
e i kish hip at vrançit te zi
kur ish ardh me Alies ish zatet
sa me rrue maxhari ish kan

510 e kish dredh vrançit perpjet
e kish nisë e q'atherë per me ikë

erdhe Alia me za i ka brit
ndal Maxhar thotë Zoti te vraft

gja te keqe me tue nuk kam
515 sal dy fjal due me te pëvete
probatin Miloshin qi e kam
qe tre dit po e lypi neper bjeshk

nuk po di çardakun me ja gjet

The bay horse spit out white
foam
495 all the while crossing the Bey's
plain,
all the while looking like flakes
of snow.
How quickly it crossed the plain!
Even quicker it climbed up the
mountain.
It galloped from mountain to
mountain
500 but was unable to catch up with
Milosh.
He searched for three days and
three nights,
but did not find the manor
house anywhere.
When he came out on a high
mountain
he met up with a Magyar on the
mountain.
505 How bold the Magyar was:
he had fine weapons and swords,
he was mounted on a black horse.
When he caught up with Ali
how clean shaven the Magyar
was.
510 He turned the black horse uphill
and started then and there to
flee.
Ali cried out in a loud voice:
"Stop, Magyar—he said—may
God strike you dead!
I have nothing bad against you,
515 I just want to ask you.
I have a blood brother, Milosh,
whom I have been looking for
three days in the mountains.
I do not know how to find his
manor house.

se jam dal Miloshin me kuntue
520 probatin maxhar m'ka qillue

se n'kamb a çue aj Bylyk Basha Muji
edhe tridhete Aga me vedi i ka marre
qe shtate dit ne bjeshk qi a dal

po na lype at Milosh Kapitanin
525 me asqer e Miloshit e me i ra
e me luft Miloshin e me i djeg
e asqerin Muja me ja pre
e zidadin bjeshken me ja qart

jam dal Miloshit me i kalzue
530 per iman maxhari kish kujtue

prej vrançit n'toke kish zdrip

per disginash vrançin e kish marrë
tu Alia me rudina a shkue

muhabet Alia i kish bâ

535 qet Alia djalin e pëvete
a din çardakun maxhar me ma gjet
e me shej maxhari ja kish kalzue

çou maxhar rruges me u fillue

tu çardaku dogri mua mem çue

540 u nise maxhari edhe pari po i pri
shkon Alia ne dorien per mas tij

kur jan votë te çardaku me hi

I have come to notify Milosh,
520 that I am his blood brother, O Magyar.

Bylyk Basha Muji has risen to his feet
and has taken the thirty Agas with him.
He has roamed the mountains for seven days

looking for Captain Milosh
525 to attack Milosh's soldiers
and to fight and burn Milosh out,
and to cut down his soldiers,
and to destroy his mountain prison.

I have come to inform Milosh."
530 The Magyar was thinking about his faith in Allah.

He climbed down to the ground from his black horse,

took his black horse by the halters
and went to meet Ali on the mountain pasture.

Ali opened a conversation with him.

535 Addressing him Ali asked the boy
if he knew how to find the manor house.
The Magyar showed him with a nod.

"Get up, Magyar, and head down the road,

direct me straight to the manor house."

540 The Magyar set off riding ahead
Ali followed behind on his bay horse.

When they went up towards the manor house,

keçyr Alia q'atherë s'kish bâ
me shpatë maxharin e kish pre

545 ja kish marre takom e salkom
vete Alia Shka kenka vesh
si maxhar tevdil tuk a bâ

arm e shpate maxharit ja ka
    marre
edhe vet Alia shpaten e ka ngjesh
550 e at jaburen me krye e paska
    vënue
e takamin vrançit ja ka hjek

maxharish dorien e ka shillue

e ne mal maxharin sa mire e ka
    msheh
edhe vrançit bjeshken ja ka
    dhan
555 vet dorjes me shpine i ka ra

kadaldale bjeshkes tue shkue

dy sahat e nate kur ja ba

tu çardaku i Miloshit pashka ra

edhe ne derë të Miloshit po i
    cokat
560 kush je n'derë Miloshi i ka brit

çelma deren jam Maxhar jabanxhi
hyzmeqar te dera ja kan çel

ne podrum dorien e paskan shti
e Alies perpara tek i kan pri
565 te Miloshi ne çardak i kan çue

zanatli Alia edhe ish kan

---

consider what Ali then did:
he cut down the Magyar with
    his sword,
545 and took off his clothing and gear.
Consider what Ali then put on:
he disguised himself like a
    Magyar.
he took the Magyar's weapons
    and sword,
Ali strapped on the sword
550 and placed the Magyar cap on
    his head.
He took off the trappings of the
    black horse
and saddled his bay horse
    Magyar style.
How well he concealed the
    Magyar in the mountains,
and turned the black horse
    loose on the mountain.
555 He himself jumped on the back
    of the bay horse
and slowly rode through the
    mountains.
When it was two hours into the
    night
he reached Milosh's manor
    house,
and he knocked on Milosh's
    door.
560 "Who is that at the door?"
    Milosh cried out.
"I am a Magyar foreigner."
A servant opened the door for
    him,
he put the bay horse in the stable.
Leading the way in front of Ali
565 he took him to Milosh's manor
    house.
Ali was quite crafty,

zhaburen prej kreje e ka hjek
mire pomozhen Miloshit ja ep
sa tazim Alia kenka hi
570 n'kamb Alia per pa u ugj

jalla u çue Milosh Kapitani
doren n'dere Alies ja ka dhan

shka ka qit Miloshi e i ka than

o hozhgjelden o Sirotin Alia
575 e Alia ish dredh e k'i fol
shuj Milosh e Zoti mos te vraft

se un maxhare ne bjeshk jam
mbet
e pa hiri çardakun ta kom gjet

se nuk mujeta ne mal e me fjet

580 qysh kujtohesh emnin me ma
ndrue
emnin turku mua me ma qit
edhe fêen ti mua me ma prish
prap Miloshi ish dredh e k'i than
vet je Sirotin Alia
585 por tevdile Alia je bâ
q'athere foli Alie e kish than
o Milosh thote he Zoti të vraft

po i ban bê ne ate Shejtin e Shen
Pjeter
kurr Alien edhe me sye s'e kam pa
590 per mysafir un sante qi te kam
ardh
mysafir dhe hiri qi po i paske
edhe mbrana kurrnjo nuk po i
lashke
doren n'xhep Alia e paska çue
e me para grushtin e ka mbush

he took the cap off his head
and greeted Milosh well.
How carefully Ali entered,
570 Ali remained on his feet without
sitting down .
By Allah, Captain Milosh got up
and extended his hand to Ali at
the door.
What did Milosh say addressing
him?
"O welcome, O Sirotin Ali."
575 Ali turned and said to him:
"Be quiet, Milosh, may God not
strike you dead,
for I am a Magyar stuck in the
mountains
and have unwillingly found
your manor house,
for I could not sleep in the
mountains.
580 Why have you thought to
change my name,
giving me a Turkish name,
and even fouling my faith?"
Milosh turned and responded:
"You are indeed Sirotin Ali,
585 but you have disguised yourself."
Then Ali spoke and said:
"O Milosh, may God strike you
dead!
I swear a *besa* by the sign of
Saint Peter,
I have never set eyes on Ali.
590 I have come to you this evening
as a guest,
a guest who comes willingly,
and you allow no one inside."

Ali put his hand into his pocket
and he filled his fist with money.

595 mysafirin Milosh po ta laj
se un po dal ne mal due me fjet

mik permbrenda kurrnjo nuk po
    lashke
e Alia q'athere ç'paska bâ
n'tavoline parat ja ka lan
600 u dredh bythprap e shkallave te
    posht
Miloshit keq edhe i ka ardh
te varbive shpejt u paska brit

shpejt maxharin ne çardak me
    ma prue
shpejt Alien bythprap e kan
    kethye
605 ty po të thrret ai Milosh
    Kapitani
u dredh Alia shkallave perpjete

te Miloshi n'ode kenka shkue
sa me qehera Miloshi e ka pritë

kabahatin maxhar me ma fal
610 mysafirt hiri si kom pas
po m'u pergave ne Sirotin Alien
e Alies sa iqrame po i bon
kah je kan e maxhar per ku je
    nise

ku je nise o maxhar rruge me
    shkue
615 thote per qef e bjeshkt me i
    kerkue
kan shtra pijen e po pinë
ven te kuqe e raki te bardhë
sa rakije te forte po e pinë

prej rakisë Alia fort po ruhet

595 "Your guest is leaving you Milosh,
for I want to go out and sleep on
    the mountain,
you do not let a friend inside."

And what did Ali do then?
He left the money on the table,
600 turned back and went down the
    stairs.
And Milosh started to feel bad.
He quickly cried out to his
    servants:
"Bring the Magyar quickly to
    the manor house."
They quickly turned Ali back.

605 "Kapitan Milosh is calling for
    you."
Ali turned and climbed up the
    stairs,
he went to Milosh's room.
How graciously Milosh received
    him:
"Please excuse my impropriety,
610 I did not receive a guest properly,
but you did resemble Sirotin Ali."
How much respect he showed Ali.
"Where are you from, O Magyar,
    and where are you setting
    out for?
Where did you set out to travel
    on the road, O Magyar?"
615 He says he searched for him in
    the mountains for pleasure.
They set out the drinks and drank
red wine and white raki.
How strong the raki they were
    drinking was.

Ali kept well away from the raki,

620 sal ne buzë goten qi po e ven

 pak pinë vet në gjykse tjeter po
  ma qet
 fort ka pi aj Milosh Kapitani
 e asqeri sa shum ju ka dhan
 shum e forte rakia ish kan
625 paska nisë asqerin me jau nxane

 mar e mrapsht ne çardak jan ra

 veç u mbet aj Milosh Kapitani
 me Alien po e gjith tue pi
 tue pie e kllapi e kish nxane

630 e ne gjumë Miloshi kanka ra
 qyge vetem Alia ish kan met
 vet me vedi ne gazep qi a ra

 tash me u çue Miloshin me e
  nxane
 po i del pije e zhurm qi po ban

635 e asqeri mbrapa ka me i ra
 e po me peshton Milosh per pa e
  lidhe
 kollaj asht thotë Miloshin me e
  pre
 po qi me duhet të Begu me e çue
 ma ka lype ajo Fatima Turkije

640 gjalle me sy vete per me e pa

 vet ka than edhe ne zidan me e
  shti
 kadaldal Alia kenka çue
 neper shkije te dera kenka dal

 e ka dal sa shpaten e ka nxjerre

620 only touching the tumbler to
  his lips.
 He drank little himself, drib-
  bling the rest on his chest.
 Kapitan Milosh drank heavily,
 and gave as much to his soldiers.
 The raki was very strong,
625 It began to take hold of the
  soldiers,
 they fell down helter-skelter
  about the manor house.
 Only Captain Milosh was left
 still drinking with Ali.
 While he was drinking dizziness
  overcame him
630 and Milosh fell asleep.
 Ali was left all by himself,
 he became quite pleased with
  himself,
 he now rose to seize Milosh,

 who vomited his drink and let
  out a loud cry.
635 The soldiers ran back
 to save Milosh from being
  bound.
 "It is easy—he says—to cut
  Milosh down,
 but I have to take him to the Beg.
 Fatima Turkija has requested
  this,
640 to see him alive with her own
  eyes,
 and to throw him, she said, into
  the dungeon herself."
 Ali rose very slowly,
 he moved over to the Slavs by
  the door
 moving as soon as he drew his
  sword.

645 nabetxhine te dera e paska pre

gja asqeri permbrenda nuk po din
por mar e mrapsht prej pijet qi jan ra
sa javash Alia qi po i pret
tonve ne fyt shpaten po jau qet

650 e prej shtatit kryte po jau hek

njo si len Alia me brit
treqind shkije q'athere i ka pre

shkoj Miloshi ne kllape per me e pre
po i bjen nder mend Fatima shka i ka than
655 c'po ban aj Sirotin Alia
dy pal pranga të forta mi ka marrë
ne kamb e ne dore t'Miloshit ja ka vuë
e q'athere sa te madhe i paska brit
me nji shkelm Miloshit i ka ra
660 çou Miloshi thotë Zoti të vraft

se te kuj at bjeshk çardakun e ki bâ

edhe zidanin n'to e ki punue

e me zollum bjeshkt e ki zapue

ske lan ne bjeshk kerkon me gjetue
665 po i ki nxane e ne zidon i ke çue

645 He killed the sentries at the door,
the soldiers inside knew nothing of it,
but helter-skelter fell down from drink.
How easily Ali killed them
lunging his sword into all their throats
650 and severing their heads from their bodies.
Ali let none of them cry out.
He then killed the three hundred Slavs.
He went to kill Milosh who was dizzy,
but he remembered what Fatima had said to him.
655 What did Sirotin Ali do?
He took two pairs of strong chains
and placed them on Milosh's legs and arms.
How loudly he then shouted.

And gave Milosh a kick:
660 "Get up, Milosh, may God strike you dead!
From the time you built your manor house in the mountains
and completed the prison on them,
and ravaged the mountains with your cruelty,
you have let no one hunt in the mountains,
665 instead you have captured them and thrown them in prison.

as ki lan nej çoban me verue

as ke lan kon travinen me e
    marre
se qe ky asht Sirotin Alia
mjeri i mjeri me te madhe paska
    brit
670 pram te kam njoft e me syë kur
    te kam pa
po rreziku Ali m'paska ardh
ne n'dore tande more Sirotin
    Alia
gjith shka duhesh more Alo ti ke
    me bâ
shka do te bajsh more halale te
    koft
675 solte shpirti prej tejet n'em
    peshtoft
n'dore tande more Alia qi kofsha
e Alia athere q'kish bâ
per çardak Miloshin e kish kap

e ka djerg per shkallave te posht
680 e n'avllia jasht e ka qit

prej podrumit dorien e ka
    nxjerre
te dy duert shkaut ja ka lidhë

edhe zidanin a shkue e ka çil

prej zidanin turqit i ka nxjerre

685 te gjitha Alies aq duva qi po
    bajne
qi na peshtove në zidan e pa u
    kalb
e çardukut zjarmin e ka shti
te dy kambët Miloshit ja ka zgide

Nor have you let shepherds
    spend the summer on them,
nor have you let them lead
    them to grassy pastures.
Look, this is Sirotin Ali!"
The poor wretch let out a cry:
670 "Last night I did recognize you
    when I set eyes on you!
Misfortune has befallen me, Ali,
we are in your hands, O Sirotin
    Ali,
you can do whatever you wish,
    Ali.
Whatever you do—may you be
    blessed—
675 just let our lives be spared by
    you.
I am in your hands, Ali."
What did Ali then do?
He led Milosh through the
    manor house
and dragged him down the steps,
680 and threw him out into the
    courtyard.
He led his horse out of the
    stable
and tied the two hands of the
    Slav.
He went to the dungeon and
    opened it
and led the Turks out of the
    dungeon.
685 They all sang ample praises to
    Ali
for rescuing them from
    festering in the dungeon.
He set fire to the manor house,
he untied Milosh's two legs,

ja lidhe duert per bishtin e dories
690 nuk vonon e çardaku ja ka djeg

rafsht me toke i thonë shpejt a bâ
e ne shpine dories edhe i ka ra

prej Judbine rrugen e ka marre
dit as natë rrugen nuk p'e ndal

695 n'kamb Miloshi gjithkune mbas tij
po i trupoje edhe bjeshkët i kaloj
n'ate fushë te Begut Alia asht ra
hajt e hajt e nji seri me e pa

keçyre c'po bon Fatime Turkija

700 çika e Begut sa fort ish merzite

i ka marre at serçali turbinë
e ne sye turbinë e ka vënue

po shikon bjeshkt per te gatit

ish merzitë Alien me e pa
705 çyqe jam taksirat paskam pas

ç'far sebep Alies qi un jam bâ

edhe krytë djali qi e ka lan
mâ me sy un e mjera s'kam me e pa
gunit vet e shupllak edhe i ka ra
710 per mbi teshat gjaku e ka mblue

hiq se ndjeu as hiq se ka shikue

and tied his hands to the tail of the bay horse.
690 It was not long before the manor house burned down,
Razed quickly to the ground— they say—
and he jumped on the back of the bay horse,
and set out on the road to Udbina.
Day and night he did not stop on his way
695 with Milosh behind him on his feet.
Cut through and crossing the mountains,
Ali reached the Beg's plain.
Come now and behold an astonishing sight!
See what Fatima Turkija was doing:
700 the daughter of the Beg was so strongly upset,
she seized a spyglass
and put the field glasses to her eyes.
She scanned the mountains to get ready,
she was upset over seeing Ali.
705 "I am all alone, having suffered bad luck,
for what reason did I give myself to Ali
and the boy was to lose his head?
I—a wretched woman—will set eyes on him no more.
An axe blade has struck his cloak
710 and blood has covered his clothes."
She had not touched him at all or looked after him at all.

267

prej marakut Alia qi a shkue	Ali has gone out of love.
e ne turbi prap çika tue shikue	The girl again looked through the field glasses.
ish ardh nana ciken tuej çortue	Her mother came up and scolded her:
715 pa te vra Zoti bije mos e lasht	715 "Daughter, may God not let you live,
ty te vraft Zoti more çika jem e bije	may God strike you dead, darling daughter,
qi e hupe atë Sirotin Ali	for causing the death of Sirotin Ali.
ska pas shoqe djali ne shate krajli	The boy has no equal in the Seven Kingdoms.
ma se sheh ori Bege kurr me syë	You will never set eyes on him again, O lady-beg!"
720 ju kan mbushe sytë plot me lot	720 Her eyes were completely filled with tears.
çou nane bre Zoti te vraft	"Get up, mother, may God strike you dead.
boll merak vete qi kom pas	I had much love for him myself
e ment prej kreje mue qi po më dalin	and I am going out of my mind."
nana çikes turbit i ka kap	Her mother grabbed the field glasses from the girl
725 e sa shpejt po i van ne syë	725 and quickly put them to her eyes.
p'e sheh n'fushë nji sende te zi	She saw something black in the plain.
ka qit çikes lokja i ka than	The mother addressed the girl and said:
drue sytë mori lum nana m'jan çart	"I am afraid your blessed mother's eyes are ruined,
shka po doket ne atë fushe te bardh	what is appearing on the white plain?"
730 nana çikes turbin ja ka dhan	730 The mother handed the field glasses to the girl.
shpejt ne syë çika i paska vue	The girl quickly put them to her eyes,
me sye të zez fushen po ma keçyre	and with her dark eyes looked across the plain.
larg Alien n'ate fushë e ka pa	Far off on the plain she saw Ali

tue ardh ne atë dorien e të kuqë

735 vet po doket si nji pllumb i bardhë
per mbas tina nji korb i zi
nanes vet e çika i ka than
po a din loke kurrgja mem
    kalzue
po vjen fushes nji san si vetima

740 e po doket me e kuqe se gjaku
e në shpinë e ka nji pllumb te
    bardhë
e p'e njek nji korbe i zi
kerkund vendin nanes ja ka lan

nana qiti çikes e i ka than

745 te dy sytë lum lokje ty të plaqin

q'aj qi asht ma i kuqë se gjaku
si vetima fushes tue ardh

aj asht loke dorija i Alies
e ne shpine aj pllumb qi ka ra

750 petka te bardhe Alia qi ka
q'aj mbas tyne nji korbë i zi
ka nxane rrob atë Milosh
    Kapitani
u gezue çika n'kamb kenkan çue

mi shtjen jeniat n'kamb
755 shpejt a djerg shkallave te posht

shpejt i çeli dyert e kallas

edhe fushen vrap e pashka
    marre
larg perpara Alies i ka dal

approaching on his reddish bay
    horse.
735 He looked like a white dove,
behind him a black raven.
And the girl said to her mother:
"Do you know of anything you
    can tell me, mother?
Something is coming across the
    plain like lightning
740 and it looks redder than blood.
On its back it has a white dove,

and a black raven is trapping it."
She made no room for her
    mother.
The mother addressed the girl
    and said:
745 "Your two eyes are getting old,
    mother dearest.
That which is redder than blood,
coming across the plain like
    lightning,
is Ali's bay horse, mother.
And the dove that has jumped
    on its back
750 are the white clothes Ali has.
And the black raven behind him
Is Kapitan Milosh taken
    prisoner."
The girl rejoiced and rose to her
    feet!
She slipped her shoes on her feet
755 and quickly climbed down the
    stairs.
She quickly opened the doors of
    the fortress
and ran full speed across the
    plain.
She stopped far in front of Ali.

hozhgjelden more Sirotin Alia

760 a ahst mymqim ti Alia me kan
edhe nji here me sye me te pa

prej marakut doren po ja rrok
n'te dy faqe puth edhe ja ka
edhe Alia ne toke a ra
765 dore m'dore edhe mbrenda
kenkan hi
hajt e hajt more nji çude me pa
dredh Alia çikes e i ka than

qe ky asht ai Milosh Kapitani
qi e ki lype te gjialle me e pa
770 treqind shkije Miloshit ja kom
pre
e zidanin ne gjeshk ja kom çart

prej zidanit turqit i kam nxjerre

e çardakut zjarmin ja kam dhan
rrafsh me toke çike ja kam bâ

775 e Miloshi n'dorë po ta la
ta çojsh çike ne zidan ke me e
shti
se un jam bâ rezille per gjum

qe shtate dit e shtate net pa fjet

Alia u ngit shkallve perpjet
780 ne ate ode e Begut kenka hi
nana e cikes e hyzmet po i ban

i ka ngjesh armët e sylahin
e ne minere gjumi e kish marrë

keçyrë ç'po ban Fatime Turkija

"It is good that you have come,
O Sirotin Ali!
760 Is it possible for me, Ali,
One more time to set eyes upon
you?"
She grasped the bay horse eagerly
and kissed it on both cheeks.
And Ali jumped to the ground,
765 hand in hand they went inside.

Come and behold this wonder!
Ali turned to the girl and said to
her:
"This is that Kapitan Milosh
whom you requested to see alive.
770 I have killed Milosh's three
hundred Slavs
and I have destroyed his
dungeon in the highlands.
I have released the Turks from
the dungeon
and I have set fire to his manse,
even leveling it, girl, to the
ground.
775 I leave Milosh in your hands.
send him away, girl, and put
him in a dungeon,
for I am ashamed about needing
sleep,
going without sleep for seven
days and seven nights.
Ali climbed up the stairs
780 and went into Beg's room.
The girl's mother taking care of
him.
He took off his weapons and belt
and sleep overcame him on the
divan.
Consider what Fatima Turkija did:

785 prej dories Miloshin e ka zgjidhe

e ka marre ne zidane me e çue

keçyre ç'kish fol aj Milosh
     Kapitani
ori çike e Begzadeje e Bukur

bije oxhakut çike qi je kan

790 po i qet bê ne din edhe iman

po i qet bê ne at lumin perendi

pash nji zot thote çike qi te ka
     dhan
sol pak duer çike te me shlirojsh
se dorija zort edhe m'ka dhan
795 tuej me ngredh zhag dhe rrfan
e konopi n'asht m'ka shkue
solte pak e çikë me mi shlirue
se pa egjel shpirti don mem
     shkue
çika e re kopilana nuk ish kan
800 shkau e rrejti e çiken e kish
     mashtrue
sol pak duert Miloshit ja ka
     shlirue
fort asgan Miloshi qi ish kan
copa copa konopët i kish bamë

qe zez dita q'aty kenka bamë

805 e per krahit çikes ja ka ngjit
per dizginash dorien i kish kap

ne shpine Miloshi i kish ra

e n'telqija çiken i kish qit
e per vedi sa mire e kish lidh

---

785 she untied Milosh from the bay
     horse
seized him to send him to the
     dungeon.
Consider what Kapitan Milosh
     said:
"Oh, my girl, Begzadeje the
     Beautiful,
daughter of the household that
     you are, girl,
790 I swear a *besa* to you on the
     Muslim faith,
I swear a *besa* to you on our
     blessed God,
for the love of God who made
     you, girl—he says—
just untie my hands a bit, girl,
for the bay horse injured me,
795 pulling and dragging me about
and the rope has been cutting me.
Just untie me a bit, girl,
because my spirit will depart
     before its appointed time."
The young girl was not clever,
800 the Slav lied to her and deceived
     her.
She untied Milosh's hands just a
     bit.
Milosh was extremely strong,
he broke the rope into small
     pieces.
There and then the day tuned
     out badly for her,
805 he grabbed the girl's arm
and seized the bay horse by the
     bridle.
Milosh jumped onto the back of
     the horse
and sat the girl on the saddle
and tightly tied her to himself.

810 me dizgina dorien e p'e ngra	810 He whipped the horse with the bridle
prej krajlish kryte e ka dredh	and turned its head towards the Kingdom.
e sa rrepte Miloshi qi po i bjen	Milosh struck it so violently,
me gjith mish lekure po ja hjek	he took off some hide and flesh.
gjam te madhe toka qi po ban	The earth let out a loud rumble,
815 ka po shkon dorija tue ladrue	815 the bay horse was on its way leaping
kullat Begut gjiamat tuej ju dridh	rattling the windows of Beg's tower
kryte ne gjam honmi e ka qit	turning all heads towards the window.
larg n'fushë Milloshin e ka pa	far off on the plain she saw Milosh.
hiq s'kish muejt çika per me brit	The girl could not cry out at all,
820 me dore gojen zue dhe ja ka	820 he had covered her mouth with his hand.
nana çikes e Alies i ka brit	The girl's mother cried out to Ali:
çou Ali e kryte mos e çofsh	"Get up, Ali, may you not lose your heard,
qjumi zi Aliet e ka marre	a deadly sleep has overcome you, Ali.
ta muer nusen Milosh Kapitani	Kapitan Milosh has taken your bride.
825 n'shpine dories edhe i ka ra	825 He has jumped on the back of his bay horse
larg ne fushë ala asht the shkue	and, oh my God, he is riding far off on the plain!"
gjumi i idhen me det i ka dal	His troubled sleep came to an end.
kryte ne gjam Alia paska çue	Ali put his face to the window.
larg ne atë fushë Miloshin e ka pa	Far off on the plain he saw Milosh
830 tuej shkue fushen e trupoje	830 riding and cutting through the plain,
p'e krajlies rrugen e filloj	setting off on his way to the Kingdom.
shka me bâ Alia veç me e nam	What could Ali do but curse?

e sa n'zorr i mjeri kenka ra

How difficult it became for the poor wretch.

e i ka ngjesh armët e sylahin

He put on his belt and weapons.

835 e shahin n'dorë e ka marre

835 Taking his falcon in his hand

e per mas Alia ju ka vënue

Ali placed it behind him.

kamb at fushen i mjeri e ka trupue

The poor wretch cut across the plain on foot,

per mbash tina kambe tue shkue

walking behind them on foot.

m'ato bjeshk Ali kur a dal

When Ali came to the highland pasture

840 ne tjerat bjeshk Miloshi e ka pa

840 he saw Milosh on another highland pasture.

ne tjerat bjeshk Alia kur a dal

When Ali came to the other highland pasture

ndoj krajli Miloshi kenka ra

Milosh had descended into some Kingdom.

fille m'ish votë te Krajleviçe Marku

He went straight to Marko Kraljević

e bakshish Fatimen ja ka çue

and handed him Fatima as a gift.

845 e per fillë krajlit i kish kalzue

845 He told the King everything in detail:

qi treqind shki Alia mi ka pre

"Ali has killed my three hundred Slavs,

e zidanin n'bjeshk ma ka qart

and has destroyed my dungeon in the highlands,

e rrafsh me toke çardakun ma ka bâ

and has razed my manse to the ground.

e rrob te gjalle Alia qi m'ka nxane

Ali captured me alive as a prisoner

850 e n'krahine mue qi m'ka çue

850 and sent me off to the Borderland."

q'athere krajli kerçyre shka ka bâ

Consider what the King then did:

treqind topa në shejlak po shprazë

He fired three hundred cannons as a signal

e shtatë krajlat ne darsem i ka thirrë

And summoned the Seven Kings to his wedding.

në bjeshk topat Alia i ka ndije

In the mountains Ali heard the cannons,

855 mire e pa Miloshi qi i peshtoj

e asht ugj ne ledin me pushue

e sa lodh Alia kanka kan
tre sahate pushime i ka bâ
ne kujtim e ne mendim qi ka ra

860 thotë jam nisum tevdile pa u bâ

un ne krajli q'ishtu per me ra

njgind krena ne trup e me i pas

njo pa pre krajlit e s'ma lan

bê kam bâ bythprape mos me u
kethye
865 boftë i Zoti e q'athere kenka çue
prej krajlish rrugen e ka marrë

kur kish marre nji bjeshken e te
poshtë
në ato male Alia tue shkue
po ma ndije i cakicë tue krisë
870 e Alia aty asht shkue
e ka gjet nji mjeshter tue punue

shkoj Alia dhe me shpate e k'i
pre
q'ata tesha e atij mjeshtrit ja ka
marre
permbi petkat veta i ka vesh

875 per non-petkash shpaten e kish
shti
e ish nxije fort ish kan çudue

edhe mustaket me gershan i
kish shkurtue

855 he realized that Milosh had
been rescued,
he sat down on the grassy
meadow to rest.
And Ali was so tired,
he rested for three hours.
He started remembering and
fell to thinking.
860 He says: "I set off without
putting on a disguise.
If I were to appear in the
Kingdom this way,
even if I had a hundred heads
on my body,
the King would not let a single
one of them go unsevered.
I have given my *besa* that I
would not turn back."
865 By the grace of God he then rose
and set off on his way to the
Kingdom.
When Ali set off down to a
mountain meadow.
While walking in the mountains
he heard an axe chopping away.
870 And Ali went towards it:
he found a craftsman working
away.
Ali went and killed him with his
sword.
He took the garments of the
craftsman
and put them over his own
clothes.
875 Under his clothes he hid his
sword.
He blackened his face and made
himself ugly,
and trimmed his moustache
with a pair of scissors.

e halatat mjeshtrit ja ma marrë
e në nji thes Alia qi i kish shti
880 e mbas krahit q'athere i ka qit

në tjetren dorë cakicen e ka
        marrë
shkon tuej mbajte rruges tuej
        shkepue
e ne fushë të krajli kur a ra

e asqerin me syë e ka pa
885 e krajli ne fushë e te ton i kish
        qit
i kish ngreh dajren e salkamin

shtate krajlit ne darsem qi i kish
        thirr
e xhevapin ne krajli e kish hap

kam marre nusen e Sirotin Alies

890 e ja kom marre dorien e
        mejdanit
ja ka marrë ai Milosh Kapitani
per bakshisht edhe mue mi ka
        prue
per shkêj tyne Alia tue shkue

edhe rreth asqerit i ka ra
895 ne pazar e q'athere kur a hi

shkon pazarit Alia tue shikjue

thesin në krah e gjith tue
        shkepue
nji mehane q'athere e ka gjet
q'at mihane Alia kenka hi
900 e të dera thesin e ka gjue
nji karrig e q'athere tuk a ugj

He took the craftsman's tools
and stuck them in a bag,
880 and then threw it over his
        shoulder.
In his other hand he took the
        hatchet
and walked keeping to the road
        and limping.
When he descended to the plain
        of the King
he caught sight of the soldiers.
885 The King had sent all of them
        onto the plain.
He had let loose drums and
        cannons,
summoning the Seven Kings to
        his wedding.
He had spread the news
        throughout the Kingdom:
"I have taken the bride of
        Sirotin Ali
890 and I have taken his bay battle
        mount.
Kapitan Milosh has stolen them
and has brought them to me as
        gifts."
Ali went walking among the
        Slavs
and fell in among the soldiers.
895 Then when he entered the
        market place,
he walked around the market
        place, looking around,
the bag on his shoulder, and
        limping all the while.
Then he found a tavern.
Ali entered the tavern
900 and placed the bag by the door.
He then sat down on a chair

nji uqarm me te madhe paska leshue	and let out a big sigh.
aty ish kan Maruka e mihanes	The tavern keeper Maruka was there,
e ka qit Alies edhe i ka than	she addressed Ali and said:
905 a po aq fort ore mjeshter qi je lodh	905 "Are you that tired, O craftsman?"
dredh Alia e me goje e k'i fol	Ali turned and spoke to her directly:
me ma prue nji gotë me raki	"Bring me a glass of raki,
se bol jam lodhe e ketu mezi kom mbri	for I am very tired and barely reached here."
q'athere Mara goten ja ka çue	Thereupon Mara brought him a glass
910 e ne dorë Alies ja ka dhan	910 and put it in Ali's hand.
dredh Alia Maren p'e pëvete	Ali turned and asked Mara:
pash i zote thotë Mare qi te ka dhan	"By the grace of God who made you—he says to Mara—
ç'far xhevapit Krajlit e i ka ardh	what news has come to the King?
qi jam kan ne bjeshk tue punue	I have been in the mountains working,
915 treqind topa ne bjeshk qi i kam ndigue	915 in the mountains I heard three hundred cannons.
kam than sheherit ton dotë ish rranue	I thought the whole city might be destroyed."
u dredh Mara Alies e i paska brit	Mara turned towards Ali and cried out,
pse po pivet e goja ty te thaft	"Why are you asking; may your mouth dry up?"
dy pal lot per faqja i kan pështue	Two streams of tears ran down her face.
920 e te zezë diten o mjeshter me te kalzue	920 "It is a dark day, O craftsman, I inform you of.
Zoti e vraft atë Milosh Kapitanin	May God strike dead that Kapitan Milosh!
i ka marre nusen Sirotin Alies	He has stolen the bride of Sirotin Ali,
e ja ka marrë atë dorien e mejdanit	he stole his bay battle mount

e bakshish të krajli ja ka prue

925 e ka ngreh dajren e salkamin

shtate krajlit ne darsem qi i ka thirr

çyqe jau te madhe paska brit

qi s'ma qet Zoti Sirotin Alien

se ndo kryte vet qi kish me e hup

930 ndo edhe Alies qi kishna me i ndihmue

u dredh Alia Maren po e pëvetë

Zoti të vraft e Maruke mehanxhija

qysh ti Turkut Maruk me i dhihmue

ku e njeh atë Sirotin Alien

935 qi per Alien kryte don me e hup

qiti Mara Alies i ka thon

kom nevoje kryte per me e hup

se nandë vjet ne Judbine kam ndej

m'ka nxane rrobi baba i Alies

940 e nandë vjet ne Judbine qi me ka mbajte

i ka fal zoti atë Sirotin Alien

ne prehen tem Alia qi a rritë

e shtate vjeç Alia qi a bâ

e q'athere per mua Alia qi ka dite

945 qi jam rrobi e nxanun prej krajlish

e babes vetë rixha i ka bâ

ore bab rrobin me ma fal

per me leshue me shkue ne krajli

---

and brought them to the King as gifts.

925 He has let loose drums and cannons,

summoning the Seven Kings to his wedding."

The wretched woman let out a loud cry:

"Why does not God send me Sirotin Ali?

For either I would have lost my own head,

930 or Ali's whom I would have helped."

Ali turned and asked Mara:

"May God strike you dead, tavern keeper Maruka,

Why would you help a Turk, Maruka?

How do you know Sirotin Ali,

935 well enough to lose your head for Ali?"

Mara addressed Ali and said:

"I need to lose my head,

for I have spent nine years in Udbina.

Ali's father took me captive

940 and held me in Udbina for nine years.

God granted him Sirotin Ali.

Ali was raised on my bosom.

When Ali became seven years old

Ali then learned all about me,

945 that I was taken captive from the Kingdom.

And he made a request to his father:

'Dear father, grant me the captive

so that I can free her go to the Kingdom,

se ka lan toke edhe belqim ka
lan shpi
950 asht merzitë e mjera per vllazni

tash nandë vjete si kam pa me
syë
atherë ç'bani baba i Alies
qi a çue e n'at ode e a shkue
i ka marrë shtateqind duket
955 e ne sob perpara mi ka prue

meri Mara me goj m'ka than

e halale Zoti e ti boft
se shum hyzmet mue m'ki bâ
n'duert tueja djali mi ka rrite

960 holashtese me ta qi jam kan
edhe rrugen prej krajlish e kam
marre
gjith the kajt rruges qi jam ardh
sa me u dhimt q'aj Sirotin Alia
e kom dit per ymer skom me e
pa
965 lot per faqe Mares tue m'ish
shkue
me Alien edhe gjith tue dertue
shka ish dredh Alia e i ka than
pash nji Zot mori Mare qi të ka
dhan
pa me jep nji besen e te Zotit
970 te m'dhaç atë besen e Perendisë
per Alien edhe diçka po te kalzoj

bese e fê Mara ja ka dhan
qi toka e çiella me u rrotullue

kuj fjalet tueja skom me ja
kalzue
975 u dredh Alia Mares i ka than

for she has left her homeland
and perhaps her family.
950 She is concerned, the poor
thing, about her brothers
whom she has not set eyes on
for nine years.'
What did Ali's father do then?
He rose and went into his room.
He took seven hundred ducats
955 and brought them down to me
in my room.
'Poor Mara—he said to me
directly—
farewell—may God bless you—
for you have served me well,
and you have raised my son
with your own hands.'
960 I bade him farewell,
and set out on the road to the
Kingdom,
crying on the road I went on.
I hurt so much for Sirotin Ali,
I knew I would not see him
again in my lifetime."
965 Tears went down Mara's face,

ever worrying about Ali.
Ali turned and said to her:
"By the grace of God who made
you, O Mara,
swear to me your sacred *besa*.
970 give me your *besa* to God,
and I will tell you something
about Ali."
Mara swore a *besa* on her faith:
"If earth and sky were to spin
around
I would never disclose your
words."
975 Ali turned and said to Mara:

un nuk muej ne mihane me të
    kalzue
ma ka marrë n'shpi e pasha çue

q'athere Alia nji grim ish rahatue
Mare djalit prap per fille i kish
    kalzue
980 une ne krajli more mjeshter kur
    jam ra
me mal Talies qirak qi jam bâ

qi kam ngreh dugaj e mihan
gjysen e sheherit temen e kam
    bâ
e per Alien e mjera kish me dit

985 shka m'kalzon ti mjeshter qi
    m'ke mashtrue

u dredh Alia q'athere ç'kish
    punue
teshat mjeshtrit permbi qi kish
    pas
e i ka hek e n'tokë i pashka gjue

shpaten e babes të ngjeshun qi e
    kish pas
990 edhe Mares ja kishe kalzue
jalla Mara n'kamb q'athere a cue

njofti shpaten edhe n'gryk e
    paska marrë

bashk per fille Alia i ka kalzue
vet jam Marë Sirotin Alia
995 bese te zotit e tanden kjofsh ra
mundesh Mara kryte me ma hup
n'oxhak tande Mara qi te kom ra

"I can not tell you in the
    tavern."
She took him and brought him
    to her house.
Then Ali relaxed a bit.
Mara again related everything
    to the boy in detail:
980 "When I came into the
    Kingdom, O craftsman,
I became an apprentice owing
    to Ali's longing.
I built up a shop and a tavern
and made half the town my
    own."
The poor thing had known
    about Ali:
985 "What are you telling me,
    craftsman who has deceived
    me?"
Thereupon Ali turned, and what
    did he do?
The craftsman's clothes that he
    had on
he took off and threw to the
    ground.
His father's sword which he had
    girded
990 he also showed to Mara.
By Allah, Mara then rose to her
    feet!
She recognized the sword and
    embraced him around the
    neck.
Ali told her everything in detail:
"I am Sirotin Ali, Mara.
995 May your sacred *besa* be granted.
You can lose your head, Mara,
over my coming to your house,
    Mara."

mundesh Mara ti edhe mem ndihmue	You can also help me, Mara."
q'atherë Mara keçyre shka ka bâ	Consider then what Mara did.
1000 me Alien n'gryke qi jan nxane	1000 She hugged Ali around the neck,
lot prej mallit Mares tuej shkue	tears of longing flowed over Mara,
nji sahat Alien nuk e ka leshue	she did not let go of Ali for one hour.
në ode vete q'atherë ma paska çue	She then sent him to her room,
tre dyshek te ri ja paska shtrue	she laid out three pillows,
1005 muhabetin q'athere ja kish fillue	1005 and started a conversation with him.
gjith shka donë goja me kerkue	Whatever he wanted he could ask for directly.
ti Alia thotë hiq mos me u mjerue	"You must not feel sorry at all, Ali,
ndo e fiki sheherin ane e mban	either the town will be demolished from one end to the other,
edhe krytë t'em Alia kam me e lan	and I will lose my head, Ali,
1010 ndo edhe ty kom per me te ndihmue	1010 or I will help you.
se un po dal ne mihane me punue	For I am leaving to work in the tavern
ndonji shkja per mos me na u kujtue	lest any Slav wonder about us."
pak kish ndej shum e s'kish vonue	She stayed there awhile, she did not wait long,
te Alia prap n'sob a shkue	and went back to Ali's room.
1015 keçyre Mara atherë ç'kish punue	1015 Consider what Mara then did:
ne hamam Alien e paska çue	she sent Ali to the steam bath,
e e kish la e ma mire e kish ndrrue	washed him and dressed him even better.
nji pal tesha çikash ja ka çue	She sent him a pile of women's clothing
e Alia teshat i ka vesh	and Ali put some clothes on.
1020 per nen-tesha shpaten e ka ngjesh	1020 Under the clothes he girded on his sword
e mustakët Alia i paska rrue	and Ali shaved off his moustache.

nande bysteksh perçen qi i kish
   punue
ka nji kryq ne maje ja k'i vënue
nji pal jenija çikash ja ka gjet

1025 me i shti n'kamb Alies e ja ka
   cue
q'athere Mara Alies e po mi pri
duelen per fushe te krajli don
   me shkue
e me hajre nusen me ja bâ

kan marrë rugen e te krajli jan
   shkue
1030 kur jan shkue n'ate deren e
   kallas
tridhete çika në bashqe qi i kan
   pa
ashtiktar Alia pak ish kan
kur i pa çikat tuej luejte
u dredh Mares Alia i ka than
1035 po na çon ne bashqe pak me
   ndej
po kom qek çikat per me i pa
masandej te krajli po shkojme

u dredh Mara Alies i ka than
ku të kesh qef more Ali duem
   me shkue
1040 por rrueje vehten more Sirotin
   Alia
se ty çikat kan edhe me te
   provue
me bâ çikat qi me te hetue
ty te nxane edhe une kam me
   marue
se nuk di mrapa qysh per me
   liftue
1045 mos ki dert Alia i ka than

Under his cap he folded his
   braid
and placed a cross on its peak.
She found a pair of women's
   shoes
1025 and handed them to Ali to put
   on his feet.
Then Mara led Ali outside,
they went off through the plain
   to go to the King
to offer their best wishes for
   the bride.
They took the road and rode to
   see the King.
1030 When they went to the door of
   the fortress
they saw thirty girls in the
   garden.
Ali was something of a flirt.
When he saw the girls dancing
Ali turned to Mara and said:
1035 "Let us go to the garden and
   stay there awhile.
I would like to watch the girls,
afterwards we can go see visit
   the King.
Mara turned and said to Ali:
"We will go, Ali, whenever you
   would like.
1040 But protect yourself Sirotin Ali,

because the girls here will also
   test you.
If the girls try to examine you,
you will be caught and I will be
   finished,
for I do not know how to fight
   back."
1045 "Do not be afraid!" Ali said.

e ne bashqe q'atherë kankan
   shkue
e me çika lojen e kan marrë

gjith me çika Alia qi po lua
kan qit çikat Mares e i kan than

1050 Zoti të vraft he Maruke
   Hanxhija
ti ketë çike Mare ku e ki marre

se jem le shoqen s'ja kem pa
as ma të mire Zoti se ka fal

sa ashike me Alien jan bâ
1055 dredh e foli Maruka Hanxija

nji dajesh mua m'ka ardh
skêj hududit kullat i kan ndodh
edhe vesht te gjitha i kan marrë

nji darsem te madhe krajli e ka
   ngreh
1060 qi kam marre nusen Sirotin
   Alies
ka pas qef në darsem per me
   ardh
e me hajre nusen me jau bâ
per hajr çikave nusen po jau
   ban
masandej te krajli thote qi due
   me shkue
1065 por te pame në bashqe tue
   luejte
patme qef me ju per me u njoft

çika e krajlit nder çika ish kan

turr Alien n'gryk e paska nxane

Thereupon they went to the
   garden
and they began dancing with
   the girls.
Ali kept dancing with the girls
and the girls addressed Mara
   and said:
1050 "May God strike you dead,
   innkeeper Mara,
where did you come up with
   this girl?
We have never seen her equal,
God has not created a better
   one."
How they flirted with Ali!
1055 Mara the innkeeper turned and
   said:
"An aunt has come to visit me,
her tower is near the border.
and she found out about
   everything,
that the King has planned a
   great wedding,
1060 and that he has taken the bride
   of Sirotin Ali.
She desired to attend the
   wedding,
and to greet the bride
and to offer her best wishes for
   the bride.
Afterwards—she says—I will go
   to see the King.
1065 But we saw you dancing in the
   garden
and desired to become
   acquainted with you."
The King's daughter was among
   the girls,
she rushed to embrace Ali
   around the neck

shum iqrame çika qi po i ban
1070 hozhgjelden ori çike i ka than
ke bâ mire n'darsem qi ke ardh

se un jam Dylber Angjelin
bashk te baba tevona kemi me
dal
dore n'dore q'athere qi po luejn

1075 e me randë atë kolen po e
kendojne
ka dy bashkë çikat qi po shkoje

gjith per bashke çikat qi po
ladrojne
sa Alia doren ja shtrengoj
qi unazen n'gisht ja paska prish
1080 e ne gishte gjaki i peshtoj
u dredh çika Alien po e nam
mori çike thote Zoti te vraft

fuqi të madhe Zoti të pashka
dhan
a po sheh ç'nishan m'ke bâ

1085 u dredh Alia e q'athere po kesh
çikes Krajlit me goje i ka than

kabahin çike me ka fol
prej ashikut doren ta kom
shtrengue
se ashik ne ty qi jam bâ
1090 sa fuqi Zoti qi me ka dhan
per iman doren me ta shtrengue
sa fuqi Zoti qi m'ka dhan
pleh t'zi doren t'a kish bamë

ne hudude shpjat qi i kam
1095 rreth bjeshkes baba i ka bamë

and she greeted him well.
1070 "Welcome, O girl—she said—
You did well to come to the
wedding.
For I am Dylber Angjelina,
we can go together to see my
father."
Thereupon they went on
dancing hand in hand,
1075 and singing ever louder.

As the girls were moving
together in pairs
and dancing all around the
garden,
Ali squeezed one's hand so hard,
he broke the ring on her finger
1080 and blood ran on her finger.
The girl turned and cursed Ali:
"May God strike you dead, oh
girl!
God has indeed given you great
strength,
but see what kind of scar you
have made."

1085 Ali turned and then laughed
and said directly to the
daughter of the King:
"Excuse my foolishness, girl,
I squeezed your hand from
being smitten,
for I was flirting with you.
1090 What strength God gave me
I used to squeeze your hand.
What strength God gave me
could have turned your hand
into foul dust.
I have houses on the border,
1095 my father built them all around
the mountain.

shndet te math Zoti mua m'ka dhan	God has given me great health."
tuej luejt e çikat tuej këndue	The girls kept dancing and singing,
sa me renda kolen po ma sjellen	dancing in a circle faster and faster.
ashiktare Alia ishte kan	Ali was smitten,
1100 nuk po mundet aj me u durue	1100 he could not stand it.
se na faqe me dham e kish kap	He bit her on the face with his teeth,
gjiaki n'tokë çikes ja ka qit	and spurted the girl's blood onto the ground.
u dredh e nami Dylber Anglielin	Dylber Angjelina turned and cursed him:
Zoti te vraft çike i paska than	"May God strike you dead, girl!
1105 kurve e madhe ti e kenka kan	1105 You are a big whore indeed!
a po sheh se nishane m'ke bamë	Look at the scar you have given me!"
u dredh çika bê edhe qi po i ban	The girl turned and swore a *besa* to him,
kush keto faqe mori çike s'mi ka prek	"No one, oh girl, has cut this face.
bê kom bâ kerkuj mos me ja dhan	I have sworn a *besa* not to give it to anyone,
1110 se i kam rruejte per Sokol Halil Agen	1110 for I am protecting it for Sokol Halil Aga."
u dredh Alia çikes i ka than	Ali turned and said to the girl:
qi ne ma dhaç nji bese te Zotit	"If you should give me your *besa* to God
shka te thom ty e kuj mo sme i kalzue	not to tell anyone what I tell you,
per Halilin kishna me te kalzue	I would have something to tell you about Halil,
1115 se probatine djali m'ka qillue	1115 for the boy is my blood-brother."
keçure shka bani Dylber Angjelin	Consider what Dylber Angjelina did:
bese e fê Alies ja ka dhan	she swore a *besa* on her faith to Ali.
fol shka të kijesh çikë per mem kalzue	"Say what you have to tell me, girl.

e kryte t'em çike per pa m'shkue
1120 ta dhash besen qi kuj s'kom me
    i kalzue
Alia çikes i ka than
un ne bashqe nuk muej me te
    kalzue
se tridhete çika rreth tuej lua

edhe mua me bâ mem ketue
1125 m'shkon ndera edhe krajli mem
    burgue
çika e krajlit Alien e ka kap
dora dora mbrenda i ka çue
ka ndej pak e shume s'kan
    vonue
gjith Alia çikes i ka kalzue
1130 qi probatin Halili m'ka qillue

n'daç n'turk çike per me u
    martue
te Halili ty qi kam me te çue
ti me e marrë at Halilin i ri
se un jam aj Sirotin Alia
1135 edhe ne bese te zotit qi te kom
    ra
n'daç ori çike mua mem ndihmue
mundesh ti erdhe sot per mem
    ndimue
edhe n'daç to besen per me e
    lan
mua m'ban mori çike per ishan

1140 q'athere çika Alies shka i ka
    than
doren e djatht ne dore ja ka
    dhan
ta dhash besen ma te forte se
    guri
kryte t'em Alia per pa e shkue
gja e ligë Alo s'ka me të gjet

before my head rolls, girl,
1120 I give you my *besa* I will tell no
    one."
Ali said to the girl:
"I can not tell you in the
    garden,
because thirty girls are dancing
    all around us
and have been looking me over.
1125 I will lose favor and the King
    will imprison me."
The King's daughter grabbed Ali
and led him inside hand in hand.
They sat for a while, they did
    not wait long.
Ali told the girl everything.
1130 "Halil is indeed my blood
    brother.
If you want to marry a Turk,
    girl,
I will send you to Halil,
so you can marry Young Halil.
For I am Sirotin Ali
1135 and have accepted your *besa* to
    God.
If you wish to help me, O girl,
you can help me this very day.

And if you wish to break your
    besa
you can, O girl, send me to my
    death."
1140 What did the girl then say to
    Ali?
She placed her right hand in
    his,
"I gave you a *besa* stronger than
    a rock,
before my head rolls, Ali,
no evil deed will befall you, Ali.

1145 por po dalin ne bashqe qi po
    luejmë
    çikat mua mos mem kujtue
    doren në dore ne bashqe prap
    jan dal
    tue luejte edhe dita kenka shkue
    ish ardh vakti ne konaqe me
    shkue
1150 atherë foli Maruka Hanxija
    Zoti te vraft ori çike i ka than

    shum marak ne Dylberen qi je
    bâ
    po as u ngine me lojë gjith
    diten
    qi na lê te krajli pa shkue

1155 e me hajr nusen me ja bâ
    atherë foli Dylber Angjielin
    kollaj asht ori Mara i ka than
    se del drit neser te krajli me
    shkue
    per hajr nusen keni me ja bamë

1160 por nji rixha tu ti qi e kom

    n'konak çiken sonte me ma lan

    se shum merak n'to qi jam
    bamë
    probatesh kismete due me e
    nxane
    u dredh Mara çikes e i ka than
1165 me besë ne Zotit çiken me ta
    lan
    pade besen çike fort ti me
    kujtue
    ç'ma gjajne çiken prej tejet e
    due

1145 But let us go into the garden to
    dance,
    lest the girls take note of me."
    Hand in hand they went back to
    the garden,
    dancing until the day ended.
    The time had come to go to
    their lodgings.
1150 Then Mara the innkeeper said:
    "May God strike you dead,
    girl—she says—
    you have taken a great liking to
    Dylber,
    not having your fill of dancing
    all day,
    which prevented us from going
    to the King
1155 and from greeting the bride."
    Then Dylber Angjelina spoke:
    "It is easy, O Mara—she said—
    "to go to the King at the break
    of day tomorrow,
    for us to give our best wishes
    for the bride.
1160 But I have one request to make
    of you:
    leave the girl in my lodging
    tonight,
    for I have taken a great liking to
    her,
    and want to take her as my
    fated blood-sister."
    Mara turned and said to the girl:
1165 "I will leave the girl for you on
    your *besa* to God,
    and remember well, girl, your
    besa.
    You are responsible for what-
    ever happens to the girl."

bese te madhe Dylberja i ka
    dhan
mos ki dert mori Maruka i ka
    than
1170 edhe Mara q'athere a fillue
e la Alien e n'mihane kenka
    shkue
keçyre shka bami Dylberja e
    Krajlit
para shkon e Dylberja po i pri

shkon Alia e gjithkun per mbas
    tij
1175 n'odat veta djalin ma ka çue
edhe muhabetin q'athere ja ka
    shtrue
po i bjen ven edhe po i bjen raki

te dy bashk e kan nise tue pi

kan pi pak e shum nuk kan
    vonue
1180 e rakin Alia e paska çue
po dron djali mos me u
    trumullue
natë a bâ e darken paskan
    hanger
po vjen vatki te nusja me shkue

çika e krajlit q'athere kenka çue

1185 e te baba n'sob i paska shkue
ne divane krajli tue ndej
q'athere qiti krajli e pëvete

ç'kije lum baba rushice i ka
    than
qi je ardh e po ri ne kamb

1190 nji rixha thotë babë me ta bamë

Dylber gave her her strongest
    besa:
"O Maruka, do not worry," she
    said.
1170 And Mara then set out,
she left Ali and went to the
    tavern.
Consider what the King's
    Dylber did:
walking ahead, Dylber led the
    way,
with Ali ever keeping behind
    her.
1175 She brought the boy to her room
and then set him at ease.

She brought him wine and
    brought him raki,
and the two of them began to
    drink together.
They drank a little, they did not
    wait long,
1180 and Ali swallowed the raki.
The boy was afraid that he
    might be deceived.
Night fell and they finished
    their dinner.
The time was coming to go to
    the bride.
The daughter of the King then
    got up
1185 and went to her father's room.
The King was sitting on a sofa.
Then he addressed her and
    asked:
"What is it, father's darling
    little rose—he said to her—
why do you come and remain
    on your feet?"
1190 "To make one request, father,

sonte nuse turkinë me ma fal

edhe sonte me to mos me ra

se fort pa qef nusja te ka qillue

krajli çikes q'athere i ka than
1195 rahat nusen sonte kam me e lan

edhe sonte te ajo skam me shkue
kem vakt tjeter herë per me
vazhdue
u dredh çika te Alia a shkue
e sonte thotë nusen e kam
peshtue
1200 the ndej e bashke tue luejt

e mjesnate q'atherë kish kalue
e Alies çika i ka than
çou Ali q'itash me u shtrengue

ne paç njetin Ali me liftue

1205 un te krajli q'itash kam me te çue
ban Alia jalla ne kamb
kenka çue Dylber Angjelina
e ka dhez nji fenerin ne dorë
e Alies çika qi po i pri
1210 e i ka marre çilsat ne dorë
gjith po shkon e dyert tue zdryë
në odë te krajli q'athere kenka
hi
mides te odes fjetun e kan gjet

gjumi rende krajlin e kish
marre
1215 tre kandila dhezun i kish pas
e Alies çika i pashka than
Baba Krajl qi tu tuk'a tue fjet

for you to leave your Turkish
bride with me tonight,
And not to sleep with her
tonight,
for the bride has no liking for
you at all."
The King then said to the girl,
1195 "I will leave the bride alone
tonight,
and I will not go to her tonight.
I will have time later to tend to
her."
The girl turned and went to Ali.
"This evening—she says—I have
spared the bride,
1200 so we can stay and amuse
ourselves together."
Midnight then passed
And the girl said to Ali:
"Get up, Ali, and gird yourself
right away
in case you have to fight
elsewhere.
1205 I have to go to the King now."
Ali bolted to his feet,
as did Dylber Angjelina.
The girl lit a lantern in her hand
and led the way for Ali.
1210 She took the keys in her hand
and went along opening doors.
Then they entered the room of
the King,
They found him asleep in the
middle of the room.
A sound sleep had overtaken
the King.
1215 He had lit three oil lamps.
And the girl said to Ali:
"My father, the King, who is
sleeping here,

kollaj asht Aliu me e pre
si gjumi dekum baben e paska
   marre
1220 e te kryte Alia i ka shkue
q'athere shpaten prej mille e ka
   nxjerre
kish hap krahin prej krajlin per
   me e pre
vet me vedi Alia ka than
mare asht ne gjum per me e pre

1225 se edhe gratë ne gjum te presin

q'athere shkelm krajlit i ka sjelle
gjumi idhun krajlit i ka dal

te madhe çika q'athere paska brit
te dy syt he djal e te plaçin

1230 me dy duert faqeve jau ka ngjit

tuej gervisht e jashta kenka dal
prej gazepit në gjak qi a mblue

ka u kujtove keshtu per me
   sharrue
ty me te nxane e mue mem
   coptue
1235 edhe sa ye jesh gjalle ne burg
   me te çue
fjalet vonojne Alia shka kish bâ

jalla n'kamb aj krajli ish kan
   çue
gadi i met ai Sirotin Alia
e me shpat per gjyse e ka
   shkurtue
1240 si i ka ra ne atë krahin të
   shmakt

is easy to kill, Ali
for a deep sleep has overtaken
   him."
1220 Ali went towards his head.
He drew his sword out of its
   scabbard,
and raised his arm to kill him.

Ali said to himself:
"It is disgraceful to kill him in
   his sleep,
1225 for even women kill you when
   you are sleeping."
Then he gave the King a kick,
and the King's embittered
   dream was ended.
The girl then let out a loud cry:
"You, boy, may both your eyes
   burst!"
1230 She slapped his face with both
   hands,
scratching him and went outside,
because of her trouble she
   covered him in blood.
"Where did you get the idea of
   ruining me?
You they will seize, me they
   will cut to pieces,
1235 and as long as you are alive you
   will be held in prison."
Her words lingered, what had
   Ali done?
My god, the King had jumped
   to his feet,
Sirotin Ali was ready for him
and he cut him in half with his
   sword.
1240 He struck him on his left
   shoulder

qit ja ka ne sjetullen e djatht

e dy copesh ne miner e ka lan

fluturim per derë kenka dal
e të çika n'sob kenka shkue
1245 po dron çika fort qi ju ka
idhnue
mos ju dhimti krajli qi ju preva

po shkon çiken Alia e pëvete
po atë u dhimti baba qi ta preva

a shka pate qi brimen e ki marre
1250 qi me gjak e çike ti kanke mblue
çfar gazepit ty keshtu te ka
ngushtue
qi per ishane faqet i paske
bamë
atherë çika Alies i ka than
baba krajl thote pak qi nuk ka
dhimt
1255 por u tuta qi kryte po ta pret

ty te pret dhe mua vendin s'ma
kish lan
e tash Ali kollaj qi po bajme

fenerin n'dore çika e kish
marre
po mi pri Alia mbas saj
1260 në derë te kallas q'athere jan
shkue
e kallan sa mire e kan gujue

te ton sheherit xhevap i ka
shku
e potera q'athere kekna çue
e preu turku Krajlin ne kalla

and cut through to his right
armpit.
He left two pieces on the
cushions.
He went flying out the door
and went to the girl's room.
1245 The girl was greatly frightened
for having angered him.
"Are you sorry that I have killed
the King?
—Ali asks approaching the girl—
were you sorry that I killed
your father?
What made you let out a cry
1250 and cover me with blood, girl?
What torment has afflicted you
like this
enough to put a scar on my
face?"
Then the girl said to Ali:
"I am a little sorry—she says—
about my father King,
1255 but I was afraid he was going to
cut off your head,
kill you and abandon me.

And now, Ali, what we are
doing is easy."
The girl took the lantern in her
hand
and was leading, Ali behind her.
1260 They went to the door of the
fortress,
how well they locked the
fortress!
News went throughout the
town
and an uproar was then raised:
A Turk had killed the King in
the fortress,

1265 paska pre aj Sirotin Alia	1265 Sirotin Ali had killed him.
e Alia trimi shka bani	What did the hero Ali do?
me gjith çike në kalla kenka shkue	Together with the girl he went to the fortress,
n'odat veta sa shpejt kenkan hi	and they quickly entered their rooms.
çojne po e marin Fatime Turkinë	They went in and got Fatima Turkija,
1270 ja bjen shkêj nusen Sirotin Alies	1270 rescuing the bride of Sirotin Ali.
fort Alie q'athere s trimnue	Ali was greatly encouraged, then,
e me vedi çikat i ka marre	and he took the girls with him.
qi a hip ne bedel te kallas	He climbed to the ramparts of the fortress,
treqind topa aty i ka gjet	and found three hundred cannons there
1275 krajli gadi per darsem i kish bâ	1275 that the King had made ready for his wedding.
sa zanat Alia edhe i kish pas	How crafty Ali was!
gryken posht te topave jau ka ugj	He lowered the barrels of the cannons
edhe me rend zjarmin jau ka dhan	and fired them one by one.
gjysen e sheherit arab e ka bâ	He blackened half the town.
1280 po lufton aj Sirotin Alia	1280 Sirotin Ali fought on,
ne të dy çoshet çikat po i ndimojne	with the girls helping him on both sides,
shum ma fort se Alia po liftojne	fighting ever harder than Ali.
ne fushë shkijet bê nder vedi po bajne	On the plain the Slavs were swearing a *besa* among themselves,
qi nuk asht vedi aj Sirotin Alia	that it was not just Sirotin Ali
1285 i ka me vedi tridhete agalar	1285 that he had with him the thirty Agas,
qi shtatë krajlit Alien me e rrethue	were the Seven Kings to surround Ali
tybe skam kurgja me i bâ	they would never be able to do anything.
kaq fort qi asqeri jan mirue	The soldiers were so demoralized,

as kur njo te kallaja s'guxojne
me shkue
1290 topat te renda Alia qi po i
shpraze
ka i piskam rallë herë po e lëshon
te ton sheherin djali qi po e
miron
hajt e hajt per nji seri me e pa
ne Jubdine Muja kenka çue
1295 ne oxhakli zjarmin e ka dhez
e gjygymin ne ate zjarm e ka shti
sheqerli kafen e paska pi

ne ate çibuk duhan po tufat
e ne qef Muja konka bâ
1300 honmi vete n'kamb tuej i ndej
ka qit Muja nuses e i ka than

me mi prue ibrik e legen
se avdes po due me e marrë
edhe sabahin me vakte me fal

1305 sot ne bjeshk kismet qi due me
dal
shpejt hyzmetin nusja ja ka bâ
po ja bjen ibrik e legen

avdes te paq aj Muja paska
marre
edhe me vakt sabahin qi po e
fal
1310 e ne sexhde Muji qi asht ugj
e teqmil namazin e ka bâ
Perendies q'athere po i lutet
ham per vedi dhe per shoket te
vet
ham per shoke dhe per imet te
Muhamet
1315 jalla n'kamb q'athere kenka çue

not one liked moving towards
the fortress.
1290 Ali was firing the heavy
cannons,
sporadically letting loose a yell.
The boy was demoralizing the
whole town!
Come and see a wondrous sight!
Muji arose in Udbina,
1295 he lit a fire in the fireplace,
placed a copper pot on the fire
and drank some sweetened
coffee.
Packing tobacco in his long pipe
Muji put himself in a good mood
1300 alone standing on his feet.
Muji addressed his bride and
said to her:
"Hand me a pitcher and hasin,
for I want to make my ablutions
and to greet the morning at the
proper time.
1305 Today I want to go try my luck
in the highlands."
His bride served him quickly:
she brought him the pitcher
and hasin.
Muji carefully made his ritual
ablutions,
and he greeted the morning at
the proper time.
1310 Muji dropped to the prayer rug
and finished saying his prayers.
He then beseeched God
for glory for himself and for his
friends,
glory for his friends and for the
name of Muhamed!
1315 Then, with a cry to Allah, he
rose to his feet

e me za Halilit i ka thirr
çou prej gjumit more Halil Aga i
    ri
se ne bjeshk e kismet duem me
    dal
e Halili sa shpejt qi a çue
1320 bacen Muji fort e kish pas
    ndigjue
u vesh e u mbath shpejt kenka
    shtregue

perpjet shkallave n'ate kalla
    kenka shkue
n'ode te Mujis e djali kenka hi
Baces Muji dhe selam i ka dhan

1325 e ma mire selamin ja paska
    marre
hajrosun Halili i ka than

ç'far xhevapit bace qi te ka
    ardh
me i zan te idhun mue qu m'ke
    thirr
neper gjume bace m'ka ra

1330 e jam tut ndoj rrezik na ka le

kurgja s'asht e Muja i ka than
por ne podrum o Halile me ra
na shtrengysh gjokun e dorine

u dredh Halili baces i ka than

1335 kollaj asht atlarët me i
    shtrengue
po per i pune ti bace mem
    ndigjue
qi te marrsh atë pushken
    habertare

and called out loudly to Halil:
"Wake up from your sleep,
    Young Halil Aga,
for we will go seek our fortune
    in the highlands."
How quickly Halil woke up,
1320 he heard his brother well.

Putting on his clothes and
    footwear he quickly girded
    himself,
he climbed up the steps of the
    fortress.
The boy entered Muji's room.
He gave greetings to his
    brother Muji
1325 and received even better greet-
    ings from him.
"Good tidings to you—Halil
    said—
what news, brother, has
    reached you
making you call out to me in an
    angry voice?
You have interrupted my sleep,
    brother,
1330 and I am afraid some danger
    has befallen us."
"It is nothing—Muji said to him—
go down to the stable, Halil,
and saddle the white stallion
    and the bay horse for us."
Halil turned and said to his
    brother:
1335 "It is easy to saddle the
    thoroughbreds,
but hear me out on one thing,
    brother.
Take your signaling rifle,

nalt me hip ne bedel te kallas

edhe pushken bace per me e
    shpraze
1340 tridhete Age bace kan me i
    ndije
e te kulla ne kan me na ardh
bashk me ta në çete duem me
    dal
ndoj rrezik ne bjeshk edhe me
    na gjet
fuqi të madhe Agët edhe kan
    me pas
1345 çdo ndoj krajl ne bjeshk me u
    zatet
ne luften baçe kemi me e fitue
mire Halilin Muja kish ndigjue
e kish marrë atë pushken
    habertare
nalt ish hip ne atë bedel te
    kallas
1350 pushken Muji q'athere e ka
    shpraze
mbas e leshoj nji piskam te
    vogel
tuej shkue malit ne bjeshk qi a
    dridh
paskan ndije tridhete agalar
keçyre Agët ne kambë kenka çue
1355 e atlaret me shpejt i kan
    shtrengue
e tu kullat Mujis i paskan shkue
Muja i çelke dyert te kallas

e Halili q'athere i ka brit
del me in ndhesh thidhete
    kraznikt
1360 se me hpejt Agët tek po vine

climb to the battlement of the
    fortress

and fire your rifle, brother.
1340 The thirty Agas will hear it,
    brother,
and will come to our tower.
We will ride out together with
    them on a raiding party.
If any danger catches us in the
    highlands,
the Agas will have great
    strength.
1345 If any King encounters us in the
    highlands,
we will win the battle, brother."
Muji listened well to Halil,
he took his signaling rifle

and climbed up to the battle-
    ments of the fortress.
1350 Muji then fired his rifle,

afterwards he let out a short
    piercing cry.
Crossing the mountains it spun
    down to the highlands,
the thirty Agas heeded it.
Look the Agas rose to their feet.
1355 They girded their thorough-
    breds even quicker,
and rode to Muji's tower.
Muji opened the doors of the
    fortress,
and then called out to Halil:
"Go outside and greet the thirty
    brave heroes
1360 for the Agas are approaching
    quickly,

e atlaret ne podrum me jau shti

shpejt Halili para u paska dal

e hozhgjelden tridhete Agalar
e atlaret Halili jau ka marre
1365 e rahat n'podrum jau ka bâ

Agët jan hip shkallave perpjete
ne atë kalla te Muja kenkan
    shkue
ne divehane Muja i paska ndesh

o hozhgjelden tridhete more Agë
1370 e mire selamin Muja jau ka
    marre
në ode te Mujes q'atherë
    kenkan shkue
ne minere gjith rreth jan ndej

me sheqer kafe po me u pjekin

po ju pjek aj Bylyk Basha Muji
1375 po ju shkep aj Halili i ri
e ne lafe q'athere jan ra
duhan të kuqë Muja qi jau ka
    dhan
i ka qite Agvet e jau ka than

more shoke ju sot qi ju kam
    thirr
1380 kam pas qef tu kulla me u
    bashkue
n'daçi mue shoke mem ndigjue

po i shtrengojme atlarët e
    mejdanit
e po i marim shpate e gargija

and put their thoroughbreds in
    the stables."
Halil quickly went outside to
    meet them
and he welcomed the thirty Agas.
He took their thoroughbreds
1365 and made them comfortable in
    the stables.

The Agas climbed up the steps
and went to see Muji in the
    fortress.
Muji greeted them in the
    anteroom.

"Welcome, O thirty Agas."
1370 And Muji nicely received their
    greeting.
They then went into Muji's
    room.
They sat down all around on
    cushions.

Coffee with sugar was being
    made for them,
Bylyk Basha Muji making it,
1375 and Young Halil kept serving it.
Then they all fell to talking,
Muji gave them red tobacco.

He addressed the Agas and said
    to them:
"I have summoned you today,
    my friends,
1380 for I wished to assemble you at
    the tower.
If you want to heed me, my
    friends,
let us saddle up our battle
    mounts,
let us take up our swords and
    lances,

e po marrim xhephane e fyshek

1385 m'ka ra huja ne bjeshke me dal

ne llugje te verdha bashk shoke
me shkue
bjeshkt e Turkut bytyn me i
suxhue
ndonji krajl a mos nau ka afrue
kan qite Agët Mujes i paskan
than
1390 gadi bace kurnjo nuk jem kan
të te na dhaç myvlet ne shpi me
shkue
me zi presim bace per me u
shtrengue
e ne at çete me ty per me dal

se ikbal gjithmon e ki pas

1395 q'athere Muja shokvet jau ka
then
sonte shkepniju ne konaqe te
ton
kur te dalin q'ajo drita e bardh

banju gadi ne llaugje per me dal

q'athere rrugen kismet kemi
me e marre
1400 q'athere Agët te gjitha jan çue
qysh thote Muja mire e kan
ndigjue
e jan djerg shkallave te posht
e atlarve ne shpine jau kan ra

e ne konaqe te gjitha jan shkue

1405 nuk vonon e nata ka kalue

let us take up our rifles and
cartridges.

1385 The urge to ride into the high-
lands has overcame me,
and to go together, friends, into
the green groves,
to examine all the highlands of
the Turk,
lest any King is approaching us."
The Agas addressed Muji and
said:
1390 "Not one of us is ready, brother.
Just give us permission to go
home,
we can hardly wait to gird
ourselves, brother,
and to ride out on that raiding
party with you,
for you have always had good
success."
1395 Then Muji said to his friends:

"Tonight retire to your
lodgings.
When the white light of day
breaks,
get ready to come out to the
meeting place.
Then we will try our luck on
the road."
1400 Then all the Agas rose.
What Muji said they well
understood.
They climbed down the stairs,
jumped on the backs of their
thoroughbreds
and they all went to their
lodgings.
1405 It was not long before the night
passed,

nata shkoj e drita kenka dal
qi u çuen tridhete more Age
vesh e mbath e mire kankan
    strengue
ne kopace shpatat i kan ngjesh

1410 ne sylha kuburat i kan shti

e atlaret e gadi i paskan bâ

e ka t'top fyshek i paskan marrë

e atlarve ne shpine jau kan ra

xhuherdare ne dore i kau marrë
1415 ne llangje te Judbines q'athere
    jan dal
kenka çue aj Bylyk Basha Muji
me Halilin gadi kenkan bâ

paskan marrë xhephane e
    fishek
prej podrumit atlaret i kah
    nxjerre
1420 e ne shpine q'athere ju kan ra
e ne fushë te dyja i kan qit

neper fushë atlaret qi po i luejn

rreth e rrotull fushen po i
    trupojne
te Agët ne llangje qi po shkojne

1425 po shkon Muja selam ju kan
    dhan
e ma mire selamin ja kan marrë

e te gjith ne kamb jau kan çue
paka kan ndej e shum s'ka
    vonue

night went and daylight came.
The thirty Agas arose,
they put on clothes and footwear
    and girded themselves well.
they jammed their swords into
    their scabbards,
1410 stuck their pistols into their
    ammunition belts
and made their thoroughbreds
    ready.
The put on their bandoliers full
    of cartridges,
jumped on the backs of their
    thoroughbreds
and took signaling rifles in hand.
1415 Then they came out to the
    meeting place of Udbina.
Bylyk Basha Muji arose
and with Halil made himself
    ready.
The took rifles and
    ammunition,
led their thoroughbreds out of
    the stable
1420 and jumped on their backs.
The two of them set off into the
    plain,
their thoroughbreds galloping
    on the plain.
Plunging round and about the
    plain
going towards the Agas at the
    meeting place.
1425 Muji went and gave them his
    greetings,
and they received his greetings
    even better.
All of them rose to their feet.
They stayed there awhile, it
    was not long,

ja mbrini aj Sokole Halili

1430 çojnju shoket agvet ju ka than

se asht vakti ne bjeshk per me dal
se un nji enderr shoke edhe e kam pa
e me hajre shoket ja kan bâ

kam has ne bjeshk nji harushe te zezë
1435 plot me zoj harusha qi ish kan

e kam mësyre harushen per me e pre
zojët mue rrethin shoket qi ma kan qit
edhe rrob te gjalle shoket mua m'kan nxane
per hajre endren Talia ka bâ

1440 o me hajr endrra qi te koft

se ajo endrra ty qi te ka kalzue

se ne krajli Alien e kan rrethe

endrra jote Halile qysh thotë
ne krajli Alia qi a votë
1445 nuses mrapa djali per me i ra
ndonji luft po gjet qi me pas bâ
e ne zidon Alia qi asht met
nuk ka kush permrapa per me i ra
prap Dezdari atij paska fol
1450 Zoti ju vraft tridhete more Age

se te kulla Alia asht ardh
q'athere u çue aj Çeto Basho Muji

before Sokol Halil approached them.

1430 "Get up, friends—he said to the Agas—
because the time has come to go into the highlands.
For I have dreamed a dream, friends,
—and his friends wished him a lucky one—
I encountered a black she-bear in the highlands,
1435 the she-bear was with many cubs.
I attacked to kill the she-bear,

her cubs turned and surrounded me, friends,
And took me alive as a prisoner."
Tali interpreted the dream favorably:
1440 "May your dream be a favorable one!
For your dream has revealed to you
that they have surrounded Ali in the Kingdom.
What your dream means, Halil,
Ali has gone into the Kingdom
1445 to bring back his bride.
He has been taken in battle
and Ali remains in a prison.
He has no one of to get him back."
In reply Dezdar then said:
1450 "May God strike you dead, O thirty Agas!
for Ali has come to the tower."
Then Çeto Basha Muji rose,

n'shpine i ra gjokut t'mejdanit

e a çue aj Ali Bajraktari
1455 e ne shpine dories i ka ra

e jan çue te tridhete agalar
e jan kan ra atlarve ne shpine

per mas Mujit te gjith jan fillue
hajt e hajt ne atë bjeshk jan dal

1460 kankan hip ne atë llugjet e
    verdha
aty ishe nji krue i ftohfte
kish fal zoti nji molik te bute

e ne atë hije atlarve u kan drip

jau kan hek frêjt prej krejtë

1465 e i kan leshue ne barë me kullot
vete po pinë uji edhe te ftohft

e jan ugj e n'ate hije po
    pushojne
paskan dhez edhe duhan qi po
    pinë
duhan pinë edhe gjith tue
    ndigjue
1470 a asht mymqym gja ne bjeshk
    per me hetue
ndonj krajl mos na kau afrue

tuej ndigjue Agët qi ishin kan
i gjam per toke te madhe e kan
    dnije
ka qite Tali shokvet jau ka than

1475 kjo asht endrra e Halilit qi e ka
    pa

he jumped on the back of his
    battle steed.
Ali Bajrakteri also rose
1455 and jumped on the back of his
    bay horse.

The thirty Agas also rose
and jumped on the backs of
    their thoroughbreds.
They all started out behind Muji.
How quickly they reached the
    highlands!
1460 They climbed up to the green
    valley,
a cold spring was there.
God had provided a lovely pine
    tree
and in its shade they dismounted
    from their thoroughbreds.
They removed the reins from
    their heads,
1465 and let them graze on the grass.
They themselves drank the cold
    water
and lay down and rested in the
    shade.
They lit up their tobacco and
    were smoking,
smoking their cigarettes and
    ever listening
1470 in case they could detect
    anything in the highlands,
if any King had gotten close to
    them.
While the Agas were listening
they heard a rumbling sound
    on the ground.
Tali addressed his friends and
    said:
1475 "This is the dream Halil has
    dreamt.

se n'krajli Alia qi asht ra
trimi i madh aj Sirotin Alia
ndonj luft o shoke qi e paska
    nise
q'athere Muja Talit i ka than
1480 a ke ndije vet a kush edhe të ka
    than
u dredh Tali Mujes edhe i paska
    than
gjithmone bace budalle je kan

ty Dezdari bace qysh me te
    mashtrue
se me na fikë Dezdari ka qillue
1485 se n'krajli Alia qi a shkue

bê ka bâ aj Sirotin Alia
ndo e nxjerri Begzaden e Bukur

ndo e pres atë Milosh Kapitani
qi ne krajli dorine ma ka çue

1490 bê te medha Ali ka ba more
    Bace
ne krajli qi kryte do ta la

u dredh Tali prap Mujes i ka
    than
me Alien more bace qi je korrit
se me ne prej sobët qi a çue

1495 edhe ne bjeshk vetem qi a
    shkue
edhe e ka nxane atë Milosh
    Kapitani
e treqind shkija bace qi ja ka
    pre
e zidanin ne bjeshk qi ja ka qart

For Ali has gone to the Kingdom,
a great hero that Sirotin Ali
he has started a battle, my
    friends!"
Then Muji said to Tali:
1480 "Have you learned of this your-
    self or has anyone told you?"
Tali turned to Muji and said:

"You have always been foolish,
    brother.
This is how Dezdar has tricked
    you, brother,
for Dezdar has done us harm.
1485 Ali indeed has gone to the
    Kingdom.
Sirotin Ali has sworn a *besa*,
either to get Beautiful Begzade
    out
and to cut down Kapitan Milosh
who took his bay horse off to
    the Kingdom,
1490 Ali has sworn a great *besa*, O
    brother,
or he will leave his head in the
    Kingdom."
Tali turned around and said to
    Muji:
"You have been shamed by Ali
because he up and left us at the
    meeting
1495 and went alone into the
    mountains
and captured Kapitan Milosh.

He killed three hundred Slavs,
    brother,
and destroyed his prison in the
    highlands,

e prej zidanit Turqit i ka
nxjerre
1500 e çardakun zjarmin ja ka dhan

rrafsh me toke Miloshit ja ka bâ
rrob te gjalle Miloshin e ka pas
nxane
te kullat Begut e ka prue

qi e ka lypë ajo Begzadeja e
Bukur
1505 rrobë te gjalle Miloshin vete me
e pa
edhe te ka than ne zidan due
me e shti
e Alia tu kulla e ka prue

e n'dore çikes ja ka lan
e ka qitun me gojë e ka than

1510 qi ky asht aj Milosh Kapitani
qi e ki lype me sy me e pa
merre çike e ne zidan ke me e
shti
taksirat aj Alia ka pas
e ish kan ba rezile per gjum

1515 vet ish hip shkallave perpjete
e Alia n'ate ode a shkue
arm e shpate me te shpejt e k'i
hjek
e gjumin e rande Alien e ka
marre
shka ka bâ bace Milosh Kapitani

1520 bê te medha çikes i ka qit
pak duert çike me mi shlirue
se konopi n'asht m'ka shkue
pa egjell shpirti qi po me del
çiken bace Miloshi e ka mashtrue

and released the Turks from
the prison,
1500 he set fire to Milosh's manor
house
razing it even to the ground.
He took Milosh alive as a
prisoner,
and brought him to the tower
of the Beg.
The Beautiful Begzade asked for
him
1505 to see the prisoner Milosh alive
for herself,
and said, 'I want to throw him
into the prison.'
And Ali brought him to the
tower,
and left him in the girl's hands.
He turned him over and said to
her directly:
1510 'This is the Kapitan Milosh
you asked to set your eyes on.
Take him away, girl, and throw
him into the prison.'
Ali had some bad luck,
he was ashamed about being
sleepy
1515 and climbed up the steps alone.
Ali went into his room.
Quickly took off his weapons
and sword
and was overcome by a deep
sleep.
What did Kapitan Milosh do,
brother?
1520 He swore a great *besa* to the girl:
'Loosen my hands a little, girl,
for the rope has cut into me.
I may die before my fated time.'
Milosh tricked the girl, brother.

1525 sol pak duert q'athere jau ka
shlirue
pak takat Miloshi i kish ardh

sa azgan more bace qi ish kan
copa cope konopët i ka bame
me nji dore bace nuses ja ka
ngjite
1530 e ka nxjerre rizen prej xhepit
edhe gojen nuses ja ka lidhe
se ka lan as hiqe per me brit
per dizginash dories ja ka ngjite

shpeit e shpejt ne shpinë i ka ra

1535 e telqi nusen e ka qite
e per vedi more bace qi e ka lidhi
prej krajlies dorien e ka dredh

me dizgina dories tuej ra

lukuren n'toke dories ja ka qit

1540 e Alies ne gjum i kan kalzue
ta muer nusen Milosh Kapitani

e prej gjumit bace kur a çue

kryte ne gjam Alia e ka qit
larg Miloshin n'ate fushe e ka
pa
1545 s'kish s'ka i ban Alia veç me e
nam
hajrli koft me rrezik kanka kan

kadaldale Alia a shtrengue
kambe mbas tina bjeshken e ka
marre
m'ato bjeshke Alia kur a dal

1525 She then loosened his hands
just a little.
A little strength returned to
Milosh.
He was so strong, brother,
that he shredded the rope to bits.
With one arm, brother, he
picked up the girl,
1530 took a kerchief out of his pocket,
and covered the girl's mouth,
not allowing her at all to cry out.
He bound her by the halters of
the bay horse
and ever so quickly jumped on
its back.
1535 He placed the girl on the saddle
and tied her to himself, brother.
He turned the bay horse
towards the Kingdom.
Striking the bay horse with the
reins,
he sent hide of the bay horse to
the ground.
1540 And Ali was told in a dream:
'Kapitan Milosh has stolen your
bride!'
And when he awoke from his
sleep
Ali put his head to a window
and saw Milosh far off on the
plain.
1545 Ali could not do anything but
curse him.
May he be lucky, he was in
danger.
He slowly girded himself,
on foot he set off after them in
the highlands.
When Ali came to one highland
clearing

1550 ne te tjera bjeshk Miloshin e ka
     pa
     ne te tjera bjeshk Alia kur a dal

     ne krajli bace Miloshi qi a ra

     thonë asht votë tu Krajleviçe
     Marko
     thonë bakshish qi nusen ja ka
     çue
1555 more bace qishtu m'kan kalzue

     e ne krajli shkoj aj Sirotin Ali

     mas shka a bâ bace nuk e di

     q'athere Muja ne mendim
     kenka ra
     asht dredh shoket e Muja po i
     pëvete
1560 qysh me bâ e hallin me ja gjet

     me te foli Budaline Tali
     na ne krajli more bace per me
     ra
     tridhete Age çfar lufte qi bajne

     tridhete Age sol qi kem qillue
1565 kur nji krajl nuk muejme per
     me e rethue
     por po e çojme at Ali Bajraktarin
     e po ja japim Sokol Halilin
     i pa prituem Halili qi a kan
     e serde Ali dorien edhe e ka

1570 e ti prinë aj Ali Bajraktari
     e poter ne krahine me e qit

     let ti mbledhin Judbine e
     krahine

1550 he saw Milosh on another one.

     When he came to the other
     highland clearing,
     Milosh, brother, had already
     reached the Kingdom.
     They say he went to Marko
     Kraljević.
     They say he brought him the
     bride as a gift.
1555 This, my brother, is how it was
     reported to me.
     So Sirotin Ali went to the
     Kingdom.
     What he did after that I do not
     know."
     Then Muji fell to thinking.

     Turning to his friends Muji
     asked them:
1560 "What can we do to handle this
     trouble?"
     Budaline Tali spoke up:
     "If we ride into the kingdom,
     my brother,
     what battle can thirty Agas
     wage?
     We are only thirty Agas,
1565 we would never be able to
     surround a King.
     But if we send Ali Bajraktari
     and give him Sokol Halil,
     Halil is unhesitating
     and just like Ali he has a bay
     horse.
1570 Let Ali Bajraktari lead
     and send an alarm throughout
     the border.
     Let them assemble Udbina and
     the Borderland.

shum asqer Alia ka me bâ	Ali will assemble many soldiers.
m'at hudud edhe na qi po dalin	We will ride out to the border
1575 e po i vënojme turbijat ne syë	1575 and put field glasses to our eyes
shikojme kullat të Krajleviçe Markut	and survey the tower of Marko Kraljević
po ja shohim asqerin se shka ka	and find out how many soldiers be has.
a thuej muejm bace per me i ra	Tell us, brother, when we might attack."
q'ashtu thone edhe q'ashtu e paskan lan	This is what they said, and this is how they left it.
1580 n'kamb u çue aj Ali Bajraktari	1580 Ali Bajraktari rose to his feet
e n'shpine dories edhe i ka ra	and jumped on the back of his bay horse,
prej krahine rrugen e ka marrë	he took the road to the border.
se vetime Halil Aga i ri	The Young Halil acted like lightning,
ne shpine dories Halili i ha ra	Halil jumped on the back of his bay horse.
1585 mdbas Alies djali asht fillue	1585 The boy set out behind Ali,
po kerkojne Judbine e Krahine	they were roaming about Udbina and the Borderland.
si telal Ali Bajraktari	Ali Bajraktari was like a town-crier,
gjith po shkon si telal tuej brit	shouting like a town-crier wherever he went:
hiq kush te jesh i gjalle edhe me shpirt	"Get up any of you who are alive and healthy
1590 me shtate vjet edhe deri ne shatedhete	1590 seven years old up to seventy,
kush te kapish pushken e me dore	whoever can hold a rifle in his hand,
m'at hudud sa shpejt per me dal	let him ride as quickly as possible to the border,
se tre krajla ne hudud jan afrue	for three Kings have approached the border
po dojn turqit trimat me mjerue	they want to bring misery to the heroes of the Turks
1595 luft me dal edhe besa burë e grue	1595 let men and women come out to battle and to *besa*."

	They roamed through Udbina
kan kerkue Judbinë e krahinë	and the Borderland,
shum asqer Alia kish bashkue	Ali assembled many soldiers.
por po u pri aj Ali Bajraktari	Ali Bajraktari led them
e per rreth Halili tuej shkue	while Halil went all among them.
1600 ne ate hudud trimat jan afrue	1600 The heroes approached the border.
ne hudud kurgja skan pa	They saw nothing at the border,
veç kan gjet te tridhet agalar	but did find the thirty Agas,
tridhete Age ne bjeshk i kan gjet	they found the thirty Agas in the highlands,
tuej keçyre hududin me turbi	surveying the border with field glasses.
1605 q'athere Muja n'kambe kenka çue	1605 Then Muji rose to his feet.
u dredh edhe keçyri Ali Bajraktarin	He turned and scrutinized Ali Bajraktari.
edhe Alia Mujis shka i ka than	And what did Ali say to Muji?
asqer te math more bace qi kem bâ	"We have formed a great army, my brother!"
sa ne qef aj Muja qi ish bâ	How pleased Muji became.
1610 ka qit Agvet me gojë jau ka than	1610 He addressed the Agas and said directly to them:
per tre vende Age qi dojme me u da	We need to split into three positions
ka trimij per shoqë me i marrë	there are three thousand men to take.
kalauza tre vetë dojme me i bâ	We need to make three men leaders.
nji ane te u pri aj Ali Bajraktari	Ali Bajraktari will lead one flank,
1615 tjetren ane aj Gjergjelez Alia	1615 Gjergjelez Alia the other one,
e nji krahin edhe Arnaut Osmani	and Arnaut Osmani one sortie."
ka qit Muja prap Agve jau ka than	Muji again addressed the Agas and said:
mbas po vij me Budaline Tali	"I will come up behind with Budaline Tali
ne boft ndoje shkja ju per me u peshtue	in the event any Slav should evade you.
1620 na pa i pre ne xhelat s'kemi me e lan	1620 We will not spare a single oppressor."

q'athere bjeshken te poshte e
    kan marrë
e ne kasabe krajlit i kan ra
asqer te math krajli i kish
    bashkue
sa forcue sheherin e kish pas

1625 nuk po muejn kurgja shka me u
    bâ
kan liftue shtatë dit e shtatë
    net
e ne krajli Agët skan muejte e
    me hi
sa merzite ish kan Sirotin Alia
qi po dron Agët edhe po thehen

1630 e s'po mujen Alien per me e
    nxjerre
çikes krajlit i ka qit e i ka than

ori çike e Dylber Anglieline
sikur moter un ty të di
se per Halilin un nuse due me
    te çue
1635 se probatin Halili m'ka qillue
ti ne Judbinë Ishalla me u
    martue
por kurr ma ngusht mori çike
    s'kan qillue
qe shtate dite e lufta si a fillue

asqer te madh shkijet kan
    bashkue
1640 a din nji fjalë çike me ma kalzue

dorinë tem krajli ku e ka çue

pash aj Zot thote çikë qi me ka
    dhan
se me pas at dorinë e mejdanit

Then they rode down the high-
    land clearing,
and came to the King's city.
The King had assembled a large
    army.
He had reinforced the city so
    strongly
1625 they were unable to do
    anything.
They fought for seven days and
    seven nights
and the Agas were unable to
    enter the Kingdom.
How distressed Sirotin Ali was!
The Agas were afraid and
    breaking up
1630 and unable to rescue Ali.

He addressed the daughter of
    the King and said:
"My girl, Dylber Angjelina,
you are like a sister to me,
for I want to send you as a bride
    for Halil,
1635 for Halil is my blood brother.
You, God willing, will be
    married in Udbina.
But never, girl, have they been
    more hard pressed.
It has been seven days since the
    battle began,
the Slavs have assembled a
    large army.
1640 Do you know anything you can
    tell me, girl?
where has the King sent my bay
    horse
for the sake of God who made
    me, girl—he says—
if I had that battle steed,

ne shpine e dories kish me i ra

1645 n'asqer perjashta kish me dal
ton asqerit dallash per me i
dhan
shum i pres me shpaten e
mejdanit
ma shum vret aj dorija me
kamb
q'athere çika djalit shka i ka
than
1650 tutem keq more Sirotin Alia

se ty shkijet rrob kan me te
nxane
se dorinë n'podrum e kam shti

vet i kam qit sonë dhe taxhi

ma rahat a kur qi nuk a kan
1655 çou Alia çikes i pashka than
te dorija edhe shpejt per mem
çue
edhe çika perparen po i pri
te dorja ne podrum e ka shti

prej podrumit Alia e ka nxjerre
1660 e putsatet ne shpinë ja ka qit

nande kollanat dories ja
shtrengoj
e dizginat ne kaltak ja ka qit

prap a hi per shkallave perpjet
në atë kalla te nusja kenka
shkue
1665 ka qit nusen me goje i ka than

drigjue e mshelma deren e
kallas

I would jump on the back of the
bay horse,
1645 I would ride out into the soldiers
and spread confusion
throughout the army.
I would cut down many of them
with my battle sword,
and my bay horse would kill
even more with its legs."
What did the girl then say to
the boy:
1650 "I am terribly afraid, O Sirotin
Ali,
that the Slavs will take you
prisoner.
For they have put your bay
horse in the stable.
I myself have brought it hay
and fodder,
It has never been calmer."
1655 Ali rose and said to the girl:
"Take me quickly to my bay
horse."
And the girl led him forward,
and put him in the stable with
his bay horse.
Ali brought it out of the stable
1660 and threw its trappings on its
back.
He saddled the horse with nine
girth belts,
and place the halters on its
pommel.
He climbed back up the steps
and went into the fortress to
the bride.
1665 He addressed the bride directly
and said:
"Be sure to close the door of
the fortress,

se un po i bij dories ne shpinë

se nder asqer po due me dal

sol nji shkja ne kalla me na hi

1670 na nuk kemi kurgja shka me i
bâ
se tash shate dit e lufta qi a nisë

me asqer Muja ka rrethue

force te madhe shkijat kan
punue
tabe te forta shkijat qi kan bâ
1675 s'po mund Muja ne kasab per
me hi
q'athere çbani Sirotin Alia
tu dera nusen e ka lan
prap ish hip ne bedel te kallas

e k'i leshue nji piskame te madhe
1680 ne majet bjeshkes Agët e ka
ndije
e kan ndije e ma mire e kan
njoft
baces Muji i ka qit e i ka than

gjalle tek asht aj Sirotin Alia
edhe kurr ma i fort Alia qi s'a
kan
1685 keçyre c'bani aj Bylyk Bashka
Muji
te dy gishtat ne vesh i ka shti
nji za te idhum Muja paska leshue
e ne bark te nanes djali me u
mjerue
mire e ndjeu aj Sirotin Alia
1690 e i piskam per mbrapa aj ka
leshue

because I am jumping on the
bay horse's back
and I am going to ride out into
the soldiers.
If just a single Slav enters the
fortress
1670 there will be nothing that we
can do.
· For now it is seven days since
the battle began.
Muji has surrounded them with
soldiers.
The Slavs have built up a great
force, ·
and have built strong defenses.
1675 Muji is not able to enter the
city."
What did Sirotin Ali then do?
He left the bride at the door,
climbed back up to the battle-
ments of the fortress
and let out a loud cry.
1680 On top of the highlands the
Agas heard it,
they heard it and recognized it
even better.
They addressed their brother
Muji and said:
"Sirotin Ali is still alive.
never has Ali been any
stronger."
1685 Consider what Bylyk Basha
Muji did:
sticking two fingers in his ears
Muji let out an angry cry,
enough for a boy in his moth-
er's womb to feel miserable!
Sirotin Ali heard it well
1690 and he let out a shout in return.

q'athere shkallave Alia a djerg
e n'oborr at dorinë e ka gjet

rreth kallaja dorija po cillet

per dizginash Alia ja ka ngjit
1695 e ne shpinë sa shpejt i ka ra
shka i ka than Dylber
Angjelines
amanet edhe nuses ja ka lan
shpejt e shpejt thote deren me
ma çel
e ma shpejt per mbrapa me
ngujue
1700 çikat deren sa shpejt ja kan çel

e aj Alia sa fort ish idhnue
si vetima dorine e ka gjue

si vetima nder asqer asht ra

per mas tina deren e kan
ngujue
1705 te dy çikat ne kalla jau hip

heçyre c'po bajne trimneshat
tue liftue
e Alia nder shkija asht ra
e per mbas luften e ka fillue

shum Alia me shpate qi po i
pret
1710 ma shum dorija qi po i vret

q'athere ndjeu aj Çeto Basho Muji
qi prej kallas Alija asht dal
edhe mrapa luften djali jau ka
nise
mer e madhe shkijet jau ka marrë
1715 po bertet ai Bylyk Basho Muji

Then Ali climbed down the stairs
and found his bay horse in the
courtyard.
The bay horse was circling
about the fortress.
Ali grabbed it by its bridle straps,
1695 quickly jumping onto its back.
And what did he say to Dylber
Angjelina?
He left the bride his last wishes:
"Quick, quick—he said—open
the door for me,
and close it behind me even
quicker!"
1700 The girls ever so quickly
opened the door.
Ali was so angered:
he struck the bay horse like
lightning
and rode into the soldiers like
lightning.
Behind him they closed the
door.
1705 The two girls climbed up in the
fortress.
Consider what the heroines
were doing fighting!
Ali rode into the Slavs
and immediately started the
battle.
Ali was cutting many of them
down with his sword,
1710 and his bay horse was killing
even more of them.
Then Çeto Basha Muji realized
Ali had come out of the fortress,
and the boy again had begun
fighting.
A great fear overtook the Slavs.
1715 Bylyk Basha Muji was shouting:

ku jeni Age se diten nau ka ardh

se jasht a dal aj Sirotin Alia
prej kalla nder shkije a ra

me zan te idhum Muja qi i ka thirr
1720 pa a qjalle je more Sirotin Alia
kurr ma i fort thote Alia s'jam kan

sal dy vete ne kalla qi i kam lan

shtate krajlit more bace per me i rrethue
kurr nji grim djelt s'kan me u mjerue
1725 ç'po ban aj Bylyk Basho Muji
sa ne qef Muja qi a bâ
me zinxhi at gjokun qi po e therr

krejt n'hava gjoku qi po çohet

si me krah gjoku qi ish kan
1730 shkum te kuqe po qitke me dham

nji sahat larg aj gjoku qi po gjue

gure e dru e gjioku me mirue

e n'toke aj gjoku kur po hidhet

teri ne gush toka po e leshon
1735 gjam te medha gjoku qi po ban

e prej tij toka tue gjimue
ton ordija e krajlit jan mjerue

qe zez dita ne qi na ka gjet
ksi mjerimit kerkush nuk ka pa

"Where are you, Agas, for our day has come?

For Sirotin Ali has come out
and has attacked the Slavs from the fortress!"
Muji called out in an angry voice:
1720 "Are you alive, O Sirotin Ali?"
"Never have I been stronger— says Ali—
I have left only two people in the fortress.

If the Seven Kings were to surround me, my brother,
the boys would not worry one bit."
1725 What did Bylyk Basha Muji do?
Muji was so delighted,
he cuts into his white stallion with his spurs.

The white stallion lifts itself right up in the sky,
as if the white stallion had wings,
1730 spewing red foam through its teeth

and shooting it one hour's distance!

The white stallion uproots rocks and trees,

and when the white stallion hits the ground
it lets fly knee-high dirt,
1735 the white stallion produced a loud rumbling

and made the earth shake.
The whole army of the King was miserable.

A dark day had befallen it.
None had ever seen such misery.

1740 fort mundohen luft per me bâ

se ashqer te fort besa krajli kish
pas
sa me topa Mujin gjith po e
gjujin
e n'hava gjioku qi po çohet

ikbalije gjoku e kish pas
1745 pushk as topë kurqysh se kish
marre
ka po cillet rreth sheherit per
gurë
zjarm e flak prej patkoit qi po
qet
prej çelikut thumat qi i lish pas
prej tumakut patkojt ja k'i vue
1750 te ton gurët po shkon tue ranue

kush po e sheh fort qi ish
mjerue
ç'po lifton aj Sirotin Alia
me dori nder shkije kenka ra

mere e madh shkijet e kish
marre
1755 para e mrapa lufta a fillue
tridhete Agë fort tue liftue
q'athere shkijat jan nise e jau
gushtue
q'athere ç'bani ai Milosh
Kapitani
treqind shkije me vedi i kish
marre
1760 nji mihane shkoj kenka gujuje

fort e fort mihanje ish qillue
si kalla krajli e kish punue

po mundohet Miloshi tuej liftue

1740 They struggled hard to carry on
the battle,
for the army had firmly sworn
a *besa* to the King.
However much they fire at Muji
with cannons
his white stallion lifts itself into
the sky.
The white stallion was fortunate,
1745 neither rifle nor cannon ever
hit it.
It was circling about the city
over stones,
sending fire and flames from its
shoes.
It had spikes made of steel
nailed to its bronze shoes
1750 and it went striking all the
stones.
Whoever watched it was very
worried.
How was Sirotin Ali fighting?
He plunged with his bay horse
into the Slavs,
a great fear had overtaken the
Slavs.
1755 The battle began on all sides,
the thirty Agas fiercely fighting.
The Slavs then began to feel
hard pressed.
What did Kapitan Milosh then
do?
He took three hundred Slavs
with him
1760 and left and locked himself in a
tavern.
The tavern was ever so strong,
the King had built it like a
fortress.
Milosh struggles while fighting,

e tre ditë q'aty qi kish qindrue
1765 me Alien Agët jan bashkue
kur jan pa me at Sirotin Alien
ne gryk kan marre e ne fy faqe
kan puth

me te foli ai Budaline Tali
pashë nji zot more Ali qi te ka
dhan
1770 ti ne kalla Ali kush ke lan

sol nji shka ne kalla me na hi

na nuk kem kurgja ska me i bâ
me te madhe keshe aj Sirotin Alia
mos ki dert more Budaline Tali

1775 se dy djelt Zoti mi ka fal

qi ne dunaja shoket nuk i kan
ti me syë Tale per me i pa

fort je pllak e ment edhe te lau

bê ban Tali ne din edhe iman
1780 shoket e tyne nana nuk i ka
bame
amanet kallan jau kam lan
shtate krajla ne kalla me i
rrethue
per pa dek djelt nuk kan me e
leshue
boll u kam lan xhephane e
fyshek
1785 e boll kan bukë edhe barrut

topa te renda ne kalla jau kam
lan
e sa mire fitilat jau kam dhez

he held out there for three days.
1765 The Agas joined up with Ali.
When they saw Sirotin Ali
they embraced him around the
neck and kissed both his
cheeks.
When Budaline Tali spoke up:
"For the sake of God who made
you, Ali,
1770 whom did you leave in the
fortress?
If just one Slav enters the
fortress
there is nothing we can do."
Sirotin Ali loudly laughed:
"Do not be afraid, dear
Budaline Tali,
1775 for God has granted me two
heroes
who have no equal in this world.
If you were to set eyes upon
them, Tali,
you would be struck flat and
you would lose your mind."
Tali swears by his faith in Allah:
1780 "No mother has made your
heroes!"
"I left them my final wish:
If the Seven Kings were to
surround the fortress
the heroes would not abandon
it before dying.
I left them many rifles and
bullets,
1785 and they have much food and
gunpowder.
I left them heavy cannons in
the fortress,
and I lit the fuses so well for
them,

kur te ngushtohen topat per
me i shpraze
harab sheherin Muji qi kan me
e bâ
1790 prap kish fol aj Sirotin Alia
ore Muji halin qish me e bâ

qi Miloshi ne mihan na esht
gujue
shum asqer edhe me vedi ka
marre
pushk as topi mehanen s'po e
çart
1795 e gjith anesh rrethin ja ka qit

trimij turq Miloshin e kan
rrethue
fort dushmani edhe paska liftue

pushk e top Miloshin qi po e
gjujne
e s'po kan mihanes shka me e
bâ
1800 shka kish fol aj Budaline Tali
ndalnju shokeju Zoti mos ju
vraft
se me jurrush Miloshin
s'muejm me e marre
por kadale Miloshin me e
gushtue
buk as uje ne mihan si ka qillue

1805 vete merzitet n'dore ka me ra

me jurrush Miloshin me e
rrethue
ne me pushk aj ka me na damtue
njo prej Agësh ne krajli per me
met

if hand pressed to fire the
cannons
they will burn the city black,
Muji."
1790 Sirotin Ali spoke back:
"O Muji, what can we possibly
do?
Milosh is locked up in the
tavern
and has taken many soldiers
with him.
Neither rifles nor cannons are
damaging the tavern.
1795 They have been surrounded on
all sides,
three thousand Turks have
surrounded Milosh,
and the enemy has fought
fiercely,
rifles and cannons that are
firing at Milosh,
cannot do anything to the
tavern."
1800 What did Budaline Tali say?
"Stop, friends, may God strike
you dead.
For you cannot take Milosh
with an assault,
but put pressure on him slowly,

there is neither food nor water
in the tavern.
1805 He will get impatient and fall
into our hands.
If we encircle Milosh with an
assault
he will injure us with his rifles.
If one of the Agas will be left in
the Kingdom

e mazun ne Judbine kemi me
   shkue

1810 per varre te idhta shoke qi kemi
   marre

na me varre gjithmonë jemi
   mesue

prap kish than aj Budaline Tali

rreth mihanet Miloshin me e
   rrethue

e istikamet te fort me i punue

1815 sa mire Talin Agët e kan ndigjue

edhe tabet te mira i kan punue

rreth mihane te gjith ku e kan
   rrethue

buk as uje s'po i lan me shkue

keçyre ç'po ban aj Sirotin Alia

1820 muer me vedi at Halilin i ri

baces Muji edhe q'atherë i ka
   kalzue

ne kalla thotë bace po due me
   shkue

i kam dy djel e gjithnji tue
   liftue

me vedi Halilin e ka marre

1825 ne dere të kallas e q'atherë qi
   jan shkue

q'atherë thirri aj Sirotin Alia

ku je ti mori Begzadeja e Bukur

ori Fatime shpejt deren me ma
   çel

se me Halilin jam ardhun ne
   derë

1830 heçyre shka bani Dylber
   Angjelina

Halil Agës zanin ja ka ndije

---

we will return to Udbina
   defeated

1810 because of the grievous wounds
   we have suffered,

we have always been used to
   wounds."

Budaline Tali said again:

"Encircle Milosh around the
   tavern

and build strong fortifications!"

1815 How well the Agas heeded Tali:

they dug strong trenches

and encircled him around the
   tavern.

They prevent food and water
   from getting through.

Consider what Sirotin Ali did:

1820 he took the Young Halil Aga
   with him,

and then he said to his brother
   Muji:

"Brother—he says—I want to go
   into the fortress.

I have two heroes fighting this
   whole time."

He took Halil with him.

1825 Then they went to the door of
   the fortress

and then Sirotin Ali cried out:

"Where are you, O Beautiful
   Begzade?

O Fatima, open the door for me
   quickly,

for I have come to the door
   with Halil!"

1830 Consider what Dylber Angjelina
   did:

She was aware of Halil Agas's
   fame,

si vetima shkallave a djerg

shpejt e shpejt at deren jau ka
çel
e permbrenda te dyja jan hi
1835 shpejt permbrapa deren po
gujojne
e ne podrum atlaret i kau
leshue
ton me gjiak atlarët qi ish
mblue
tuej pre me asqer e tuej coptue

ne at kalla bashk kenkan hip

1840 prap po flet aj Sirotin Alia
pa ndigjo moj Dylber Angjelin
qi ky asht ai Halil Aga i ri
per to çike mue qi me ki vete

probatin Halili m'ka qillue
1845 sikur moter ty qi te kam desht
Halil Agën ishalla me e martue
e Dylberja more qi ish kan ra

ka ugj kryte ne turb thej
mendue
e Alia çikes i ka than
1850 nuk asht vakti ori çike per me
kujtue
na jem ardh mori çike per me
të pëvete
ne ate mihan qi Miloshi asht
ngujue
me asqer edhe gjith e kem
rrethue
me i pas kraht edhe me fluturue
1855 tybe gjalle moj çike nuk kem
me leshue
çika u dredh edhe Alies i ka than

like lightning she climbed down
the stairs
and opened the door for them
as fast as she could.
And the two of them went inside,
1835 quickly closing the door behind
them.
They left their thoroughbreds
loose in the stable,
thoroughbreds that were all
covered in blood
from fighting and slaughtering
the soldiers.
They climbed up the fortress
together.
1840 Again Sirotin Ali says:
"Listen, dear Dylber Angjelina,
this is Young Halil Aga,
the one you had asked me
about, girl.
Halil is my blood brother.
1845 I have wanted you, like a sister,
to marry Halil, God willing."
And Dylber was overcome with
longing,
she lowered her head, embar-
rassed, pondering.
Ali said to the girl:
1850 "This is not the time, O girl, to
be thinking.
We have come, O girl, to ques-
tion you.
Milosh has locked himself in
the tavern,
we have completely encircled
him with soldiers.
If he had wings and could fly.
1855 Dear girl, I would never let him
get away alive."
The girl turned and said to Ali,

315

mua krajlica nji fjal ma ka lan

"The Queen has left word with me,

nji gjephane ne mihan qi a kan

that there is a munitions room in the tavern.

ne kalla Ali e per me hip

Climb to the top of the fortress, Ali,

1860 e dy topa te randa qi jau kan

1860 there are two heavy cannons there.

q'ata topa n'muejsh ti Ali me i goditë

If you can aim those cannons, Ali,

edhe gryken me jau kethye ne mihan

and turn the barrels on the tavern

edhe zjarmin q'athere me jau dhan

and then fire them,

per ishan Miloshin ke me e bâ

you can make Milosh a target

1865 q'athere merret Miloshi Kapitani

1865 then Kapitan Milosh can be taken

nuk ka qare ne dore pa ra

he would have no choice but to fall into your hands."

e n'kalla Alia tek a shkue

And Ali went straight to the fortress.

me Halilin topat i ka punue

He operated the cannons with Halil:

prej mihanes e gryken jau ka dredh

he turned the barrels on the tavern

1870 q'atherë flakë e topate jau kan dhan

1870 and then fired the cannons.

topat te randa krajli kish pas mbush

The King had loaded the cannons

shtate krajlive xhevap me jau dhan

to send news to the Seven Kings.

e mihanes me topat i ka ra

Ali hit the tavern with the cannons

bitevi mblojen ja kan hjek

and took off the whole roof,

1875 gjith Miloshin ne to tuej liftue

1875 but Milosh kept on fighting.

prap Alia n'kalla ç'kish bâ

What did Ali do back in the fortress?

perseri topat i ka mbush

He loaded the cannons again.

gjylet te randa te topa paska shti

He placed heavy cannon balls in the cannons

e po stjen barrute pa mas

1880 prap mihanes me to ja ka venue

edhe flake te dyja jan dhez
e nji kat mihanes ja kan rrezue

sa e nalt mihanje qi ish kan
prap Miloshi n'to tuej liftue
1885 keçyre ç'po ban aj Sirotin Alia
e Halili djalit i ka brit
nuk po din e topat per me i
 mbush
teri ne gjyshe barrut me u dhan
ka dy gjyle ne ta me i shti

1890 a mymqyn Miloshin me e marre
po me vjeu keq Halil me kalzue
kaq shum Miloshi me na
 qindrue
me barrute topat i kan mbush

e ka dy gjyla ne to i kan shti

1895 prej mihanes q'athere i kan
 dredh
zjarm e flakë topave u kan dhan

sa fitilat të mira qi jau kan dhez
e mihaves me ta i kau ra
deri themelin gjysen e kan
 rrezue
1900 shum asqeri Miloshit ju ka
 damtue
e ka mesye at mehanen me dal

kesh me ike a mondet me
 peshtue
me batare Argët tue gjue

and packed them with plenty of
 powder.
1880 He again took aim with the
 cannons at the tavern
and fired the two of them.
They leveled one story of the
 tavern,
the tavern was so tall!
Milosh was back fighting.
1885 Consider what Sirotin Ali did!
He cried out to the hero Halil:
"Don't they know how to load
 the cannons?
Fill them half up with powder,
and load two cannon balls into
 them.
1890 It is possible to take Milosh.
But I feel bad, Halil, to admit
how well Milosh has stopped
 us."
They filled the cannons with
 powder
and loaded two cannon balls
 into each one.
1895 Then they turned them on the
 tavern.
They put fire and flame to the
 cannons.
How many good fuses they lit!
They hit the tavern with them
and leveled half of it to the
 foundation.
1900 They injured many of Milosh's
 soldiers.
He emerged to get out of the
 tavern
as if to escape and struggle to
 save himself.
The Agas took aim with their
 batteries

e shtate varre Miloshit ja kau
dhan

1905 rrob e zuni Arnaut Osmani

ka nxane rrob e Mujit ja ka çue

ka qit Mujit e me goje i ka than
amanet Miloshin dua me ta lan

amanet ne Judbin per me e çue

1910 se kan borxh burrat me liftue

ton asqeri q'athere ish bashkue

Muja qiti Agvet jau ka than
fukaraja faje edhe nuk ka
veçse krajli mall te vet edhe
shkaka

1915 kimetli mallin me ja marre
e n'ate fushe Tale per me dal

Muja trimi q'athere ç'k'i bâ
ne derë t'kallas Alies i paska
shkue
ku je ti thotë more Sirotin Alia

1920 a po do e deren me ma çel

a me çika ne kalla je ngujue

nuk bjen mend per krajl e as
per mue
paska ndije aj Sirotin Alia
te madhe Mujit i kenka germue

1925 qysh kujtohesh bace mem
qortue
se ne sahit Zotit e taudin kam
liftue
fluturim e shkallave kenka djerg

and gave Milosh seven wounds.

1905 Arnaut Osmani took him
prisoner,
took him prisoner and deliv-
ered him to Muji.
He said to Muji directly:
"As a pledge I want to hand
Milosh over to you,
I entrust him to you to send
him to Udbina,

1910 because men have a duty to
fight."
He then assembled his whole
army.
Muji addressed the Agas and said,
"The poor are not guilty,
but the King's own possessions,
whatever is valuable,

1915 is worth taking as plunder,
for Tale to take out into the
plain."
What did the hero Muji then do?
He went to the door of Ali's
fortress.
"Where are you, Sirotin Ali—he
says—

1920 Are you going to open the door
for me
or be locked in the tower with
the girl,
without thinking about the
King or about me?"
Sirotin Ali heard that.
He thundered loudly at Muji:

1925 "How can you think of scolding
me, brother,
for I have fought on our God's
behalf."
He went flying down the stairs

baces Muji deren ja ka çel

mrenda Muji ne kalla kenka hi
1930 tridhete Age edhe shkojshin
    per mbas tij
sore te madh ne kalla per me pa

çfar fuqije ne kalla qi ka
çfar fuqije krajli ka mbarue

qi me dy çika ja ka liftue
1935 e sa dite ne kalla ka qindrue

nuk kan pas kurgja shka me i bâ
sa te fort krajli qi i kish pas bâ
me te foli aj Sirotin Alia
baca Muji dy fjal me mi ndigjue
1940 qi kjo çike e krajlit qi me ka
    peshtue
ka nderè vehten bace edhe ty e
    mua
se te krajli misnatë m'ka çue

q'athere vehten bace e ka pague
ka pre krajlin bace edhe kam
    liftue
1945 ton asqeri dhe mua m'ka
    rrethue
si nji trim çika ka liftue
kamb per kamb me mue tue
    shkue
dore me dore e kamb per kamb
nji bese te madhe çikes ja kam
    dhau
1950 per Halilin nuse me ja dhan
tridhete Age me hajr ja kam bâ

q'athere Agët keçyre shka kan
    punue

and opened the door for his
    brother Muji.
Muji entered inside the fortress,
1930 The thirty Agas walking behind
    him
to see the great stones in the
    fortress.
What strength the fortress had,
What strength the King had
    created!
He fought with two girls,
1935 and for all the days he resisted
    in the fortress,
they were unable to do anything.
So well had the King fortified it.
Sirotin Ali spoke up:
"Brother Muji, heed my words!
1940 This daughter of the King who
    saved me
has brought honor to herself and
    to you and to me, brother.
For she went to the King in the
    middle of the night
and then paid him back herself.
She killed the King, brother,
    and we fought on.
1945 All the soldiers encircled me as
    well.
The girl fought like a hero,
going with me step for step,

hand in hand, step for step.
I swore a great *besa* to the girl
1950 to give her to Halil as a bride."
The thirty Agas congratulated
    him.
Then consider what the Agas
    did:

e kallas kan hap e kan shikue	they opened the fortress and looked it over,
kimetlije mallin ja kan marre	and grabbed valuable plunder.
1955 e ne fushe q'athere jan dal	1955 Then they rode out to the plain.
e Miloshin rrob qi e kishin marre	They had taken Milosh prisoner,
shum asqer e rrobije kan nxane	they seized many soldiers and prisoners.
e dy nuset ne fushe e kan qit	and they sent the two brides into the plain.
e shka bani Sirotin Alia	And what did Sirotin Ali do?
1960 nji koçi ne sheher e ka marre	1960 He took a carriage in the town
te dy nuse ne to i ka shti	and put the two brides in it.
amanete Talit ja ka dhan	He entrusted them to Tali:
deri ne Judbine Koçijat me i dryë	"Keep the carriage locked all the way to Udbina,
se pak pune ne sheher qi e kam	for I have a few things to do in the town."
1965 muer me vedi at Halilin i ri	1965 He took with him the Young Halil
e ne pazar te dyja jan dal	and the two of them went out to the market place
po ma lypin Maruken Hanxhi	searching for the innkeeper Maruka.
e ne mihane te dy kenkan hi	The two of them entered the inn
ne gryk e muer ai Sirotin Alia	and Sirotin Ali embraced her around the neck.
1970 ku je ti e Maruke Hanxija	1970 "Where have you been, innkeeper Maruka?"
p'e merr n'gryk aj Sokole Halili	Sokol Halil embraces her around the neck.
u dredh Alia e Marukes po i kalzon	Ali turns and says to Maruka:
qi ky asht aj Halil Aga i ri	"This is Young Halil Aga.
n'daç me e njoft mori Maruka Hanxhi	perhaps you know of him, O innkeeper Maruka.
1975 ka shkue zani i djalit ne shtate krajli	1975 The boy's fame has traveled to the Seven Kingdoms.
as nuk ka ma mire as ma daji	There is no one better or braver.
shum iqrom Maruka qi po ban	Maruka paid him much respect.

pak kan ndej e shum nuk kan
vonuë
u dredh Alies e Mara shka i ka
than
1980 itiza more Ali kur te bajne

ja mesye kullat Maruka
Hanxhise
ndo se e shkrije mallin bitevi

ndo edhe vet une qi kom me
marrue
ndo ty edhe qi kom me te
ndhimune
1985 me Maren q'aty jan halalue

keçyre Alia athere ç'kish punue
pash nji zot thotë Mara qi te fal

a asht mymqym ne darsem per
mem ardh
lot per faqe Mares i kan peshtue
1990 kish me ardh Ali po s'kom me e
guxue
edhe Mara u dredh po e flet nji
fjal
tjeter Zoti Ali s'kish me e dasht

veç ne darsem ty kesh me te
ardh
por krajlit Ali ata vesh me
marre
1995 qi ty mik Ali qi te kam dal
njiqind mashkull n'oxhak e me
i pas
njo pa pre more Ali nuk ma lan

por udha marrë u pjekshim me
hajr

They sat for awhile, they did
not delay long.
Turning to Ali what did Mara
say?
1980 "O, Ali, when they make
reparations
just remember the towers of
the innkeeper Maruka
either all my property will be
completely wasted,
and I myself will be
dishonored,
all for having assisting you."

1985 Then he exchanged farewell
blessings with Mara.
Consider what Ali then did:
"Mara—he says—by the grace
of God who made you,
is it possible for you to come to
my wedding?"
Tears ran down Mara's face.
1990 "If only I could come, Ali, but I
do not dare to."
Mara turned and said a few
words:
"There is nothing else I would
want, master Ali
besides attending your
wedding.
But if the King should get word,
Ali,
1995 that I have befriended you,
if I had a hundred males in my
family
they would not leave one alive,
Ali.
But fare you well, may we meet
again on a happy occasion,

e nuses ate hajrin ja pash

2000 e e gezofsh Ali e trashgofsh

e shum gajret Ali qi ke bâ

ki martue at Sokol Halil Agen

q'ashtu duket per mike e me
liftue
probatin Halili qi te ka qillue

2005 nuse muer e ishalla ka me e
gezue

me Marukun q'athere jan da
edhe rrugen djelt e paskan marre
e n'fushë te baca kenkan dal

q'athere gadi të ton kekan bâ

2010 tuej shkue rruges jan fillue
shpejt u kethye aj Sirotin Alia
diçka shoke ne kalla e kam
harrue
nuk kam qajre ne kalla per pa
shkue
e dorinë bythprape ma ka
dredh
2015 si vetima ne kalla te ka hi

ne dere te kallas at dorinë e ka
lidh
e vet a hip shkallave perpjet

e ne teboj Alia kenka shkue
nji fitil e q'aty e paska dhez
2020 në at xhephana fitilin e ka lan

and may you rejoice with your
bride.

2000 May you enjoy her, Ali, and
have children.
You have been very coura-
geous, Ali,
you have married off Sokol
Halil Aga.
That is how one must fight for
his friends,
as Halil is indeed your blood
brother.
2005 He has taken a bride and, God
willing, will be happy with
her."
Then they parted with Maruka.
And the heroes took to the road
and came out on their brother's
plain.
Then they all made themselves
ready
2010 and started riding along the road.
Sirotin Ali quickly turned around:
"I have forgotten something in
the fortress, my friends,
I have no choice but to go to
the fortress."
And he turned his bay horse
back.
2015 He flew like lightning to the
fortress.
He tied the bay horse to the
door of the fortress
and he himself climbed up the
stairs.
Ali went to the arsenal,
there he lit a long fuse
2020 and left the fuse in the ammu-
nition room.

shpejt shkallave te posht adjerg

ne shpine dories shpejt i ka ra

e per mrapa Agve ju ka venue
e n'ate fushe Agët qi i ka nxane

2025 tue shkue fushes qi ishin kan
me nji here ne bjeshk jan zatet

i kan marre bjeshken edhe
perpjet
kur jan dal n'ate majen e
bjeshkes
e ka gjetun nji krue te ftohfte
2030 prej barutit fort qi ishin kan
lodhë
s'ju kish ra ne mend me ngran
as me pi
po per uje per te cillen ishin
kan shkri
kan pi uje e sa mire po
pushojne
turbit Muji p'e xhepit i kish
nxjerre
2035 e ne sye trimi paska vue

po i shikon fushat e krajlive

nji rê te zeze ne at fushe ka pa
çud po i vjen e s'po mundet me
e njoft
shkove vet edhe Muja qi jau ka
than
2040 Pash nji Zot shoke qi jau ka
dhan
pa a thuj dini kurgja mem
kalzue
a por sytë mua m'ka qorue

He quickly climbed down the
stairs,
he quickly jumped on the back
of his bay horse
and rode back to the Agas.
And on the plain he caught up
with the Agas
2025 as they were crossing the plain.
In a short time they reached
the highlands.
They began climbing up the
highlands.
When they came up to the edge
of a highland meadow
they found a cold spring.
2030 They were exhausted by the
gunpowder,
eating and drinking had not
entered their minds,
except for the water they had
melted.
They drank some water and
were nicely resting.
Muji took his field glasses out
of his pocket
2035 and the hero put them to his
eyes,
he was looking across the
plains of the Kings.
He saw a black cloud on a plain,
he was amazed because he was
not able to recognize it.
Muji said to his friends:
2040 "For the sake of God who made
you,
tell me, is there anything you
can tell me?
Have my eyes gone blind,

nji rê te zeze ne krajli qi a çue

or has a black cloud appeared on the plain?"

q'athere foli Sirotin Alia

Then Sirotin Ali spoke up.

2045 ore bace Mujit i ka than
nji fitil ne xhephana e kam lan

2045 "O my brother—he said to Muji—
I left a fuse in the ammunition room.

krejt hava kallaja tek a çue

The fortress has just blown sky high.

gjysen e sheherit bace e ka pervlue
pak kan ndej e shum nuk kan vonue

It has scorched half the city, brother."
They delayed for a while, it was not long,

2050 per Judbine rrugen e kan fillue

2050 and set out on the road to Udbina.

ja mysyn kullat Sirotin Alies

They espied the towers of Sirotin Ali,

me asqer tu kulla i kan ra

reaching the towers with their soldiers.

nana e Alies perpara jau ka dal

Ali's mother came out to meet them:

ju hozhgjelden djelm a keni muejte me ardh

"Welcome, my boys, it is good that you have managed to come!

2055 pa a thuej e kam Alien të gjalle
se edhe nusen e tij ja kan pas marrë
me te foli ai Budaline Tali
ori loke Tali i ka than
muhabete sonte me na bâ

2055 Tell me, is my Ali alive,
Because they have taken his bride, too?"
At that Budaline Tali spoke up:
"O dear mother—Tali said—
Tonight make pleasant conversation with us

2060 se dy nuse Alia i ka marre
e ate te vehen ishalla ka me e gezue
e Halil ages njo ja ka fitue

2060 for Ali has taken two brides.
God willing, he will enjoy his own,
The better one he has won for Halil.

e ma mire Halilin e ka martue

And how well he has married off Halil,

se e ka marre at Dylber Anglielinen

for he has taken Dylber Angjelina,

2065 qi ne shtate krajlit shoqen nuk
e ka
as ma soj as ma mire per me pa

keçyre ç'bani aj Sirotin Alia
si telal n'asqer qi a dal

gjth me za Alia tue brit
2070 kush ne luft e ne krajli qi je kan

kush a plague ishalla ka me
peshtue
kush a mbet shehit a shkue
e ne hajiret ishalla kemi me u
pjek
kush te jesh i gjalle e me shpirt

2075 mua ne dasem shoke mem ardh

per nande dite dasem due me
bâ
ton asqerin ne fushe e ka ndal
sa zjarmijet ne fushë i ka dhezë

ka i tabak per zjarmi jau ka çue

2080 e ne qelyma fushen e ka shtrue
e verdhe ish kan e kuqe e kish
bâ
rahatue asqerin qi e kish pas
e Miloshin q'athere i kish marre
e ne zidon Miloshin e ka shti
2085 njiqind shkije me vedi i kish
nxane
me Miloshin ne zidan i ka çue

te dy nuse prej koçeje i ka
nxjerre
nanes vet Alia i ka brit
te dy nuse nana me na i marre

2065 who has no equal in the Seven
Kingdoms,
and none more noble or beau-
tiful to be beheld."
Consider what Sirotin Ali did!
He went among the soldiers
like a town crier
and loudly cried out:
2070 "Whoever fought and was in
the Kingdom,
whoever was wounded and,
God willing, rescued,
whoever became a martyr,
with luck we will meet again,
God willing,
whoever is alive and with a
breath of life
2075 come, my friends, to my
wedding.
I want to have a nine day
celebration."
He kept the army on the plain.
How many campfires he lit on
the plain!
He provided a tureen for each
fire
2080 and covered the plain with rugs.
It had been yellow, he made it
red.
And rested his soldiers.
He then took Milosh
and put him in prison.
2085 He had taken one hundred
Slavs with him
and sent them to prison with
Milosh.
Ali took the two brides out of
the carriage
and he shouted to his mother:
"Mother, take our two brides

2090 e ne kulla bashke me na i shti

me ju dhan nane me hanger e
    me pi
per nande dit q'aty qi te rrin

sa te jene dasme nane edhe e
    fillue
hiq te nuset nuk dona me shkue
2095 i ka ngreh dajre e salkamin

treqind desh Alia qi ka prue

kasaphanen ne ledin e ka
    ngresh
ka treqind n'dite qi po i pret

e ne fushe dajren tue bâ

2100 nuk kish kulla asqerin me i
    nxane
tupanxhite q'athere i ka mbledh
syrlaxhite Alia i ka bashkue
ton Judbina q'aty kenka mbledh
me hajr nusen Alies po ja bajne

2105 te koft me hajr Fatime Turkije

e te koft me hajr Ali e Gazija

she shum gajret Ali e ki bâ

rrob te gjalle Miloshin qi e ke
    nxane
kan bâ dajre nande dit e nande
    net
2110 nuk kalzohen ç'kan hanger
    ç'kan pi
veç nande dite q'athere kur jan
    mbush

2090 and put them together in our
    tower.
Give them something to eat and
    drink, mother,
enough to remain there for
    nine days.
As soon as the wedding begins,
    mother,
I will not go to the brides at all."
2095 Ali gathered together drums
    and pipes,
and provided three hundred
    rams.
He set up a slaughterhouse in
    the meadow
and slaughtered three hundred
    of them a day,
and the drums resounded on
    the plain.
2100 The towers could not accom-
    modate the army.
Ali assembled the drummers
and gathered the pipers,
then all of Udbina assembled
wishing Ali good fortune with
    his bride.
2105 "May good fortune be yours,
    Fatima Turkija!
May good fortune be yours, Ali,
    hero of Islam!
For you have shown much
    courage, Ali,
you took Milosh alive as a
    prisoner."
They celebrated for nine days
    and nine nights,
2110 words cannot tell how much
    they ate and drank.
But when the nine days then
    came to an end,

paska fole Bylyk Basho Mujo
pa ndigjon more Sirotin Alia
asht ardh vatke dasmen e me e
   ndrrue
2115 te Halili krushqit e me i çue
n'daç Ali Halilin me e martue

me te foli Sirotin Alia
nuse te mire Halilit ja kam
   marre
edhe gadi nana ja ka bâ

2120 kon e boj çikes ja ka ngjite

si me kan e vedja e ka
   shtrengue
e n'koçi at çiken e ka shti
e n'ate fushe Alia e paska hi
ka qit Mujit Alia i ka than
2125 q'itash gadi nusen te kon bâ

tridhete Age q'athere jan çue
jau kan e ra atlarvet n'shpine

po mu pri ai Ali Bajraktari
e mbas tina Agët jan fillue

2130 e mbas Agvet trimij dasmor

aj ma i mrami Sokole Halili
shka i ka than Sirotin Alies
çou Ali ne darsem per mem
   ardh
se un pa ty hajrin mos ja pasha

2135 qe nandë dit nusen ma ki ndal

s'em ki lan as me sy per me e pa

Bylyk Basha Muji spoke up:
"Listen well, O Sirotin Ali.
The time has come to move the
   wedding celebration
2115 and to send the guests to Halil's
if you intend, Ali, to marry off
   Halil."
Sirotin Ali spoke up:
"I have taken a fine bride for
   Halil
and my mother has made her
   ready.
2120 She has decorated the girl with
   henna and blush,
dressing her as if she were her
   own."
Putting the girl in the carriage,
Ali rode into the plain.
Ali addressed Muji and said:
2125 "I have just now made the bride
   ready for you."
The thirty Agas then rose
and jumped on the backs of
   their thoroughbreds.
Ali Bajraktari led them,
and behind him followed the
   Agas,
2130 and behind the Agas the three
   thousand wedding guests,
the last being Sokol Halil.
What did he say to Sirotin Ali?
"Get up, Sirotin, to come to my
   wedding,
For without you I would not
   have seen good fortune.
2135 You have detained my bride for
   nine days,
not even letting me set eyes on
   her.

se une te shpija Ali dua me te
çue
edhe ty prej nuses me te largue

per nande dit ne darsem qi
m'ke mbajt
2140 tetemdhete e pa te ndal nuk e
lâ
q'athere nusen mire e kan fillue

per mbas krushqit ne Judbine
jan shkue
e tu kulla e Mujit i kan râ
shum oxhak aj Muji qi ish kan
2145 darsem te madhe q'athere
paska ngreh
e i ka mbledh Judbine e Krahinë

jau ka shtrâ pijen e salkamin

sheqerli kafet tue pjek
vene te kuqe rakije te bardhe

2150 per tri jave dasem se ka da

nuse te mire Halili e paska marre
me gajret djalin e ka martue

nuk len kon ne Krajli me u
gezue
pesh te madhe Zoti e ka çue
2155 kush nuk mundet me dal e
perballe
shtate krajlit e zani qi a hap

keshtu luftoj aj Sirotin Alia
nuse te mire Halilit i ka dhan
keshtu ka than atje s'jam kan

I want to send you to my house,
Ali,
and to keep you away from
your bride.

For the nine days you kept me
at your wedding celebration,
2140 I will not let her go eighteen
days without going out."
They then set out nicely with
the bride.

They rode to Udbina behind
the wedding guests
and reached Muji's tower.
Muji had many kinfolk,
2145 he then arranged for a large
wedding celebration.
He assembled Udbina and the
Borderland,
he set out for them drinks and
food,
roasting coffee with sugar,
and providing red wine and
white raki.
2150 He did not stop the celebration
for three weeks,
Halil took a fine bride indeed.
He married the hero off with
great zeal,
he let no one in the Kingdom
rejoice.
God gave him great importance,
2155 none could oppose him,

his reputation awed the Seven
Kingdoms.
This is how Sirotin Ali fought!
He gave Halil a fine bride.
This is how they told of it, I was
not there.

2160 por pa kan nuk kishin than

gjithmon Zotyn na ndihmoft
e dushmanat Zoti i poshtoft

e per ne mbret rinoft

2160 But had it not happened, they
would not have told of it.
May God ever help us,
and may He bring down our
enemies,
and may our Emperor live long!

LAN 79. Rexhep Zeneli, *Kanga e Halilit qi ka nxane Jovan Kapidanin*

Rexhep Zeneli; Puka; October 6, 1937
Kanga e Halilit qi ka nxane Jovan Kapidanin
The Song of Halil Who Seized Jovan Kapidani
Legendary song. Zeneli learned this song from Qorr Hysa.

	Tridhete agë ne llangjë ishin mbledh		Thirty Agas were gathered at the meeting place,
	kan marre llafin e po llafojne		they made conversation and were saying,
	p'e qortojne Çeto Basho Mujin		they were criticizing Çeto Basho Muji:
	pse p'e len Halilin pa u martue		"Why do you leave Halil unmarried?
5	Zotyn mall boll ta ka dhan	5	God has granted you possessions enough."
	q'atherë foli Çeto Basho Muja		Then Çeto Basho Muji said:
	Zoti mall boll m'ka dhan		"God has granted me possessions enough.
	pa martue per mall se kom lan		I have not left him unmarried because of possessions.
	por mik per qef nuk kam gjet		But I have not found an in-law to my liking.
10	kur kam gjet mikun per qef	10	When I have found an in-law to my liking
	çikë per qef nuk kam gjet		I have not found a girl to my liking."
	q'athere foli Ali Bajraktari		Then Ali Bajraktari said:
	mik e çike te dueja po ti gjaj		"I will find you both an in-law and a girl."
	mik e çike te dueja me mi gjet		"If you find me both an in-law and a girl,

15 un per mall ne e la pa e nxane	15 I will not let her go unbetrothed
	because of possessions."
po edhe mikun po ta kallxoj	"I will even tell you who that
	in-law is:
i thon per emen Beg Alaj Begu	They call him Beg Alaj Beg.
se ne Budim kullat i ka	He has his towers in Budim,
ai ma ka Begzaden e bardhë	and he has Begzade the White.
20 per Halilin qato per me e nxane	20 the one for you to betroth to
	Halil."
Muja n'kamb qathere kanka çue	Muji then rose to his feet:
çou Ali Muji paska than	"Get up, Ali—Muji said—
n'kullat mija sonte dom me shkue	tonight we will go to my towers.
me Halilin derte dom me bâ	We will take the concern up
	with Halil
25 dom me shkue çiken me ja lyp	25 and go to ask for the girl's hand."
me Alijen bashk kokan çue	He and Ali rose together
n'kullat Mujes te dy kokan	and the two went to Muji's
shkue	towers.
me Halilin derte paskan bâ	They took their concern up
	with Halil
per me e nxane Begzaden e	about the betrothing of Begzade
bardh	the White.
30 kur e fali Zotyn sabahin	30 When God granted morning light,
te dy krazhnikt bashk konkan	the two border warriors arose
çue	together
ja mësyn kullat Beg Alaj Begut	and appeared at the towers of
	Beg Alaj Beg.
hyzmetqarët para u kan dal	Servants came out in front of
	them.
mire se vjen o Muja me Alinë	"Welcome, O Muji and Ali."
35 mire se ju gjaj Muja ju paska than	35 "Well met," Muji said.
e perpjet shkallave Muja kanka	Muji climbed up the stairs
hip	
deren e odes e paska çel	and opened the door to parlor,
n'ode i gjet dymdhete vezira	in the parlor he finds twelve
	viziers,
n'ode i gjet dymdhete pashalar	in the parlor he finds twelve
	pashas,
40 qi jan shkue çiken me ja lyp	40 who had come to ask for the
	girl's hand.

por selam Muja jau paska dhan

mire selamin Mujis ja kan marre
ne vend te madh Mujin e kan ungj

po pin kafe e llafe qi po bajne

45 asht ardh darka e dark e paskan ngran

Muja i thojke Beg Alaj Begut
ton keta miq mbrend qi kan hi

kan ardh çiken ty me ta lyp

q'atherë foli Beg Alaj Begu
50 nuk muej çiken kerkuj me ja dhan

veç ko te don çika per me marre

Muja i thojke Beg Alaj Begut
shko ti Beg e çiken per me pëvet
ko te do çika Beg per me marre

55 athere u Çue Beg Alaj Begu
ne hareme Begu koka shkue
oj Begzade begu i paska than
per sherr tem Zoti te paska fal

se plot kulla me miq mu ka mbush
60 ty po te lypin dymdhete vezira

ty po te lypin dymdhete pashalar

ty po te lype Muja per Halilin

koh te duesh bij ne ta per me marre
athere foli Begzadja e Bardh

Nevertheless Muji gave them his greetings.

They received his greetings well,
and seated Muji in a place of honor.

They drank coffee and made conversation.

45 Suppertime came and they had supper.

Muji says to Beg Alaj Beg:
"All these guests who have come inside,

have they come to ask for your daughter's hand?"

Then Beg Alaj Beg said:
50 "I can not give my daughter to anyone,

except the one she wants to marry."

Muji says to Beg Alaj Beg:
"Go, Beg, and ask your daughter
who your daughter wants to marry."

55 Then Beg Alaj Beg got up
and went for the harem.
"O Begzade—the Beg said to her—
God has made you the cause of my troubles.

The tower is completely filled with guests,
60 twelve viziers are asking for your hand,

twelve pashas are asking for your hand,

Muji is asking for your hand for Halil.

Marry the one you want, daughter!"
Then Begzade the White said:

65	tash prej kulla kollaj po ti heki	65	"I will now remove them easily from the tower."
	ne jemenit kamb i ka shti		She stuck her feet in peasant slippers
	sofrabezin per fytyr e ka shtrue		and laid a tablecloth over her body.
	perpjet shkalleve çika konka ngjit		The girl climbed up the stairs
	deren e odes çika kenka çel		and opened the door to the parlor.
70	mire se rini burra u ka than	70	"It is good that you are waiting, men," she said to them.
	mire se vjen oj Begzadje e Bardh		"It is good that you have come, O Begzade the White."
	tash nji fjale une po jau thom		"Now I have a few words to say to you.
	keni ardh mua per mem pëvete		You have come to ask for my hand in marriage.
	tjeter burr nuk kam per me marre		I will marry no other man
75	veç kush te dalin n'Kotorr per me shkue	75	but the one who will leave to go to Kotorr
	me ma pre at Jovan Kapitanin		to cut down Jovan Kapitan.
	se shtate vllazen une i kam pas		For I had seven brothers,
	ton Jovan nder shpat mi ka shti		and Jovan put them all to the sword,
	sod m'ka lan moter pa vlla		leaving me today a sister without a brother.
80	kush të ma presin Jovan Kapitanin	80	Whoever kills Jovan Kapitan
	se per per burr hajrin ja pasha		let me have the good fortune to take for a husband."
	qysh jan kan dyemdhete vezira		How the twelve viziers groaned!
	kryte per toke te ton i kan ulë		All of them lowered their heads to the ground,
	njo me gojë as pak nuk po flet		not one uttered a word from his mouth,
85	njo ka njo per dere qi po dalin	85	one by one they went out the door.
	si jan kan dymdhete pashalar		How the twelve pashas groaned!
	kryte per tokë te gjitha kan ulë		All of them lowered their heads to the ground,

njo me goj as pak nuk po flet	not one uttered a word from his mouth,
njo ka njo per deret qi po dalin	one by one they went out the door.
90 Muja n'gujë qatherë konka çue	90 Muji then rose on his knees.
Zoti te vraft oj Begzade i ka than	"May God strike you dead, O Begzade—he said to her—
krejt nafaken vedit ja ki këput	"you have completely ruined our chances.
nuk ka burrë n'Kotorr per me shkue	There is no man to go to Kotorr
qi me e prê Jovan Kapitanin	who can kill Jovan Kapitan,
95 se tri herë ne Kotorr qi jam kan	95 for the three times I have been to Kotorr
me zarar gjith herë qi jam da	I wound up with injuries each time
ka shtate varr ne trup i kam marre	taking seven wounds on my body.
shume shokve kryte jau kom lan	Many of my comrades lost their lives.
gjoku i mire me shpirt qi m'ka peshtue	My fine grey-white horse coura-geously saved me.
100 lum tu mire prej kullash jan çue	100 Good luck to you!" They left the tower.
n'kullat Mujis me Alien jan shkue	Muji went to his tower with Ali
q'ato fjal Halilit ja kan kalzue	and reported these very words to Halil.
se ne kamb Halili a çue	Halil rose to his feet,
te madhe Mujes ju ka germue	and thundered loudly at Muji:
105 vet n'Kotorr due me shkue	105 "I want to go to Kotorr by myself.
por ndo se e pres Jovan Kapitanin	I will either cut down Jovan Kapitan,
ndo kam kryet n'Kotorr per me e lan	or lose my life in Kotorr."
zavend kopil Muja i paska than	"You little brat—Muji said to him—
se n'Kotorr ti kurr s'je kan	"you have never been to Kotorr!"
110 mire athere Halili u çue n'kamb	110 Fine then! Halil jumped to his feet.
motres vet Kunes po i ban za	and called out to his sister Kuna:

me mi gjet teshahat e tevdilit	"Find me clothes for a disguise."
ja ka prue teshat maxharrisht	She brought him Magyar-style clothes.
dymdhete kryqa ne gjykse i ka vënue	placed twelve crosses on his chest,
115 nji zhabure ne krye po e venon	115 put a fur hat on his head,
maxharrisht o gjogun p'e shtrengon	and girded the grey-white horse Magyar-style.
bash ne shpine djali po mi bjen	The boy jumped right on its back
p'e Budimi rrugen e ka marrë	and set out on the road for Budim.
i shkoj te dera Beg Alaj Begut	He went to the home of Beg Alaj Beg
120 bash ne derë Begut po i cokat	120 and knocked right on Beg's door.
koka dal Begzadja e bardh	Begzade the White came outside:
kush je ti n'dere qi cokat	"Who is that who is knocking on the door?"
une jam Sokole Halili	"I am Sokol Halil."
hajde mbrend o Halil n'daç me hi	"Come inside, O Halil, if you wish to enter."
125 nuk kam ngê o brenda per me hi	125 "I have no time to come inside.
fjal mbas fjale une qi kam ndije	Word for word I have heard
qi bê n'Zoten ti qi ke bâ	that you have sworn a *besa* to God:
tjeter burre nuk kam per me marre	'I will marry no other man
vec kush te dalin n'kotorr per me shkue	but the one who will leave to go to Kotorr
130 me ma pre Jovan Kapitanin	130 to cut down Jovan Kapitan
qatij burrin hajrin qi ja pasha	I will be fortunate to take for a husband.'
un jam nise ne Kotorr per me shkue	I have set out to go to Kotorr,
veç jam ardh ty per me te kalzue	and have just come to inform you."
ketheu Halil çika i paska than	"Turn back, Halil!" the girl said.
135 krejt Kotorrin qitash dom me lan	135 "Forget right now completely about Kotorr,
se bukuri o Zotit paska fale	for God has favored you with beauty."

bê n'Zoten Halili po e ban
nuk e la ne Kotorr per pa shkue

ndo me pre Jovan Kapitanin

140 ndo se kryte n'Kotorr kam me lan
udha e marë çika i paska than

prej Kotorrit rrugen e ka marrë
gjith per trup bjeshket po i
    trupon
si vetima shpejte qi po shkon
145 se n'Kotorr djali konka dal
ja mësyn kullat Jovan Kapitanit

dymdhete katash kullat i kish pas
nebetlit n'dere tuj rruejte

ndal maxharo nebet i kan than

150 se ne gjum aj Jovani a ra
nuk munt la ma mbrenda per
    me hi
maxharrisht Halili paska fol
Zoti ju vraft o juve nebetxhi

nuk ka qare une mbred pa hi

155 se kam punë me Jovan
    Kapitanin
nebetqit apet nuk p'e leshojne

Halil aga fort o ish idhnue
teri n'gjyse shpaten e ka nxjerre
bê n'Zoten djali qi po ban
160 qitash kryete una jau shkurtoj

edhe rrugen nebet jau kan lshue

Halil swears a *besa* to God
not forgetting about going to
    Kotorr.
"I will either cut down Jovan
    Kapitan
140 or I will lose my life in Kotorr."
"Safe journey to you," the girl
    said to him.
He set out on the road to Kotorr,
cutting straight through the
    highlands,
traveling with lightning speed.
145 When the boy reached Kotorr
he appeared at Jovan Kapitan's
    towers.
His towers had twelve stories,
sentries were standing guard at
    the door.
"Halt, Magyar—a sentry said to
    him—
150 for Jovan has fallen asleep.
I can not allow anyone inside."

Halil said in Hungarian,
"May God strike you dead, O
    sentries!
I have no other choice but to go
    inside,
155 for I have dealings with Jovan
    Kapitan."
The sentries again do not let
    him pass.
Halil Aga was greatly angered,
he drew his sword halfway out,
swearing a *besa* to God:
160 "I will cut off your heads right
    now!"
And the sentries made way for
    him.

e n'oborr t'kulles djali konka
shkue
e n'oborr gjogun e ka lshue

perpjet shkallve djali kenka ngjit
165 n'kullë t'Jovanit djali konka hip
se ne gjum Jovanin e ka gjet
kambsh e duersh djali ja ka lidh
po me shkelem ne gjykse i ka ra
po ne gjum aj Jovan pse me fjet

170 a e njeh ti Sokole Halilin
qi shtate Krajla sherrin ma kan
pa
e per krahit djali ja ka ngjit
ço Jovan se n' Kladush due me të
çue
sol nji pushk n'mue per me kris
175 un nder shpate se la per pa të
shti
ne vidhet gjokun Jovani ma qiti

e shtrengoj me rypat e shpates

edhe vet ne gjok paska hip

shpaten çel ne dore e ka marrë
180 nebetqit pushket i kan ngreh
don me qit ne Sokol Halilin

u ka brit Jovan Kapitani
ndalne doren të zeze o nebetxhi

sol nji pushk ne Halilin per me
kris
185 mue nder shpat Haili qi pom
shtjen
nebetxhit doren e kan ndal
edhe rrugen djali e ka marre
prej Kotorrit shndosh kanka dal

The boy went to the courtyard
of the tower
and turned his grey-white horse
loose in the courtyard.
The boy climbed up steps
165 and went up into Jovan's tower.
When he found Jovan asleep,
he bound him hand and foot
and kicked him in the chest.
"Hey, Jovan, why are you
sleeping?

170 Do you not recognize Sokol Halil,
from whom the Seven Kings
have experienced trouble?"
The boy grabbed him by the arm:
"Get up, Jovan, for I want to
take you to Klladusha.
If just one rifle fires at me,
175 I will not hesitate to put you to
the sword."
He placed Jovan on the rump of
his grey-white horse,
girded him with the belt of his
sword
and jumped on the grey-white
horse himself.
He bared the sword in his hand.
180 The guards raised their rifles
and were about to fire at Sokol
Halil.
Jovan Kapitan yelled out to them:
"Lower your hands, you
wretched sentries!
If just one rifle fires at Halil

185 he is going to put me to the
sword."
The sentries lowered their hands
and the boy took to the road.
He came out of Kotorr safely.

ja msyne kullat Beg Alaj Begut

190 se ne Budime djali qi po shkon
bash ne dere Begut po i cokat

aty Begu at di s'ish qillue
koka dal o Begzadja e bardh
mire se erdhe o Sokole Halili

195 mire se te gjejta o Begzade i ka
than
ja çel deren e mbrenda e ka shti

se n'podrum gjokun po ja lidh
perpjet shkallve djali konka hip
bash ne kulla Begut i ka zhdrip

200 oj Begzade djali i ka than
qe tri dite buke nuk kam ngran

qe tri net as gjum nuk kam fjet
qe ky asht ai Jovan Kapitani

kambsh e duersh e lidh ta kom
prue
205 mem prue buke se po do me
hanger
edhe çika buken ja ka prue
edhe buke djali paska ngran
oj Begzade djali i paska than
kambsh e duersh lidh jam tuej
ta lan
210 une me fjet ne gjum due me ra
kambsh e duersh lidh ja ka lan
e me fjet n'xhum paska ra
gjumi rande djali e ka marre
keçyre Jovani thiu qa ka bâ
215 oj Bgzade Jovani i ka than
a e din ti rahmetin e Zotit
kambt e duert pak mi shlirojsh

He appeared at the towers of
Beg Alaj Beg,
190 For the boy was going to Budim.
He knocked right on the door of
the Beg,
the Beg was not there that day,
Begzade the White came out.
"It is good that you have come,
Sokol Halil!"
195 "It is good that I have found
you, Begzade!" he said.
She opened the door and led
him inside
and tied up his horse in the cellar,
The boy climbed up the stairs,
and stepped inside the tower of
the Beg.
200 "O Begzade—the boy said to her—
I have not eaten any food for
three days,
nor have I slept for three nights.
This is none other than Jovan
Kapitan.
I bring him to you bound hand
and foot.
205 Bring me some food for I want
to eat."
The maiden brought him food,
and the boy ate the food.
"O Begzade—the boy said to her—
I am leaving him with you
bound hand and foot.
210 I want to lie down and fall asleep."
He left him bound hand and foot,
and he fell asleep.
A deep sleep overcame the boy.
Consider what the bull Jovan did.
215 "O Begzade—Jovan said to her—
If you know of God's mercy,
loosen my feet and hands a little,

fort Halili mue m'ka shtrengue	Halil has tied me up too tightly.
ndihma vllaznit une ti kam pre	I know I have killed your brothers,
220 po sal ni fije mue mem shlirue	220 but loosen me just a tiny bit."
edhe çika keqi ish mashtrue	And the girl was badly deceived.
u avit duert me ja shlirue	She drew close to loosen his hands,
mire konopët jali ja grabiti	the boy had roped him well,
edhe duert Jovani qi mi zgjidhi	and Jovan loosened his hands.
225 e per krahi Begzades ja ngjiti	225 He grabbed Begzade's arm
i tha shpejt o kambët me mi zgidhe	he said to her: "Untie my feet quickly,
ndo se kryte me shpat po ta pres	or I will cut off your head with my sword!"
te madhe briti Begzadje e Bardh	Begzade the White let out a loud cry:
çou Halil e Zotyn e te vraft	"Get up, Halil, may God strike you dead,
230 se mu zgidh ky Jovan Kapitani	230 Jovan Kapitan has untied himself!"
gjumi i rand Halilin e kish marre	A deep sleep had overcome Halili
as pak gjumi djalit nuk po i del	and the boy could not wake up at all.
deren m'shel mrapa i kish pas	He had closed the door behind him,
n'tjeter ode kta i kish pase lan	and left them in the other room.
235 edhe kambët Jovani i ka zgjidhe	235 Jovan untied his feet
e per krahi çikes ja ka ngjite	and held onto the girl's arm.
te posht shkallvet te dyja paskan zdrip	The two of them climbed down the stairs.
ja ka marrë gjokun e Halilit	He took Halil's grey-white horse,
ne vidhet gjokun Begzaden e vënoj	placed Begzade of the rump of the horse,
240 p'e Kotorrit rrugen e ka marr	240 and set out on the road for Kotorr.
gjith sa mundet çika tue bertit	The girl shouted as loudly as she could.
po aj Halili gjumi i ka dal	At last Halil awoke from his sleep,
por qat za larg e ka ndije	hearing her cry from far off.
shpaten vjerun djali e ka marre	The boy took hold of his trusty sword.

245 mjeri un i mjeri per diten e sodit
shum rrezik o sod qi m'ka gjet

mue m'pështoj aj Jovan Kapitani

e ma muer Begzaden e Bardh

shpaten n'dorë djali e ka marre

250 se prej kulla jashte kanka dal
mbas Jovanit djali konka nise
gjogu i shpejt s'mundet per me
e nxane
se Jovani n'Kotorr kanka shkue
e Begzaden n'Kotorr e ka çue
255 shume popin aty ja ka çue
po don fêen çikes me ja ndrrue
don Jovani me e marre per grue

s'asht e muejtun hiq fêen me ja
ndrrue
rixhaxhi shume i ka çue
260 feen e Turkut ti me e ndrrue
edhe un po te marre per grue
se ty Halili t'ka mashtrue
s'asht menqym feen me ja
ndrrue
Halili Aga shum ka vanue

265 dymedhet dit per rrugë tue
shkue
e krejt kepucet ju kan coptue
edhe teshat ju kan shkaterrue

se n'Kotorr konka shkue
se ne nji han i kan afrue
270 nji plak e moçme ne han ish
qillue
q'asaj plake Halili i ka than

---

245 "Woe is me this very day!
Great misfortune has found me
today.
Jovan Kapitan has gotten away
from me
and has carried off Begzade the
White."
The boy took hold of the sword
in his hand
250 and went outside the tower.
The boy set off after Jovan.
The fleet grey-white horse
could not be overtaken
for Jovan had gone to Kotorr,
and taken Begzade to Kotorr.
255 He sent many priests there
wanting to change the girl's faith.
Jovan wants to take her for his
wife
but is not at all able to change
her faith.
He sent many intercessors to her
260 to change her Turkish faith.
"I will take you for my wife
for Halil has deceived you."
It was impossible for them to
change her faith.
Halil Aga lagged behind for a
long time.
265 Walking on roads for twelve
days,
his shoes were torn all to pieces
and his clothes were torn to
shreds.
When he came to Kotorr
he approached an inn.
270 An old woman advanced in years
happened to be in the inn.
Halil said to the old woman:

a asht mymqym q'at bashqe me
    ma dhan
se sevap shum kije me bâ

edhe plaka boshqen ja ka dhan

275 mire q'at boshqe Halili e ka vesh
nder qat boshqe shpaten e ka
    ngjesh
e po shkon Kotorrit perpjet
ne nji hotel djali ish zatet
aj hotel me dit kush a kan
280 i thon per emen Velike Kokan
edhe djalin n'rruge e ka pam
e perpara djalit i ka dal

e Halil o mire se ki ardh

atherë foli Sokole Halili
285 zoti te vraft moj Velike Kokona

keshu qi e bon Sokole Halilin
une jam fukara i mbetun
un kam dal dunjan me merzite

fol mos tutë Velika i ka than

290 se Muja rrob mue m'kapa nxane
dymdhete vjet n'Kladush q'i
    m'ka mbajt
se ne guh teme une qi te kam
    rrite
probotin me Mujin si e kam

ç'far nevoja qikoh qi te ka qit

295 fije per fije punet ja kalzoj

se ne hotele mbrenda e ka shti

"Is it possible for you to give me
    that shawl,
for you will be doing a great act
    of charity?"
And the old woman gave him
    the shawl
275 and Halil put the shawl on well.
Under it he girded on his sword

and went straight on to Kotorr.
The boy happened upon a hotel.
He knew who owned that hotel:
280 her name was Velike Kokona.
She saw the boy on the road
and came outside in front of the
    boy.
"Halil it is good that you have
    come!"
Then Sokol Halil said:
285 "May God strike you dead,
    Velike Kokona,
for mistaking me for Sokol Halil!
I am a poor man without kin
and have come out to pester
    people."
"Talk, do not be afraid—Velike
    said to him—
290 for Muji did take me captive
and kept me for twelve years in
    Klladusha.
I raised you on my knee

as if I had Muji for a sworn
    brother.
What need has brought you
    here?"
295 He told her everything little by
    little.
She led him into the hotel.

q'asaj pune kollaj po ja bajme

se n'hamam djalin po ma çon
me sapun mire po ma lan
300 ni pal tesha çikave ja gjet

bash si çikat djalin e ka bâ

mbrenda teshat shpaten e ka
vesh
nji pashqyre n'dore ja ka dhan
p'e sheh vehten Sokole Halili

305 be n'Zoten djali qi po ban
bash si çike une kokna bâ

po ç'po ban o Velike Kokona
nji tepsi baklav po ma mbush

q'asaj çike n'dore ja ka dhan
310 vet perpara Velika i prine

ja mesyne kullat Jovan Kapitanit

bash ne due Velika cokat
hyzmetqaret deren ja kan çel

perpjet shkallve bashk konkan
ngjit
315 ish shkue n'ode Jovan Kapidanit

mire se te gjaj Jovan Kapitani

mire se vjen o Velika Kokona

muhabet o Velikes po mi ban

po u pjek kafe edhe po u qet
duhan

"We will easily handle this
matter."
She takes the boy to the hamam
washes him well with soap
300 and finds him a pile of girl's
clothes.

She made the boy look just like
a girl,
and fitted a sword inside his
clothes.
She placed a mirror in his hand.
"Can you see yourself, Sokol
Halil?"

305 The boy swears a *besa* to God,
"I have been made to look just
like a girl!"
But what does Velike Kokona do?
She fills a serving tray with
baklava
and puts it in the girl's hands.
310 With Velike herself leading her
forward
they appear at Jovan Kapitan's
towers.
Velike knocks right on the door,
servants opened the door for
them.
The two climbed up the stairs

315 and went to Jovan Kapitan's
room.
"It is good that I have found
you, Jovan Kapitan."
"It is good that you have come,
Velike Kokona."
He makes pleasant conversation
with Velike
roasting them coffee and
offering them tobacco.

320 per hajrë nuse Velika ja ban	320 Velike extends best wishes to him on his bride.
e hajrë paç Jovani i ka than	"Best wishes to you—Jovan said—
po ket çike Velike e kom	"But who is this girl, Velike?"
keto e kam nji çike prej katundi	"This is a girl from my village.
hyzmetqare une e kam marre	I have taken her on as a servant,
325 na jem ardh nusen me ta pa	325 we have come to see your bride."
hajt Velika Jovani i ka than	"Come, Velike—Jovan said to her—
n'paçi qef nusen per me e pamë	"If you desire to see the bride.
n' tjetren ode nusen qi e kom	I have the bride in the other room."
lum te mire o Velika i ka than	"Bless you—Velike said—
330 se po shkojm nusen me ta pamë	330 "We are going to see the bride."
se ne ode Velika konka shkue	Velike went into the room
me Begzaden q'aty jan takue	and they encountered Begzade there.
dymdhete popa aty i kishin çue	Twelve priests had been sent there,
u mundojshin feen me ja ndrrue	they were struggling to change her faith.
335 se prej shndete çika ish mbarue	335 The girl was wasting away because of her health:
dymdhete dit buke pa kerkue	not asking for food for twelve days,
dymdhete net hiq pa fjet	not sleeping for twelve nights.
me Halilin q'aty jan zatet	Right there she met up with Halil
e Halili çiken po ma pëvete	and Halil asked her:
340 ty prej shndetit ty shka t'ka gjet	340 "What has happened to your health?
buk pa ngran as gjum per pa fjet	No eating food or going to sleep,
lot e gjak prej sysh po qet	shedding tears and blood from your eyes?"
mire Halili turqe qi po i flet	Halil was speaking kindly to her in Turkish:
hajt Begzde ti o mos ki dert	"Come, Begzade, do not worry
345 se Halili ty te ka ardh opet	345 For Halil has come for you again!"
po Begzadja Velikes i ka than	Begzade then said to Velike:
a asht mymqym kete çike me ma lan	"Is it possible for you to leave this girl with me,

se keto tri net nuse kam me u
bame
qef po kom çika ketu me kan

350 e Velika çiken ja ka lan
vet Velika than u çue ne kamb

e Jovanit Velika i ka than
un q'at çike te nusja ta kom lan

due shndosh teslim me ma
bamë
355 mos kije dert Jovani i ka than

kom teslim shndosh me ta bamë
por Jovani q'athere qa punon
per rixha çiken po ja çon

thote ishalla Begzadja te
ndigjon
360 edhe feen ishalla p'e ndrron

edhe çika rixha po i ban
e Begzadja mire o ma nigon

po me fjal feen po ma ndrron
e Jovani darsem qi po ban

365 shume krushqit Jovani i
bashkon
edhe dhanderr Jovani po shkon

Halil aga q'atherë shka punon

po ne dere n'kamb qi po rrin
mire se erdhe Jovan i ka than

370 se Begzaden gadi ta kom bamë

for in three days I will be made
a bride?
I would be pleased to have the
girl here."

350 Velike left her the girl.
Velike herself—they said—rose
to her feet,

Velike said to Jovan:
"I have left the girl with your
bride,
I want her to restore her to
good health."

355 "Do not worry—Jovan said to
her—
I will restore her to good health."
But what does Jovan do then?
He sends the girl to intercede
for him,

saying: "God willing, Bezade
listens to you,
360 and, God willing, will change
her faith!"

And the girl intercedes.
And Begzade understands her
well.

She professes to change her faith,
and Jovan makes arrangements
for the wedding.

365 Jovan assembles many wedding
guests
and Jovan goes off to become a
groom.

Consider what Halil Aga then
does,
standing on his feet by the door:
"It is good that you have come,
Jovan—he says to him—
370 for I have made Begzade ready
for you."

me dy duert me shpatë i ka ra	He struck him with his sword with both hands
kryte ne tokë ja ka qit	and sent his head to the ground.
deren e odes Halili ja ka mëshel	Halil closed the door to the parlor
edhe teshat Jovanit ja deshi	and took off Jovan's clothes.
375 q'ato tesha vet i paska vesh	375 He dressed himself in the clothes,
per mbi seter shpaten e ka ngjesh	girding the sword over his wool jacket.
saba Zoti shpejt e ka bam	God soon granted the morning light.
nebetxhive urdhen ju ka dhan	He gave an order to the sentries:
nji koçi shpejt me ma prue	"Bring me a coach quickly,
380 me Begzaden bashk do te shetiti	380 I want to take a ride together with Begzade."
nebetxhite koçin ja kan prue	The sentries brought him a coach
mire Begzaden n'koçi e ka shti	and he deftly lifted Begzade into the coach.
edhe çilsat Jovanit ja muer	He took Jovan's keys
krejt kallan çel ja kish pas	and opened the entire fortress.
385 shka ka gjet mall e kymetli	385 Whatever goods and valuables he found
krejt n'koçi Halili e ka shti	Halil loaded them all onto the coach,
nji fitil ne gjephana ja ka lan	leaving behind a fuse in the munitions room.
vet Halili n'burg konka ramë	Halil himself rushed to the stable.
gjogun e vet ne burg e ka marre	He took hold of his grey-white horse in the stable.
390 shpejt e shpejt godi e ka bame	390 Making it ready as quickly as he could
bash ne shpine djali i paska ramë	the boy jumped on its back
krah per krah me koçije a dal	and rode out side by side with the coach,
trup pazarit bashk i kan ramë	Together they passed straight through the market place.
ne fushe Kotorrit djali kur a dal	When the boy came out on the plain of Kotorr
395 p'e koçije çiken e ka marre	395 he took the girl from the coach.

mire gjephanja ne kalla kanka kal
se krejt kulla ju kallen ne zjar

Halil aga rrugen e ka marre
se ne Budim shndosh konka dal

400 Alaj Begut n'dere po mi shkon
bash ne derë begut po i cokat

edhe begu n'dere konka dal
lumju lumju mire se keni ardh

bash ne kulle te dy mi ka hip

405 muhabet e shume po mi ban

krejt vakit Halili ja kalzon

aferim o Begu i paska than

qito pune burrat si mi bajne
qishtu burrat gjithmone kane punue

410 mire Halili leter ma ka shkrue
Mujes n'Kladush Halili ja ka çue
treqind krushq bashk me mi bashkue
se ne Budim me mi çue
se Begzaden me e marre per mue

415 nder shpatë Jovanin e kam shkurtue
edhe kullat ja kam rafshue
edhe Muja q'athere a gezue
treqind krushq i ka bashkue

se ne Budine i ka çue
420 me Halilin jan bashkue
e kan marre nusen e jan fillue

The munitions room in the fortress exploded loudly,
and the whole tower went up in flames.

Halil Aga set off on the road
and reached Budim safe and sound.

400 He went up to Alaj Beg's door
and knocked right on the Beg's door.

The Beg came to the door:
"Praised be that you have come back all right!"
He showed the two of them right into the tower

405 and they made pleasant conversation for a long time,
with Halil all the while reporting to him.
"Well done!—the Beg said to him—
such deeds that brave men do
brave men have ever managed."

410 Halil wrote a well-writ letter
And sent it to Muji in Klladusha:
"Gather together three hundred wedding guests
and send them to Budim
to get Begzade for me.

415 I have put Jovan to the sword,

and have destroyed his towers."
Muji then became happy!
He assembled three hundred wedding guests
and sent them to Budim.
420 They met up with Halil,
got the bride and set out.

shndosh e mire ne Kladush jan shkue
e q'aj mundim mos me u harrue
fal na fajin se u kam shurdhue

They went to Klladusha safe and sound.
May my pains not be forgotten.
Excuse our mistakes, for I have worn you all out.

APPENDIX 1

PHOTOS

Plate 1. Recording apparatus. Photo by Milman Parry or Albert B. Lord.
Courtesy of the Milman Parry Collection of Oral Literature.

Plate 2. Salih Ugljanin, Novi Pazar (Serbia), November 1934. Photo by
Milman Parry or Albert B. Lord.
Courtesy of the Milman Parry Collection of Oral Literature.

Plate 3. Gjergj Pllumbi and his audience, Theth, sometime in the 1930s.
Photo by Shan Pici. Courtesy of *Shêjzat*.

Plate 4. Gjergj Pllumbi and his audience, Theth, sometime in the 1930s.
Photo by Shan Pici. Courtesy of *Shêjzat*.

Plate 5. Embroidery sellers in the "Christian market," Shkodër,
September, 1937. Photo by Albert B. Lord.
Courtesy of the family of Mary Louise and Albert B. Lord.

Plate 6. Pjeter Trepshi, Shkodër, September, 1937. Photo by Albert B. Lord.
Courtesy of the family of Mary Louise and Albert B. Lord.

Plate 7. Peter Preka writing at the dictation of Gjok Pjetri, second chief elder, Kastrat, September, 1937. Photo by Albert B. Lord. Courtesy of the family of Mary Louise and Albert B. Lord.

Plate 8. Gjok Pjetri, his brother, and their families, Kastrat, September, 1937. Photo by Albert B. Lord. Courtesy of the family of Mary Louise and Albert B. Lord.

Plate 9. Albert B. Lord, Kastrat, September, 1937.
Photographer unknown.
Courtesy of the family of Mary Louise and Albert B. Lord.

Plate 10. The 'goat well,' dedicated to Skanderbeg, Boga, September, 1937.
Photo by Albert B. Lord.
Courtesy of the family of Mary Louise and Albert B. Lord.

Plate 11. Nik Toma, chief elder, Boga, September, 1937.
Photo by Albert B. Lord.
Courtesy of the family of Mary Louise and Albert B. Lord.

Plate 12. Trail to church, Theth, September, 1937.
Photo by Albert B. Lord.
Courtesy of the family of Mary Louise and Albert B. Lord.

Plate 13. Rest stop on the journey from Theth to Abat, September, 1937. *Çirixhis* [draymen] consume cheese and bread. Photo by Albert B. Lord. Courtesy of the family of Mary Louise and Albert B. Lord.

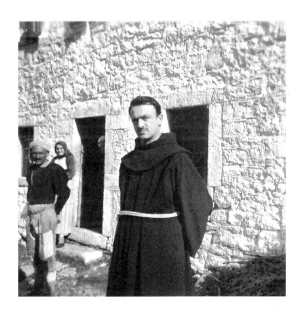

Plate 14. Father Bernardin Palaj, Abat, September, 1937. Photo by Albert B. Lord. Courtesy of the family of Mary Louise and Albert B. Lord.

Plate 15. Peter Preka, Father Bernardin Palaj, Father Rrok Gurashi, and Adem Brahimi at the Franciscan church at Abat, September, 1937. Photo by Albert B. Lord. Courtesy of the family of Mary Louise and Albert B. Lord.

Plate 16. Sokol Martini, Palç, September, 1937. Photo by Albert B. Lord. Courtesy of the family of Mary Louise and Albert B. Lord.

Plate 17. The home of Albert Lord's host in Geghysen, September, 1937.
Photo by Albert B. Lord.
Courtesy of the family of Mary Louise and Albert B. Lord.

Plate 18. Girl dressed for Monarchy Day, Tirana, September, 1937. Photo by
Albert B. Lord. Courtesy of the family of Mary Louise and Albert B. Lord.

Plate 19. Franciscan church, Theth, October, 2017.
Photo by Nicola Scaldaferri

Plate 20. Shala Valley, October, 2017. Photo by Nicola Scaldaferri.

APPENDIX 2

LETTERS BY ALBERT B. LORD,
FROM NORTHERN ALBANIA

Put Meda Pucića 10,
Kod Jakobušić,
Dubrovnik, Jugoslavija
29 Juna, 1937

Dear folks,

Got mother's letter this morning, and was, as always, very glad to hear from you all. Everything with you apparently is moving along in its accustomed circles, or curves, or straight lines, or what have you. How interesting to have met up with Lucia again! I should like to see her, for some strange reason. Has she changed at all?

And things here are also progressing hopefully, if not alarmingly fast—not today at least. Yesterday we seemed to cover so much ground in the translation, that today we are rather out of inspiration, and a bit tired of it. So it goes. One has to take it as comes, and on our less brilliant days, do the routine work which is necessary, but neither significant nor difficult.

We have really done little else but work, eat and sleep since we arrived. Dubrovnik is the same charming place it always was, and the family here just as before. Not one of them seem a day older or a mite different. Of course our work is ordered differently, and one misses the big house down below, and the Parry's. With two secretaries to keep supplied with work and satisfy, I sometimes feel that there is little time for thinking out our theories, but that is after all work which can perhaps best be done in Cambridge, and really these chaps are a great help. Jack does al[l] the typing for me, takes down my translation from dictation, leaving me free to pound the dictionaries, and think out the sentences, besides giving very valuable suggestions as to style of English, words, etc., which he really knows so well. He works with me up at Jakobušić's, and Nikola works alone down in the room across the street, transcribing the records.

One day last week we went swimming—needed a bath, you know, and that was the only way—and we hired a little boat for five dinars an hour. But we had never tried to launch one of the dainty little things before, and it was a rough day, and the breakers picked up me and the skiff together, because I was foolish and put it into the water sideways, not as I should have, prow first, and the result was that the boat and I got a bit scrambled in the beach, and my legs are still black and blue and sore. And then to top the climax the man at the bath house said that we had nearly ruined the *boat!* Well it was all very funny, and when we got the thing in the water, I was scared to perdition that it would turn over, because the sea was not calm, and that I would drown—which amused Jack, who was piloting the damned craft. At any rate we had a good time, and will repeat it one of these days, preferably when the sea is calm.

June 30

Today and tomorrow are the days of reckoning, when the various people in and out of one's employ are paid off, when we enter larger sums than movies and ice cream in our expense book.

H[a]ve arranged with an Albanian chap here in Dubrovnik to give me four or five lessons in his language as a start on pronunciation and the essentials. He is very decent, and will not charge me anything for them.

By the way, the exchange is much more favorable than it was two years ago. We are now getting 47.50 dinars to the dollar as compared with the 42 average of those days. That helps considerably on our budget.

You know, I have not forgotten that Dad's birthday is July 5, but I really do not know what to send through the mails. I think that the best is to send some money with this letter, consigning it to registered mail. We have sent valuable manuscripts that way before with no trouble.

So, my dear, here's a five spot for ye, and may God bless it to you, and grant you long life. Have a good time with it. I shall cable you a message on the auspicious day, that you won't think your son has forgotten.

Incidentally *don't* send me anything on my birthday, because (a) I don't know where I'll be, and (b) I'ld [sic] have to pay the devil's own price in customs.

And now, remember that beneath my levity there's a real deep feeling, and so I send you my love, as always, wishing you all the best of everything.

AB

Do continue to write. Your letters give me courage, and remind me that if all these other structures fail, my folks are still with me.

Please keep the pictures for me—don't paste them into anything!

Put Meda Pucića 10,
Kod Jakobušić,
Dubrovnik, Jugoslavija.
August 1, 1937

Dear folks,

It is really such a long time since I wrote you. Do forgive me. Somehow, I have no great feeling for writing anything, not even such comparatively pleasant things as letters. No doubt when I return there will be plenty of writing to do—things which I really should be writing or planning now.

Since I saw you last not much has happened. Jack and I went on a trip to Stolac for a few days, to hear the *gusle* again, ride horseback, and get out of the rut of Dubrovnik routine. We did all right. Left suddenly in a rush one noon by train for Chapljina. In so much of hurry in fact that I forgot to take my passport with me, and you know in this country one needs one['s] papers constantly. So when the police on the train asked for my passport there I was, feeling very foolish, and telling them that I was an American professor studying their folk songs, with my assistant (who fortunately had his passport with him), but that I had forgotten my papers, and left them on the table in Dubrovnik, etc. etc. Well I got along all right, and strangely enough on the return trip on the train no questions were asked.

Getting to Chapljina we refused to pay the exorbitant price asked for a car to Stolac, about twenty miles, and so walked. Got about six kilometers, and Jack sort of caved in. We got a horse from there, and took turns riding him. Lot of fun. Jack recuperated shortly, so we went all the distance that night, getting to Stolac just about midnight. The moon was beautiful, the landscape, as always, mysterious beyond words. The night was cool.

The next day was spent in looking up old friends, singers, and sitting about in the cafes, eating cantelope and drinking coffee. That night we went to hear one of our guslars sing. It was a glorious experience again, lying at ease on heavy woolen blankets—like those I brought back to America—hearing our Moslem friend, an old man of seventy, sitting beside his fireplace, on the floor, of course, cross-legged, singing the old songs we know so well. There was a thrill in it, the thrill which comes from meeting an old acquaintance after long years have passed.

And we hired horses too, and tried to find some singers at a village about five miles out, without great success. We found one, but the *gusle* he had was not in good shape, so he couldn't sing for us. That was a grand ride up the ravine, in the burning sun, and back at nightfall, the horses breaking easily into a gallop and racing one another on the way home, eager to get back to their stalls.

Back at Dubrovnik, there seems to be nothing new, except that I have bought myself some white short pants to wear about. It is frightfully hot here. My legs aren't anything to write home about, but I don't care especially, as long as I am comfortable.

Got your letter, Muttie dear. Thanks a lot. It's good to hear all the little things which are going on at the farm, and I am very much interested of course in the success of garden and chickens. Which reminds me, had a letter from Sam Bayard, whom Dad will remember, who sends greetings, and best wishes to him and the chickens. Also one from Tommy McClure, who is up at Harvard, working at the laboratory on some experiments, this summer, and goes back to Rutgers in the fall. Card from Fred Packard, who is in Mexico. I'm not sure yet as to what he is doing there, but a letter with details is on the way some where [sic]. Have you heard anything from Win and Pauline? I haven't for some time, but it's my own fault because I have not written. Just don't seem to get around to write anybody these days.

Have very little time to myself. Just Sundays, like today, when none of my people work. Jack and I are together even on these days some of the time, very often we go down to town for supper, just for the change. Food here gets rather monotonous.

The work proceeds well enough. Nikola has gotten into his stride with the transcriptions, and is very much interested in the work. He probably has a greater knowledge of the details of these poems and their language than any other living person. I am fortunate in having him. The typist is slow, but accurate, and the texts, I know, are hard going for a Dal[ma]tian. Jack is at present engaged in typing Serbian texts, and does amazingly well, since of course he has no idea of what he's writing. We shall have plenty of results to present to the University for this summer's work. Only I myself am dissatisfied with the amount I do on reading and theory and writing. But there is so much planning to do, so much administration!

Well my dears, take care of yourselves. I must go into town now to mail this, and to have Sunday night supper.

By the way, am probably off for Albania, as I have already written Cal, on the thirtieth of this month, arriving in Tirana the following day. You see it is not very far. Shall have no address, except in an emergency, the American Legation, Tirana. They could probably get in touch with me. At any rate, I'll probably write again before I go.

Love to you all,
    AB

m/n Vulcania [letterhead of ship]

August 25, 1937.

Dear folks,

Here's a last long letter before I set of[f] on the Albanian venture.
And some pictures.

Bought a new camera, because the other was too complicated an affair. How do you like it? Please keep the pictures 'til I get back.

First of all, before I forget. I want you to get in oil for heating the house this winter—and let me take care of the bill—I will not have you fiddling around with those smelly and unhealthy stoves this coming winter. Heat the house as you should and I'll worry about the money. There's no arguing on this matter—so do as you're told! Please let me help—for I owe you much, and want to show my appreciation.

Your letters seem cheerful, and business must be good from the number of chickens you tell of selling. How about eggs? Are you putting up a lot of vegetables and things for winter? When do you go home? Hope you can come to N.Y. to meet us. Have written Cal about the baggage. I know he'll help me with it.

Little new here. Politically quiet. Town overrun with tourists now and then.

Jack's not going to Albania with me, but is off to Paris for about a month. I don't think his health could stand the bad food etc. in Albania. But he is coming back to Dbk [Dubrovnik], may even come to meet me somewhere in Albania for a short time. Then we come back to USA together.

Am well prepared for Albanian trip. Slight knowledge of the language. Am expected in Tirana, and even have a guide and interpreter, picked out by the American Legation, waiting for me there. Have the names of some singers all ready, and have even collected one Albanian song in Dbk. Films and cameras are ready. Have written to Jacques, and hope I'll get an appointment to take a trip south into his part of the country.

Jack and I went up to Stolac for a few days, hired horses and spent a night under the stars on the mountain. Found a deserted mill in the valley with an empty stable, where we left the horses, and then built a fire of dry thorn and spread our blankets on the ground. The moon was full, the sky clear. Everything ideal.

Nikola and native typist still keep on working here during my absence. Jack is taking some work with him to Paris also.

Well, there's not much to write—and I must get to work again.

Take care of yourselves.
See you later,
much love,
    AB

Am trying to find you a dress or blouse with embroidery, mother! Hope I succeed. Will bring many things home this time. Bought a little dress for Nan, a blouse for sister, and one for Betty too!

Hotel Kafe Park [letterhead of hotel]

Shkoder, 6 Sept. 1937

Dear folks,

Just about to jump off for the mountains. All has gone amazingly well. The authorities have given us recommendations, informing all police posts in the mountains of our approach, with orders to care for us.

Have already done a little collecting here in Scutari. Am encouraged that shall find what I'm looking for.

Shall get no mail until Oct 1 when I am having it forwarded to Kuk[e]s, with the hopes I can get there on that date.

Don't fear, we have papers with the signature of the minister of the interior, who, next to the king, is the most powerful man in the country.

Now I must go to the first stop, Kastrati.

Love

AB

Boga
Sept. 11, 1935.

Dear folks,

High in the mountains now—and delayed a day by weather, which is very irritating. The worst of the road lies ahead of us in the next three or four weeks. So far we have proceeded by auto, but in another 15 miles the road ends, and we go on foot and by horse.

It is still hard to say how successful the trip is. We have found singers, and the songs are interesting, but I do not yet know enough to judge.

The country is fascinating, though rough. More time is required for everything than I had reckoned. The customs demand that much time be spent in talking, talking around a subject, before getting to work.

A few days ago we were entertained in one of the villages by the chief elder. They killed a sheep in our honor. First, according to mountain custom, we sat crosslegged on the floor and had a kind of brandy accompanied by raw onions, fresh cheese, and roast liver. This took, with conversation, nearly an hour. They never leave a glass empty, or even partly filled, but the host must keep all glasses full. You see, when a blood feud is going on, the man who has yet to kill an enemy, who has not yet avenged his family's blood, has before him a half-filled glass of brandy, to ever remind him of his duty. Hence it is an insult to leave a guest's glass half full.

Then a short round table was brought, and still sitting on the floor we surrounded it. The women brought coarse corn bread, salted cheese, and finally the sheep whole, on the spit on which it had just been roasted. Portions were given us—and I tell you it was delicious.

For desert [sic] came a bowl of fresh milk, from which we each spooned our share. The whole business took more than two hours.

Before dinner they dressed me in mountain garb and we had our pictures taken. Some fun.

The wind is coming up now and perhaps the clouds will lift for us to proceed this afternoon. We have to cross a pass, which is at the moment covered. There may even be snow there.

For your comfort, be it known I am well dressed for this trip. In Dubrovnik I bought heavy tramping shoes, and Jack lent me his riding boots. My socks are all wool, and have been replenished by peasant socks here. I wear riding pants, colored shirts, and have two sweaters beside my regular suit coat and my short heavy jacket. In Tirana, I bought a fine raincoat with a hood, which covers me literally from top to toe, and also a heavy blanket for sleeping.

We have our own food supplies for the more remote places—bread, coffee, sugar and cheese. The gendarmes will furnish us with guns if it is necessary against wolves, or with an escort, whenever we need it.

Yesterday the wolves ate 16 sheep on the mountains near here! But they won't attack men until dead winter, so we are quite safe.

Lunch is ready. See you later.

~~

Then we went in the rain to visit a family in a wooden hut not far from here. On the way I heard that last night wolves attacked and ate a horse! Nice place, huh!?!

Well we sat by the fire and got smoke in our eyes. One of the girls is to be married shortly, and we were shown the new clothes she is making. Fine sets of dresses etc, before she is married, because after marriage she won't have time to do anything of that sort.

Wives are still bought in the mountainous parts of this country. One pays from eight to sixty napoleons for a wife. That's between fifty and 370 dollars. The bargaining is done by representatives of both sides, and the boy and girl do not see each other before marriage. This particular lass is only sixteen!

Another sidelight on the primitive state of these people is the cure for fever. An old man here in Boga has power given him by a Turkish priest to "tie up" a fever. He ties a piece of red string around the right wrist of the patient. It's as simple as that—and he takes no pay. I was present talking with him when one mountain woman came and had her fever "tied up." And a singer who has just now left us had the same red string around his wrist. Does the fever stop? Who knows?

~~

What a life! It's raining like hell, and the roof leaks. We can't proceed, and I'm dying of boredom, anxious to go on because our time is so limited.

Cars have just come up, saying that the road below us is almost impassable. What can it be higher in the mountains?! Now is thunder and lightning—and my lamp fails so I must stop.

If God grants, tomorrow will be good.

Tell Cal that I shall not forget his birthday though it shall be late. Heaven knows when you'll get this letter, because there is no post. It is just given to somebody going to Scutari, and, then—God care for it.

Love,
 AB

Supper over. Things are looking up. The inspector of roads just arrived in his own car, and has offered to take us as far as the road goes tomorrow. God be praised.

In bed now, and getting sleepy.

Well, my dears, how are you all. Although not really homesick—I'm a hardened traveller now—I do think much of you all, of Boston, New London, and Cambridge. Do you feel angry that I write so little? Writing of all sorts usually bores me. I prefer reading or pure action.

Will Nancy know her Uncle Albert when he returns? I guess so.

Now I must write a few letters to Dubrovnik with instructions—so

Good night and love,
 AB

Tropoja, Krasniqi
Sept. 23, 1937.

Dear folks,

When I last wrote, we had just entered the mountains. Now we are out of the big ones, and on the Jugoslav border. From here we move south to Kuk[e]s and Dibra, following the boundary.

There are three of us now, myself, Peter, and an old man, Adem, who has a horse. He's a Moslem, knows this region well, is the best singer we've struck yet, and his horse carries our baggage. He gets no salary, but volunteered his services from love, and whatever we wanted to give him. He's proved very helpful, and will probably go with us as far as Kuk[e]s.

Sept. 24 –

You see, I never get very far with a letter. Have little inclination to write.

Tomorrow we probably go on from here. This has been the best place so far for our work.

We were given a royal reception here. A gendarme was sent to meet us, and the moment we arrived another was put at our disposal for whatever we needed. The schoolmaster cleared out of his room and bed to give it to me. Good singers were brought. When we go walking, our man, Adem, follows behind at a respectable distance, carrying my cameras. It's ridiculously amusing. And the gendarme also looks over my bills before they're paid to be sure no one cheats me! That last is remarkable!

But I think much of home and the university, and shall be glad to be back for a while. Am a bit tired of being forever on the move. No more than two or three days in each place.

I have commissioned the schoolmaster here, a very nice young lad, to collect songs for me during the winter and send them to Harvard. There'll be another chap in Scutari, and thus the work will go on in my absence from the country.

We are in exclusively Mohammedan country now, and the tradition is more interesting for me. In the mountains I have sat next the fire with our man opposite brewing coffee, while others sat about on cushions in true Turkish style and talked of heroes and exploits, smoking and sipping coffee constantly. Such scenes are described in the poems.

And then at meal times we sit about a round table on the floor. The host divides the bread and cheese and pickles, and the youngest son, or brother[,] stands and waits, brings water to wash our hands, and to drink. Whenever an important person enters this "selamlik," all jump to their feet and salute with a "long life to you!" This is all in the poems also.

The selamlik has windows on one side, and is very low. This is the plan:

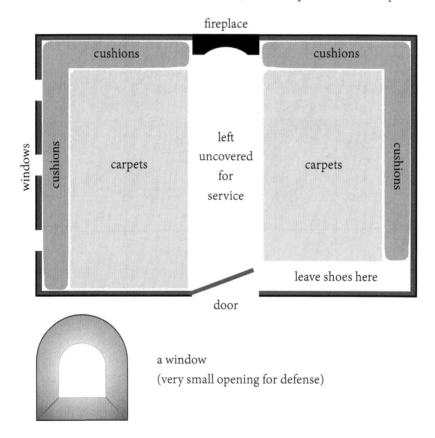

Have just bought myself a complete Albanian costume. Not expensive. Wait till you see it!

Love and kisses,
    AB.

There's post here, so must get this off.

Pukë, Dukagjin.
Oct. 5, 1937.

Dear folks,

Just a note. We are out of the difficult travel zone now. Came in here by horse last night after three full days from Kukës, where I got some mail—from you, the birthday card; thanks a lot; it was nice to hear. Now we travel all by auto.

The trip has been quite successful. I've uncovered some very interesting and important material. We go on to Scutari, Gurz, Kavaje and Tirana. Then we are through. If there is time then I shall run down to Korça to see Ed Jacques. On the twentieth I'm off to Dubrovnik, and on the 26th, as you know (if our reservations come through, which I shall not know until we get to Tirana) I'm on the way home. Arrive N.Y. ("Saturnia") on Nov. 9, I think. I should be delighted if you could come with the car to meet me. Would, indeed, be willing to pay some of the expense. But may stay a day or two in N.Y. in order to see a few people.

I'm a bit tired of trotting around, and will be glad to stick at home a few months.

How did the chicken business turn out? I'm wondering about you folks.

This letter must go now.

Be seeing you soon.

Love,
Albert

Tiranë
Oct 15

Dear folks,

Just a note. Arrived back here yesterday after exactly six weeks of travel. Although the trip was rather difficult, and occasionally dangerous, we passed without the slightest mishap, and are many times better in health now than when we started. From the point of view of the work too, it was highly enlightening and successful, though actually I did not find the exact thing I was looking for, only traces of it. For various reasons it is harder to get at than I had expected, and needs more time in "breaking ice."

Now I am looking forward to returning. Tomorrow I leave here for Durazzo, and at midnight board an Italian boat for Dubrovnik. Then on the 26th the "Saturnia." We have excellent reservations, double cabin with private bath. Since my funds are very low, I shall probably go almost directly to Cambridge—not *more* than one night in N.Y., if that. Depends on the time of day we arrive. So I *hope* you'll be down to greet me—and don't forget to get "pier passes"!

I got your birthday letters and cards. Thanks a lot, my dears. Was glad to hear that things at the farm turned out so well. Expect more mail in Dbk.

See you all later

Love
Albert

This is the last I shall write until I get to N.Y.

APPENDIX 3

MANUSCRIPT REPRODUCTIONS

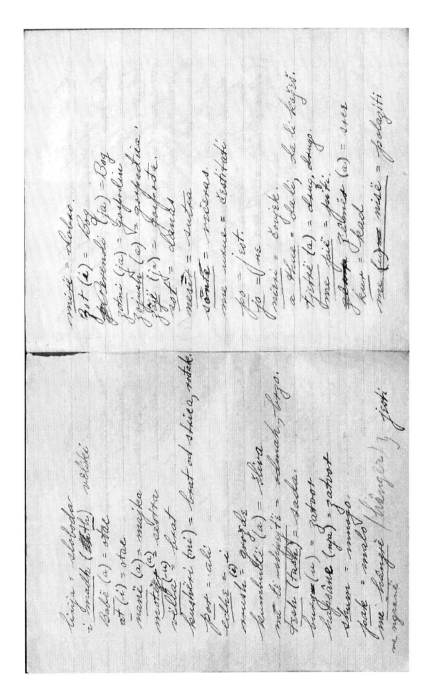

Pages from the notebook Albert B. Lord kept in connection with the Albanian lessons he took in Dubrovnik, July, 1937.

LAN 26. Gjergj Pllumbi: Biographical information and repertoire
(list continues for two more pages).

642

September 24/ 1937. al Tropojë.
Adem Brahimi   Dorëshkrim N. 60

Kanga e Sirotin Alis

Lum të na për të lumin Perendi'
qi s'jem kon e ojna ka falë
konka dalë sabah o'rita e bardhë'
e prej gjumit Alija ish eue
nanes vet Alija i ka thirë"   5
Në oshakli zjermin më na dhezë"
Nana vet sa mirë' e kish ndigjue
e m'oshak zjermin po ja dhezë"
e zhzgyrmat nr zjarmin e ka shti
po ja pjek kafen me sheqer   10
pin Alija në gyp loko bë
n'mët nargile duhan qi ka dhezë"
pak ka ndej e nuk ka vonue
se po dron sabahi don me i shkrue

LAN 60. *The Song of Sirotin Ali,* dictated by Adem Brahimi.

APPENDIX 4

MAPS

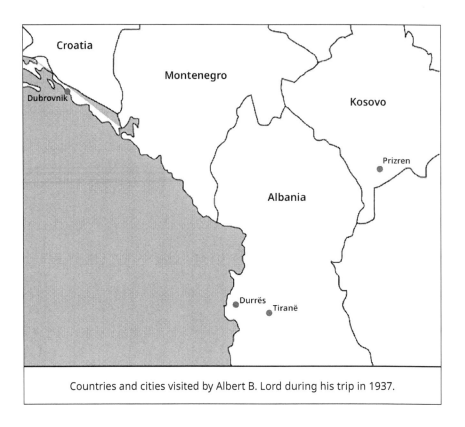

Countries and cities visited by Albert B. Lord during his trip in 1937.

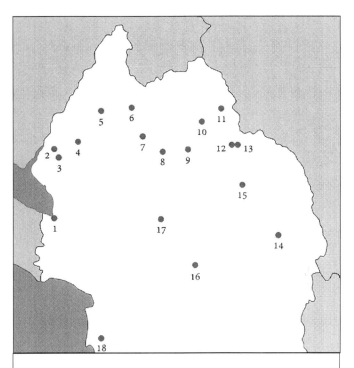

1. Shkodër. September 4–6
2 Bajza (Kastrat). September 6–7
3. Pjetroshan (Kastrat). September 8
4. Dedaj (Kastrat). September 8
5. Boga. September 9–11
6. Theth. September 12–13
7. Abat. September 14–15
8. Palç. September 16–17
9. Geghysen. September 19–20

10. Kolgecaj. September 20–21
11. Tropoja .September 22–24
12. Pac. September 26
13. Kam. September 26
14. Bicaj. October 1
15. Va Spas. October 3
16. Spaç. October 4
17. Puka. October 5–7
18. Gurrëz. October 10–13

Places touched by Albert B. Lord in Northern Albania
during his research in 1937.

Glossary

In this synthetic glossary are included terms and names relevant for the texts presented in the anthology. For a more exhaustive glossary in English about Albanian epic, see Elsie and Mathie-Heck 2004: 367–374; in Albanian, important glossaries can be found in Haxhihasani 1955: 306-325; *Këngë Kreshnike* III: 427-434; Neziri 2009: 251-261; Neziri 2011: 377-389.

Aga
Ottoman title, roughly equivalent to 'lord', describing a landowner, official, or esteemed person. The Thirty Agas are the frontier warriors of Judbina, lead by Muji.

Ajkuna
Also: Hajkuna, Kuna.Wife of Muji and mother of Omer.

Ali Bajraktari
Warrior among the Agas; symbol of fidelity to *besa* (one's word of honour).

Arapi [Arab]
A menacing, dark-skinned figure in Balkan tales and epics.

Arrnaut (Arnaut) Osmani
Warrior among the Thirty Agas. *Arnaut* means 'Albanian.'

Bajraktar
Chief of a tribe, literally 'standard-bearer.'

Bac
Older brother. Term of respect for an older male relative. Sokol Halil uses it to address his elder brother Muji.

Baloz
A monster in Albanian mythology; usually rises from the sea and exacts tribute in the form of food, wine, and young maidens.

Besa
Literally 'faith' (in the sense of 'fidelity') and also 'pledge', 'trust', 'belief', 'word of honor', 'sworn oath', 'truce', depending on context. The term is considered quintessentially representative of Albanian culture and especially the Albanian concept and value of honor.

Blood brothers
Popular custom of the Balkan countries: two young men who were emotionally attached to one another could decide to become blood brothers for life and undertake the same obligations as kinship toward one another.

Çeta
Band of fighters, guerrillas; a squadron of a tribal brotherhood.

Gavran
Literally 'raven'. Name of a Slavic warrior from the Kingdom of the Christians, also called Gavran Kapetani.

Gjergj Elez Alia
Legendary warrior, symbol of fraternal fidelity. Known in Bosnian as Ðerđelez Alija; in Turkish as Gürz Ilyas.

Hadji
A title originally given to a person who completed the pilgrimage to Mecca; honorific title for a respected man.

Halil
Younger brother of Mujo. Also: Sokol Halil (Falcon Halil). Known in Bosnian as Halil Hrnjica.

Halva
A sweet, served also during the funeral wake.

Hodja
A religious muslim master.

Januka
A fair maid.

Jovan
A Christian Slav from Kotorr.

Judbina
Udbina in what is today western Croatia.

Kaçanik
Town in Southern Kosovo. According to legend, Marko Kraljević and Musa fought in the Kaçanik gorge, close to the town.

Kapetan (Kapitan, Kapidan)
Captain; the term refers to a leader or powerful warlord.

Kismet
Fate, destiny, in different languages, including Albanian, Serbo-Croatian, and Turkish.

Klladusha
Town in the Bihać region of northwestern Bosnia now known as Velika Kladuša. Home of Muji and Halil.

Krahina
Territory, province. In Albanian epics refers to Muslim territories around Judbina, as opposed to the *krajli*, the Christian kingdom.

Kreshnik
A frontier warrior or hero. In Bosnian, *krajišnik*.

Kotorr
Also Kotorri i ri (New Kotorr) or Ravni Kotari (Flatland Kotari), 15 km east of Zadar in Croatia.

Kulla
Fortified tower or multi-storeyed dwelling.

Kulshedra
A dragon-like figure of Nothern Albanian mythology.

Marko Kraljević
A popular Balkan legendary hero, inspired by the Serbian King Marko.

Muji
Also Muja; Gjeto (Çeto) Basho Muji; Bylykbasho Muji. Hero and leader of the Thirty Agas. Known in Bosnian as Mujo Hrnjica. The form *Mujo* is a Bosnian hypcoristic for Muharrem.

Musa Qesexhi (or Qeshexhi)
Albanian highwayman; a popular Balkan legendary villain, rival of Marko Kraljević. Known in Bosnian as Musa Kesedžija.

Oka
Unit of weight in the Ottoman Empire, equivalent to 1.24 kilograms or 2.75 pounds.

Omer
Son of Muji and Ajkuna.

Ora
Good fairy, a supernatural female figure of northern Albanian mythology.

Primore
Primorje in western Croatia, near Gorski Kotar (mountain Kotar).

Raki
Unaged fruit brandy.

Selam
Muslim greeting, from Turkish, which is from Arabic salām 'peace.'

Seven Kings (*Shtatë krajli*)
Usually refers to the Great Powers which negotiated with the Ottoman Empire before the First World War; they represent the great kings of Europe.

Shkja
Slavic speaker. In this context, Christian Slav.

Stambol
Istanbul, the city of the Emperor.

Tali Budaline
Warrior among the Agas, armed with a mace.

Zana
Mountain fairy, a supernatural female figure of the northern Albanian mythology.

Zuk Bajraktari
Young warrior among the Thirty Agas.

Bibliography

Ahmedaja, A. 2012. "Songs with Lahutë and Their Music." In Bohlman and Petković 2012:101-132.

———. 2012b. *Discovering Albania: World Premiere of the Earliest Sound Recordings from 1903 and from a Milestone Expedition in 1957.* Tirana. With audio CD.

Aikhenvald, A., and R. W. M. Dixon, eds. 2003. *Studies in Evidentiality.* Amsterdam.

Alimusaj, N. 2009. *Nga Lahuta e Dukagjinit (këngë kreshnike dhe balada).* Prishtina.

Altimari, F., and E. Conforti, eds. 2008. *Omaggio a Gerolamo De Rada/Homazh për Jeronim De Radën.* Rende.

Andromaqi, G. 1986. "Etnosi ynë në epikën legjendare." *Çështje të folklorit shqiptar* 2:103–119.

Arps, B. 2016. *Tall Tree, Nest of the Wind: The Javanese Shadow-Play Dewa Ruci Performed by Ki Anom Soeroto; A Study in Performance Philology.* Singapore.

Auslander, P. 1999. *Liveness: Performance in a Mediatized Culture.* London and New York.

Bakker, F., and K. Ahuvia, eds. 1997. *Written Voices, Spoken Signs: Tradition, Performance, and the Epic Text.* Cambridge, MA.

Bardhoshi, N. 2016. *Antropologji e Kanunit.* Tirana.

Barnie, J. 1978. "Oral Formulas in the Country Blues." *Southern Folklore Quarterly* 42:39–52.

Bartók, B. 1978. *Yugoslav Folk Music.* Ed. B. Suchoff. 4 vols. Albany.

Bartók, B., and A. B. Lord. 1951. *Serbo-Croatian Folk Songs.* New York.

Berisha, A. N. 1987. *Mbi letërsinë gojore shqipe. Studime e artikuj.* Prishtina.

———. 1998. *Qasje Poetikës së letërsisë gojore shqipe.* Prishtina.

———. 2008. *Antologji e kangëve kreshnike shqiptare.* Prishtina.

Berisha, R., S. Fetiu, and A. Zejnullahu, eds. 1991. *Këngë kreshnike II.* Prishtina.

Bllaca, R. 1997. *Këngë popullore 1.* Ed. R. Berisha, S. Fetiu, and J. Ahmeti. Prishtina.

Bohlman, P. V., and N. Petković, eds. 2012. *Balkan Epic: Song, History, Modernity.* Lanham.

Bonifazi, A., and D. F. Elmer. 2012a. "Composing Lines, Performing Acts: Clauses, Discourse Acts, and Melodic Units in a South Slavic Epic Song." In Minchin 2012:89–109.

———. 2012b. "The Meaning of Melody: Remarks on the Performance-Based Analysis of Bosniac Epic Song." In Harris and Hillers 2012:233–247.

Buda, A. 1986. "Eposi dhe historia jonë." *Çështje të folklorit shqiptar* 2:46–55.

Buturović, Đ. 1976. *Studija o Hormannovoj zbirci muslimanskih narodnih pjesama.* Sarajevo.

Chansonnier epique albanais. 1983. Tirana.

Clayton, M., ed. 2008. *Music, Words and Voice: A Reader.* Manchester.

Cocchiara, G. 1977. *Storia del folklore in Europa.* Torino.

Cohen, R. D., ed. 2010. *Alan Lomax Assistant in Charge: The Library of Congress Letters, 1935-1945.* Jackson.

Coon, C. S. 1950. *The Mountains of Giants: A Racial and Cultural Study of the North Albanian Mountain Ghegs.* Cambridge, MA.

Cordignano, F. 1941. "Kangë kreshnikësh në Shqypnín e verit [Parathanje — Shenim bibliografik — Të him]." *Hylli i Dritës* 3–5:147–154.

———. 1943. *La poesia epica di confine nell'Albania del Nord.* 2 vols. Vol. 1, Venezia, and vol. 2, Padova.

Çabej, E. 1939. "Për gjenezën e literaturës shqipe." *Hylli i Dritës* 3–7:149–180.

Çetta, A., ed. 1974. *Këngë kreshnike I.* Prishtina.

Çetta, A., F. Syla, M. Mustafa, and A. N. Berisha, eds. 1993. *Këngë kreshnike III.* Prishtina.

Daja, F. 1982. "Disa karakteristika të gamave në këngët e epikës heroike." *Kultura Popullore* 1:87–96.

———, ed. 1983. *Rapsodi kreshnike: tekste e melodi.* Tirana.

De Rada, G. 2017. *Canti di Milosao.* Ed. F. Altimari. Soveria Mannelli.

Desnickaja [Desnickaya], A. V. 1975. "Mbi lidhjet boshnjake-shqiptare në lëmin e poezisë epike." *Gjurmime Albanologjike: folklor dhe etnologji* V:41–61.

———. 1988. "Mbi formulat e gjuhës dhe formulat e poezisë epike shqiptare." *Gjurmime Albanologjike: folklor dhe etnologji* XVIII:65–82.

———. 2007. "Për studimi e traditave epike të ballkanit. Ngjashmëritë dhe dallimet e ciklit epik shqiptar 'Muji e Halili' me eposin e Bosnjës." In Skendi 2007:307–342.

Dietrich, W. 2000. *The Singing of Albanian Heroic Poetry.* In Reichl 2000:82–94.

Di Lellio, A. 2009. *The Battle of Kosovo 1389: An Albanian Epic.* London

Durham, E. 1909. *High Albania.* London.

Đorđević, T. 1932. *Naš narodni život,* VI. Belgrade.

Elliot, J. 2016. *Albanian Scholarship and the Epos of the Frontier Warriors after the Second World War.* In Neziri and Sinani 2016(2):89–108.

Elmer, D. F. 2013. "The Milman Parry Collection of Oral Literature." *Oral Tradition* 28/2:341–354.

Elsie, R. 1994. *Albanian Folktales and Legends: Selected and Translated from the Albanian.* Tirana.

———. 2001. *A Dictionary of Albanian Religion, Mythology, and Folk Culture.* London.

————. 2010. *Historical Dictionary of Albania*. Lanham.

Elsie, R., and J. Mathie-Heck, eds. 2004. *Songs of the Frontier Warriors: Albanian Epic Verse in a Bilingual English-Albanian Edition. Këngë Kreshnikësh*. Wauconda.

Erdely, S. 1995. *Music of Southslavic Epics from the Bihać Region of Bosnia*. New York.

Ernst, W. 2013. *Digital Memory and the Archive*. Minneapolis.

Faye, E. 2015. *Parathënie*. In Kadare 2015:7–9.

Ferrarini, L., ed. 2011. *L'Esperienza del Corpo*. Milan.

Fico, A. F. 2016. *Zbulimi i eposit sqiptar në Harvard*. New York and Tirana.

Fishta, G. 2010. *Lahuta e Malcis*. 16th ed. Shkodër.

Foley, J. M. 1988. *The Theory of Oral Composition: History and Methodology*. Bloomington.

————, ed. and trans. 2004. *The Wedding of Mustajbey's Son Bećirbey as Performed by Halil Bajgorić*. FF Communications 283. Helsinki. eEdition at http://oral-tradition.org/zbm/. Accessed January 2018.

————. 2005. *The Singer of Tales in Performance*. Bloomington.

Foster, H. W. 2000. *The Textualization of South Slavic Oral Epic and Its Implication for Oral-Derived Epic*. In Honko 2000:71–88.

————. 2004a. "The Role of Music in South Slavic Epic." In Foley 2004:223–260.

————. 2004b. "Jazz Musicians and South Slavic Oral Epic Bards." *Oral Tradition* 19(2):155–176.

Friedman, V. A. 1982. "Admirativity in Bulgarian Compared with Albanian and Turkish." In Kosev 1982:63–67.

————. 1994. "Surprise! Surprise! Arumanian Has Had an Admirative!" *Indiana Slavic Studies* 7:79–89.

————. 2003. "Evidentiality in the Balkans: With special Attention to Macedonian and Albanian." In Aikhenvald and Dixon 2003:189–218.

————. 2010. "The Age of the Albanian Admirative: A Problem in Historical Semantics." In Kim et al. 2010:31–39.

————. 2012a. "Enhancing National Solidarity through the Deployment of Verbal Categories: How the Albanian Admirative Participates in the Construction of a Reliable Self and an Unreliable Other." *Pragmatics and Society* 3(2):189–225.

————. 2012b. "Perhaps Mirativity is Phlogiston, but Admirativity is Perfect: On Balkan Evidential Strategies." *Linguistic Typology* 16(3):505–527.

García, J. F. 2001. "Milman Parry and A. L. Kroeber: Americanist Anthropology and the Oral Homer." *Oral Tradition* 16(1):58–84.

Gërcaliu, M. 1986. "Tipi i rapsodit të këngëve të kreshnikëve." *Çështje të folklorit shqiptar* 2:290–304.

Gitelman, L. 1999. *Scripts, Grooves, and Writing Machines: Representing Technology in the Edison Era*. Stanford.

Gjeçaj, D. 2007. *Gjergj Fishta: jeta dhe vepra.* Shkodër.

Gjeçov, Sh. K. 2010. *Kanuni i Lekë Dukagjinit.* Shkodër. Orig. pub. 1933.

Gjinaj, M. 2016. *100 vjet "Botime Françeskane."* Shkodër.

Gjonbalaj, H. 1986. *Kelmendi-gjenealogjia e familjes Nikçi.* Peja.

Gurakuqi, K., and F. Fishta, eds. 1937. *Visaret e Kombit I. Kângë trimije dhe kreshnikësh.* Tirana.

Halili, R. 2016. "Epica heroike-legjendare në Sanxhakun e Pazarit: një krahasim midis kërkimeve të Parryt dhe Lordin dhe gjendjes së sotme." In Neziri and Sinani 2016(1):499–511.

Harris, J., and B. Hillers, eds. 2012. *Child's Children: Ballad Study and Its Legacies.* Trier.

Hart, M. 2003. *Songcatchers: In Search of the World's Music.* Washington.

Havelock, E. A. 1963. *Preface to Plato.* Cambridge, MA.

Haxhihasani, Q., ed. 1955. *Kënke popullore legjendare.* Tirana.

———, ed. 1966. *Epika legjendare (Cikli i kreshnikëve). Vëllimi i parë. Folklori shqiptar II.* Tirana.

———. 1983. "Vështrim kritik i disa koncepteve antishkencore rreth epikës sonë heroike legjendare." *Kultura popullore* 2:31–46.

———. 1986. "Vështrim kritik i disa koncepteve antishkencore rreth epikës sonë heroike legjendare." *Çështje të folklorit shqiptar* 2:56–76.

———. 1991. "Mendësi zotëruese në ciklin e kreshikëve." *Gjurmime Albanologjike: folklor dhe etnologji* 21:33–50.

Herzfeld, M. 1985. *The Poetics of Manhood: Contest and Identity in a Cretan Mountain Village.* Princeton.

———. 2005. *Cultural Intimacy: Social Poetics in the Nation-State.* New York.

Herzog, G. 1951. "The Music of Yugoslav Heroic Epic Folk Poetry." *Journal of the International Folk Music Council* 3:62–64.

Honko, L., ed. 2000. *Textualization of Oral Epics.* Berlin.

Hoxha, H. 1987. *Struktura e vargut të këngëve kreshnike.* Prishtina.

Ivanova, R. 1999. "Once More About the Kosovo Epos and Its Utilisation." *Ethnologia Balkanica* 3:181–195.

Jakobson, R., and E. J. Simmons, eds. 1949. *Russian Epic Studies.* Philadelphia.

Jakova-Merturi, G. 1904. *Grammatica della lingua albanese.* Frascati.

Jelka, R. 1991. "The Legend of Kosovo." *Oral Tradition* 6/2 3:253–265.

Jensen, M. S. 1986. "Studimi krahasues i epikës. Disa konsiderata." *Çështje të folklorit shqiptar* 2:206–213.

Jousse, M. 1969. *L'anthropologie du geste.* Paris.

Kadare, I. 1987. "Eposi dhe kultura shqiptare." *Çeshtje të folklorit shqiptar* 3:328–331.

———. 1997. *The File on H.* Trans. D. Bellos. New York.

———. 2000. *Elegy for Kosovo.* Trans. P. Constantine. New York.

———. 2002. *Autobiografia e popullit në vargje.* Tirana.

———. 2015. *Tri gëngë zie për Kosovën.* Tirana. Orig. pub. 1998.

Kalfus, K. 1998. "Balkanizing Homer: An Albanian Novel Raises Questions About the Greek Epics." *The New York Times,* March 1, 1998..

Katalog i Ekspozites Dokumentore te Rilindjes Kombetare. 1937. Tirana.

Katiçiq, R. 1988. "Mbi gjuhën e ilirëve." *Fjala* 21–22:1–7.

Katz, M. 2005. *Capturing Sound: How Technology Has Changed Music.* Berkeley.

Kay, M. W. 1995. *The Index of the Milman Parry Collection 1933-1935: Heroic Songs, Conversations and Stories.* New York.

Këngë popullore shqiptare së Kosovës dhe Metohisë. 1952. Prishtina.

Kim, R., N. Oettinger, E. Rieken, and M. Weiss, eds. 2010. *Ex Anatolia Lux: Anatolian and Indo-European Studies in Honor of H. Craig Melchert.* Ann Arbor.

Koliqi, E. 1937. *Epica popolare albanese.* Padova.

———. 1942. "I rapsodi delle Alpi Albanesi." *Rivista d'Albania* 3:83–92

———, ed. 1957. *Poesia popolare albanese.* Firenze.

———. 1959, 1960. "Rapsodi e rapsodie delle Alpi Albanesi." *Shêjzat* 3:350–355, and 4:113–119, 168–170, 320–329.

Kolsti, J. 1975. "A Song About the Collapse of the Noli Government in Albania." *Journal of the Folklore Institute* 12(2/3):189–202.

———. 1985. "From Courtyard to Cabinet: The Political Emergence of Albanian Women." In Wolchik and Meyer 1985:138–151.

———. 1990. *The Bilingual Singer: A Study in Albanian and Serbo-Croatian Oral Epic Traditions.* New York.

Kosev, D., ed. 1982. *Bulgaria Past and Present.* Sofia.

Krasniqi, F., and S. Krasniqi. 2007. *Këngë popullore, 1.* Prishtina.

Kurti, D. 2007. *Lojët komtare.* Shkodër.

———. 2010. *Zakone e doke shqiptare.* Shkodër.

———. 2013. *Pralla kombëtare.* Shkodër.

Kurti, L. 2016. "Dreit eposit të krëshnikëve dhe kodifikuesve të parë të tij: Bernardin Palaj-Donat Kurti." In Neziri and Sinani 2012(2):109–142.

LaBelle, B. 2014. *Lexicon of the Mouth: Poetics and Politics of Voice and the Oral Imaginary.* New York.

Lambertz, M. 1917. *Die Volkspoesie der Albaner: eine einführende Studie.* Sarajevo.

———. 1922. *Albanische Märchen und andere Texte zur albanischen Volkskunde.* Vienna.

———. 1958. *Die Volksepik der Albaner.* Halle (Saale).

———. 1998. "Epika popullore e shqiptarëve." *Çështje të folklorit shqiptar* 6:5–95.

Lassiter, L. E. 2005. *The Chicago Guide to Collaborative Ethnography.* Chicago.

Lawson, F. R. S. 2010. "Rethinking the Orality-Literacy Paradigm in Musicology." *Oral Tradition* 25/2:429–446.

Leach, M., ed. 1949, 1950. *The Dictionary of Folklore, Mythology and Legend, I, II.* New York.

Lewis, I. M., ed. 1968. *History and Social Anthropology.* London.

Lomax, A. 2003. *Selected Writings 1934-1997.* London and New York.

Lord, A. B. 1948. "Homer, Parry, and Huso." *American Journal of Archaeology* 52(1):34–44.

———. 1968. "Homer as Oral Poet." *Harvard Studies in Classical Philology* 72:1–46.

———. 1984. *The Battle of Kosovo in Albanian and Serbocroatian Tradition.* In Pipa and Repishti 1984:65–83.

———. 1991. *Epic Singers and Oral Tradition.* Ithaca.

———. 1995. *The Singer Resumes the Tale.* Ed. M. L. Lord. Ithaca.

———. 2000. *The Singer of Tales.* 2nd edition. Ed. S. Mitchell and G. Nagy. Cambridge, MA.

———. n.d. "Interrelationship Among the Genres of Balkan Oral Traditional Lore." Unpublished papers of Albert B. Lord. Milman Parry Collection of Oral Literature. Cambridge, MA.

Maretić, T. 1966. *Naša narodna epika.* Zagreb. Orig. pub. 1909.

Martucci, D. 2016. "La *purezza della razza* e lo scandalo Cordignano." *Palaver* 5:231–300.

McMurray, P. 2015. "Archival Excess: Sensational Histories Beyond the Audiovisual." *Fontes Artis Musicae* 62/3:262–275.

———. 2020. "There Are No Oral Media? Multisensory Perceptions of South Slavic Epic Poetry." *Classics@* 14: https://classics-at.chs.harvard.edu/classics14-mcmurray/.

Medenica, R. 1974. "Arbanaške krešničke pesme i naša narodna epika." In *Rad XIV kongresa Saveza folklorista Jugoslavije u Prizrenu 1967.* Belgrade.

Mehmeti, E. 1996. *Studime në fushën e letërsisë gojore.* Tetovo.

Meyer, G. 1897. *Albanesische Studien. Beiträge zur Kenntniss verschiedener albanesischer Mundarten.* Vol. VI. Wien.

Mićović, D., ed. 1981. *Albanske junačke pesme.* Prishtina.

Minchin, E., ed. 2012. *Orality, Literacy and Performance in the Ancient World.* Leiden.

Miso, P. 1987. "Roli dhe funksioni etnoartistik i lahutës." *Çështje të folklorit shqiptar* 3:27–44.

Murati, Q. 2000. *Këngë të moçme kërçovare.* Tetovo.

Murko, M. 1951. *Tragom srpskohrvatske narodne epike. Putovanja u godinama 1930-32, I-II.* Zagreb.

———. 1990. "The Singers and their Epic Songs." *Oral Tradition* 5/1:107–130.

Nagy, G. 2000. *Epic as Music: Rhapsodic Models of Homer in Plato's Timaeus and Critias.* In Reichl 2000:41–67.

Neziri, Z. U. 1997. *Epika Legjendare e Rugovës V.* Prishtina.

———. 1999. *Këngë të kreshnikeve.* Prishtina.

———. 2001 "Veçori të këngëve të kreshnikëve." *Educologia* 73–77.

———. 2002. "Lahutarët e sotëm në Kosovë. Model: Isë Elezi-Lekëgjekaj (1947)." In *Seminari XX Ndërkombëtar për GJLKSH* 20/1:185–191. Prishtina.

———. 2003a. *Këngë të kreshnikëve.* Prishtina.

———. 2003b. "Tri fazat e mendimit të E. Çabeit për etimologjinë e emrit *kreshnik*." In *Rëndesia e veprës së Prof. Eqrem Çabeir për studimet albanologjike* 341–345. Prishtina.

———. 2004. "Këngë të kreshnikëve nga Kelmendi në Koleksionin e Allbert Llordit në Universitetin e Harvardit." *Gjurmime Albanologjike: folklor dhe etnologji* 32:101–111.

———. 2005. "Halil Beka-lahutar i njohur i Rrafshit të Dukagjinit." *Epoka e re* 19. Prishtina.

———. 2006. *Studime për folklorin I: Eposi i kreshnikëve dhe epika historike.* Prishtina.

———. 2008. *Studime për folklorin II: Epika gojore dhe etnokultura.* Prishtina.

———. 2009. *Epika Legjendare e Rugovës I.* Prishtina.

———. 2011. *Epika Legjendare e Rugovës II.* Prishtina.

Neziri, Z. U., and N. Scaldaferri. 2016. "From the Archive to the Field: New Research on Albanian Epic Songs." Classics@14. http://nrs.harvard.edu/urn-3:hlnc.essay:NeziriZ_and_ScaldaferriN.From_the_Archive_to_the_Field.2016

Neziri, Z. U., and S. Sinani, eds. 2016. *Epos of the Frontier Warriors: A Monument of the Albanian Cultural Heritage (Eposi i Kreshnikëve: monument i trashëgimisë kulturore shqiptare).* Vol. 1–2. Prishtina and Tirana.

Osmani, H. 1999. *Epikë popullore shqiptare (mbledhur në Tetovë e Gostivar me rrethinë).* Skopje.

Palaj, B. 2005. *Vepra.* Ed. A. Cirrincione. Shkodër.

Palaj, B., and D. Kurti. 1937. "Hymje." In *Visaret e Kombit II*:VII–XVI.

Palaj, B., and D. Kurti, eds. 1937. *Visaret e Kombit II. Kânge Kreshnikësh dhe Legjenda.* Tirana.

Panajoti, J. 1986. "Epika heroike legjendare dhe proza jonë popullore." *Çështje të folklorit shqiptar* 2:214–235.

Parry, M. 1971. *The Making of Homeric Verse.* Ed. A. Parry. Oxford.

Pennan, R. P., C. P. Panagiotis, and A. Theodosiou, eds. 2013. *Ottoman Intimacies, Balkan Musical Realities.* Helsinki.

Pipa, A. 1978. *Albanian Folk Verse: Structure and Genre.* Munich.

———. 1984. "Serbocroatian and Albanian Frontier Epic Cycles." In Pipa and Repishti 1984:85–102.

Pipa, A., and S. Repishti, eds. 1984. *Studies on Kosova*. Boulder.

Pistrick, E., N. Scaldaferri, and G. Schwörer, eds. 2011. *Audiovisual Media and Identity Issues on Southeastern Europe*. Newcastle upon Tyne.

Prennushi, V. 1911. *Kângë popullare gegënishte. Visari komtar I*. Sarajevo.

Progni, K. 2000. *Malësia e Kelmendi*. Shkodër.

Pulaha, S. 1987. "Fshatarësia e lirë e Shqipërisë së Veriut gjatë shek. XV-XVIII dhe cikli i kreshnikëve." *Çështje të folklorit shqiptar* 3:174–189.

Ranković, S. 2012. "Managing the Boss: Epistemic Violence, Resistance, and Negotiations in Milman Parry's and Nikola Vujnović's *Pričanja* with Salih Ugljanin." *Oral Tradition*. 27/1:5–66.

Reece, S. 2019. "The Myth of Milman Parry: Ajax or Elpenor?" *Oral Tradition* 33/1:115-142.

Reichl, K., ed. 2000. *The Oral Epic: Performance and Music*. Berlin.

Rhodes, N. 2009. "On Speech, Print, and New Media: Thomas Nashe and Marshall McLuhan." *Oral Tradition* 24/2:373–392.

Roberts, H. H., and L. Thompson. 1935. "The Re-recording of Wax Cylinders." *Zeitschrift für vergleichende Musikwissenschaft* III, 3–4:75–84. Repr. 1963. In *The Folklore and Folk Music Archivist*, IV, 2.

Roka, M., ed. 1944. *Visaret e Kombit X. Lahuta e Kosovës*. Tirana.

Roy, A. E. 2015. *Media, Materiality and Memory: Grounding the Groove*. Farnham and Burlington.

Sako, Z., and Q. Haxhihasani. 1966. "Hyrje." In Haxhihasani 1966:7–49.

Sako, Z., Q. Haxhihsani, and A. Fico. 1974. *Folklor shqiptar, I-II*. Tirana.

Samson, J. 2013. *Music in the Balkans*. Leiden and Boston.

Saussy, H. 2016. *The Ethnography of Rhythm: Orality and Its Technologies*. New York.

Scaldaferri, N. 2008. "Appunti per un'analisi della versificazione tradizionale arbëreshe." In Altimari and Conforti 2008:351–382.

———. 2009. "Vargu arbëresh i traditës gojore." *Gjurmime Albanologjike: folklor dhe Etnologji* 39:9–26.

———. 2011. *Voce, memoria, ritmo, movimento corporeo. Esempi di performance dei canti epici dei Balcani*. In Ferrarini 2011:145–163.

———. 2012. "Remapping Songs in the Balkans: Bilingual Albanian Singers in the Milman Parry Collection." In Bohlman and Petković 2012:203-223.

———. 2014. "Voice, Body, Technologies: Tales from an Arbëresh Village." *TRANS-Revista Transcultural de Música/Transcultural Music Review* 18 (accessed January 2018).

Schmaus, A. 1934. "Nekoliko podataka o epskom pevanju u pesmama kod Arbanasa (Arnauta) u Staroj Srbiji." In *Prilozi proučavanja narodne poezije* 1:107–112. Belgrade.

———. 1970. "Poezija epike shqiptare." *Shêjzat* 14(4–6):115–130.

SCHS I. 1953. *Serbocroatian Heroic Songs.* Ed. A. B. Lord. Cambridge, MA, and Belgrade.

SCHS II. 1953. *Serbocroatian Heroic Songs.* Ed. A. B. Lord. Belgrade and Cambridge, MA.

Schwandner-Sievers, S., and B. J. Fischer, eds. 2002. *Albanian Identities: Myth and History.* London.

Sejko, V. 2002. *Mbi elementet e përbashkëta në epikën shqiptaro-arbëreshe dhe serbokroate.* Tirana.

Shala, D. 1985. *Rreth këngëve kreshnike shqiptare.* Prishtina.

Sienaert, E. R. 1990. "Marcel Jousse: The Oral Style and the Anthropology of Gesture." *Oral Tradition* 5/1:91–106.

Sinani, S. 1993. "Rreth kohës dhe vendit të formimit të eposit të kreshnikëve." *Kultura popullore* 1–2:11–24.

———. 2006. *Mitologji në eposin e kreshnikëve.* Tirana.

Sirdani, A. D. 1934. "Duro Jabanxhija [Ki falë Zoti kreshnikë prej vaktit. Bogë, 2.III.1924]." *Leka* VI/10:358–360.

Skendi, S. 1953. "The South Slavic Decasyllable in Albanian Oral Epic Poetry." *Slavic Word* II:339–348.

———. 1954. *Albanian and South Slavic Oral Epic Poetry.* Philadelphia.

———. 2007. *Poezia epika gojore e shqiptareve dhe e sllaveve të jugut.* Tirana.

Sokoli, R. 1954. "Prozodia the metrika jonë popullore." *Nëntori* 8:177–227.

———. 1984. "Lahuta dhe kënget e kreshnikëve." *Nëntori* 1:186–205.

Sokoli, R., and P. Miso. 1991. *Veglat muzikore të popullit shqiptar.* Tirana.

Suchoff, B., ed. 1976. *Béla Bartók Essays.* New York.

Suta, B. 2009. "Linguaggio poetico in funzione del gesto etico di segno opposto nel poema romantico balcanico: il caso albanese del *Liuto della montagna* di P. Giorgio Fishta." *Romània Orientale* XII:209–231.

———. 2016. *Funksioni i eposit gojor në poemën epike romantike: Fishta dhe autorët sllavo-jugore.* In Neziri and Sinani 2016:397–410.

Swire, J. 1930. *The Rise of a Kingdom.* New York.

Tarifa, F. 2008. "Of Time, Honor, and Memory: Oral Law in Albania." *Oral tradition* 23/1:3–14.

Tate, A. P. 2010. "'There Were Two Foreigners and One of Ours': Parry and Lord in Kijevo, Croatia, 24 September 1934." *Folklore* 121:311–320.

———. 2016. "Matija Murko, Wilhelm Radloff, and Oral Epic Studies." *Oral Tradition* 26/2:329–352.

Tedlock, D. 1979. "The Analogical Tradition and the Emergence of a Dialogical Anthropology." *Journal of Anthropological Research* 35/4:387–400.

Thomaidis, K., and B. Macpherson, eds. 2015. *Voice Studies: Critial Approaches to Process, Performance and Experience.* London and New York.

Thomas, R., and D. Gerstle, eds. 2005. "Performance Literature I." *Oral Tradition* 20/1.

Tirta, M. 2004. *Mitologjia ndër shqiptarë*. Tirana.

Todorova, M. 1987. *Imagining the Balkans*. New York and Oxford.

Tole, V. S. 2007. *Enciklopedia e Iso-polifonisë popullore shqiptare/ Encyclopedia of Albanian Folk Iso-Polyphony*. Tirana.

Treitler, L. 1974. "Homer and Gregory: The Transmission of Epic Poetry and Plainchant." *The Musical Quarterly* 60:333–372.

Turin, M. 2013. "Orality and Technology, or the Bit and the Byte: The Work of the World Oral Literature Project." *Oral Tradition* 28/2:173–186.

Uçi, A. 1986. "Epika heroike dhe roli i saj në folklorin shqiptar." *Çështje të folklorit shqiptar* 2:5–45.

Valtchinova, G. 2002. "Ismail Kadare's The H-File and the Making of the Homeric Verse. Variations on the Works and Lives of Milman Parry and Albert Lord." In Schwandner-Sievers and Fischer 2002:104–114.

Van Orden, K. 2015. *Materialities: Books, Readers, and the Chanson in 16th-Century Europe*. New York and Oxford.

Varèse, E., and C. Wen-chung. 1966. "The Liberation of Sound." *Perspectives of New Music* 5/1:11–12.

Vidan, A. 2003. *Embroidered with Gold, Strung with Pearls: The Traditional Ballads of Bosnian Women*. Cambridge, MA.

Whitaker, I. 1968. "Tribal Structure and National Politics in Albania, 1910-1950." In Lewis 1968:253–296.

Wolchik, S. L., and A. G. Meyer, eds. 1985. *Women, State, and Party in Eastern Europe*. Durham, NC.

Xhaferi, H. 1996. *Epika popullore e trevës së Kërçovës*. Tetovo.

Xhagolli, A. 1984. "Vendi që zënë këngët e kreshnikëve në realitetin folklorik bashkëkohor." *Kultura popullore* 2:97–104.

———. 1999. "Këngët e kreshnikëve në Kelmend." *Seminari i dytë ndërkombëtar «Shkodra në shekuj», II*, Shkodër:163–166.

Young, M. 2015. *Singing the Body Electric: The Human Voice and Sound Technology*. Farnham.

Zheji, G. 1986. "Rreth tipareve të vargut të këngeve të krshnikëve dhe të instrumentit të tij." *Çështje të folklorit shqiptar* 2:375–384.

———. 1987. *Vargu i këngëve të kreshnikëve. Studim*. Tirana.

———. 2000. *Folklori shqiptar*. Tirana.

Zojzi, R. 1962. "*Ndamja krahinore e popullit shqiptar*." *Etnografia shqiptare* 1:16–62.

Zumthor, P. 1990. *Oral Poetry: An Introduction*. Trans. K. Murphy-Judy. Minneapolis.

Online Resources

Hylli i Drites online, Digital Public Library Martin Barleti, Shkodër
  http://bibliotekashkoder.com/digital/hylli_i_drites

"Early Photography in Albania," website by Robert Elsie
  http://www.albanianphotography.net

Marubi Albanian National Museum of Photography
  http://www.marubi.gov.al

"Mirash Ndou, Albanian singer of tales", website by Minna Skafte Jensen
  http://albanian-tales.net

Milman Parry Collection of Oral Literature, Harvard University
  https://mpc.chs.harvard.edu

Ethnomusicology and Visual Anthropology Lab, University of Milan
  http://www.leav.unimi.it

Index of Names and Places

Subject Index